12975751

WITHDRAWN

ORIGINS OF NURTURANCE
Developmental, Biological and Cultural Perspectives on Caregiving

ORIGINS OF NURTURANCE
Developmental, Biological and Cultural Perspectives on Caregiving

Edited by

ALAN FOGEL
GAIL F. MELSON
Department of Child Development and Family Studies
Purdue University

LAWRENCE ERLBAUM ASSOCIATES, PUBLISHERS
1986   Hillsdale, New Jersey   London

Copyright © 1986 by Lawrence Erlbaum Associates, Inc.
All rights reserved. No part of this book may be reproduced in
any form, by photostat, microform, retrieval system, or any other
means, without the prior written permission of the publisher.

Lawrence Erlbaum Associates, Inc., Publishers
365 Broadway
Hillsdale, New Jersey 07642

Library of Congress Cataloging in Publication Data
Main entry under title:

Origins of nurturance.

Includes bibliographies and indexes.
1. Nurturing behavior in children.   2. Nurturing
behavior.   I. Fogel, Alan.   II. Melson, L. Gail.
[DNLM: 1. Child Care.   2. Child Rearing.   3. Parent-
Child Relations.   WS 105.5.F2 069]
BF723.N84075   1986   155.4'18   85-29301
ISBN 0-89859-643-2

Printed in the United States of America
10 9 8 7 6 5 4 3 2 1

Contents

Preface

I: CHILD–INFANT INTERACTIONS   1

1. **Nurturance in the Home: A Longitudinal Study of Sibling Interaction**   3
   Jan Pelletier-Stiefel, Debra Pepler, Kim Crozier, Linda Stanhope, Carl Corter, and Rona Abramovitch

   Observations   8
   Results and Discussion   9
   Conclusions   17
   References   23

2. **Young Children's Responses to Babies: Do They Foreshadow Differences Between Maternal and Paternal Styles?**   25
   Phyllis W. Berman

   Attraction to Infant Features   26
   Observational Studies of Interactions
     With Toddlers   29
   Sex Differences in Response to the
     Caretaker Role   34
   Responses to Adults' Caretaking
     Requests and Instructions   36
   Summary of Observational Studies   42
   Help, Sharing, and Donations to a
     Younger Child   43
   Summary and Future Directions for Research   47
   References   50

3. **Conceptualizing the Determinants of Nurturance: A Reassessment of Sex Differences** 53
Alan Fogel, Gail F. Melson, and Jayanthi Mistry

Nurturance, Empathy and Altruism 54
Four Dimensions of Nurturance 56
Sex Differences in Nurturance 59
Nurturance and Society 65
References 66

4. **The Study of Nurturant Interactions: From the Infant's Perspective** 69
Gail F. Melson, Alan Fogel, and Jayanthi Mistry

Indirect Measures of Interest 71
Cognitions About Infants 73
Behavioral Interest 77
Contingent Responsiveness 83
Summary 88
References 89

II. **PERSPECTIVES ON THE DEVELOPMENT OF NURTURANCE: CULTURE, BIOLOGY, AND RISK** 91

5. **Another Style of Competence: The Caregiving Child** 95
Carolyn Pope Edwards

Rational Versus Conventional Moral Rules and Reasoning 98
Nurturance and Prosocial Responsibility as Aspects of Interchild Behavior 100
The Material for this Study 104
Aggression Towards Small Children 107
Aggression Towards Animals 108
Positive Action to Meet the Needs of Others 109
Conflicts Over Turn-Taking and Sharing (Positive Justice) 112
Children's Discussions About Task Assignment 112
Commands Concerning Proper Social Behavior 116
Summary and Conclusion 118
References 120

6. **Becoming Nurturant in Japan:
   Past and Present**   123
   Hideo Kojima

   Introduction   *123*
   Japanese Traditional Attitudes Toward Children:
     Historical Background   *123*
   Problems of Nurturing Children in Present-Day
     Japan   *127*
   References   *137*

7. **Psychobiology of Maternal Behavior in Rats,
   Selected Other Species and Humans**   141
   Alison Fleming and Gail Orpen

   Functional Features of Maternal Behavior
     in the Rat   *142*
   Sensitization of Maternal Behavior in the
     Virgin Rat   *144*
   Hormonal Control of Maternal Behavior in
     the New Mother   *145*
   Sensory Control of Maternal Behavior in
     the New Mother   *156*
   What Hormones May Be Doing to Promote
     Maternal Responsiveness   *169*
   Neural Control of Maternal Behavior   *174*
   Where in the Brain Do Hormones Act?   *182*
   Biological Control of Maternal Behavior in
     Human Mothers   *185*
   References   *196*

8. **Antecedents of Early Parenting**   209
   *S. Shirley Feldman and
   Sharon Churnin Nash*

   Prenatal Antecedents of Parenting:
     Direct Effects   *213*
   Prenatal Antecedents of Parenting:
     Indirect Effects   *226*
   Concluding Comments   *229*
   References   *231*

9. Antecedents and Consequences of Parenting: The Case of Adolescent Motherhood   233
J. Brooks-Gunn and Frank F. Furstenberg, Jr.

Parenthood and Parenting   233
Approaches to the Study of Parenting   234
Prevalence of Teenage Motherhood   236
Parental Practices   238
Antecedents of Parenting   239
Consequences of Parenting Upon Children's Development   246
Issues in Teenage Parenting   251
References   254

10. Nurturing Under Stress: The Care of Preterm Infants and Developmentally Delayed Preschoolers   259
Susan Goldberg and Sharon Marcovitch

The Parent-Child Dyad   260
Stress and Support   261
Preterm Infants   262
Developmental Delays: Down's Syndrome and Other Etiologies   267
Summary   272
References   274

Author Index   277
Subject Index   287

Preface

In recent years, the importance of caring for and nurturing the young has moved from the private concern of families to the public agenda. This has been due in part to some of the failures of childrearing within the family, as shown in instances of abuse, neglect, and incest. Other symptoms that also may be related to the stresses inherent in contemporary parenting are latch-key children, delinquency, adolescent suicide, and substance abuse among children and adolescents.

The family does not exist in isolation, but is embedded in a societal context, and changes in this context have many implications for the quality of caregiving within the family. For example, the dramatic influx in recent years of mothers of young children and infants into the work force has led to reliance on alternative caregiving, in day care centers, day care homes, or other informal arrangements. The individual family's main concern is finding adequate child-care, but looked at from a broader perspective, this movement toward supplementary parenting has broadened the societal definition of who may be a caregiver, and has drawn in a variety of other persons into what previously had been a more private, family realm.

These changes have increased the flexibility of parents' options but at the same time have increased the risks that children may not receive optimal care. For example, there is no clear consensus among parents or professionals concerning the qualities necessary for good caregiving, nor do we have an acceptable system of evaluating or monitoring outside-the-home care. While alternative caregiving can pose risks for the child, it must be recognized that where the home provides a less than adequate environment for the child's development, supplemental care can be beneficial.

Defining Nurturance

These changes within the family and within society have raised the question of how to define caregiving toward the child. The term, "care-giving," which appeared in the preface of Lewis and Rosenblum's 1974 edited volume, *The Effect of the Infant on the Caregiver,* expanded the notion of caretaking to include a broader range of competencies and behaviors related to child care. Following Bell's (1968) call to examine multidirectional effects in the parent-child interaction, Lewis and Rosenblum focused on the infant's contribution to its own care. Subsequently, Bronfenbrenner's ecological framework (1979), Belsky's triadic analysis of family interaction (1981) and Garbarino's (1982) concept of sociocultural risk factors in child maltreatment have been influential in calling attention to a broader range of influences on caregiving.

In addition to the influences of the child and the social context, there is a growing amount of evidence suggesting that experiences during the caregiver's childhood may affect the caregiving competencies of adults. Moreover, research on the development of prosocial behavior and empathy shows that even from an early age, children are aware of some of the needs of both peers and children younger than themselves, and that often they can act sensitively to respond to those needs when encouraged by adults to perform child-care tasks.

This volume brings together recent research that illustrates how caregiving develops in young children and how experiences in childhood may contribute to later parenting and adult caregiving. This is the first time that caregiving has been examined systematically within a developmental perspective. This may give us additional insights into how individual adults respond to the pressures and stresses of caring for children in contemporary society.

In addition, we want to go beyond Lewis and Rosenblum's notion of caregiving within the family context to include caregiving outside the family, and to go beyond the idea of caregiving as mere interaction. Our concept not only includes behaviors designed to meet the immediate needs of the young, but also encompasses behaviors that are intended to contribute to the long-term, future development of the child. We will use the term, *nurturance,* to refer to this broadened concept of caregiving. In addition, as we discuss in the chapter, "Conceptualizing the determinants of nurturance: A reassessment of sex differences," nurturance can be applied to a wide variety of endeavors that seek to enhance the developmental potential of other humans, or even animals or objects.

This conceptualization does not preclude other ways of defining nurturance; indeed, throughout the following chapters, the reader will find varied definitions employed. However, most approaches would agree that the concept of nurturance need not be applied uniquely to children, but can be extended to the care of the elderly, sick, or others in need. When looked at in this way, we can find evidence of nurturance throughout the life-span, in a variety of activities performed by both children and adults. Indeed, although the chapters in this volume consist of studies of the development of nurturance in childhood and early adulthood, we can conceptualize nurturance as following a life-long developmental path.

In addition, this approach calls our attention to nurturing experiences not directly related to child-care, which may nonetheless affect an individual's developing capacity and willingness to nurture young children or others in need. Such experiences might include caring for pets, or empathic responses toward peers (cf. chapter by Fogel, Melson, & Mistry).

Implications of a Developmental Perspective on Nurturance

A developmental perspective on nurturance views the individual's personal history as an important determinant of his or her nurturing ability. However, just as caregiving by parents has been shown to be affected by the marital relationship and other aspects of the family context, the child's capacity and willingness to nurture also is affected by family context variables. Finally, the wider societal and cultural milieu can be expected to influence the conditions under which children are exposed to opportunities and incentives to nurture others.

Part I of this volume focuses on the developing child's responses to infants and younger children as possible precursors of later nurturance. The research studies outlined in this section provide detailed descriptions of the range of responses of children of different ages to the young. In addition, they call attention to person and situational variables—such as gender, sibling status, adult encouragement, and the infant's own responses to the child—that appear to modify children's behavior during child-infant interaction.

Part II extends the developmental course of nurturance by examining early parenting and its determinants. In addition, cultural contexts and biological influences are examined for their potential impact on the developmental course of nurturance. Each part contains an overview detailing the contributions of each chapter.

REFERENCES

Bell, R. Q. (1968). A re-interpretation of the direction of effects in studies of socialization. *Psychological Review, 75,* 63–72.

Belsky, J. (1981). Early human experience: A family perspective. *Developmental Psychology, 17,* 3–23.

Bronfenbrenner, U. (1979). *The ecology of human development.* Cambridge: Harvard University Press.

Garbarino, J. (1982). Sociocultural risk: Dangers to competence. In C. Kopp & J. B. Krakow (Eds.), *The child: Development in a social context.* Reading, MA: Addison-Wesley.

Lewis, M., & Rosenblum, L. (Eds.). (1974). *The effect on the infant on its caregiver.* New York: Wiley.

To our children:
Ephram and Menasheh, Sara and Josh

ORIGINS OF NURTURANCE
Developmental, Biological and Cultural Perspectives on Caregiving

CHILD-INFANT INTERACTIONS

The chapters in Part I all focus upon the early development of children's positive responses to those younger than themselves, both within and outside the family. Chapter 1, "Nurturance in the home: A longitudinal study of sibling interaction," by Pelletier-Stiefel and colleagues examines positive, caring responses between siblings in a longitudinal study of spontaneous sibling interactions in the home. Using the rich data base this investigation has generated, the authors address the possible influence of age, birth order, sex composition of the sibling pair, and interval on the expression of sibling nurturance. They also demonstrate the complex, reciprocal influences operating over time that suggest that sibling interactions may be an important context for developing nurturant responses.

Chapter 2, "Young children's responses to babies: Do they foreshadow differences between maternal and paternal styles?" by Berman looks at children's responses toward infants and younger children outside the family context. In a review of literature on the determinants of responsiveness toward unfamiliar babies, the effects of age, gender, and situation are examined in an effort to explain how caregiving toward infants becomes integrated into the sex-role identity of individuals as they develop.

In Chapter 3, "Conceptualizing the determinants of nurturance: A reassessment of sex differences," Fogel,

Melson, and Mistry re-examine evidence for sex differences in children's responsiveness toward infants and suggest that the concept of nurturance be broadened in several ways. First, they argue that nurturance can be thought of as including a variety of behaviors designed to foster the developmental potential of others. Second, they propose that individuals may choose a variety of individuals or objects to nurture. Thus, nurturance is conceptualized as a capacity developed by both males and females but often actualized in behavior in differing ways.

Finally, Melson, Fogel, and Mistry, in Chapter 4, "The study of nurturant interactions: From the infant's perspective," document evidence that infants themselves contribute in important ways to their own nurturance. Using data on encounters between young children and unfamiliar infants, they demonstrate how varying characteristics of babies—their age, gender, and appearance—have differential effects on even preschoolage children. Moreover, behavioral analysis of infants with older children is used to show how infants signal their needs to children and attempt to draw them into interaction and maintain their interest.

Taken as a whole, these chapters illustrate the complex nature of children's interactions with infants and younger children both within and outside the family. Both person and situational variables appear to interact in determining even short-term responsiveness to the young and when interactions are part of ongoing relationships, as they are among siblings, the developmental history of the relationship also becomes important.

1 Nurturance in the Home: A Longitudinal Study of Sibling Interaction

Jan Pelletier-Stiefel
Debra Pepler
Kim Crozier
Linda Stanhope
Carl Corter
Rona Abramovitch
Erindale College, University of Toronto

The sibling relationship, a unique blend of friendship and parenting, has been viewed as fostering the development of both positive, nurturant behaviors and negative, rivalrous behaviors. In this chapter, our attention is on the former, and on the factors that may be related to nurturance between siblings. Within the framework of their play together, siblings have the unique opportunity to "try out" parenting behaviors. Although young children are limited in their abilities to perform caretaking acts which resemble those of parenting, they nevertheless are able to give positive, supportive care, such as helping and physical affection, which may be the rudiments of later adult-like caretaking behavior. Attitudes of helpfulness, as well as particular nurturant behaviors, could also be fostered, or not, in sibling relationships.

This chapter describes nurturance in siblings as examined in a longitudinal study of sibling interaction in the home (Abramovitch, Corter, & Lando, 1979; Abramovitch, Corter, & Pepler, 1980; Corter, Pepler, & Abramovitch, 1982; Corter, Abramovitch, & Pepler, 1983; Pepler, 1981). Our previous papers have described general patterns of prosocial, agonistic and imitative interaction according to the variables of sex composition of the dyad, the age-spacing or interval between siblings, and the age of the individual child (older or younger child within the dyad). Here we focus on nurturance in relation to these same variables. We examine more closely the prosocial category of behavior, and in particular, a subset of nurturant, prosocial acts. Finally, we present observations from a final longitudinal follow-up not reported in our previous papers.

A renewed interest in recent years in family functioning and in social development in general has raised questions about the sibling relationship. From a practical standpoint, sibling research may have implications for family planning, such as the choice of age-spacing between children. Research into sibling interaction should also lead to a better understanding of the role of other children in a child's development. Piaget's theoretical view of declining egocentrism as a function of interaction with other children might have implications for the sibling relationship and for nurturance in particular. As children learn to take the perspective of other children and to respond to the emotional needs of others, we might expect to see an increase in nurturant behavior. Likewise, the role of siblings must be considered when examining birth order differences. It is increasingly recognized that parental treatment is not the only mediator of such differences (Kendrick & Dunn, 1983).

In order to describe nurturance in siblings, we first must be able to distinguish nurturant behaviors from other forms of interaction in our observations. The traditional connotation of nurturance involves caring for someone needier, in most cases, younger. In reference to siblings, that would limit consideration to the older child's nurturance toward the younger sibling. However, as Bryant (1982) points out in a review, both the older and younger child may play a part in sibling caretaking. Similarly, our observations revealed helping, teaching, and comforting behaviors by the older siblings as well as sharing and affectionate behaviors by both younger and older siblings. These behaviors demonstrate the mutual caring and concern of both siblings. Of course, it is possible that a number of characteristics of our sample may have made for more equal nurturance between older and younger siblings than in other kinds of families. The younger children in this study were not infants. The youngest siblings were 18-months-old and it is possible that a child of this age would not elicit as much nurturant behavior by the older child, as an infant sibling would (Samuels, 1977). The age of the older child may also be important—perhaps the older children in this study were not old enough to give "real" care. In addition, this study is limited to two-child families. There is evidence that children may be more nurturant in larger families (Bossard & Boll, 1956). Finally, in our families, older children were not assigned caretaking roles. Therefore, in families different from the kind we observed, even more extensive caretaking activities might be seen. However, we did not limit our definition of nurturance to physical caretaking; we chose to define it to include prosocial behaviors that have elements of psychological nurturance—behaviors such as comforting, praising, giving, sharing, co-operating, helping, and physical affection. To set the stage for the analyses of these nurturant behaviors, we briefly review how they may relate to variables such as sex and age according to the existing literature.

A variety of types of evidence suggest that female siblings, particularly older ones, should be especially nurturant in their interactions with their brothers and sisters. For instance, it is more common for girls, than for boys, to be assigned caretaking roles with younger siblings. Barry, Brown, and Child (1957) found that girls were expected to be more reasonable and nurturant than were boys.

Older sisters, in fact, get more caretaking experience than boys (Bossard & Boll, 1956). Similarly, the cross-cultural research of Whiting and Whiting (1975) and of Weisner and Gallimore (1977), indicates that girls between the ages of three and six are assigned more caretaking responsibility than boys of the same age. Based on their research, Whiting and Whiting (1975) suggest that caretaking experience may lead to more nurturant behavior. Hence, one might expect sisters to be more nurturant even beyond their direct caretaking obligations.

Indeed, a number of lines of evidence from novel tasks or situations reveal that females appear to be more nurturant outside of their everyday caretaking roles. Cicirelli's (1973) laboratory research on teaching between siblings has demonstrated that older sisters teach more effectively than older brothers. Cicirelli (1976) suggests that role theory may explain these findings; girls are more likely than boys to identify with the role of mother and school teacher and perceive the caretaking role as predominantly feminine. Evidence also shows that when asked to look after an infant, older females are more responsive to babies than older males or younger children (Berman & Goodman, 1984). In addition to being the most responsive group, they also provided physical care, not simply play activities. They were also most responsive in imitating caregiving activities previously modeled by an adult. This raises the question of whether the older females are guided more by social desirability. In other words, girls may simply have been more "eager to please" than the older boys or younger children were and therefore appeared to be more nurturant with the infant. On the other hand, Bryant (1982) maintains that older sisters do not necessarily help the younger sibling in specific ways modeled by the mother; they acquire the intent to caretake but may lack particular skills. Berman and Goodman (1984) suggest that there is a normative age for the emergence of nurturant behaviors; girls over 5 years tended to show the pattern, whereas girls under 5 years did not.

The evidence above suggests that it is better to have a first-born daughter than a first-born son, at least from the standpoint of potential second-borns. However, this conclusion may be premature, given the many unresolved issues. First, there are methodological problems. Most of the data on nurturance or caretaking and sibling interaction have been collected indirectly, by questionnaires, rather than by naturalistic observations (Weisner & Gallimore, 1977). Second, the cross-cultural evidence suggests that this pattern of sex differences may not exist in every culture or across all ages. For example, Whiting and Edward's (1973) examination of sex differences in seven societies revealed that only older girls over 7 years were more nurturant than boys and there were no sex differences prior to that age. Third, Maccoby and Jacklin's (1974) review reported no sex differences for overall nurturance in peer interaction and in our own sibling data Pepler (1981) found no evidence of sex differences in teaching. Fourth, it may be that the heightened prosocial behavior of girls does not provide the most optimal developmental milieu for the younger sibling; in other words, there may be "too much of a good thing." For instance, Berman and Goodman's (1984) work reveals that older females may provide care which is inappropriate, perhaps acting as more intrusive caretakers than boys. Such behavior may be seen in their tendency to "smother" rather than "mother" their infant wards. A similar tendency may also be seen in the laboratory study by Cicirelli (1973), who noted that younger children would accept help from an older sister more readily than from an older brother, but worked more independently in the presence of the older brother. Older brothers, therefore, could be viewed as fostering independence in their younger siblings in the same way that some parents might.

As noted above, although Whiting and Edward's (1973) cross-cultural research illustrates a relationship between sex and nurturant behaviors, these differences were only apparent in older children. Likewise, Berman and Zahn-Waxler (1983) report the emergence of more "nurturant" behaviors on the part of females after 5-years-of-age in their observations of children's responsiveness to babies. This evidence is consistent with Stewart's (1983) attachment study in which he discovered that children who were more advanced in perspective-taking ability were more nurturant in response to their infant sibling's distress. Thus, it may be that maturing cognitive abilities allow for greater sensitivity and greater likelihood of nurturant responses in older children. Dunn and Kendrick's work on empathy between siblings provides theoretical support for this statement (1982). In any case, the evidence suggests that older children, particularly females, are often placed in caretaking roles and, in general, are more nurturant than younger children.

In most of the studies already discussed, as well as our own, age is confounded with birth order. In other words, the more nurturant older sisters are not only older, but are generally first-borns. There are few studies which have disentangled these variables in analyzing sibling interaction. Minnett, Lowe-Vandell, and Santrock (1983) compared interaction between first-born 8-year-olds and a younger sibling with second-born 8-year-olds and an older sibling; they found birth-order differences in behavior, including nurturant behaviors such as praising and teaching. First-borns were also found to be more dominant and more positive than second-borns. Although their design controlled age in comparing birth orders, it confounded the age of the partner with birth order.

Finally, with respect to the possible effects of age interval between siblings on nurturance, there is little positive evidence. Lamb's (1978a, 1978b) laboratory research, Dunn and Kendrick's (1982) home observations, and our own, show almost no effect of interval on any measure of interaction at any time. There is, nevertheless, considerable speculation about interval in relation to the question of nurturance. For example, in Bryant's (1982) discussion of siblings as therapeutic caretakers, she notes that closely spaced dyads may provide more conflict than support. Because there is greater rivalry for mother's attention, it would seem to follow that there would also be less nurturance. However, our own work has failed to support such speculation, since no interval differences have been found for any behavior. Although Minnett et al. (1983) did find more nurturance in widely spaced dyads, their study is based on older children in a nonnaturalistic setting, and therefore is quite different from the naturalistic studies of Dunn and Abramovitch and their colleagues. Thus, there is little evidence that age spacing is a factor in sibling nurturance.

Having looked at past research in areas related to sibling nurturance, we now turn to our longitudinal study. Sibling dyads were observed at three points in time—first when the younger children were 1½ and their older siblings were either 3- or 4½-years-old (34 same-sex and 36 mixed-sex dyads); second when the younger children were 3-years-old (28 same- and 28 mixed-sex dyads); and third when the younger children were just under 5-years-of-age (24 same- and 24 mixed-sex dyads). Previously reported findings were based on the first two observations; these findings may be summarized as follows:

1. Overall prosocial behavior increased with time; agonistic behavior did not increase, although there was a tendency for verbal aggression to increase in younger siblings and in mixed-sex dyads. Thus, the siblings seemed to be "getting along" more as time went on.

2. Older children initiated more prosocial behavior as well as more agonism than younger children at all times.

3. Older females initiated more prosocial behavior than males at time 1 in same-sex dyads and at time 3 in mixed-sex dyads, but there were no differences at time 2 in either same- or mixed-sex dyads. In other words, there was no consistent effect for sex of the individual child.

4. There were no consistent effects for sex composition of the dyad.

5. Finally, the most remarkable finding was the repeated lack of an interval, or age-spacing, effect.

This finding stands in sharp contrast to the speculation cited earlier and to expert advice on ideal age spacing. For example, Burton White (1980) contends that intervals less than 3 years are ill-advised. Although we expected to find such effects, our failure to do so is consistent with the findings of Dunn and Kendrick (1982) and Lamb (1978a, 1978b) who, as was noted earlier, were equally unsuccessful in uncovering significant interval effects.

Our longitudinal research allowed examination of prosocial, agonistic and imitative behaviors of both same- and mixed-sex sibling dyads across a span of several years. Previously, we have reported frequencies of these behaviors along the dimensions of age, sex, and interval. Here the focus is on the "more nurturant" prosocial behaviors and how they relate to the variables of age, sex, and interval according to multivariate analyses of variance and correlational analyses. In addition, we report analyses designed to tease apart the age/birth order issue.

Previously, our prosocial data included a category of requests (requests made by either the younger child or the older child to the sibling, but not necessarily conveying or soliciting a nurturant tone). The age changes in prosocial behavior may have been inflated due to the increasingly verbal interaction of the children as they got older. In other words, perhaps siblings talk to each other more as they get older but are not necessarily more nurturant. In order to distinguish nurturance from the general prosocial category, the analyses reported here include an examination of prosocial behavior without requests; analyses of the broader category of prosocial behavior with requests are also included for comparison. The category of nurturance comprises sibling affection (physical and verbal), comforting, sharing, helping, and cooperating. Although some of these behaviors may not reflect common definitions of nurturance, they all involve a sense of emotional caring and/or fostering of mutuality and helpfulness. In fact, these seem to be the categories the children themselves use in describing the positive aspects of the sibling relationship. When asked what they liked best about their siblings they gave responses like the following:

(Y = younger sibling; O = older)

Mixed Sex:
- Y "She kisses me with small kisses."
- Y "He lets me sleep with his teddy bear at night."
- O "He listens when I tell him not to do something."
- O "He shares most of his stuff. He finds things and says this is for you. The way he imitates me makes me feel sort of good."

Same Sex:
- Y "She always lets me sit on her chair with her to watch TV."
- Y "She helps me learn a cartwheel."
- O "When I fall down, he picks my bike up. I might lose a shoe—he might get it for me."
- O "If you're hurt, she'll come and kiss me."

OBSERVATIONS

All observations were made in the home by one of several female observers, except for assessment of observer agreement when two observers were present, at a time of day when the children were likely to be together. During the observations mothers were asked to go about their normal routine. All exits and entrances by the mother were noted and timed. An initial 10–15 min period preceded each session to allow the children to become accustomed to the observer's presence. Each sibling pair was observed for two 1-hour observation periods on different days, except at time 3, when they were observed for one 1-hour period. At times 1 and 2 the observer kept a written record of a number of nonverbal and verbal target behaviors and responses. At time 3 interaction had become more verbal, so each session was recorded on audio cassette. In addition, the observer recorded a number of nonverbal behaviors using the same procedure as described above for times 1 and 2.

The verbal prosocial behaviors recorded and/or coded from the transcripts of the audio tapes were verbal affection and comfort, praise and approval, and requests (for help, objects, or some desired behavior). To be coded as prosocial behavior, requests had to be stated in a polite, positive manner. The nonverbal prosocial behaviors recorded by the observer were physical affection and comfort, give and/or share an object, and cooperate and/or help. The verbal agonistic behaviors were directive commands, insults, disapproval, threats of physical aggression, and tattle-telling. Commands with reason, territorial claims, repetitions of mother's commands, and bribing were added to this category at time 3. The nonverbal agonistic categories consisted of physical aggression, struggles over objects, and, at time 3, physical teasing. More specific details of the procedure and definitions for all of the behaviors mentioned above, plus verbal and physical imitation and play-related behaviors are included in our previous publications. Observer agreement for all of the behaviors was high. Specifically, agreement for the category of prosocial behavior averaged 83% across the three time periods.

RESULTS AND DISCUSSION

The first analysis of the longitudinal data is a multivariate approach to repeated measures (McCall & Applebaum, 1973). It treats the sibling dyad as the unit of analysis with age of sibling (older or younger) and time (times 1, 2, and 3) as the repeated factors, and sex of the older child (male or female), sex composition (same- or mixed-sex), and interval (small or large spacing) as between-subjects factors. Although this analysis differed from our previous univariate analyses of prosocial behavior, the results were essentially those reported before. There were no effects of sex, sex composition, and interval and these factors did not enter into any interactions. There were main effects of time (multivariate $F[2,39] = 72.39$, $p<.0001$), age ($F[1,40] = 34.35$, $p<.001$), and these factors interacted ($F[2,39] = 6.34$, $p<.005$). Prosocial behavior increased over time; older children were more prosocial, and the differences between the older and younger children were significantly greater at time 3, than at time 2 or time 1 (see Table 1.1).

The second analysis was identical to the above except that it analysed prosocial behavior excluding requests in order to focus on more nurturant behavior (see Table 1.1). Again, there were no main effects for sex or interval and there was a significant main effect of age ($F[1,40] = 4.42$, $p<.05$). Older children were more nurturant, even when verbal requests were excluded. However, in contrast to the first analysis, there was no effect of time and there was a main effect of sex composition ($F[1.40] = 5.21$, $p<.03$). Same-sex dyads had significantly higher frequencies of nurturant acts than mixed-sex dyads (see Fig. 1.1).

TABLE 1.1
Mean Frequency per Two Hours of Nurturant (and Prosocial) Behaviors for Older and Younger Siblings in Each Group at Each Time

	Same Sex							
	Small Interval				Large Interval			
	Female		Male		Female		Male	
	Younger	Older	Younger	Older	Younger	Older	Younger	Older
TIME								
Time 1	6.0 (6.7)	11.6 (17.0)	3.2 (4.0)	6.0 (8.8)	5.7 (5.9)	15.1 (16.4)	4.5 (4.7)	6.4 (7.7)
Time 2	6.1 (18.1)	12.9 (33.4)	5.3 (18.3)	14.5 (32.1)	6.6 (30.2)	23.4 (43.4)	8.4 (19.6)	13.5 (29.0)
Time 3	5.7 (32.2)	25.0 (83.0)	2.8 (31.2)	7.2 (54.4)	4.0 (45.2)	10.0 (69.6)	3.3 (43.0)	15.3 (80.3)

	Mixed Sex							
	Small Interval				Large Interval			
	Female Older		Male Older		Female Older		Male Older	
	Younger	Older	Younger	Older	Younger	Older	Younger	Older
TIME								
Time 1	3.0 (3.1)	13.5 (16.4)	4.6 (5.5)	9.3 (15.6)	6.1 (6.5)	17.0 (29.1)	5.3 (7.3)	9.4 (14.2)
Time 2	2.7 (18.4)	12.3 (34.9)	4.2 (23.4)	7.4 (30.9)	2.5 (14.5)	9.0 (26.5)	4.4 (17.9)	9.1 (31.7)
Time 3	1.1 (26.9)	8.3 (82.0)	2.3 (35.7)	10.3 (50.0)	2.5 (34.5)	12.5 (72.0)	2.9 (26.9)	4.0 (29.4)

The finding of differences between same- and mixed-sex sibling pairs is consistent with Dunn and Kendrick's (1982) report that same-sex dyads show more positive social behavior toward each other than mixed-sex pairs. For example, they reported that upon the arrival of the second-born child into a single-child family, first-born boys were more friendly toward a male sibling than toward a female sibling.

Finally, there was a time × sex × sex composition × interval interaction ($F[2,39] = 3.42$, $p<.05$). Although interpretations of four-way interactions are quixotic, some details of the interaction may help to elucidate the lack of a main effect for time. For most types of same-sex dyads, nurturant behavior increased from time 1 to time 2 and decreased from time 2 to time 3. While mixed-sex dyads started at roughly the same levels as same-sex dyads at time 1, they decreased slightly to time 2. There was no consistent pattern for mixed-sex dyads from time 2 to time 3; the changes varied with interval and whether the male or female was the older child. Thus, levels of nurturance did not demonstrate the consistent increase across time that we found for the overall category of prosocial behavior. The increase for prosocial behavior was not surprising since it was due

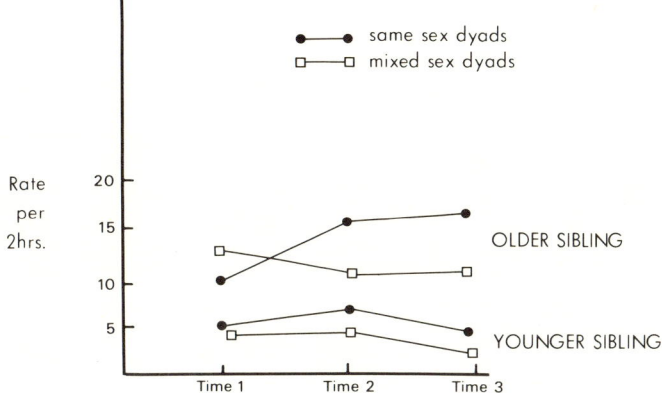

FIG. 1.1. Age and sex composition differences in nurturance.

largely to the increasing frequency of verbal requests. On the other hand, the failure to find increasing nurturance as children got older was surprising. As noted earlier, increasing social cognitive skills might be expected to produce more nurturance as children get older and, in fact, researchers have reported greater nurturance among older children. Nevertheless, we also pointed out that statements about age are often complicated by birth-order differences. For example, differences between older and younger siblings have been the most consistent positive findings in our results to date; at all times older children have initiated substantially more prosocial, nurturant, and agonistic behavior than their younger siblings. Yet, we did not know the extent to which these differences were due to age per se as opposed to birth order, or relative standing in the family. The analyses that follow attempt to examine the separate contributions of these factors.

The analyses involved comparisons of the older sibling at one point in time with the younger sibling at a later point when the younger was the same age as the older had been previously. Thus, we compared small-interval older children at time 1 with younger children at time 2, when both were approximately 3-years-old; we also compared small-interval older children at time 2 with younger children at time 3, when both groups of children were approximately 4½- to 5-years-old. The results depended strongly on whether or not requests were included in the analysis (see Fig. 1.2). When requests were included, there were no differences between first- and second-born children. That is, children of the same age, but of different birth order, were relatively similar in the frequency of prosocial behavior in both comparisons. However, when we focus only on the more nurturant behaviors excluding requests, we find that across sexes, first-

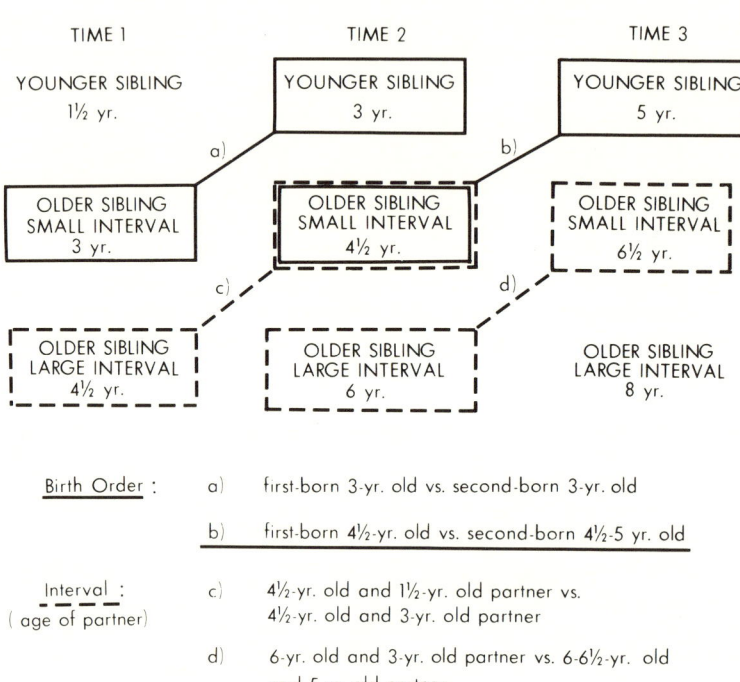

FIG. 1.2. Analyses of birth order and intervals.

born children are indeed more nurturant than second-born children in the time 1/time 2 comparison ($t[87] = 4.36$, $p<.001$; mean frequencies were 10.4 for first-born children and 5.1 for second-born children) and in the time 2/time 3 comparison ($t[76] = 5.94$, $p<.001$; mean frequencies were 11.6 for first-born children and 3.2 for second-born children).

For the sake of balance, a similar analysis was conducted for agonistic acts with the idea that we might find that although first-born children are "nicer," they are also "nastier." In fact, our hypothesis was corroborated by the data. First-born children were significantly more agonistic than second-born children at time 1/time 2 ($t[87] = 4.21$; mean of 17.5 for first-born and 7.8 for second-born) and at time 2/time 3 ($t[76] = 3.75$, $p<.001$; mean of 19.0 for first-born and 8.7 for second-born). Therefore, our data suggest that greater nurturance (and aggression) is not a function of increasing cognitive functioning but of relative position in the family.

However, one obvious objection to the above exercise is that we have confounded age of partner in our attempt to tease apart age and birth order. In other words, the finding that a first-born 3-year-old is nicer and nastier than a second-born 3-year-old is complicated by their having either younger or older partners. An easy answer to this objection is that this confounding of birth order and age of sibling partner is inevitable in the two-child family—part of what it means to be a first- or second-born sibling.

Nevertheless, the role of the age of partner is an important question. In fact, our previously reported comparisons of large- and small-interval dyads were designed to determine whether interaction differed when second-born siblings of a given age interacted with first-born siblings who were either 1½- or 3-years-older. The findings revealed no effect of age interval (or age of partner). In one last look at the question, we decided to test the role of interval or age of partner by comparing same-age first-borns interacting with second-born siblings of different ages.

Our design allowed us to do this by comparing one group of 4½-year-old first-borns interacting with 1½-year-old siblings (large-interval dyads at time 1) with another group of 4½-year-old first-borns with 3-year-old siblings (small interval dyads at time 2). These two groups of first-borns were also compared when they were 6-years-of-age. The comparisons revealed that the first-borns' nurturance did not vary with the age of the younger sibling; measures for nurturance were nearly identical for the two groups of first-borns at both 4 and 6 years. On the other hand, when the groups were compared in terms of the broader category of prosocial behaviors, we found an interval, or age-of-partner effect—there were twice as many prosocial behaviors among first-borns whose younger siblings were close in age ($t[66] = 4.02$, $p<.001$ at 4 years; $t[50] = 3.28$, $p<.005$ at 6 years). Since prosocial behavior consists of nurturance plus requests, it appears that having a more verbal younger sibling may simply spur the older child to use requests more frequently. These analyses reinforce our general findings that relative age or birth order within the dyad is an important factor while age spacing or age of partner is not, when one is looking at the patterning of sibling interaction.

Sex Differences

Although the analyses of variance revealed consistent age differences, the results were also surprisingly consistent in failing to reveal any effects of interval or sex of the individual child. The lack of sex differences was especially surprising in light of numerous suggestions of greater nurturance on the part of females and the frequent finding of sex differences in peer agonism (Maccoby & Jacklin, 1974). It is possible that differences were obscured by the global nature of our nurturance behavior category; with a finer-grained analysis, sex differences might emerge. Based on the possibility that males might be more physical and females more verbal in their interactions, we looked for sex differences in physical and verbal affection, and for balance, in physical and verbal agonism. These categories were defined as follows: Verbal affection was comprised of the categories of praise and verbal comfort (e.g., "I think you are nice" or "Do you feel better now?"). Physical affection was positive physical contact (e.g., hug, kiss, pat). Verbal aggression was defined as remarks which were insults, scolds, or commands (e.g., "You're a dummy" or "I don't like you"). Physical aggression was negative physical contact (e.g., hit, push, bite, pull hair).

Despite the different measures, no sex differences among the younger siblings were found. However, there were differences for older siblings. These emerged in chi-square comparisons of males and females, summed across time periods and the factors of interval and sex composition. A median-split was done and children were classified as low or high on physical affection and verbal affection (0 or 1 acts vs. 2 or more), physical agonism (0–5 acts vs. 6–34 acts), and verbal agonism (0–29 acts vs. 30–112 acts). Nearly two-thirds of all older sisters were high in verbal affection while only one-third of the older brothers were ($X^2[1] = 4.09, p<.05$). In contrast, there were no differences in physical affection or verbal aggression—males and females were approximately evenly divided between the high and low groups for both variables. On the other hand, three-fourths of the older brothers were in the high physical aggression category, which contained fewer than one-third of the older sisters ($X^2[1] = 10.1, p<.002$). It is important to note that these sex differences emerge only when the data of the children from all of the cells are examined together. Thus, it could be argued that although some siblings display typical sex-typed behavior, sex-stereotyping is not pervasive in sibling interaction.

The findings presented above indicate that older siblings are both more agonistic and more nurturant than their younger brothers' and sisters and that more positive behavior may characterize same-sex dyads. However, we also know that there are striking individual differences in affective tone within these broad groupings, as Dunn and Kendrick's work with younger dyads has shown (Dunn & Kendrick, 1981). In the following section, individual differences in affective quality of sibling interaction are examined in two ways. The first is to determine whether the degree of nurturance/agonism on the part of one sibling is related to the degree of nurturance/agonism on the part of the other. The second type of analysis is to determine whether there is stability in the quality of interaction from one longitudinal assessment to the next.

In an attempt to look at these issues we first calculated correlations based on the *frequencies* of behaviors. On the whole, these resulted in some positive correlations between the prosocial behavior of one partner and the prosocial behavior of the other, particularly at time 3. On the other hand, there were no correlations between the prosocial behavior of one child and the agonistic behavior of his/her sibling and almost no individual stability for either prosocial or agonistic behavior across time. We suspected that the absence of associations might be due to the confounding effect of differences in activity level across dyads, and across time. Therefore, we carried out a correlational analysis in which activity level was partialed out—activity level was defined as the sum of the prosocial and agonistic behaviors of the dyad. The resulting correlations revealed a very consistent negative relationship between the nurturant behavior of one sibling and the agonistic behavior of the other. This relationship held across all three time periods and across the four types of dyads (same-sex male, same-sex female, mixed-sex male older, and mixed-sex female older). The results are summarized in Table 1.2. The median correlation for the twelve resulting correlations between the younger's nurturance and the older's agonism was r = −.60 (range .17 to −.96) and eight of the twelve correlations were significant. The median correlation for the twelve resulting correlations between the younger's agonism and the older's nurturance was r = −.39 (range, .38 to −.93) and five of the twelve correlations were significant. Having found a relationship between the positive behavior of one child and the negative behavior of the other, we proceeded to look at the relationship between nurturant behavior of the younger and older siblings. To capture affective quality, rather than quantity of interaction, correlations were based on the proportion of each child's nurturant

TABLE 1.2
Complementarity and Individual Differences: Partial Correlations Between the Nurturance of one Partner and the Agonism of the Other

	Same Sex			
	Female		Male	
	YN-OA[a]	YA-ON	YN-OA	YA-ON
TIME				
Time 1	−.40	−.35	−.60*	−.15
Time 2	−.60*	−.27	−.90*	−.35
Time 3	.17	−.93*	−.28	−.96*

	Mixed Sex			
	Female Older		Male Older	
	YN-OA	YA-ON	YN-OA	YA-ON
TIME				
Time 1	−.70*	−.71*	−.80*	−.60
Time 2	−.50*	.38	−.44	−.62*
Time 3	−.60*	−.42	−.70*	−.37

[a] Y = younger child, O = older child, N = nurturance, A = agonism
*$p < .05$

behavior out of the total of that child's nurturant plus agonistic behavior. Almost all of these correlations were positive at the different times and for different types of dyads (see Table 1.3). Specifically, the median correlation for the twelve correlations was r = .49 (range, −.02 to .88) and six of twelve correlations were significant, although three of these were accounted for by one dyad type, the same-sex females. Nevertheless, nurturance is tied to the overall affective tone of the dyad, in the sense that nurturance of one child correlates positively in some cases with nurturance of the other and in many cases negatively with the agonism of the other child.

The evidence for stability of individual differences was not as clear. As noted above, previous correlations based on frequency revealed no evidence for individual stability. Therefore, correlations were recalculated based on the proportion of nurturant behavior; these were calculated for the dyad as a whole, for the younger sibling alone, and for the older sibling alone. Correlations were calculated between time 1 and time 2 and between time 2 and time 3 for each of the four types of dyads, resulting in eight correlations for dyads, eight for younger siblings and eight for older siblings (see Table 1.4). For dyads, the median correlation for proportional stability of nurturant behavior was r = .35 (range, −.48 to .76); two positive correlations and the single negative correlation were significant. For younger siblings, there was more evidence of stability. The

TABLE 1.3
Complementarity and Individual Differences: Proportional Correlations Between the Nurturance of One Partner and the Nurturance of the Other

	Same Sex	
	YN-ON Female	YN-ON Male
TIME		
Time 1	.49*	.26
Time 2	.49*	.09
Time 3	.84*	.88*

	Mixed Sex	
	YN-ON Female Older	YN-ON Male Older
Time		
Time 1	.48*	.22
Time 2	−.02	.34
Time 3	.31	.77*

Y = younger child, O = older child, N = nurturance
$p < .05$

TABLE 1.4
Stability of Individual Differences in Level of Nurturance: Proportional Correlations Across Time for Individuals and Dyads[a]

	Same Sex					
	Female			Male		
	Y	O	Dyad	Y	O	Dyad
Across Times 1 & 2	.34	.70*	.76*	.71*	.41	.36
Across Times 2 & 3	.00	.37	.15	.77*	.41	.43

	Mixed Sex					
	Female Older			Male Older		
	Y	O	Dyad	Y	O	Dyad
Across Times 1 & 2	.31	-.47	-.48*	.50*	.22	.33
Across Times 2 & 3	.66*	.49	.58*	.28	.31	.21

[a]Based on the proportion of nurturant acts out of the frequency of prosocial and agonistic acts for a child or dyad.
*$p < .05$

median correlation was r = .42 (range, −.31 to .77); four of seven positive correlations were significant. Finally, the lack of stability of dyads may reflect the greater variability of the older sibling across times since there was less stability in their behavior taken alone. The median correlation was r = .41 (range, −.47 to .70); one of seven positive correlations was significant.

It is notable that predicting behavior from one time to another is more difficult than predicting the behavior of one child from the behavior of his/her sibling at any given time. The power of the second type of prediction clearly reflects the importance of mutuality and reciprocity in sibling interaction. If you are nasty your sibling will not be nice, but if you are nice your sibling will be as well. The balance for the dyad might change over time, but the reciprocity in the relationship will not.

CONCLUSIONS

This analysis of nurturance between siblings addressed the following themes: how nurturance relates to the variables of sex, age, birth-order, and interval; how the nurturant behavior of one sibling relates to the nurturant and agonistic behavior of the other sibling; and how individual differences and changes over time might relate to the development of nurturance. The results revealed that older children were more nurturant than their younger siblings. This difference suggests that the sibling relationship is at least somewhat complementary. The older siblings seem to perceive the needs of their younger brothers and sisters and respond accordingly, with nurturant behaviors such as helping, comforting, and praising. The nurturant behavior of the older siblings was generally supportive and often reflected unselfish motives. For example, in the following account of one of the same-sex male dyads one can observe the way in which the older boy (O) forfeits a win by helping his younger brother (Y) in a game of checkers.

> Y: "Oh no, you're about to jump me!"
> (O pauses, as if to think.)
> O: "No, there's no other choice . . . no, don't do that . . . I think this is your safest move."
> (Y accepts the advice and moves his checker man to the recommended spot and wins the point.)
> Y: "Crown me!"

Although this 7-year-old boy may have enjoyed the win himself, he nevertheless considered the needs of his younger brother and chose to help him win instead.

It may be that the younger siblings also contribute to the complementary nature of nurturance by seeking out their older siblings for help and expertise. However, there were actually very few specific requests by the younger child for help—for example, in direct requests for teaching (Pepler, 1981). It appears, therefore, that the older child assumes the dominant role and offers nurturance even when it is not solicited. A reasonable hypothesis about the spontaneous nurturance on the part of the older siblings is that it results from their more advanced perspective-taking skills. However, the data on age versus birth-order suggest that it is not the result of more mature cognitive functioning since age per se did not seem important. Rather, having someone younger around to nurture may be the key. Of course, some level of perspective-taking is necessary, if not sufficient, for some of the sensitive nurturing we observed. In the following example, again of two brothers, note how the older child is concerned with not just the safety and comfort of his younger brother, but especially with his sibling's feelings. Note also, the difference in the younger child's perspective of the interaction—a more egocentric, or at least single-minded, view of their activity.

> The boys were playing ball hockey in the basement and it was now the younger sibling's turn to be in goal.
> O: "Do you have a shinguard? I'll do that up for you, Matt."
> Y: "No hard shots."
> O: "When you see a slapshot coming . . . you see one slapshot coming at you, Matt . . . Matt, don't get frustrated if I score."
> Y: "Right . . . um . . . um . . . Don't take a hard shot, O.K.?"

Although the data revealed significantly greater nurturance on the part of older siblings, the contribution of the younger children should not be overlooked. The nurturance data indicate that the younger children initiated approximately one-fourth of all the nurturant behaviors. Even though they were not equal partners, the younger siblings were certainly nurturing in their interactions with their older siblings—indicating that the sibling relationship is reciprocal as well as complementary. The following account of a play sequence in an older-female, younger-male dyad, reflects the ability of the younger child to maintain or extend the interaction when faced with the possibility that his older sister may give up, should she become too frustrated by external forces (in this case, a closet door). His offers to close the door evidence nurturance, helping, and verbal reassurance.

O & Y are playing in the cupboard. Toys are spilling out, making it difficult for O to close the door.

    O: "I can't shut it!"
    Y: "OK, I will shut it." (Toys start to spill out.)
    O: "Oh no!"
    Y: "OK, I will shut it." (Y gets the door closed.)
    O: "We did great work, right?" (Both laugh.)

Surprisingly, the analyses revealed no effect for sex of the individual child in overall nurturance, contrary to general expectations of greater nurturance by females. The unexpected nurturance of young males is illustrated by a little boy's interest in nurturant play in the face of sex stereotyping by his older sister in the following account from the time 3 data. O is playing with her doll and carriage.

    Y: "Karen, can I play with you?"
    O: "You can do that (she points to something else) but you can't stroll. I'm strolling."
    Y: "Is . . . is this strolling?" (he demonstrates)
    O: "No! . . . I drove the carriage. You don't stroll the baby . . . I do!"
    Y: "I do . . . I want to . . . Mom, Mom! Karen won't let me have a stroll with the baby!"
    O: "Jason . . . you can't . . . you're a boy!"

Nevertheless, we did find a sex difference in comparing boys and girls on physical versus verbal nurturance and agonism. Older girls were verbally more nurturant and older boys were physically more aggressive. Thus, the styles of both nurturant and aggressive interactions may differ for older brothers and sisters.

When we turned from sex of the individual child to sex composition of the dyad, we began to see clearer effects on nurturance. Same-sex dyads initiated significantly more nurturant behaviors than mixed-sex dyads especially at times 2 and 3. This finding may indicate that the quality of a same-sex sibling relationship is more positive as compared to a mixed-sex relationship. As noted earlier, Dunn's observations of younger sibling dyads in Britain revealed more positive social behavior and less aggressive behavior in same-sex dyads than in mixed-sex dyads.

Dunn and her colleagues (Dunn & Kendrick, 1981) propose that these differences reflect the impact of the mother on the nature of sibling interaction. They have found that the mother is especially positive with an infant who is not the same sex as the older sibling; they speculate that this leads to greater jealousy on the part of the older child in a mixed-sex dyad and to less positive sibling interaction. In a more positive vein, it could be that there is simply more opportunity for an older same-sex sibling to be nurturant since the mother is not so solicitous with her new child. Alternatively, the same-sex older child may identify more with the younger child. Dunn describes the same-sex older child as more frequently "sharing" toys with the baby. In any case, our own findings concerning the mother's role and sex composition differences do not fit neatly with Dunn's analysis. There were sex composition effects at times 2 and 3 but not at time 1 when the sample was closest in age to Dunn's and when jealousy might be expected to be at the peak. Furthermore, a previous paper (Corter, Abramovitch, & Pepler, 1983) reported no differences in positive or negative maternal behavior toward children in mixed-sex versus same-sex dyads. On the other hand, in same-sex dyads there were larger correlations between the mother's positive behavior toward the older and younger child, as well as between her negative behavior toward the older and younger child. Thus mothers appear to be more consistent in their treatment of same-sex children and it is possible to imagine how differences in maternal consistency could effect sex composition differences in nurturance. For example, more inconsistency in mothers' treatment of their mixed-sex children could lead to more resentment and less positive, nurturant behavior between the siblings.

Another plausible interpretation of the sex-composition difference is that same-sex dyads develop more common interests and shared activities than mixed-sex dyads, having received reinforcement for sex-appropriate play behavior via parents, peers, or television, etc. Therefore, there may be more opportunities for them to interact directly by helping, giving or sharing. Siblings in mixed-sex dyads may engage in different activities and therefore interact more "at arm's length" by verbal exchange. In fact, there were indications of increasing differentiation in the mixed-sex dyads, such as a more rapid decrease in imitation by younger siblings in mixed-sex dyads.

Once again, we have found that the nature of interaction is not affected by interval or, as we have considered it here, age of partner. This was the case even though we adopted a different strategy in the analyses just reported in which we compared same-age first-borns with either closely or widely spaced younger siblings; previously we had compared same-age second-borns with either closely or widely spaced older siblings and found no differences. There was one minor exception—requests were much more frequent when the older sibling interacted with a closely-spaced younger sibling, presumably because of the greater verbal skills of the closely-spaced younger siblings.

The examination of individual differences in the affective quality of sibling dyads revealed two general points. First, the golden rule is generally at work in the sibling dyad in that the degree to which one sibling is nurturant correlates with the other sibling's degree of nurturance. Second, there is very little stability in the affective quality of sibling interaction across 18-month time periods. There are a number of possible explanations for this somewhat unexpected lack of stability. It may be that the changing face of the sibling dyad reflects the decreasing needs of the younger sibling for comfort, affection, help, etc. as she or he matures. This developmental change may interact with other developmental trends, such as the increasing sensitivity and perspective-taking of the older sibling in different ways in different dyads. It is also possible that there is stability but our method was not adequate to capture it. Thus, it is possible that our definitions of behavior may have contributed to the lack of stability. We used the same operational definitions across the entire span of this study and may have inadvertently "missed the intent" behind some of the behaviors observed. As an example, the definition of nurturance was limited to a subset of prosocial behaviors, but it may be that some agonistic behaviors of the older child are motivated by caring or concern for the younger child's needs. In this vein, Bryant (1982) notes that differences between adult-child caretaking and sibling-sibling caretaking may reflect a lack of caretaking skills on the part of the older sibling. Although the intent to help may be present, the skills necessary to perform adult-like caretaking are not, and consequently unskilled helping strategies may appear to be agonistic. Consider the following example seen at our time 3 observation: The mother had asked the children to play in the same room and had then gone upstairs. Mary-Leah (older) is wandering around the room singing. Randy (younger) is kicking a doll.

- O: "Randy, where are you?"
- Y: "Here."
- O: "What did you see?"
- Y: "Get you, get you." (he takes O's doll and clowns around with it)
- O: "Randy! We're supposed to play, and not be so bad, like you are!" (O then slaps Y)

Is this aggression or some form of sibling caretaking? Although Mary-Leah's intent may have been to replicate her mother's efforts to control the younger child, she nevertheless did hit Randy and her behavior was recorded as an act of agonism. Bryant's point is certainly worth considering but it should be noted that we were unable to find other examples of aggression that might have served a caretaking function in our time 3 data.

Aside from issues of definition, other methodological limitations of the study might have masked individual stability in the affective quality of the interaction. Among these, limitations in sampling merit particular mention. A total of 5 hours of naturalistic observation, across three points in time, separated by 18 mon, is a rather modest look at the complexion of a complex relationship. To take this point further, our observers reported that the context of the interaction between siblings was important in determining affective quality on some occasions. For example, in some observations, the children might spend most of their time in a single activity which fostered a particular quality of interaction. Thus, coloring at the kitchen table could produce a high frequency of nurturant acts such as giving objects (crayons) and very little agonism. Given that the observations were unstructured, it was unlikely that the dyad would be observed in the same context eighteen months later. Naturally, such variability would obscure stability in the quality of the sibling relationship. On the other hand, most of the observations sampled a variety of activities on the part of the children and were not as limited as the preceding example. Even so, the negative findings concerning stability in the sibling relationship must not be taken as the final word on this issue.

In summary, the observations of sibling interaction indicate that there is a considerable amount of nurturant, supportive behavior between brothers and sisters. Although there is also negative, aggressive behavior, the popular conception of the sibling relationship as *basically* hostile and rivalrous is clearly wrong. Lest the reader think we have slanted our analyses toward the positive, having been duped by sampling a middle-class veneer of nurturant social convention, masking the deeper reality of sibling rivalry and competition, we should recall the cross-cultural observation that caretaking by older siblings is commonplace. In an even broader view, a review of mammalian sibling interaction by Bekoff (1981) shows that alloparental care by siblings is common in a number of species. Although there are notable examples of competition, such as piglets jostling for teats, Bekoff's review revealed that ". . . there are very few substantive data concerning selfish sibling rivalry in nonhuman mammals" (p. 324).

Although the size of our sample was not large, the general pattern of results was quite consistent over time and we feel that these results are reasonably representative of two-child middle-class families. The clearest part of the pattern of results is the difference between the older and younger sibling. We have shown that across times and types of dyads the older child is more nurturant but also more agonistic. In this chapter we have taken the analysis of this variable further than in previous papers by showing that it is not age per se that produced this difference since the age of child or age of partner did not account for differences in interaction. Instead, it is the relative age of older/younger—or in other words, birth-order—that seems to be the key. This finding provides important support for accounts of birth-order effects that include differential sibling experiences for different birth-order positions.

Aside from isolating the effects of birth-order, we were less successful in delineating other factors which account for variability and individual differences in sibling interaction. The results suggest that it is too simplistic to think that age spacing or sex will account for much of the variability in sibling behavior. A next step in studying the determinants of sibling interaction is to consider the development of these behaviors within the broader framework of family interaction and to identify the formative processes and the directions of influences. We are currently studying such factors as the relationship between mother and first-born before the arrival of the second child, infant temperament, and paternal involvement. It is also of interest to trace the development of the sibling relationship beyond early childhood into adolescence and adulthood (cf. Cicirelli, 1980). With respect to early childhood, however, there are still many unanswered questions about the sibling relationship; more answers about siblings may provide new perspectives on the development of social understanding and nurturance.

REFERENCES

Abramovitch, R., Corter, C., & Lando, B. (1979). Sibling interaction in the home. *Child Development, 50,* 997–1003.

Abramovitch, R., Corter, C., & Pepler, D. (1980). Observations of mixed-sex sibling dyads. *Child Development, 51,* 1268–1271.

Barry, H., III., Brown, M. K., & Child, I. L. (1957). A cross-cultural survey of some sex differences in socialization. *Journal of Abnormal and Social Psychology, 55,* 327–332.

Bekoff, M. (1981). Mammalian sibling interaction. In D. Gabernick & P. Klopfer (Eds.), *Parental care in mammals.* New York: Plenum.

Berman, P., & Goodman, V. (1984). Age and sex differences in children's responses to babies: effects of adults' caretaking requests and instructions. *Child Development, 55*(3), 1071–1077.

Berman, P., & Zahn-Waxler, C. (1983, April). *Children's nurturance to younger children: Age, sex, and the situation.* Presented at the meeting of the Society for Research in Child Development, Detroit.

Bossard, J., & Boll, E. (1956). *The large family system.* Philadelphia: University of Pennsylvania Press.

Bryant, B. K. (1982). Sibling relationships in middle childhood. In M. Lamb & B. Sutton-Smith (Eds.), *Sibling relationships: Their nature and significance across the lifespan.* Hillsdale, NJ: Lawrence Erlbaum Associates.

Cicirelli, V. G. (1973). Effects of sibling structure and interaction on children's categorization style. *Developmental Psychology, 9,* 132–139.

Cicirelli, V. G. (1976). Siblings teaching siblings. In V. L. Allen (Ed.), *Children as teachers.* New York: Academic Press.

Cicirelli, V. G. (1980). A comparison of college women's feelings towards their siblings and parents. *Journal of Marriage and the Family, 42,* 111–117.

Corter, C., Abramovitch, R., & Pepler, D. (1983). The role of the mother in sibling interaction. *Child Development, 54,* 1599–1605.

Corter, C., Pepler, D., & Abramovitch, R. (1982). The effects of situation and sibling status on sibling interaction. *Canadian Journal of Behavioural Sciences, 14,* 380–392.

Dunn, J., & Kendrick, C. (1981). Social behavior of young siblings in the family context: Differences between same-sex and different-sex dyads. *Child Development, 52,* 1265–1273.

Dunn, J., & Kendrick, C. (1982). *Siblings: Love, envy and understanding.* Cambridge, MA: Harvard University Press.

Kendrick, C., & Dunn, J. (1983). Sibling quarrels and maternal responses. *Developmental Psychology, 19,* 62–70.

Lamb, M. (1978a). Interaction between 18-month-olds and their preschool-aged siblings. *Child Development, 49,* 51–59.

Lamb, M. (1978b). The development of sibling relationships in infancy: A short-term longitudinal study. *Child Development, 49,* 1189–1196.

Maccoby, E., & Jacklin, C. (1974). *The psychology of sex differences.* Stanford, CA: Stanford University Press.

McCall, R. B., & Applebaum, M. I. (1973). Bias in the analysis of repeated measures designs: some alternative approaches. *Child Development, 44,* 401–415.

Minnett, A. M., Lowe-Vandell, D., & Santrock, J. W. (1983). The effects of sibling status on sibling interactions: Influence of birth order, age spacing, sex of child and sex of sibling. *Child Development, 54,* 1064–1072.

Pepler, D. (1981, April). *Naturalistic observations of teaching and modeling between siblings.* Paper presented at the Biennial Meeting of the Society for Research in Child Development, Boston.

Pepler, D., Corter, C., & Abramovitch, R. (1982). Social relations among children: Siblings and peers. In K. Rubin & H. Ross (Eds.), *Peer relationships and social skills in childhood.* New York: Springer-Verlag.

Samuels, H. R. (1977, March). *The role of the sibling in the infant's social environment.* Paper presented at the meeting of the Society for Research in Child Development, New Orleans.

Stewart, R. B. (1983). Sibling attachment relationships: Child-infant interactions in the strange-situation. *Developmental Psychology, 19,* 192–199.

Weisner, T., & Gallimore, R. (1977). My brother's keeper: Child and sibling caretaking. *Current Anthropology, 18,* 169–180.

White, B. (1980). *A parent's guide to the first three years.* Englewood Cliffs, NJ: Prentice Hall.

Whiting, B., & Edwards, C. P. (1973). A cross-cultural analysis of sex differences in the behavior of children aged three through eleven. *Journal of Social Psychology, 91,* 171–188.

Whiting, B., & Whiting, J. W. M. (1975). *Children of six cultures.* Cambridge, MA: Harvard University Press.

2 Young Children's Responses to Babies: Do They Foreshadow Differences Between Maternal and Paternal Styles?

Phyllis W. Berman
National Institute of Child Health and Human Development

Although mothers have entered the labor force in increasing numbers, mothers' caregiving parental roles remain unmatched by fathers. When and how do the sex differences in orientation to the young begin? This chapter is devoted to an exploration of early sex and age differences in children's nurturance to younger children. The study focuses on interactions between age, sex, and situational variables, that is, on variables that are specific to the social context, the task at hand, or to ways in which children construe the situation.

As might be expected, age is an important variable. Research has demonstrated that children are capable of performing caring acts towards others as early as the second year of life (Rheingold, Hay, & West, 1976). Motivation for these acts is obviously not entirely dependent upon highly developed cognitive abilities, thought to be typical of only older children. In addition, the relationship between age and nurturing is neither simple nor linear and age often interacts with sex and social setting.

Similarly, although females are often believed to be more nurturant than males to infants and young children, this is often not so (Berman, 1980). In our research we have found that the social setting is of great importance in determining male and female children's responses to younger children and babies and, consequently, to the existence and size of sex differences.

Various social situations pose demands for different types of responses associated with nurturance. Therefore, this chapter includes an examination of age and sex differences in a variety of responses to the young such as attraction, spontaneous play, instructed and uninstructed caretaking behavior, and altruistic acts such as helping, sharing, and donating.

ATTRACTION TO INFANT FEATURES

Proximity is a necessary, although not sufficient condition for nurturance and, therefore, attraction to babies is an important precondition for most, if not all of the behaviors with which we are concerned. We know that even infants can distinguish between persons on the basis of age (Brooks & Lewis, 1976) but we do not know whether young children are *attracted* to younger children and infants. If so, what is the course of developmental changes in attraction toward the young for girls and for boys throughout childhood and adolescence? Does attraction begin early, grow or decline with age, and does it follow a different course for females and males?

Only Lorenz's (1943) theory provides a definitive hypothesis. An "attraction-to-babies" response is attributed to innate mechanisms. The behavior is thought to be released by the sight of physical characteristics typical of infants: a head that is large in proportion to body size; a forehead that is large in proportion to facial size; large eyes; short, heavy, large-footed limbs; round protruding cheeks; and soft elastic skin. Lorenz was not explicit about possible age or sex differences in this unlearned response, but he described examples of the response in his daughters who were less than 2-years-old, comparing their responses to dolls and, in one case, to a ball of wool from a knitting basket, to a mature woman's responses to a baby.

Although the theory was, and still is incompletely specified, it is quite clear that the most potent aspects of the baby stimuli are visual. Therefore, picture stimuli seem appropriate to test the theory but there have been few tests of the developmental course of children's responses to this type of stimuli. However, in 1976 Fullard and Reiling reported that they had presented pairs of slides of infant and adult humans and animals to graduate students and to school children in grades 2, 4, 6, 8, and 12, asking them to choose between infant and adult in animal and human pairs, the picture that was liked best. Children from grades 2 through 6 preferred adults to infants, but subjects from grade 8 and above preferred infants. The younger subjects' preference for adults was significantly greater in females than males but the sex difference was reversed for the older subjects. Interestingly, there was a significant interaction that indicated male subjects preferred infants more often when the stimuli were pictures of animals, rather than human babies, but separate data were not presented for the two types of stimulus pictures. Fullard and Reiling's data were difficult to interpret because details were not provided about sex, age, and particularly, about the physical attractiveness of the pictured individuals.

It is important to trace the course of children's preference for pictures of infants while controlling for the sex, age, and physical attractiveness of the stimuli. In order to have some check upon our method and on the generality of our results, two replications of a preference study were designed, one replication with white subjects and stimulus pictures of white individuals, and another, with

2. CHILDREN'S RESPONSES TO BABIES   27

black subjects and stimulus pictures of black individuals. No pictures of animals were used. Forty-nine university student volunteers served as judges, each dividing four large pools of pictures into three groups of equal size: high-, medium-, and low-attractive pictures. That is, each judge chose pictures of high-, medium-, and low-attractive individuals from four groups: pictures of 12-month-old baby girls, those of 12-month-old baby boys, those of women judged to be between 35- and 55-years-old, and those of men judged to be in the same age range. Black students judged pictures of black individuals, and white students judged pictures of whites.

Thus, all subjects were presented with pictures of individuals of their own race, chosen by judges of the same race. Forty pairs of pictures of middle-attractive individuals were presented to white subjects and 32 pairs of pictures of blacks were presented to black subjects. Figure 2.1 shows three sample stimulus pairs used. For each of the replications, on half of the trials (target trials) a picture of a baby was paired with a picture of a middle-aged adult of the same sex and race. Half of the target pairs were pictures of males; half were pictures of females. On the remaining (nontarget) trials a picture of a male was paired with a

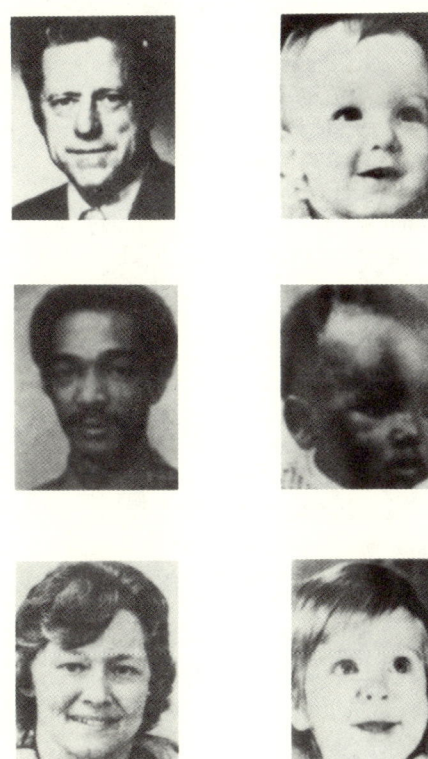

FIG. 2.1. Three pairs of choice stimuli used for the infant-adult picture preference study.

picture of a female in the same age group. (See Berman, Goodman, Sloan, & Fernander, 1978, for details.)

Two samples of subjects were drawn from the research school of Florida State University: 68 white subjects and 74 black subjects from grades 2, 3, and 4 in the younger groups, and grades 9, 10, and 11 in the older groups. The percentage of target trials on which infants were preferred to adults by black and white younger and older children is shown in Table 2.1. Although the black and white subjects responded to different stimuli, the pattern of results was similar for the two samples. Girls preferred infants significantly more often than boys did. Age was not a significant variable for blacks or whites and age did not interact with sex in either sample. Except for the fact that preadolescent black girls preferred infants considerably more often than preadolescent white girls, the two samples were remarkably similar in their preferences for infants.

It appeared that by the time children reached second grade both girls and boys showed a preference for the physical features of infants although this preference was stronger for girls than it was for boys. These results were in accord with Lorenz's hypothesis. However, we don't know how early the preference for infants becomes established, if it is native or acquired and, if learned, what circumstances control the acquisition of this preference. The same questions might be asked about the sex differential in the preference for infants. It should be noted that self-report studies such as this, that utilize rather minimal representations of infants, such as static, two dimensional illustrations of infant faces, may yield results that are very much influenced by the demand characteristics and social context of the experiments (cf. Berman, 1980). For that reason each subject completed the task in private without the presence of an experimenter or other subjects. (Younger subjects were first trained with other materials to report their preferences.) Nevertheless, the information that can be gleaned from self-

TABLE 2.1
Preference for Infants expressed as a percentage of the Total number of Choices made by Black and White Adolescent and Preadolescent Children

Subjects' Grade:	Subjects' Sex:	
	Male	Female
2, 3, & 4	Black 54	72
	White 56	63
9, 10, & 11	Black 57	77
	White 57	72

report preference studies is probably quite limited. We therefore planned a series of studies of children's behavior in situations where they were free to give varied responses to live babies.

OBSERVATIONAL STUDIES OF INTERACTIONS WITH TODDLERS

Private day care centers in Tallahassee, Florida provided an excellent environment to observe the responses of young children to infants and toddlers. Those centers with facilities for the care of babies housed infants and children separately so that the older children's experience with infants and toddlers was generally limited to brief contacts while arriving at and leaving school and sometimes shortlived teacher-supervised contacts on shared outdoor playgrounds. Sibling status could not always be established for each child, but most of the subjects were children of working women and of college students, and few of the children had younger siblings. Tallahassee is the capital city of the state with two universities, one of which is predominantly white and the other, largely black. The children we observed represented a well-integrated population of middle class families, approximately 10 to 15 % black, and the remainder white. Most of the parents were the clerical or managerial employees of the state government or students, faculty, or staff of one of the two universities. Our subjects generally attended preschool, kindergarten, or first grade at the centers but a few of the oldest children attended public school and were transported to a center for after school care. The babies with whom the children were observed were enrolled at the same centers.

Each of the observational studies was preceded by a period when we became regular guests or volunteer aides at the host center. This helped us to understand the structural and social conditions at the centers and design each study so that it asked questions that were meaningful in terms of the specific routines and conditions at the center. Having established that by second grade there was a significant sex difference in children's preference for pictures of babies, we wanted to know how early a reliable sex difference could be established, and whether this sex difference in preference for infant stimuli extended to a difference in attraction to live infants. We decided to measure attraction in terms of physical proximity and to pose attraction to a baby against attraction to other desirable objects and activities were available. It was possible to do this without greatly altering the daily routine of the children enrolled in one of the larger day care centers in the city. We chose to study a group of children from 32 to 63-months-old because our observations led us to believe that this is an age period when considerable sex typing in play activities takes place, and sex differences in attraction to babies may be only one of a complex of differences that arises during the preschool period.

The study was conducted in an extremely large room of a private day care center, a classroom with 43 girls and 43 boys who participated in daily activities at home-base tables, each with a home-base teacher. However, each morning at approximately the same time children were free to choose from a number of activities such as art, dance, and nature study. Each activity took place in a designated area of the room. From time to time the center had visitors who brought some animals or objects to show to the children. We, therefore, set up a visitor's area to compete with the other free play activities on each of seven consecutive days. Children were free to enter and leave this 85 x 116 inch area as they pleased during the 30-min period each day.

On all seven days of the study the area contained a playpen, flanked by three observers. There were three preliminary sessions to adapt the children to the observers, materials, and procedure, and to establish a baseline. On these days the playpen was empty. On two of the four test days (baby days) a 13-month-old white baby girl occupied the playpen. On the remaining two days the baby was absent but a large, rectangular fish tank with a goldfish was in front of the playpen. Thus, days 1 through 3 were preliminary days, days 4 and 7 were fish days, and days 5 and 6 were baby days. Fish days were scheduled as a control for novelty. When the usual announcement of free choice activities was made each day, immediately before observational recording began, the teacher added on days 1 through 3, "We have some visitors at the end of the room. They will be busy working so they won't be able to talk to you, but you may go over to see them if you like." During the following test sessions she said instead, "Our visitors are here and they have a goldfish (baby) with them today." Attendance and behavior in the visitors area (which was marked on the floor with chalk) were recorded for three 5-min periods per session interspersed with 5-min periods when reliability was checked.

Each child wore a card with an identifying number. Recorded behaviors included: (1) approaches to the observers, playpen, and fish tank when accompanied by focused looking at the object approached; (2) touching observers, peers, playpen, or fish tank; (3) verbalizations and other behaviors (e.g., kisses) directed toward the infant, observers, peers, or goldfish. Activities were classified as being directed to the observers, peers, fish (or fish tank), or to the infant (or playpen). Further details about the procedure are given in Berman, Monda, & Myerscough (1977). Whenever necessary, the observers told the children not to reach inside the playpen or fish tank, or not to touch the baby.

Girls spent significantly more time in the area than boys did when the baby was present, but not on other days. Figure 2.2 shows girls' and boys' attendance in the area on baby days and fish days as a percentage of all possible periods that might have been spent in the area. The bar graph on the left represents data from all subjects who were in school on each of the baby days or fish days. It was thought possible that some subjects might have been involved in other activities to the extent that they may never have been in the immediate locale of the

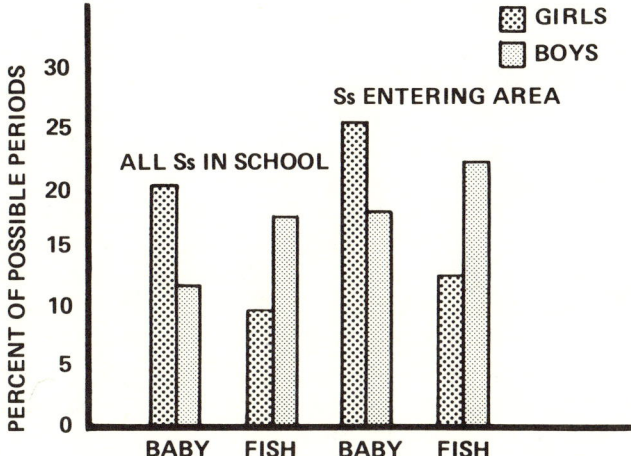

FIG. 2.2. Percent of possible periods girls and boys spent in the area surrounding the baby or the goldfish. Percentages are presented separately for all subjects in school on test days, and for only those who entered the area at least once.

visitors' area and they may have had less opportunity to spend time in the area. For this reason, data are presented in the bar graph on the right for only those children who entered the visitors' area at least once on the baby days and on the fish days. In each case, girls spent more time in the area than boys on baby days. Even more interesting was the finding that older boys within this group spent significantly *less* time in the area on baby days than younger boys did, a finding that might be expected if the older boys had acquired gender-role attitudes that were incongruent with attraction to infants. This age relationship did not hold for boys on days when the baby was not present. Examination of the data for girls showed no age trend.

This study was planned to examine attraction to a baby rather than qualitative aspects of young children's interactions with the baby, but the data are of interest because they illustrate how important situational variables are in determining interactions with babies. It cannot be assumed that children's behavior is simply the product of the stimulus qualities of the baby and of organismic conditions of the children studied. The children were studied in their usual group situations and the social qualities of these groups were major determinants of children's behavior. It was not at all unusual for a child to call to, or to physically lead a friend into or out of the visitors' area. The children's behavior in the visitors' area was obviously under adult control, as it was in all other areas of the schoolroom. Although the observers were far less responsive than the other adults (teachers) were, they were nevertheless adults and were therefore understood to be in control. Because there were many children and only one infant, there was some concern about her safety. Therefore, her mobility was restricted and if children reached into the playpen, they were asked not to do so. It is also probably of some importance that, although our observers were two female adults and one male, all of the teachers and school personnel were female. Again, this is not an atypical environment for preschool children, and it is probably the case that in most situations when preschool children have an opportunity to interact with babies, a female adult exercises considerable control.

Figure 2.3 shows the major types of baby-oriented behaviors that occurred during preliminary days, fish days, and baby days, and the proportion of total time in the area during which the boys and girls there engaged in each activity. The most common of these involved approaches to the playpen, establishment of proximity, when possible, by touching or holding onto the playpen, and focused looking. At times, too many children surrounded the playpen for each child to touch it, and therefore, two categories of behavior were combined: approach to the playpen with focused looking, and playpen touching. Although playpen touches were sometimes brief they were rarely casual, and most often they were combined with a period of sustained and deliberate attention. Although the baby was not present on preliminary days or fish days children responded to the

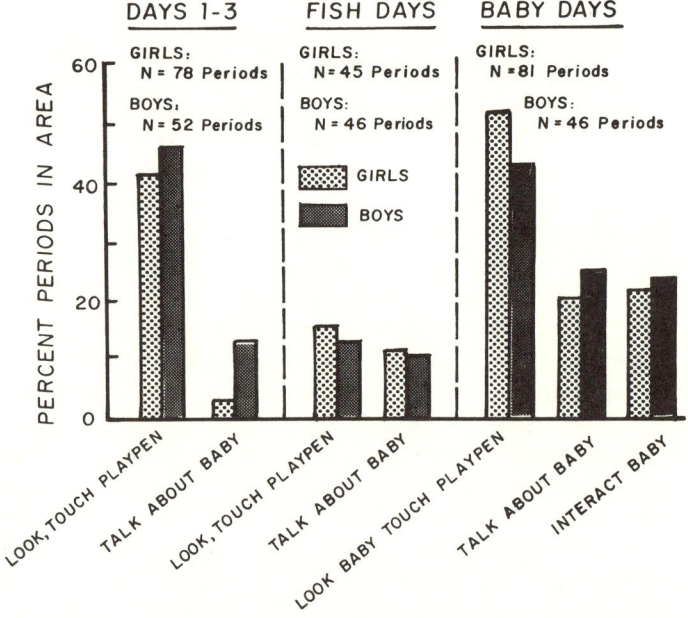

FIG. 2.3. Percentage of total number of periods boys and girls spent in the area on experimental days during which they engaged in various baby-related activities. (Reprinted from: Berman, P. W., Monda, L. C., & Myerscough, R. P. Sex differences in young children's responses to an infant: An observation within a day-care setting. *Child Development*, 1977, 48, 711–715.)

presence of the playpen and talked about babies. In fact, boys spent more of their total time in the area at the playpen on days 1 through 3 when it was unoccupied, than when the baby was present.

Direct interactions with the baby occurred during approximately a fifth of the time girls and boys were in the area in her presence. One-third of the girls and one-sixth of the boys who were in school on both baby days engaged in interactions with her. This sex difference was due to the fact that fewer boys were in the area, but boys and girls there spent the same proportion of their time there in direct interactions with her. Verbalizations to the baby were uncommon (only four children talked to her) and when they occurred they were simple and short. This is particularly interesting since verbalizations about the baby were so frequent.

Attempts to touch the baby were, by far, the most common type of interaction despite prohibitions against reaching into the playpen. The baby, a very sociable 13-month-old, during most of her time in the playpen stood at the railing or walked around its perimeter, holding the railing, sometimes reaching out, and on ten occasions touching one of the children. Those children who were nearest her, who reached toward her, or in some way attracted her attention, were most likely to be touched and it was often impossible to determine whether the child or the baby initiated the contact. However, it was obviously rewarding, since nine of the ten children whom she touched subsequently engaged in further interactions with her. Overtures to the baby and attempts to hold her attention were common. For example, one boy spent five of the six periods when the baby was present in varied but totally nonverbal interactions with her, snapping his fingers in front of her, making noises to her, positioning a chair near her playpen, climbing on it several times so that he could be seen above the other children who were at the playpen blocking her view of him, and holding up papers for her to see. Other children smiled and laughed to and kissed the baby.

The two major findings of this study were that both age and sex were important variables determining attraction to a live infant, and that the baby's behavior was of greatest importance in initiating and sustaining interactions once children were nearby. The children were in a group situation and the presence of a large group of peers was probably important. The limitations were that individual subjects' behaviors could not be studied in fine detail as they came into and left the area, and also that children's interactions with the baby had to be restricted. Therefore, a further study was planned in order to observe the behavior of individual children who were segregated with a toddler in a small space through no choice of their own. It was also decided to widen the age range studied. The age trend found for boys' attraction to a toddler was unexpected and we wanted to know if it could be replicated in another sample, and in a situation without the presence of peers. It was also thought that the age range studied might have been too narrow to reveal a trend which might be expected for girls: that is, that older girls might be more responsive than younger girls to babies. Still another important reason for planning another study was to test whether children's responses to babies could be manipulated by varying the social circumstances in which the responses take place.

SEX DIFFERENCES IN RESPONSE TO THE CARETAKER ROLE

A review of the literature (Berman, 1980) showed that sex differences are more likely when subjects are asked to take responsibility for a baby than when spontaneous play is expected. Therefore, two conditions were included in the next study: one in which young children were asked to assume the role of caretaker for the baby while available adults were "busy" and one in which spontaneous play was permitted but not required. It was hypothesized that a caretaking request is an explicit social cue with significance that depends on gender role expectations that are usually acquired late during the preschool period, probably between ages 4 and 5. Older boys were expected to respond less than younger boys to the baby, and sex differences were expected only in the older group. Differences were expected to be particularly large in a caretaking condition compared with a spontaneous play condition.

As subjects for the next study we enlisted 38 children from a different cohort of students at the same daycare center. On the basis of our previous data, boys were expected to decrease in responsiveness to babies at approximately age 4½. Therefore, we divided the available children into a group of 10 younger boys and 10 younger girls from 3½ to 4½-years-old and a group of 9 older boys and 9 older girls from 4½ to 5½-years-old. Observations took place in an unused room at the center. A small play area that was virtually littered with an abundance of toys was partitioned off from the rest of the room with bookcase dividers 3 feet tall. A male and a female toddler, 13- to 16-months-old, served in the study.

One toddler was brought into the area before each session, and after he or she was playing contentedly, the older child was escorted to the play area for 6 min of spontaneous play followed by a caretaking assignment. Specifically, children were first told that they could "play with the toys or the baby or do whatever (they) would like to do" while the observers (who were outside the partitioned play area) "work(ed) over here." The observers listened to a low volume tape with earphones. The tape signaled the beginning and end of time intervals when observations were recorded. The following types of behavior were observed: solitary play, toy interactions (offering, giving, accepting, mutual play with, or touching the same toys), physical touch, verbal or vocal interactions, verbalization or vocalization to the self, any sort of response to observers (See Berman, Sloan, & Goodman, 1979).

After 6 min subjects were told, "We're really having a hard time doing our work, and we'd like you to take care of the baby for a few minutes so we can work. You take care of the baby for us now." Observations continued for an additional 3 min in the caretaking condition.

The most frequent activity in which children engaged was solitary play (on 82% of all intervals). In contrast, interactions with the baby were only about ⅕ as frequent. Children played with, touched, or vocalized to the baby during 17% of all intervals. The most frequent interactions involved use of a toy (9% of the time), physical contact (6%), and verbalizations or vocalizations (5%). There were few verbalizations to self (3%), or to the observers (1% of the time).

Amount of baby-directed activity during spontaneous play (with verbal, physical, and toy-interactions combined) was not significantly related to age, sex, or their interaction. However, after the caretaking request there were large significant differences between all groups in amount of interaction with the baby. In this condition as predicted, older girls interacted with the baby most (43% of all intervals), and older boys the least (2% of all intervals), with younger boys and girls at intermediate levels (26% and 13% respectively). Thus, older girls interacted with the baby significantly more than any other group, older boys significantly less than any other group and, surprisingly, younger boys significantly *more* than younger girls.

To sum up then, we did find that in the main our hypotheses were verified. Assignment to caretaking roles elicited behavior that was even more traditionally sex-typed than behavior during spontaneous play. When sex differences were found they partly replicated the results of the earlier study, with older boys engaging in fewer interactions with the baby than younger boys. In addition, older girls were far more baby-directed than younger girls.

We then examined the quality of the interactions with the baby. Qualitatively distinguishable behaviors were analyzed in terms of number of episodes of various types. Episodes were defined as uninterrupted series of intervals during which a particular activity took place. That is, a brief kiss and a more extended activity, such as rolling a ball back and forth, each counted as one episode. These were tallied over all 9 min of the study for all groups and are presented in Fig. 2.4. Because episodes most often involved physical touch or interaction with a toy, with the older child either initiating positive interactions with the baby or engaging in mutually initiated interactions, the frequency of mutually initiated and older child-initiated episodes were compared for the four groups. Girls over age 4½ were the only group of children who initiated interactions more often than they engaged in mutually initiated interactions with the baby. In this respect the older girls' behaviors were more like adults' behaviors than those of the other groups. Older girls initiated approximately two episodes per session on the average. Younger children initiated few, if any episodes. Most episodes involved use of toys. Although they did not often interact with the baby, when they did interact, the boys most often engaged in mutually initiate toy interactions, exchanging toys or touching the same toy from time to time. This pattern of activities was also typical of the younger girls. The babies made few approaches

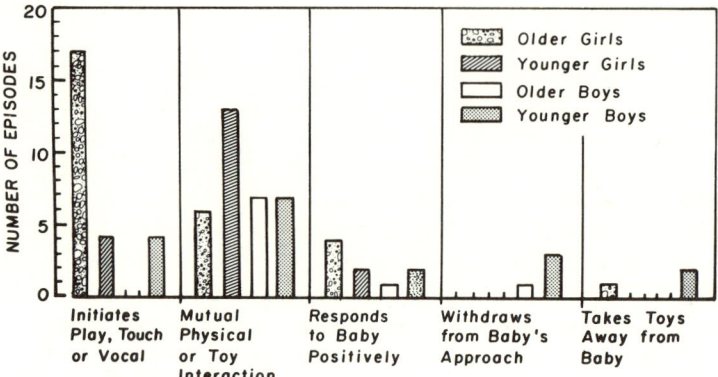

FIG. 2.4. Number of episodes when children in four age-sex groups engaged in several types of baby-related activities.

to the older children. When an approach was made, boys withdrew as often as they responded positively. The toddlers approached older girls more often than the other children, perhaps because they most often were approached by the older girls. When approached, all of the girls responded positively. However, children and babies spent a very large proportion of their time in solitary play with toys and it is difficult to draw any firm conclusions about the nature of the interactions which did occur. Therefore, another study was planned that incorporated conditions designed to elicit a greater number of interactions.

RESPONSES TO ADULTS' CARETAKING REQUESTS AND INSTRUCTIONS

It is likely that young children have limited ability to independently devise ways to initiate and maintain successful interactions with babies. It is also true that in our culture young children seldom interact with babies without some degree of adult supervision and direction. We therefore designed a study to attempt to replicate age and sex differences in children's interactions with a toddler after assignment to a caretaker role and, in addition, to observe children's responses to an adult's direct instructions concerning interactions with the toddler. Several other changes were also made in the design of this study.

Because adults' instructions always followed a period of time when children were asked to assume the caretaker role without any further instructions, a double baseline design was used so that it would be possible to distinguish the effects of the adults' instructions from the effects of simply spending time with the baby in the uninstructed caretaker condition. Moreover, previous experience had convinced us that children's interactions with toddlers were greatly affected by wide variations in toddlers' temperament and maturity. We therefore planned to enlist a large number of toddlers in this study to avoid any possible bias stemming from the idiosyncratic behavior or appearance of a particular baby. Children's level of engagement in interactions with the babies should also be highly dependent on the attractiveness of competing activities. In the previous experiment, many attractive toys had been provided. Although we had taken care to provide toys which could be used in interactive play with the baby, the older children had preferred to play by themselves with the toys. We therefore decided to reduce the competitive valence of alternative activities by providing only a few very simple toys that could be used by the older child and baby alone or in interactive play before instructions were given by an adult. We then randomly selected one toy each session and an adult instructed the child in the use of the toy to engage the baby in playful interactions.

The setting for the study was another day care center in the same city with a population of students similar to the subjects in the previously described studies. A wider age range of subjects was used in this study: 12 girls and 12 boys between 2½ years and 5 years, 3 months were subjects in the younger group; 12 girls and 12 boys between 5 years, 9-months-old and 7 years, 8-months-old were subjects in the older group. The babies with whom the subjects interacted were all regular attendees at the same center. Babies were chosen who were mature enough to approach and interact with the older children, but not mature enough to be considered peers, even by the youngest subjects. Six male and five female babies met these criteria and served in the experiment. All were able to walk but none had a vocabulary of more than a few words. The baby for any particular session was chosen on a random basis from those of the group who were awake and available, with the restriction that close to half of the 12 subjects (5–7) in each of the groups would be paired with girl babies and the remaining subjects, with boy babies.

The research area, a small triangular area, approximately 100 square feet, was the corner of a large unoccupied playroom at the center. The area was blocked-off from the rest of the room by low bookcase dividers, with the observers outside the area. Four sets of toys were provided: several balls, a set of blocks, toy trucks and cars, and a bean bag toss game. After the baby began playing, the older child was brought to the area and told, ". . . we really need someone to help us while we do some work. We're going to a room with some toys in it and a baby, and we'd like you to take care of the baby while we work. This is the baby we'd like you to take care of. We'll be doing some work right over here and it's important that no one bother or interrupt us while we do our work so we'd like you to stay right in this area with the baby. You take care of the baby now."

In a double-baseline design, half of the children in each of the four age-sex groups were randomly chosen to be in the baseline (uninstructed) caretaking condition for 6 min, and the other half, for 3 min before an experimenter entered the area for the demonstration. A toy interaction was chosen for the demonstration because our previous research had shown this to be the most likely type of interaction with the baby to occur for both sexes and each of the age groups. The experimenters each used one of the four toys saying, "I'd like to show you something. Watch me a minute." The experimenter then used the randomly selected toy in a scripted manner, picking up the toy, showing the toy to the baby, and trying to induce the baby to reach for the toy. After the demonstration the experimenter left the area and the observation was continued for another 3 min. The sex of the experimenter was balanced over the four age-sex groups.

Data recorded within 10-sec intervals included solitary play, toy interaction, accidental physical touch, all other physical touch, verbal or vocal interactions, verbalizations or vocalizations to the self, and any response to the observers. The nature of the observed behavior and initiator of the behavior were noted. The baby's behavior and the older child's behavior were observed, and at the end of each session each observer wrote a narrative account of activities and behaviors observed. (See Berman & Goodman, 1984, for a detailed description of procedures.)

Table 2.2 shows the mean percentage of all intervals before and after the demonstration when the children in each group engaged in particular activities. Total-interaction scores were determined for each subject in order to assess the extent of his or her overall interactions with the baby. These scores were the total of the three percentage scores: toy interaction plus verbal or vocal interaction plus nonaccidental physical interaction. Two scores were determined for each subject, one for the period before, and another for the period after the caretaking demonstration. The effects on children's behavior of the amount of time spent in the research situation were tested in two ways. Data from each of the age-sex groups were examined separately. For those children with a 6 min predemonstration period there was little change in the amount of interaction with the baby from the first, to the second 3 min spent in the experimental situation. There were also only small, insignificant differences within groups in the extent of postdemonstration interaction with the baby, when children with longer and shorter predemonstration periods were compared. Therefore, data from the 3- and the 6-min predemonstration subjects were combined for all further analyses.

The data presented in Table 2.2 show that efforts to reduce the extent of solitary play were successful (from 82% of all intervals in the previous study to 54%). It was the most common activity for all groups but the older girls. The most striking feature of the data is the contrast between the older girls' interactions with the toddlers and those of the other groups. In fact, the older girls' total interaction scores for the predemonstration period were almost three times as high as the younger boys' and girls', and more than seven times as high as the older boys'. The contrast between older girls' postdemonstration scores and those of the other groups' was even more striking.

TABLE 2.2
Mean Percent of all Intervals Before and After the Demonstration When Subjects in Each Group Engaged in Particular Activities (N per group = 12)

Group:	Older Girls		Younger Girls		Older Boys		Younger Boys	
Before or After Demonstration	Before	After	Before	After	Before	After	Before	After
Interaction with toys	22.7	58.3	15.7	20.8	9.3	15.3	18.8	20.4
Verbal/vocal interaction	27.8	38.9	2.8	0.9	1.4	0.9	8.3	9.7
Physical interaction	25.2	15.7	8.6	7.4	0.0	0.0	0.0	0.0
Solitary play with toys	25.9	27.3	57.6	59.7	58.6	67.6	66.0	71.3
Vocalization to self	3.5	3.2	6.9	12.0	2.1	0.9	14.8	9.0
Accidental touch	1.4	0.5	0.7	0.5	0.0	0.0	0.0	0.0
Responses to observers	0.0	0.5	0.7	1.4	0.2	0.0	0.7	1.9

Reprinted from: Berman and Goodman (1984). Age and sex differences in children's responses to babies: Effects of adults' caretaking requests and instructions. *Child Development, 55,* 1071-1077.

Analyses (cf. Berman & Goodman, 1984) showed that subjects' sex and age were significant variables, but that the high interaction scores of the older girls were responsible for these effects. That is, there was a highly significant interaction between age and sex. As predicted, there was little difference between younger boys and girls, but a large significant difference between older boys and girls. Although older boys interacted less with the baby than did younger boys, the difference was not significant. However, older girls interacted with the baby significantly more than younger girls did.

The demonstration was an effective way of stimulating interactions with the toddlers, and male and female adults were equally effective as demonstrators. However, the demonstration was reliably effective only for the older group, perhaps because younger children were not capable of modeling their behavior after the adult's or of following instructions as brief as these. It should be noted that, not only was the demonstration a very brief and modest intervention, but also that its effects were tested for only a very short period immediately following the demonstration. It is interesting that this sort of intervention did measurably affect the older children's behavior. However, its lack of effect for the younger children, and the lack of difference due to the demonstraters' sex should be tested with a longer-term intervention.

Older girls' behavior was strikingly different from the other children's in several ways. Not only did the older girls interact with the baby more than other children did, but they interacted in a variety of ways. For example, physical interactions were common for the older girls but less frequent for the younger girls and entirely absent for boys of both age groups. Although verbal or vocal interactions were frequent only for the older girls, they were observed in all groups. In order to examine the nature of children's interactions with the baby more closely a classification system was devised for the observers' descriptions of interactions. Independent judges sorted these descriptions and categorized them according to this system with a .92 reliability (Pearson r). Table 2.3 lists the number of children in each group who initiated each type of interaction. All activities initiated by at least 3 of the 48 subjects are included. Baby-initiated interactions were quite rare and were therefore excluded.

Although most of the children in each group did spend some time interacting with the baby using toys, these episodes were often brief and similar to younger children's play with age mates. At times toy play with the baby included showing, offering, or giving toys to the baby, but often it involved only mutual play with the same toys, albeit cooperative play. Older girls' behaviors contrasted with the other children's behaviors in that they appeared to be "nurturant." They included greeting, talking to, patting, and embracing the infant, lifting or taking the infant on the lap, demonstrating or offering toys, and other behaviors seemingly designed to facilitate contact and mutual play, or to direct the baby's activities by prosocial means. However, although these behaviors appeared to be strikingly adult-like, they often seemed to be poorly directed. At times, the baby

TABLE 2.3
Number of Children in Each Group Who Initiated Specific Types of Interactions With the Baby Before and After the Demonstration (N per group = 12)

Group:	Older Girls		Younger Girls		Older Boys		Younger Boys		All Ages	
Before (B) or After (A) the Demonstration	B	A	B	A	B	A	B	A	B	A
Interactions:										
Mutual play	6	12	5	7	4	6	7	5	22	30
Offer, give, show	8	8	2	3	4	4	4	3	18	18
Any toy interaction	10	12	7	10	5	8	8	8	30	38
Greet, call	7	0	0	2	1	2	2	1	10	5
Instruct, command	6	6	1	0	1	1	1	0	9	7
Reassure, reinforce	3	1	1	0	1	0	1	1	6	2
Other talk	8	8	1	0	0	0	2	2	11	10
Any verbal interaction	9	10	3	2	1	3	3	4	16	19
Pick up, hold	5	3	0	2	0	0	0	0	5	5
Touch, carry, lead	7	4	3	3	0	0	0	0	10	7
Any physical interaction	7	5	3	4	0	0	0	0	10	9

Reprinted from: Berman and Goodman (1984). Age and sex differences in children's responses to babies: Effects of adults' caretaking requests and instructions. *Child Development*, 55, 1071-1077.

reciprocated the older child's initiatives and the interactions were prolonged, but at other times the behavior seemed inappropriate or badly timed. This was particularly true of physical interactions that sometimes seemed to confine the baby, and at times the baby struggled to become free. When this occurred the girls often persisted in their attentions to the baby or attempted to resume physical interactions after a short time.

It is not surprising that the older girls often greeted or called the baby, and that their attempts to control or direct the baby included quite a few instructions and commands to the baby. However, at least one child in each age-sex group responded to a fussy baby with verbal reassurance, reinforcement, or soothing words. Thus, it appears that at least some of the boys and girls, even the younger ones, were capable of responding to the baby appropriately when the demand for such behavior was great enough.

It may be that some of the difference between the older girls and boys is related to differences in the interpretation of an adult's request to "take care of" the baby. Although younger boys were very active in the research situation, engaging actively and noisily in solitary play, many of the older boys seemed somewhat inhibited. Four of the older boys, but only one of the older girls, spent at least 1 min in the situation with no recordable behaviors. Observers' descriptions indicated that these children watched or "stared at" the baby during this time. Watching a baby may be a rather passive form of infant caretaking that is in keeping with a young child's interpretation of the appropriate masculine role. This type of behavior is in obvious contrast with the very actively baby-oriented behavior of many of the older girls who, at times, were not only controlling, but intrusive.

SUMMARY OF OBSERVATIONAL STUDIES

Three different observational studies conducted in two day care centers with three different groups of children with somewhat different age ranges all yielded one important result. An interaction between sex and age was found such that older preschool boys were less baby oriented than younger boys, but older preschool girls were more baby oriented than younger girls. These age changes are in accord with the increasingly divergent gender roles assumed by young children. In the first study, when a large group of 32 to 63-month-old children was given a choice of activities, older boys spent less time near a toddler than younger boys did but there was no age effect for girls. In this situation possible interactions with the toddler were quite limited because she was kept within a playpen with adults nearby and children were asked not to touch the baby.

In a second study children from 42 to 66-months-old were individually paired with a toddler and they chose to interact with the baby or to play alone under two different conditions. In a spontaneous play situation the age × sex interaction was not significant, however, when children were given the responsibility for baby care a significant age × sex effect emerged. Boys over 4½-years-old interacted less with the baby than did any other group. In contrast, girls over 4½ interacted more with the baby than any other group did.

This general age × sex effect was replicated later in a third study in another day care center under similar conditions. That is, 30 to 92-month-old children were each asked to care for the baby when they entered the situation. An adult's demonstration of playful interactions with the toddler was successful in raising older boys' and girls' levels of interaction with the baby but there was no significant effect of the demonstration for younger girls and boys.

Several qualifications are in order. All of the observations were for very brief periods and treatments such as the caretaking instructions and demonstration were not extensive. Children's activities are greatly affected by the alternative choices available such as toys and other activities. It is also undoubtedly true that the quantity and quality of interactions with the toddler were greatly affected by many characteristics of the toddler. However, we chose to measure the older child's response while varying those elements of the situational context that might tap children's growing perceptions of gender roles that are appropriate for them. Pressure to assume responsibility for caretaking appears to be an important factor. Finally, it should be noted that although we have found sturdy, replicable effects there are obvious individual differences and we are not able, at this point, to relate these differences to differences in prior experience, sibling status, parent variables, etc.

The situations presented in these studies either allowed spontaneous interactions during play or posed a demand for caretaking while the available adults were "too busy" to care for the toddler. The request for caretaking was designed to be somewhat ambiguous in order to study age and sex differences in children's conceptions of "appropriate" caretaking roles. In fact, in our culture few children at this age have had sufficient experience or instruction to acquaint them with the realities involved in the care of toddlers. It is interesting, therefore, that after a male or female adult demonstrated how one might care for a baby, older boys, as well as older girls, significantly increased their interactions with the babies. Another study was, therefore, designed to avoid the ambiguities associated with children's interpretation of caretaking roles and to determine whether similar differences between older boys and girls would persist when a younger child is clearly in need of a specific type of help.

HELP, SHARING, AND DONATIONS TO A YOUNGER CHILD

Although girls are often thought to be more altruistic than boys (cf. Shigetomi, Hartmann, & Gelfand, 1981) there is little research to support the belief that there is a consistent, generalized tendency for girls to help, share, and donate more than boys do. Most research has examined young children's altruistic responses to age mates rather than to younger children. This is particularly surprising because early sex differences in nurturance to the young have been cited as justification for the belief that females are "naturally" more fit for parenting than males are. We, therefore, designed a study (Weinstock, 1979) to investigate possible sex differences in a series of situations structured so that some specific kinds of helping, sharing, or donating to a younger child would be appropriate. Our subjects were 32 5- and 6-year-old children enrolled in another day care center with a population of students very similar to the subjects in the other studies described in this chapter. Toddlers were not available to this center but 3- and 4-year-olds were. The 3-year-olds were housed in a building set aside for younger children, while the 4-year-olds were housed in the same building as our subjects, but in separate classrooms. In a donation situation our 5- and 6-year-old subjects were asked to donate to a pictured baby, but in the helping and sharing situations our subjects were confronted with 3- and 4-year-old schoolmates who needed help, or with whom they might share. Each of the 16 girls and 16 boys was paired with a younger child of the same sex on two occasions; once with a 3-year old, once with a 4-year old, with approximately 2 weeks between sessions. Experimenters' sex and order of pairing by partners' age were balanced over subjects' sex. During each session, in different rooms of the center, a variant of each situation was embedded within routine school-type activities. In these situations interobserver reliability for all measures ranged from .99 to 1.00.

In the cookie-sharing situation each subject was given a box of 11 cookies just before entering the room to sit next to a younger child who was occupied with play materials, but had nothing to eat. The experimenter said, "Here is a box of cookies. You may share some of these cookies if you like." Observers recorded the number of cookies the subject offered during the first 5 min after entering the room.

In the crayon-sharing situation the two children were asked to draw while seated next to each other. Each child was given a paper and pencil. In addition the older child was given a box of 20 crayons and was told, "If you would like to share these with _____(younger child's name), you may." The number of crayons offered during the next 5 min was recorded.

The helping situation was structured so that the younger child would move and spill a container with a loose bottom which was full of very small objects which s/he needed for a game. The container was situated approximately 2 feet from where the subject was sitting. The experimenter then gave a sturdy container to the younger child, stated that s/he had work to do in another room, asked the younger child to pick up the objects, and then left the room. Observers recorded whether or not the subject helped the younger child by picking up, verbally directing the younger child, or offering other help. To avoid ceiling effects, recording was continued for only 4 min. We had determined from pilot tests that pairs of children at this age could not complete the task in less than this time.

In the donation situation, the experimenter took the subject to an empty room and gave the child a tumbler with 21 candies saying, "Here are some candies for you. You can have as many as you want. If you would like to give some to a poor child, we are saving some for him/her. Here is a picture of a boy (girl) your age (or baby) that you can help." Half of the subjects were shown pictures of children the subject's sex, and half, the other sex. All of the pictures had been judged to be in the middle range of attractiveness by a group of adult judges. For each subject, on one session the pictured child was a 1-year-old baby and, on the other session approximately the same age as the subject. A partly filled glass for donated candies was given to each subject. Presentation order was balanced over subjects' sex.

The major result of this study was a consistent sex difference across the situations. Boys, *not* girls, helped, shared, and donated most, and there were no substantial or consistent differences which depended upon the age of the child who was the potential recipient. Within each sex, older subjects generally were more altruistic than younger subjects, a difference that was significant only for the girls in the cookie sharing and donation situations.

Boys gave more cookies across the two sessions (mean = 8.8) than girls did (mean 1.8). Because most of the girls did not share any cookies, parametric tests could not be used. Thirteen boys shared some cookies during at least one session, compared with six girls, $\chi^2 (1) = 6.34$, $p<.05$.

Although most of the younger children appeared to want cookies, some seemed to prefer using a pencil instead of crayons, and some of the younger children grabbed crayons before they could be offered so that some data were excluded. However the trend was in the same direction as cookie-sharing. Boys gave twice as many crayons over the two sessions (mean = 4.2) as girls did (mean = 2.0). Again because so many children failed to share, the data were not suitable for parametric analyses. A Chi Square test failed to reach significance.

In the helping situation subjects gave some sort of help on 59 of the 64 sessions, most frequently by actually picking up spilled objects. Boys helped significantly more often than girls did (on 84% of all intervals, compared with 60%), $t(30) = 2.154$, $p<.05$.

In the donation situation boys gave somewhat more candy on each session (mean = 4.3 pieces) than girls did (mean = 3.1), but many children, particularly girls, did not donate at all. Only nine of the sixteen girls donated at all compared with twelve of the sixteen boys, a nonsignificant difference. For both male and female subjects differences that depended upon the age and sex of the pictured "needy" children were small and insignificant.

The results of this study lend no support to the notion that 5- and 6-year-old girls will be more nurturant to a younger child than boys will be, when nurturance is defined as helping, sharing, and donating in situations where the younger child is in need of a particular type of help. This was the case in the donation situation when the younger child was a pictured baby. It was also the case in the situations designed to elicit sharing with, and helping a 3- or 4-year-old. However, a serious limitation of the study was that babies were not available for face-to-face sharing and helping in situations when such behavior might be appropriate. In the earlier studies many girls over 5 appeared to be strikingly attentive to toddlers who were between 8- and 19-months-old. These behaviors might not generalize to helping and sharing with 3- and 4-year-olds. Would girls this age be of greater help than their male peers if the child in need of help were a toddler? This question should be explored with a variety of populations of girls and boys, potential recipients, and situational contexts. A structured classroom setting with "teacher" directed-tasks might have been a factor which elicited more prosocial behaviors from boys or encouraged passivity in girls. The specific type of help and sharing might also be important. While there is need for a great deal of research to explore these issues, there is some recent relevant research which offers important evidence about girls' and boys' responses to a baby in distress.

Zahn-Waxler, Friedman, and Cummings (1983) studied the responses of children from 4-years-old to sixth grade to taped infant cries from a room adjacent to one in which they had previously seen a baby and its mother. There were no age or sex differences in children's emotional responses to these cries. Few of the children attempted behavioral interventions, perhaps because the baby was not in the room and was presumed to be with its mother. When the mother reentered the room where the child was seated, saying that she was looking for the baby's bottle, most of the children at each age level provided some type of help. Although older children helped significantly more than younger children, there were no significant sex differences in amount of help offered. Later in the session children were interviewed about their responses to taped baby cries. It is most interesting that during the interview girls verbalized significantly more empathy for the crying baby than boys did, but they did not verbalize greater intent to help. It may be that just as others believe girls to be more empathic than boys (Shigetomi et al., 1981), girls, themselves, believe that they are particularly empathic. This belief would have much support from widespread stereotypes about the natural proclivities of women, particularly when the empathy is directed toward babies. It may be that girls are, in fact, more empathic than boys toward infants, toddlers, and younger children; however, it cannot be assumed that greater empathy is accompanied by greater instrumental response, or even by greater intent to respond with prosocial behavior.

SUMMARY AND FUTURE DIRECTIONS FOR RESEARCH

In their review of the literature on sex differences Maccoby and Jacklin (1974) observed that the existing literature had, "seldom focused on a child's offering of nurturance to an infant or younger child, that is, on behavior that might be considered a precursor to later child care," (p. 220). In the decade since Maccoby and Jacklin's book was published, such research has proceeded to the point where it is no longer fruitful to ask whether boys or girls are more nurturant to the young. Instead, research on age and sex differences in children's responses to babies may help us to redefine the complex of behaviors that are categorized as "nurturant," specify the developmental course of the components of this group of responses in the repertoire of males and females, and better understand the experiential and situational variables which are associated with these nurturant responses. Because of our interest in the widespread sex differences in adults' orientation to the young we have concentrated our research on an age period when sex differences emerge and on situations that appear to elicit responses to babies and young children in varying degrees.

Our first studies were of young children's attraction to babies. Although Lorenz proposed some 40 years ago that the physical features of infants are uniquely attractive, only lately have researchers been concerned with this kind of attraction, how early it is manifested, and possible changes for males and females in attraction to babies throughout the life course. Our research demonstrates that preference for pictures of infants is established for both sexes, at least by second grade, although the degree of preference is greater for girls. Physical attraction should make it more likely that children would come into close enough proximity with babies to be able to interact with them. Since girls showed a greater preference for infant pictures, it was not surprising to find that girls in another sample spent more time than boys near a baby when other attractive activities were available in a day care center.

However, we must ask to what degree does physical attraction guarantee that nurturant responses will occur. Lorenz believed that a *specific* type of response is elicited by babies' physical characteristics (Lorenz 1943, 1971). His theory is explicit: Infant characteristics act as releasors for specific unlearned emotional and motor responses. Perhaps it is the widespread acceptance of Lorenz's theory and maternal instinct theory over many years in the history of psychology (see Shields, 1975, 1983) that has led to the general acceptance of the idea that positive responses to the young can be considered as a unitary group of highly correlated responses which depend on the eliciting power of baby characteristics and nature (most importantly, sex) of the respondent, without regard to the social situation at hand.

A review of the literature (Berman, 1980) reveals that the linkage between physical attraction to babies and the tendency to interact behaviorally with babies, in nurturant fashion or otherwise, is quite weak. Certainly social variables are of great importance in determining the extent and quality of the interactions which occur. Our long range goal is to understand the changes which occur in boys' and girls' relationships with babies and younger children from the preschool to the middle-childhood years. What we want to know is not only how children respond to babies, but also, to what social cues do they respond. This is an important issue although major changes may be expected later and throughout the life span (cf. Feldman & Nash, 1978, 1979a, 1979b) and although there are important sources of individual differences besides gender. It is nevertheless possible during this age period to begin to identify some reliable differences between male and female children's responses to babies which, at least on the surface, bear remarkable similarity to the differences between adult men and women. We have not found sturdy sex differences among very young children but, some time between ages 4 and 5 years distinct differences emerge. We believe that these differences are associated with growing differences between girls' and boys' perceptions of their "proper" life roles and the early, but important, stages of acquisition of the different social scripts which males and females call into use in situations where there is the possibility of, or demand for, relationships with infants or very young children.[1]

What is important in this conception is that sex differences are not in response to babies alone, but to the total situation. It is in a variety of situations where babies are encountered that children learn what is expected of males and females. In our society such expectations are often, but not always, sex differentiated. Although men and women share many attitudes and behaviors in their relationships with children, responsibility for caretaking is most often delegated to women. It is probable that children learn very early to distinguish between situations in which males and females behave similarly to the young, and those in which they do not.

In our work with young children we have found that boys and girls generally respond to unfamiliar babies and toddlers in a positive manner. Boys and girls are capable of soothing an unhappy baby, and boys were at least as likely as girls to donate to a "poor" baby and to help or share with a younger child thought to be in need. Whiting (1983) in her crosscultural work found that girls and boys respond nurturantly far more often to infants than to other individuals. We have

---

[1]The term "social script" is used in the same sense as Gagnon and Simon (1973) use it to deal with sexual scripts, and we are indebted to them for the clarity with which they have analyzed the social elements involved in the performance of activities which are widely regarded as "natural" and biologically "given." Interactions with the young often appear to have the same spontaneous quality as sexual interactions but can profitably be analyzed from the same theoretical viewpoint.

found that differences do exist between boys and girls beyond age 5. However, they are largest when children are explicitly asked to take responsibility for the care of babies. Similarly, when older children and adults have been studied in situations where they could be assumed to be "in charge" or responsible for babies, sex differences are most likely to be found (cf. Berman, 1980, pp. 681–682).

There is good reason to believe that children understand and fully appreciate the sex differential in caretaking as early as the preschool years (Kuhn, Nash, & Brucken, 1978; Weeks & Thornburg, 1977) and, in fact, young children are probably less ambivalent than their parents about these common role divisions. Young girls may welcome the opportunity to establish their authority in a sphere that is widely acknowledged to be *feminine,* and boys probably respond with the avoidance of the *feminine* which is typical of young males at certain ages. Indeed, when in situations that offer the opportunity or demand for caretaker behavior, many boys over 5 appear to be passive or subdued, albeit watchful (Berman & Goodman, 1984), whereas girls that age are often described as overwhelming, smothering, and abrasive (Blakemore, 1981; Berman & Goodman, 1984; Stewart, 1983; Berman, Sloan, & Goodman, 1979). These behaviors seem to be exaggerated versions of stereotypic *masculine* and *feminine* attitudes to the young, fragments of male and female scripts that have not yet been fully developed or integrated into mature patterns of behavior. We are mindful that over the years before and during parenthood males and females will modify, expand, and radically change their parental scripts, but we believe that even very young children have acquired the beginnings of sex-differentiated parental scripts.

To date we have only explored a handful of situations and all our studies have involved cross-sectional age comparisons. Also, we have had very little information about the family backgrounds and life experiences of our individual subjects. The crosscultural work and longitudinal studies of children's interactions with their younger siblings reported elsewhere in this volume provide much needed data on children's interactions with familiar babies under a variety of conditions, data collected with methods which allow direct assessment of developmental trends.

Our data indicate that it may be well worthwhile to construct and test the effects of training programs that bring young boys and girls together with babies under the tutelage of male and female adults. Such programs are rare (see Herzig & Mali, 1980) and participants are almost always self-selected and usually limited to females. Children in the United States rarely bear responsibility for the young before adolescence, are increasingly isolated in small families with few siblings and, for the most part, are in age-segregated school systems. After surveying a broad array of data concerned with the responses of many mothers and fathers to parenthood, Miller and Newman (1978, p. 421) concluded that we must improve preparation for parenthood in two ways, ". . . first, through increased contact with babies during childhood and adolescence, especially for boys, for example, by including these age groups in the activities of child care centers; and second, through increased education for parenthood at all levels in the school system by including the relevant substantive material in coursework, field experience, and counseling." Our data base to evaluate possible effects of programs such as this is extremely poor. It may be time for behavioral researchers to turn their attention to the potential that such an approach holds.

ACKNOWLEDGMENT

The program of research described in this chapter was planned and executed while the author was at Florida State University beginning in the mid-1970s. Many graduate and undergraduate students were associated with this effort but the research program owes a great deal to Vickie Goodman and Vicki L. Sloan (Smith) who, as graduate students spent their time, creative energy, and thought on many phases of the work. Stuart C. Weinstock and La Verne Fernander each assumed responsibility for a substantial project within the program.

REFERENCES

Berman, P. W. (1980). Are women more responsive than men to the young? A review of developmental and situational variables. *Psychological Bulletin, 88,* 668–695.

Berman, P. W., & Goodman, V. (1984). Age and sex differences in children's responses to babies: Effects of adults' caretaking requests and instructions. *Child Development, 55,* 1071–1077.

Berman, P. W., Goodman, V., Sloan, V. L., & Fernander, L. (1978). Preference for infants among black and white children: Sex and age differences. *Child Development, 49,* 917–919.

Berman, P. W., Monda, L. D., & Myerscough, R. P. (1977). Sex differences in young children's responses to an infant: An observation within a day-care setting. *Child Development, 48,* 711–715.

Berman, P. W., Sloan, V. L., & Goodman, V. (1979, March). *Development of sex differences in response to an infant and to the caretaker role.* Paper presented at the meeting of the Society for Research in Child Development, San Francisco.

Blakemore, J. E. O. (1981). Age and sex differences in interaction with a human infant. *Child Development, 52,* 386–388.

Brooks, J., & Lewis, M. (1976). Infants' responses to strangers: Midget, adult, and child. *Child Development, 47,* 323–332.

Feldman, S. S., & Nash, S. C. (1978). Interest in babies during young adulthood. *Child Development, 49,* 617–622.

Feldman, S. S., & Nash, S. C. (1979a). Changes in responsiveness to babies during adolescence. *Child Development, 50,* 942–949.

Feldman, S. S., & Nash, S. C. (1979b). Sex differences in responsiveness to babies among mature adults. *Developmental Psychology, 15,* 430–436.

Fullard, W., & Reiling, A. M. (1976). An investigation of Lorenz's "babyness." *Child Development, 47,* 1191–1193.

Gagnon, J., & Simon, W. (1973). *Sexual conduct*. Chicago: Aldine.
Herzig, A. C., & Mali, J. L. (1980). *Oh Boy! Babies!* Boston: Little Brown & Co.
Kuhn, D., Nash, S. C., & Brucken, L. (1978). Sex role concepts of two- and three-year olds. *Child Development, 49,* 445–451.
Lorenz, K. (1943). Die angebornen Formen moglicher Erfahrung. *Zeitschrift fur Tierpsychologie, 5,* 235–582.
Lorenz, K. (1971). *Studies in animal and human behavior,* vol. 2. London: Methuen & Co.
Maccoby, E. E., & Jacklin, C. N. (1974). *The psychology of sex differences*. Stanford, CA: Stanford University Press.
Miller, W. B., & Newman, L. F. (1978). *The first child and family formation*. Chapel Hill, NC: University of North Carolina Press.
Rheingold, H. L., Hay, D. F., & West, M. J. (1976). Sharing in the second year of life. *Child Development, 47,* 1148–1158.
Shields, S. A. (1975). Functionalism, Darwinism, and the psychology of women. *American Psychologist, 30,* 739–754.
Shields, S. A. (1983). "To pet, coddle, and 'do for'": Caretaking and the concept of maternal instinct. In M. Lewin (Ed.), *In the shadow of the past: Psychology examines the sexes, 1800–1900* (pp. 256–273). New York: Columbia University Press.
Shigetomi, C. C., Hartmann, D. P., & Gelfand, D. M. (1981). Sex differences in children's altruistic behavior and reputations for helpfulness. *Developmental Psychology, 17,* 434–437.
Stewart, R. B. (1983). Sibling attachment relationships: Child-infant interactions in the strange situation. *Developmental Psychology, 19,* 192–199.
Weeks, M. O., & Thornburg, K. R. (1977). Marriage role expectations of five-year old children and their parents. *Sex Roles. 3,* 189–191.
Weinstock, S. C. (1979). *Preschool children's sex differences in prosocial behaviors directed toward a younger child*. Unpublished honors thesis, Florida State University, Tallahassee, FL.
Whiting, B. B. (1983). Prosocial behavior. In D. Bridgeman (Ed.), *The nature of prosocial development: Interdisciplinary theories of strategy* (pp. 221–242). New York: Academic Press.
Zahn-Waxler, C., Friedman, S. L., & Cummings, E. M. (1983). Children's emotions and behaviors in response to infants' cries. *Child Development, 54,* 1522–1528.

3 Conceptualizing the Determinants of Nurturance: A Reassessment of Sex Differences

Alan Fogel
Gail F. Melson
Purdue University

Jayanthi Mistry
University of Utah

Infants and children are cared for in a wide variety of situations, and the responsibility for their care is related to decisions made by the society in which the children are reared. These cultural decisions concern where children will be reared, how, and by whom. The focus of this paper is on the latter category of choice: Who takes care of infants and children. We further simplify the issue by breaking the "who" into two groups: male and female. We argue that in spite of a clear majority of female caregivers around the globe, both sexes possess the ability to nurture the young.

Ability in this context is used in the sense of *competence* as distinct from *performance*. Clarke-Stewart (1977), in discussing differences in time spent with children by fathers vs. mothers in American society, suggested that if fathers were given more social support they might be able to demonstrate a potentially equal competence to nurture through actual caregiving performance.

If, however, males are given few opportunities to nurture the young, how can we conclude that they might have equal ability? One could reason from the results of a few special cases; for example, fathers who "time-share" with mothers in child-rearing duties, or study those few societies in which men and boys are responsible for the majority of child care. Although we review some of this evidence in what follows, it is not sufficient to make the conclusion, as in those situations we may be witnessing the behavior of a few self-selected androgenous males.

We shall approach this issue in two ways. First, we need to take a critical look at the concept of nurturance. We shall show that nurturance can be thought of rather generally, and thus is not limited only to the care of the young, but to a wide range of human endeavor that is accessible to members of both sexes.

Second, we review some of the evidence from experimental manipulations of subject's responses to infants and young children. In these studies, random samples of males and females, in age groups ranging from preschool children to the elderly, are observed during exposure to stimuli relating to infants, and to infants themselves. The results of these studies speak to the specific issue of the nurturance of the young, and have the potential to be generalized to the population of potential caregivers.

NURTURANCE, EMPATHY AND ALTRUISM

In the literature on child caregiving, there is no standard definition of the concept of nurturance. Nurturance is usually thought of as being composed of empathy, altruism, and affection in a caregiving context, but even these related concepts have gone without clear conceptualization. For the purposes of this chapter we outline the definitions of altruism and of empathy based on our review of the literature. From there, we construct a definition of nurturance.

Altruism refers to giving assistance, comfort, or resources to another individual without apparent reward or reciprocation, and often at great personal sacrifice (even death). This definition is based on the sociobiological concept of altruism related to parenting behavior (Wilson, 1975). Altruistic behavior can occur even in simple species, and does not require any cognitive or even emotional reaction to the recipient of the altruistic behavior. Altruism, in its simplest form, can be activated by a simple stimulus response mechanism, and is often an unconditioned response. Furthermore, we need not conceptualize an independent altruistic motivation. An act may be motivated by the altruistic individual's goals and needs, a sense of obligation or duty, feelings of later reciprocity, or doing one's part for society (Krebs, 1978; Mussen & Eisenberg-Berg, 1977). The end result may involve personal sacrifice to that individual, and gain to another.

In discussion of *empathy,* quite a different set of themes occurs, typically related to the ability of one individual to infer, or to experience vicariously, the thoughts or feelings of another individual (Eisenberg & Lennon, 1983). Unlike altruism, empathy does not require an action component, although empathy is often inferred from behavioral acts subsequent to one's empathic perception of another person. We shall follow a number of other recent researchers in defining empathy as an affective response to someone else's emotional experience (Eisenberg & Lennon, 1983; Hoffman, 1977). In humans, there may be cognitive components to empathy; as a result of role taking, identification, or conscious evaluation of another's state (Feshbach, 1977; Hoffman, 1977).

Certainly, altruism does not always require empathic motivation, and empathy—as an affective experience—need not be accompanied by an altruistic act, although in practice the two may co-exist. But what is nurturance?

Let us consider parenting, for the moment, as a prototypical example of nurturant behavior. Our ideal concept of parents often includes elements of empathy and of altruism. We expect parents to identify emotionally with their children's needs and limitations, and we also expect parents to exert a certain degree of self-abnegation, deferring to the more urgent needs of the child.

In real situations, however, the behavior of parents is not limited to altruism, nor bound by empathic responses. Parents often forego the child's needs in favor of other considerations. This might be because the parent fails to comprehend the nature of the child's affective state, or because ecological factors beyond the control of the parent prohibit the display of appropriate parental behavior. On the other hand, parents may perceive the child's need, have the ability to meet it, and still avoid carrying out the necessary actions. Parents often deliberately withhold their resources in order to encourage the child to develop on his or her own, or to encourage independence. Parents may create a situation in which they will provide only part of what the child needs, and allow the child to complete the action on his own. For example, in studies of parental teaching of children during a problem situation, parents often lead the child toward a solution, but step back at a time when they think the child can use his own resources to complete the task (Kaye, 1982; Wertsch, McNamee, McLane, & Budwig, 1980).

One way to analyze this common pattern of parental behavior is in terms of the concept of empathy. The parent can be presumed to empathize not only with the child's current desire to solve the puzzle, but also with the parent's vision of some future condition of the child (for example, as more competent and more independent of the parent's guidance). This kind of conceptualization severely stretches the concept of empathy, since one would have to distinguish between both current states and future states of the child. Furthermore, the child's later developmental status does not necessarily have affective components. It is this distinction, however, that we wish to argue is the core of the concept of nurturance. *Nurturance is the provision of guidance, protection and care for the purpose of fostering developmental change congruent with the expected potential for change of the object of nurturance.* In the example we have been discussing, nurturance can be combined with empathy in order to explain the parental behavior. In the case of a parent meeting the immediate needs of the child—exhibiting both empathy and altruism perhaps—there may also be a nurturant component, so long as the parent provides the resource with the intention of fostering the child's development.

One can imagine both empathy and altruism without a nurturant component in the case of an immediate response, devoid of developmental significance (that is without any thought that the empathic perception or act will lead to change in the other), as in a direct response to someone's distress. On the other hand, there can be nurturant behavior without an altruistic or empathic component. For example, a nonempathic a parent could foster development in a child that was contrary to the needs and potentials of that particular child, and that was founded in the parent's own needs and goals. Indeed, all parents probably put their own personal and cultural goals for children into the process of making parenting decisions. Altruism would not always be adaptive for the maintenance of the parent's own goals, while responses on the basis of empathic perceptions of the current needs of the child are not always adaptive for the future development of self-regulation and independence in the child.

This conceptualization of nurturance was derived using the specific example of parenting behavior. If we think of "fostering developmental change" in general terms, we need not limit our perspectives only to nurturance of children. Individuals can nurture other individuals of any age. Furthermore, such a concept of nurturance, when conceptually divorced from the related concepts of empathy and altruism, need not even apply to another human being. People can nurture animals of other species, or they can nurture inanimate and even insubstantial things. So long as nurturance is defined in terms of fostering developmental change within the potentials of the nurturant object, it can apply to many kinds of human endeavor (such as a job or a sport), to nonliving objects (such as a painting or a stamp collection), and to abstract entities (such as mathematical thinking or spiritual growth). One can, in a sense, foster the development of each of these things for one's own personal satisfaction (that is, nonaltruistically), and without need of an affective identification (that is, nonempathically).

In the next section we develop theoretically the notion of nurturance as fostering development, and we show how this concept can apply to the understanding of sex differences in nurturant behavior. Following this, we present evidence from a small number of research studies in support of our argument, and finally we can suggest directions for future research, and for society's conception of male vs. female roles and abilities related to nurturance.

FOUR DIMENSIONS OF NURTURANCE

In the previous section, nurturance was defined as fostering developmental change within the potentials of growth of the nurturant object. In addition to being flexible with regard to the choice of nurturant object, this definition also allows for individual variation in the performance of nurturant behavior, in the individual's awareness of their own or other's needs to be nurtured, and in the individual's motivation to nurture in relation to the other factors already mentioned. Further, such a conceptualization serves to account for differences between groups (e.g., sex, culture), as well as ontogenetic differences.

Choice of nurturant object

Objects of nurturance can be divided into at least four categories: human, nonhuman and animate, inanimate and substantial, and insubstantial (see Table 3.1).

TABLE 3.1
Classification of Nurtured Objects

Category	Examples
Human	Infants, Children, Age-Mates, Elderly
Nonhuman, Animate	Pets, Plants, Forests, Crops
Inanimate, Substantial	Art, Hobbies, Products of Work
Insubstantial	Athletic Skill, Theorizing, Spiritual Growth

Within the first category we include response to infants and children, but also interactions between age-mates, and care of the elderly and sick. The main requirement is that there be an intention to change the object as a result of the subject's behavior. The second category includes objects such as pets, wildlife, in fact all flora and fauna with which one may enter a relationship for the purpose of nurturance. This includes not only taking care of one's pet, but environmental protection and conservation in the broadest sense. Agricultural activities are certainly included, and so is growing houseplants. Although it may strike one as odd, including babies and houseplants in the same category (nurturant objects), we argue that the human capacity to foster development is generalizable to a wide range of rather different endeavors, leading to the conclusion that different individuals may choose to display nurturant capacities in relation to different objects and in different styles. Our concept of nurturance is similar, in this regard, to Erikson's (1952) idea of "generativity."

In the third category falls nurturance of physical objects. In this we can include works of art and literature, hobbies such as collecting or constructing of objects, jobs that require articulation of physical objects, etc. Not all work with physical objects, nor all interaction with animate objects, is nurturant. Again, it depends on the existence of the intention to foster development of that object, either for personal gain or for an altruistic goal. Finally, we include the development of higher human intellectual and spiritual potentials as legitimate objects of nurturance, including academic and athletic achievement, theoretical thinking, spiritual growth, etc. Nurturance involves the development of these aspects of human endeavor, regardless of the ultimate purpose of the individual.

Expression of Nurturant Feelings

As defined earlier, nurturance is related to a subjective intention to foster development, and can be directed to any number of different objects. The expression of nurturance refers to the behavioral style with which the desire to foster development is expressed. The expression of nurturance will depend on the type of object chosen. For example, the specific behaviors used in infant care will differ from those used in the care of a pet, or in the development of athletic ability. Expression, thus, is the performance component of nurturance.

At present, we are not able to demarcate behaviors that are nurturant, and we would have even more difficulty trying to classify behavior into a four-fold table formed by the intersection of nurturant vs. nonnurturant, and empathic vs. nonempathic. This would be one of the essential tasks of future research using this point of view. Here, we merely suggest that this approach can lead to a number of fruitful questions regarding the nature and origins of nurturance.

Could it be that all individuals express nurturance, at least to some object? In what ways are nurturant behaviors object-specific? Could we use this performance component of nurturance to verify that there is equal competence between the sexes? For example, is the stereotypical male-role nurturance of a profession (or the family car or the front lawn), in some way equivalent to the stereotypical female-role nurturance of the children (or the family meals or the household interior)? As for the traditional male nurturance of the job or profession we might argue that it is nurturance without empathy or altruism, primarily intended to increase personal satisfaction for the male. However, some males may devote energy to their work as an indirect form of nurturance for the family and children, that is, as a partly altruistic and empathic service to the family's financial well-being. Although we might complain that the male who works too much is losing the opportunity to enjoy his children, it still may be the case that his behavior is nurturant in the sense of attempting to foster development in his children by providing some of the necessary resources for their proper growth. Family division of labor, therefore, may not necessarily be a division of the nurturant function of parenting. In families where both parents work and both spend time with children, then there is a diversity of nurturant expression within the same person, rather than a parental division of labor vis-à-vis childcare.

Motivation to Nurture

Related to the style of nurturance and the identity of the nurturant object is the individual's desire to nurture. Here we can admit social influences related to a particular individual's nurturance of a particular object. Thus, if we assume equal competence to nurture between the sexes, then society can educate (socialize) its members toward nurturance of specific objects that are either limited by norms to members of one or the other sex, or to which both sexes have equal access and for which they receive equal encouragement.

Thus, we might ask whether the motivation to nurture is spontaneous toward a particular object, as opposed to a social obligation. Such a question can be posed at the group level—differences between the sexes in motivation to nurture particular objects—or at the individual level. Even if nurturance is spontaneous, it may not necessarily derive from empathic or altruistic sources of motivation, so we must attempt to keep these various independent dimensions conceptually separated, at least until further research has shown that they are related, and in what ways.

Awareness of Nurturance

This component refers to the individual's awareness of their own, or another's need to be nurtured. In a sense, this is a kind of "empathy for nurturance." In the strict definition of empathy we mean, usually, an awareness of another's affective state. A need for nurturance, however, may not be directly reflected in the current affective state, but part of a social cognition of self, others and objects as "in the process of development." Thus, awareness of nurturance can be conceptualized as the degree of articulation of an individual's concepts of their own and other's developmental processes.

This concept has recently been investigated by Sameroff and Feil (1984). They found that there were different levels of parental understanding of children's developmental potentials. At the "symbiotic" level parents respond to the "here-and-now," and fail to see beyond caring for the child's immediate needs. At the next level, the "categorical," a parent can see that the child has independent feelings and needs, but believes that the child has intrinsic tendencies that are relatively unchanging, such as the good child, the bright child, the pretty child, etc. At the "compensating" level, parents view their children as changing as a result of complex organismic and environmental experiences, but see the child's changes as an inevitable outcome of the *stage* of development. If a child is still dependent, for example, beyond the stage at which the parent deems this appropriate, then the parent is likely to see this as deviant behavior. At the final, or "perspectivistic" level the parent sees development as the result of individual experience in a specific environment. In this view the child has no preformed nature, except as the result of a series of life experiences. Remediation is possible, and deviations in development can be analyzed critically.

The dimensions of awareness may relate to other dimensions of nurturance. It could be that one's choice of a nurturant object is related to one's knowledge of the developmental needs and limitations of the object. For example, it could be that females are more likely to be involved in the care of infants and young children simply because they have received differential training in the needs of these nurturant objects, and therefore feel better prepared for these tasks than men.

SEX DIFFERENCES IN NURTURANCE

Given this four component model of nurturance we can proceed to conceptualize potential sources of influence that lead to individual differences in each of the components. Rather than thinking of nurturance as a "trait" tied to a specific task, we propose that it can be defined in terms of the subjective experience of the nurturer, and in relation to the general function of "fostering developmental change." One can then see between individual and between group (sexes, cultures, etc.) variation in the forms of nurturant expression, rather than arguing about the *presence* or *absence* of nurturance in one group relative to another. The goal here is to suggest possible hypotheses for future research, since the existing evidence is scanty or nonexistent.

The main theme of this paper is sex differences in nurturance. If we presume that there are no sex differences in the competence or ability to nurture, as argued below, then it follows that observed sex differences in performance are the result of situational factors. What might some of these factors be? Although we cannot explore each of these factors in detail, Table 3.2 is a suggested list of sources of influence that may mediate sex differences, as well as nonsex-related individual differences.

Such factors may be included in research designs related to understanding the types of backgrounds and experiences that seem to lead to high levels of nurturant behavior in different object contexts. Such research may ultimately tell us more about the origins of nurturant behavior, and its developmental course over the life span.

In this section we review evidence suggestive of a lack of overall sex differences in the ability to nurture. We have hypothesized, based on the model of nurturance presented earlier, that we should find differences between the sexes in the objects of nurturance and in the form of expression of nurturance, but that both sexes would have the motivation to display nurturance in some form and with some object. The hypothesis further states that sex differences in nurturant behavior are therefore a function of the society's sex role socialization practices,

TABLE 3.2
Sources of Variation in Nurturance

Age
Sex
Culture
    Values
    Attitudes
Family of Origin Experiences
Prior Experience and Training
Physiological Factors
    Stress Levels
    Hormonal Priming
Situational Constraints
    Support, Supervision, Mediation
    Familiarity of Setting
Familiarity with Object of Nurturance
Relationship to Object of Nurturance
Characteristics of the Object of Nurturance

and of the particular ecological constraints that are placed on an individual's behavior.

The data that we report come from studies of young children's responses to infants during the formative years of sex-role identification. In a series of studies, children between the ages of 2 and 8 years have been observed responding to pictures and to stimuli related to infants, or have been observed in interaction with infants. The studies have been done using both sibling pairs, and pairs of unfamiliar infants and young children. The major result of these studies is that few sex differences are found in responsiveness to infants before the age of 6 years. Given that gender-role socialization becomes solidified at about the same time, we suggest that prior to the formation of culturally defined, gender-role specific responses to infants, all children share an ability to nurture infants, and therefore, to nurture anything else. It is after the age of 6 that children may direct their nurturant motives to different objects, depending upon gender-role considerations.

Methodological Issues

It seems that sex differences in interest in infants interacts with the context of measurement. Neither school-aged boys and girls, nor their mothers and fathers, differed in their physiological responses (heart rate and Galvanic skin response) to pictures of infants and recordings of infant cries. When they were permitted to interact with the infant, however, the females of both ages were more likely to stay close to the babies than were the males (Frodi & Lamb, 1978; Frodi, Lamb, Leavitt, Donovan, Neff, & Sherry, 1978). Moreover, there is some evidence that boys and girls do not differ in their cognitions about infants and their care.

For example, in a study using a semistructured interview to assess preschoolage and 2nd grade children's ideas about infants and their care (Melson, Fogel, & Toda, in press), boys and girls did not differ in their knowledge about infant characteristics or in their ideas concerning the ways different caregivers might nurture an infant. Both sexes expressed equal readiness to care for an infant themselves. A recent meta-analysis of sex differences in empathy revealed a similar result. When measures used were either physiological or nonobtrusive observations of empathic behavior, few significant sex differences were found across studies. When the measures were self-report or subjective assessments, highly significant differences were found in the ability to respond to another person's affective state, favoring females. (Eisenberg & Lennon, 1983).

Because of these problems, studies of young children have the advantage of the relative naivete of the subjects with regard to their own awareness of sex-role expectations. We can also observe children during spontaneous interaction in relatively naturalistic situations.

Observations of child-infant interaction

Studies of siblings in the home have revealed few overall sex differences, in the older sibling's response to the younger, although the research has consistently yielded an effect of the sex composition of the older sibling-infant pair. Thus, Abramovitch, Corter, & Lando (1979) and Dunn & Kendrick (1979) found that older females were more prosocial with their younger sisters. In another study, an opposite cross-sex effect was found to be confined primarily to males, who favored their younger sisters (Stewart & Marvin, 1984). This study also revealed that female infants were more likely to be recipients of caregiving responses than were male infants. Abramovitch et al. (1979) reported that boys were more aggressive and less prosocial with their younger brothers in the home, than with younger sisters.

Studies of the same age-group of children paired with unfamiliar infants in laboratory settings have yielded similar patterns of findings. For example, Melson & Fogel (1982) found a same-sex attraction between children aged 2- to 3-years and 6-month-old infants. In the 4- to 5-year-old age group, the same-sex effect held only for females, while the older boys tended to prefer girl infants and display aggressive behavior to the males. In this study, however, there were no overall sex differences between the preschool children at either age in the display of infant-directed behavior.

At slightly older ages, however, sex differences begin to emerge. Blakemore (1983), for example, found sex differences in spontaneous responsiveness to infants for children only after the age of 5. In a series of studies by Berman and her colleagues (Berman, Monda, & Myerscough, 1977; Berman, this volume; Berman & Goodman, 1984) sex differences that are unconfounded by sex composition of the pair were found in groups of children older than 6 years during interaction with unfamiliar infants. In general, boys between the ages of 5 and 8 interacted less with babies than did boys younger than 5, or girls of the same age, and the 5- to 8-year-old girls interacted more with babies than any other group. In these studies, although the boys' behavior appeared to be more passive in response to the infants, the girls' behavior was not necessarily responsive to the baby. Older girls often interacted to excess with the infants, and were at times controlling and intrusive.

Experimental manipulations of child-infant interaction

Situational factors have also been found to play a role in the elicitation of differential responsiveness between the sexes. Five- and 6-year-old children were asked to share cookies with toddlers and to help the toddlers to pick up spilled cookies. In this situation, boys did more sharing and helping than girls. When children of the same age-group were asked to "take care" of the baby, sex differences were found favoring girls (Berman, this volume). A similar effect of task demands has also been found for adolescents (Feldman & Nash, 1979).

If children's responsiveness to infants is mediated by situational factors, as might be predicted from our hypothesis, then attempts to minimize sex differences by environmental manipulations should be successful. Unfortunately, we have few such studies. In an unpublished pilot study, for example, Blakemore (1983) found that when older boys were shown videotapes and books in which men were seen caring for infants, they tended to increase their responsiveness to babies.

Our own research also lends support to this view. We compared the responses of 71 preschool children who interacted with a 6-month-old infant when the mother of the infant was present, but not involved with those of 48 children who were exposed to the babies while the mothers tried to involve the children with their infants. In all cases the infants were unfamiliar to the children. In the "mother-involved" condition there was a significantly higher number of children who became involved with the infants, and there were fewer negative responses to the infants. More specifically, while there were effects of the sex composition of the child-infant pair during the noninvolved condition, those effects were not found in the mother-involved condition. In the mother-involved condition there was a tendency for the preschool girls to talk more to the infant's mother than the boys. This finding may represent a greater tendency for girls to vocalize their interest in the baby than for boys. It may also be a reflection of the interaction between the sex of the child and the sex of infant's parent. Boys might have been more willing to talk if the adult were the infant's father, or some other male (Fogel, Melson, Toda, & Mistry, in press).

Discussion of the research findings

These studies suggest that prior to, or during the critical years of sex-role formation, boys change their responsiveness to infants in significant ways. During the period from 2- to 6-years, approximately, few overall sex differences can be found in responsiveness to infants, although there is a sex-of-pair-effect that is symmetrical between boys and girls (girls like girl babies and boys like boy babies).

Between the ages of 4 and 6, approximately, there are still no overall sex differences in responsiveness to infants, but boys seem to shift their object of interest from male to female infants, and home-based studies show that female infants are more likely to receive attention from older siblings than are male infants. Thus, although we can say that the same amount of nurturant, or potentially nurturant, behavior directed toward infants is seen in both boys and girls, boys begin to shift in their choice of nurturant object.

After the age of 7 years, and continuing into adulthood and even grandparenthood (Feldman & Nash, 1979), females show more interest in infants. These results are summarized in Table 3.3. Why? We could say that boy's nurturant abilities shown early in life simply fall behind those of the girls. Our

TABLE 3.3
General Trends in Choice of Infants as a Nurturant Object by Sex and Age of Child

Sex of Child	Age of Child		
	2 to 4 years	4 to 6 years	6 to 8 years
Male Child	Male Infant	Female Infant	No Infants
Female Child	Female Infant	Female Infant	All Infants

model predicts that instead, boys may continue to show behavior suggestive of nurturance, but to objects other than infants. For example, at this age boys are more likely than girls to respond to pictures of animal young by naming more ways in which the pictures are "like babies" (Melson, Fogel, & Toda, in press). Thus, we should see a continuation of the pattern observed at 4- to 6-years; that is, boys choosing alternative nurturant objects, and moving farther away from what they perceive to be typically female forms of nurturant expression. Alternatively, as suggested by Berman et al.,'s research, boys may continue to express nurturant interest in infants, but express this in ways that are different from the girls', that is, by more "protective," "watchful," and "helpful" behavior, rather than by providing direct caregiving responses.

Future Research Directions

Future research could be directed at looking for male-defined nurturant objects, and expanding the behavioral definition of nurturance as direct child care into a definition that encompasses other kinds of action that may have a direct or an indirect impact on the infant. Furthermore, these studies deal primarily with responses to infants. We need to learn whether such responses are actually nurturant, that is, done with the intention of fostering development. What is needed is an investigation of the ages at which children develop the concepts here ascribed to nurturance—that is, the potential for their own and for other's developmental changes, and their own role in that process. It may be that young children's responses to infants are "proto-nurturant," i.e., behavioral responses reflecting an interest in babies, but without a clear conceptualization of response to infants as part of a developmental process.

Our review of the literature on sex differences in nurturance suggests that there are no sex differences in "ability" to nurture per se, and that both sexes do display nurturance in some form. If we can presume that both sexes are capable of being nurturant, then the observed sex differences in performance must be the result of situational factors. The heuristic utility of the four component model of nurturance can be evaluated by examining whether predictions of sex differences in choice of objects for nurturance, in expression, motivation, and awareness, can account for (or support) the observed differences, not just at any one age, but developmentally as well. Table 3.2 is a suggested list of sources of influence that may mediate sex differences, as well as nongender related individual differences. For example, the role of societal factors (such as a lack of a provision for paternity leave, attitudes and values emphasizing mother's role as primary caretaker) in affecting how nurturance is expressed could be examined. Changes in some of these factors (e.g., increasing societal approval of father's involvement in caretaking) could be related to changes in males' expressions of nurturance to infants and children in ways that are similar to females.

NURTURANCE AND SOCIETY

When nurturance is defined specifically as "giving care to those in need of care," then one finds that over the life span, and across cultures, females exhibit higher levels of nurturant behavior than males. For example, single parent families in the United States are disproportionately headed by women.

Cross-culturally, similar patterns emerge. In a review of the ethnographic data from the Human Relations Area Files from 50 cultures it was found that responsibilities are assigned differentially to children by sex (Rogoff, Sellers, Piorrata, Fox, & White, 1975). Girls are assigned child-care roles and boys are given jobs outside the home, such as tending the animals. As a result of these experiences, some writers have suggested that girls develop more prosocial behavior. Older girls in the *Six Culture* study, aged 7 to 11, offered more help and support to others than did the boys (Whiting & Edwards, 1973). No such sex differences appeared before the age of 6, which precedes the assignment of girls to childrearing tasks.

A study of Luo boys from Kenya (Ember, 1973) found the opposite effect. In this group the boys were expected to do the housecare and child-care chores, and these boys were more prosocial than boys who were not chosen for this kind of work. Studies such as these, however, are not conclusive since male children may be either self-selected for childrearing, or chosen on the basis of already existing "feminine" traits.

Nevertheless, it seems clear that societies define nurturance as "feminine" by simple association of females with traditionally nurturant (childcare) tasks. It is likely that such an association is also made by children at an early age. We found that preschoolers were more likely to identify an adult female as more suitable to take care of a baby than an adult male, or a male or female adolescent or elderly person. Moreover, preschool and 2nd grade girls with younger siblings had more ideas than singleton girls, or boys in general, about ways in which a child or adolescent might care for a baby (Melson et al., in press). These developing cognitions about who is appropriately involved in nurturing infants undoubtedly affects both boys' and girls' choices of objects of nurturance. While we are not arguing for a more "masculine" concept of nurturance, we are suggesting that a more general concept—one that recognizes differences in object, expression, motivation, and awareness—may be more suitable in helping to understand the ways in which all individuals can contribute nurturant motivations and skills to the family and to society.

Certainly, the nurturance of infants and children is more important for the society as a whole than the nurturance of sports or hobbies. But, if it is the nurturance of children that we are aiming to comprehend, we must admit to other manifestations of the general nurturant function in order to trace developmental changes, and thus to understand better how to nurture each person's nurturant abilities in a wide range of settings. In industrialized countries, there are fewer opportunities for children to be exposed to younger children and infants, due to a decrease in family size and an increasing tendency to educate children in age-segregated settings. In such situations, fostering the development of nurturance will require a better understanding of its nature and origin. Perhaps fostering nurturance of other objects can lead to the development of generalizable nurturing skills.

ACKNOWLEDGMENT

Portions of this paper were presented at the Society for Research in Child Development meeting, Detroit, 1983.

REFERENCES

Abramovitch, R., Corter, C., & Lando, B. (1979). Sibling interaction in the home. *Child Development, 50,* 997–1003.

Berman, P., & Goodman, V. (1984). Age and sex differences in children's responses to babies: Affects of adult's caretaking requests and instructions. *Child Development, 155,* 1071–1077.

Berman, P., Monda, L., & Myerscough, R. (1977). Sex differences in young children's response to an infant: An observation within a day-care setting. *Child Development, 48,* 711–715.

Blakemore, J. (1983, April). *Interaction with an infant by preschoolers: An attempt to modify the sex difference.* Presented at Society for Research in Child Development, Detroit.

Clarke-Stewart, A. (1977, April). *The father's impact on mother and child.* Presented at Society for Research in Child Development, New Orleans.

Dunn, J., & Kendrick, C. (1979). Interaction between young siblings in the context of family relationships. In M. Lewis & L. Rosenblum (Eds.), *The child and its family.* New York: Plenum.

Eisenberg, N., & Lennon, R. (1983). Sex differences in empathy and related capacities. *Psychological Bulletin, 94,* 100–131.

Ember, C. (1973). Feminine task assignment and social behavior of boys. *Ethos, 1,* 424–439.

Erikson, E. (1952). *Childhood and society.* New York: Norton.

Feldman, S., & Nash, S. (1979). Sex differences in responsiveness to babies among mature adults. *Developmental Psychology, 15,* 430–436.

Feshbach, N. D. (1977). Studies on the empathic behavior of children. In B. Maher (Ed.), *Progress in experimental personality research* (Vol. 8). New York: Academic Press.

Fogel, A., Melson, G., Toda, S., & Mistry, J. (in press). Young children's responses to unfamiliar infants: The effects of adult involvement.

Frodi, A., & Lamb, M. (1978). Sex differences in responses to infants: A developmental study of psychophysiological and behavioral responses. *Child Development, 49,* 1182–1188.

Frodi, A., Lamb, M., Leavitt, L., Donovan, W., Neff, C., & Sherry, D. (1978). Fathers and mothers responses to the faces and cries of normal and premature infants. *Developmental Psychology, 14,* 490.

Hoffman, M. (1977). Sex differences in empathy and related behaviors. *Psychological Bulletin, 54,* 712–722.

Kaye, K. (1982). *The mental and social life of infants.* Chicago: University of Chicago Press.

Krebs, D. (1978). A cognitive-developmental approach to altruism. In L. Wispe (Ed.), *Altruism, sympathy and helping: Psychological and sociological principles.* New York: Academic Press.

Melson, G., & Fogel, A. (1982). Young children's interest in unfamiliar infants. *Child Development, 53,* 693–700.

Melson, G., Fogel, A., & Toda, S. (in press). Children's ideas about infants and their care.

Mussen, P., & Eisenberg-Berg, N. (1977). *The roots of caring, sharing, and helping.* San Francisco: Freeman.

Rogoff, B., Sellers, M., Piorrata, S., Fox, N., & White, S. (1975). Age of assignment of roles and responsibilities to children: A cross-cultural survey. *Human Development, 18,* 353–369.

Sameroff, A., & Feil, L. (1984). Parental concepts of development. In I. Sigel (Ed.), *Parental belief systems: The psychological consequences for children.* Hillsdale, NJ: Lawrence Erlbaum Associates.

Stewart, R., & Marvin, R. (1984). Sibling relations: The role of conceptual perspective-taking in the ontogeny of sibling caregiving. *Child Development, 55,* 1322–1332.

Troll, L., & Bengston, V. (1979). Generations in the family. In W. R. Burr, R. Hill, F. I. Nye, & I. L. Reiss (Eds.), *Contemporary theories about the family* (Vol. I). New York: The Free Press.

Wertsch, J., McNamee, G., McLane, J., & Budwig, N. (1980). The adult-child dyad as a problem-solving system. *Child Development, 51,* 1215–1221.

Whiting, B., & Edwards, C. (1973). A cross-cultural analysis of sex-differences in the behavior of children aged three through eleven. *Journal of Social Psychology, 91,* 171–188.

Wilson, E. (1975). *Sociobiology.* Cambridge, MA: Harvard University Press.

4 The Study of Nurturant Interactions: From the Infant's Perspective

Gail F. Melson
Alan Fogel
Purdue University

Jayanthi Mistry
University of Utah

In recent years, there has been increasing attention paid to the issue of how children contribute to their own development (Lerner & Busch-Rossnagel, 1981). Ever since Bell's (1968) call for a reinterpretation of the socialization literature in terms of children's effects upon parents, researchers have recognized the impact that children have on those with whom they come into contact. This impact affects how others will respond to them, which in turn can be expected to modify the child's own behavior, cognitions and affect. Thus, from a unidirectional model of socialization, contemporary child development has "graduated" to a multidirectional, systemic view of the developing child in the context of relationships. Although research design often has lagged behind recognition of the systemic complexity of relations involving the child, there is widespread agreement that children contribute in significant ways to their own socialization.

When children's interactions with nonsocializing agents have been the focus of interest, this same multidirectional approach is less common. The study of young children's responsiveness to infants has attracted research interest because it has the potential of addressing important developmental questions. First, because nurturing the young is a sex-typed activity in virtually every society, the origins and developmental course of sex differences in responsiveness to infants has received considerable attention (cf. Berman, 1980, for review; Feldman & Nash, 1979; Feldman, Nash, & Cutrona, 1977; Fogel, Melson, & Mistry, this volume; Nash & Feldman, 1981). Second, because parenting that is responsive to a child's developmental needs is essential to the continuation of any society, we look at children's behavior and emotional expression directed at babies for clues to the beginnings of later parenting styles. Finally, because nurturing an infant often involves a high degree of altruism and empathy, the developmental

69

course of these constructs may also be illuminated by examination of children's responsiveness to infants (Fogel, Melson, & Mistry, this volume; Zahn-Waxler, Friedman, & Cummings, 1983). In all these research areas, however, the focus has been on the child, while the infant has been conceptualized as a stimulus.

From the point of view of the infant, participating in nurturant interactions has consequences for development. Nurturant interactions and the relationships that may grow out of them, can be thought of in terms of the provision of a secure base by one individual for another through the satisfaction of the latter's needs. Thus, the infant may be expected to benefit from nurturant interactions generally, in terms of security of attachment and its sequelae. Second, as Lewis and his associates (Lewis & Feiring, 1979) have shown, infants and toddlers have relationships with a variety of individuals, including mother, father, siblings, peers, and others. This complex social network provides infants with opportunities to engage in a greater range of social activities than previously had been assumed under socialization models that focused only on the mother-child relationship.

There is evidence that infants as young as 3-months-of-age behave differently toward other infants than toward either familiar or unfamiliar adults (Field, 1979; Fogel, 1979). Moreover, infants respond differently to children than to adults (Brooks & Lewis, 1976). Both in the laboratory playroom (Lamb, 1978) and in the home (Pelletier-Stiefel et al., this volume), infants and young children find older children particularly attractive. Younger siblings exhibit more interest in older siblings—by watching, following, and imitating them—than do the older sibs in younger siblings (Lamb, 1978). Infants are also highly responsive to children outside their family. Thus, a variety of sources of evidence concur that interactions of children with infants may have important developmental implications for both of them.

In this chapter, we present evidence bearing on the ways that infants and toddlers play a role in eliciting, maintaining, and terminating nurturant responses toward them. Taking the position that infant-child responsiveness occurs within the context of interactions, we review available studies on the topic demonstrating how studies that investigate child-infant interaction in more dyadic terms recognize the contributions of infant characteristics and behaviors to children's expressions of nurturance towards them. In order to elucidate the argument, we review studies of children's interest in infants, categorizing studies into a hierarchy of methods used, from indirect measures to ones that focus on analysis of interactions. In each section, we examine the infant's contribution to children's expressions of nurturance. Although we limit ourselves to studies of children in interaction with babies outside their families, our perspective is applicable to other situations, such as sibling interaction within the home and infant-adult interaction both outside and within the family.

There is little agreement in the literature about what constitutes nurturant behaviors by children toward infants. Some studies focus on measures of interest toward symbolic depictions of infants, such as pictures, (Berman, Goodman, Sloan, & Fernander, 1978; Feldman & Nash, 1979; Fullard & Reiling, 1976), while others assess behavioral interest toward live infants (Berman & Goodman, 1984; Berman, et al, 1977; Feldman & Nash, 1979; Melson & Fogel, 1982). Still other studies include a measure of *contingent* responsiveness, which assesses children's behavior immediately following selected infant behaviors, such as cries or vocalizations (Berman & Goodman, 1984; Feldman & Nash, 1979). Finally, one study (Mistry, Fogel, & Melson, in press) examines the contingent responsiveness of child to infant and infant to child across a wide range of behaviors.

It may be useful to think of these different measures in terms of a hierarchy of simple to increasingly complex conceptualizations of children's nurturance toward infants. Picture preference measures assess only simple child preference for indirect representations of infants. Behavioral interest measures a wide range of child behaviors, such as looks, approaches, touches, vocalizes, etc. toward a live baby, but ignores the possible impact of the infant's behavior. Measures of contingent responsiveness conceptualize nurturance in dyadic terms, examining the extent to which the child's behavior is responsive to infant "signals," although generally only a few infant behaviors are considered. Finally, when child-infant *and* infant-child contingencies are examined across a wide range of behaviors, it becomes possible to assess not only how the child may be responding to particular infant behaviors, but how the child's responses in turn may subsequently modify infant behaviors. These altered infant behaviors may then affect the child's next responses. Thus, at its most complex level, children's nurturant behaviors toward infants are viewed as embedded within the feedback loops of a dyadic analysis.

At each increasing level of complexity, there is increased recognition of the possible contributions of infant characteristics and behavior to children's expressions of nurturance toward them. In a sense, as we view children's nurturance toward infants in more dyadic terms, the infant moves from a shadowy stimulus to a source of significant variation in children's behavior. However, even in studies where the infant is present only as a "baby picture," perceived infant characteristics such as gender, physical attractiveness, or age (newborn vs. toddler) may be affecting children's expressed preferences.

INDIRECT MEASURES OF INTEREST

Elsewhere in this volume, we defined nurturance as *the provision of guidance, protection and care for the purpose of fostering developmental change congruent with the expected potential for change in the object of nurturance* (Fogel, Melson & Mistry, this volume, p. 55). In terms of this definition, little evidence of nurturance exists in most investigations of young children with infants or toddlers. We know almost nothing about when and under what conditions children develop ideas about the developmental potential of infants and their own role in fostering change. Beyond this, children must have a repertoire of behaviors appropriate to the fostering of developmental change and be able to match behavior to perceived need. Thus, nurturance as defined above appears to pose cognitive and behavioral regulation demands that are presumed to be beyond the capacities of preschoolage children.

However, researchers have reasonably assumed that for children, particularly young children, *interest* in an infant—a necessary, but not sufficient condition for nurturance by older children and adults—would constitute the set of behaviors most likely to index the beginnings of nurturance. Interest or attraction is viewed as basic to other expressions of nurturance, indeed a precondition of them, by Berman (this volume), Melson & Fogel (1982), and Feldman and Nash (1979, 1981).

Lorenz's argument (1943) that the physical features of the young of many species act as releasers of instinctual attraction to those young led to studies using static visual depictions of infants as elicitors of expressions of children's interest. Operationally, interest has been measured by picture preference tests (Berman et al., 1978; Feldman & Nash, 1979; Fullard & Reiling, 1977; Nash & Feldman, 1981) in which children are either asked to choose between paired presentations of an infant and an adult, (Berman, this volume) or to select preferred pictures from a larger set containing stimuli of various ages. Picture choice and duration of looking at pictures constitute the measures of interest in depicted representations.

Surprisingly, almost no studies utilizing this approach have employed preschoolage subjects (cf. Berman, 1980 for a review). Nash and Feldman (1981) administered a picture preference measure to a sample of 4-5 year-olds, but reported no details concerning their findings. Thus, we know almost nothing about when (and if) young children first begin to respond preferentially to visual depictions of infants.

The meaning of such preference measures is, of course, dependent upon the number and type of other stimulus pictures presented, since interest is always relative to the other choices available. Since the set of stimulus pictures presented to older children varies in different studies (Berman et al., 1978; Feldman & Nash, 1979; Fullard & Reiling, 1976), the preference measures are not strictly comparable. Berman et al. (1978) presented pairs of infant and adult stimulus figures, while Fullard & Reiling used both animal and human pairs of young and adult figures.

A second, more serious problem with picture preference measures as indicators of interest in infants deals with the relation between interest in infants, a measure of affect, and cognitive constructions about infants. Implicit in the interpretation of the results of picture preference studies in terms of interest in *infants* is an assumption that children are using the same age discriminations as are adults. When infant figures are presented in pairs with adult figures, and children are able to discriminate between them, one can only conclude that they are perceiving an adult-nonadult distinction, but not that they perceive the infant pictures as infants per se. For example, would preschoolage children label toddlers as "babies"? What age discriminations do young children make? What are the attributions that children make to stimulus figures they label as "babies"? Do such attributions change with age and experience with infants?

Edwards (1984) presented children between 2- and 4-years-of-age with an array of photographs of individuals and a display of realistic doll figures ranging from age 1 year to 60 years and elicited spontaneous labels with the question: "What do you call this one?" She found that all children readily labeled the stimuli and tended to use terms like "baby," "boy," "girl," "man," and "woman" rather than supraordinate terms of reference, like "child" or "adult." Rather than use the term "toddler," preschoolers differentiated between "little baby" and "big baby."

In a subsequent sorting task, Edward (1984) found that preschoolers applied the term "baby" to photographs of individuals under 2-years-of-age and "little children" to those from 2- to 6-years-of-age. Older preschoolers (age 3–4) made fewer errors in age assignment than did younger preschoolers, who may have become confused by the task.

These results suggest that young children do perceive infants as distinct from "little children," but lack the category label of "toddler." Thus, there is some validity in assuming that preference for infant pictures in comparison to exemplars of older children or adults does represent an underlying conception of the infant as a separate age category.

COGNITIONS ABOUT INFANTS

Little is known, however, about the characteristics differentially ascribed to infants, and whether male vs. female infants are perceived differently. Moreover, while the category label "toddler" is not used, preschool children may ascribe different characteristics to depictions of individuals between 1- and 2-years-of-age.

To determine what cognitions are elicited by pictures of infants vs. other age categories, we devised an interview procedure using picture stimuli. We presented a set of black and white line drawings, each 8½" × 11", to 43 preschoolers and 42 second-graders, equally divided between males and females. The 16-picture set contained two pictures, one of a female and one of a male, of each of the following age groups: infant less than 12 mos, toddler standing, child, adolescent, adult, elderly person, young animal (puppy and kitten), adult animals (dog and cat). An example of two stimulus figures is shown in Fig. 4.1. We purposely used only a minimal number of conventional indicators of age and sex

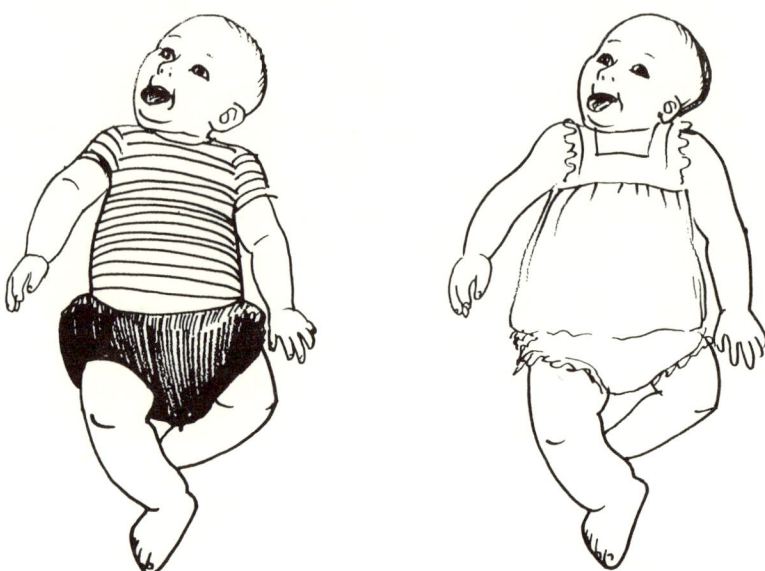

FIG. 4.1. Sample drawings from Melson, Fogel, & Toda (in preparation).

so that the stimulus figures would serve as prods for eliciting children's age discriminations and the attributions on which they were based rather than their ability to identify the characteristics of particular stimuli presented to them.

The order of presentation was randomized. Before the pictures were presented, the interviewer, an adult female familiar to the children, explained that she wanted to find out what children know about babies and had brought along some pictures to show. As she held up each picture, she asked: "Is this a baby?" Following a "yes" answer, she asked: "Why is this a baby?" To elicit all of the child's ideas, she often followed up this with "How do you know this is a baby?" What do babies do? What else do babies do?"

Each interview was audiotaped and transcripts were made for analysis. Each child's responses to the question "Why is this a baby?" and its followup questions were coded in terms of the following categories: *positive affect* (smiles, laughs), *motor behavior* (kick, crawl, turn, wiggle), *aggression* (bite, pull hair, scratch), *oral behavior* (chew, suck, lick, eat), *vocalizations* (baby noise, hiss, make sounds), *play, state* (sleep, cry), *babyishness* (small, little ears, diapers, can't understand, falls down), *dislike* (smells, drools, wets pants, gets into trouble), and *like* (holds onto you, lets you pet them, likes to be taken care of). Eight transcripts were independently recorded by a second coder and reliabilities computed for each of the categories ranged from 54–100% (M = 89.88%)

The results indicated that infant picture stimuli were immediately and clearly identified as "babies" by virtually all children (84 of 85). However, only 13 of the preschoolers and 18 of the second-graders considered the toddler pictures to be "babies."

When the characteristics children named to justify the term "baby" were examined, the results showed that children made most frequent reference to *babyishness*—the small size and relative helplessness of the infant. As Table 4.1 indicates, children attributed significantly more infant-like characteristics to infant pictures than to those toddler or animal young pictures also labeled as "babies."

It appears that children as young as 3-years-of-age easily discriminate depictions of infants from those of other young children and use visual characteristics, such as small features, in making these discriminations. In this sense, the results support Lorenz's emphasis on the perceptual salience of "babyish" physiognomy and suggest that such physical features are used by children to decide whether or not to apply the label "baby." In addition, however, children's responses revealed an emphasis on behavioral cues. Babyishness was defined for children in terms of inability to locomote unaided, common infant states, such as sleeping and crying, frequent oral behaviors such as sucking, chewing, and licking, and playfulness. A stimulus figure depicted as standing unaided was significantly less likely than one shown lying down to be labeled as a "baby."

These results suggest that preschoolers do have some conception of the developmental characteristics of infants. Since such knowledge is part of an understanding of developmental potential and how it might be fostered, the findings of this interview study raise the possibility that young children are capable of higher levels of nurturant behavior than expressions of interest alone.

TABLE 4.1
Characteristics Attributed to Human Infants, Toddlers, and Animal Young[a]

Characteristics	Infants MEAN(SD)	Toddlers MEAN(SD)	Animal Young MEAN(SD)
POSITIVE AFFECT	.11(.39)	0(0)	.04(.26)
MOTOR	.96(1.23)	.41(.89)	.49(.82)
AGGRESSIVE	.15 .56)	.04(.43)	.31(.80)
ORAL	.90(1.14)	.38(.86)	.37(.81)
VOCAL	.12(.37)	.03(.24)	.22(.44)
PLAY	.76(.84)	.22(.62)	.45(.82)
STATE	.64(.89)	.17(.49)	.15(.47)
BABYISH	2.60(4.81)	.74(2.49)	1.78(6.16)
LIKE, NOT	.03(.24)	0(0)	.03(.24)
TOTAL	6.30(5.42)	2.03(3.84)	3.36(4.67)

[a]From Melson, Fogel, and Toda, in preparation.

The Contribution of the Infant

Picture preference studies have not systematically varied infant characteristics to determine whether variations in infant appearance or (if videotapes or live presentations are used) infant behavior yield different child preferences or cognitions about infants.

Perhaps the most salient infant characteristic for adults is gender. The question most likely to be asked of new parents (Intans-Peterson & Reddel, 1984) is: Is it a boy or a girl? How salient is this difference to young children? Do their cognitions about infants vary depending upon the perceived sex of the infant?

In order to begin to answer these questions, we examined children's responses to the infant male vs infant female, toddler male vs toddler female pictures used in the interview study explained above. As Fig. 4.1 shows, only a few conventional indicators of sex—differences of clothing, hair, and appearance—were used to differentiate the pictures. We purposely did this to see if young children would employ this shorthand of gender assignment.

All but 5 preschoolers and 5 second-graders labeled infant and toddler pictures conventionally as male or female. Responses to the question: "Why is this a boy (girl) baby?" were analyzed in terms of references to clothing (female infants had ruffled dress), hair (female infants had longer, curlier hair) and appearance (references to differences in face, body shape, or general "look").

Although both the preschoolers and second-graders were quite sensitive to conventional indicators of gender, they did not go beyond the depicted differences in clothing or hair to attribute behavioral differences to infants based on gender. For example, they did not describe male infants as more active, vocal, or aggressive, nor did they view female infants as more "babyish" or delicate. In short, they showed awareness of the ways in which adults modify infants' appearance to signal their gender—putting bows in hair, for example—but beyond this did not describe male and female babies differently.

However, when perceived infant gender and child gender are both taken into account, children's responses to male vs. female infant pictures revealed some evidence of what has been called a "like-me" effect. This refers to the hypothesis, first advanced by Lewis and Brooks-Gunn (1979) that children will be more responsive to others whom they perceive as like them in important ways. Since gender identity is first formed as early as 18-months-of-age and is certainly well-established and salient for preschool children, it is possible that perceptions that infants are like them in this way may influence cognitions about infants and preferences for infants based on pictorial representations.

In support of this hypothesis, we found that preschool boys named more infant characteristics ($M = 4.45$) than did preschool girls ($M = 2.13$) when viewing a picture of an infant they perceived to be male ($F = 6.44$, $p < .01$). Similarly, preschool boys responded with more descriptors ($M = 1.35$) in response to a depicted toddler male than did preschool girls ($M = .57$) ($F = 3.53$,

$p < .06$). However, there were no comparable "like me" effects among second-graders.

Contrary to the hypothesis, boys of both age groups actually gave more responses to the infant female picture ($M = 4.12$) than did girls ($M = 2.37$) ($F = 7.14$, $p < .009$). Thus, based on this first, exploratory study of children's cognitions about babies, we must conclude that little consistent evidence for a "like me" effect is operating in terms of responses to depicted representations. However, perceived infant gender and child gender were interacting in complex, not easily understood ways.

Additional research is needed on how children respond in terms of preference and cognitions to variations in infant characteristics. Physical attractiveness, activity, fussiness, or rate of smiling are all potential elicitors of differing child responses. Moreover, interactions between child and infant characteristics need to be explored.

Critique of Picture Measures

In investigating such questions, responses to pictorial representations of infants and other persons are of limited value. Many of the most salient infant characteristics emerge only when behavior can be observed. Moreover, picture preference measures are not consistently related to behavioral orientation either in children, adolescents, or in adults. (Berman, 1980; Feldman & Nash, 1981). This is not surprising, since responses to depicted representations contain only information about certain limited physical features of infants, while behaviorally expressed interest in response to a live infant allows interest to be reflective of the full interactive contribution of the other person. (Berman, 1980) Behavioral expressions of attention toward infants and interest in them are inevitably affected by a variety of situational variables, among which the infant's own behavior figures prominently.

BEHAVIORAL INTEREST

Because of this, the majority of studies of children's interest have employed observational measures of behavior toward an infant. For example, Melson and Fogel (1982) define interest in terms of looks, approaches, touches, smiles, verbalizations, proximity, toy-mediated play (offer or takes toys), and face-to-face interaction. This last category of behavior refers to instances in which children place their faces up against the faces of the infants, often touching noses. (To do this when infants are sitting or lying on the floor requires the child to stretch out on the floor.) Finally, Melson and Fogel (1982) considered as examples of indirect interest, children's talk to the infant's mother about the baby and play with a life-size doll also present in the playroom.

Berman and her colleagues (Berman & Goodman, 1984; Berman, this volume) have employed a smaller, but overlapping set of categories in their studies of interest in toddlers—toy interaction, touch, accidental touch and verbalizations or vocalizations to baby. Feldman, Nash, and Cutrona (1977); Feldman & Nash (1979); Nash & Feldman (1981) in their studies of the responses of individuals of different ages to infants code looks, funny faces/gestures, talks, smiles, touches, proximity, noises, demonstrates toy, and gives object. Based on the pattern of intercorrelations, summary measures of proximal and distal interaction are usually derived.

While considerable overlap thus exists in the behavioral categories used to index interest or attraction, certain differences remain. One difference concerns the degree to which individual behaviors are related and hence, the utility of summary measures of interest. While the Feldman & Nash studies have used summary measures, Melson & Fogel (1982) found that behavioral categories did not cohere in clusters, suggesting that individual children expressed interest in varying ways. Such differences in the ways different behavioral indications of interest are related could well be affected by subtle variations in the situation in which child and infant meet.

One situational characteristic of importance in interpreting interest measures is the presence or absence of other novel and interesting stimuli in the situation. Only when attractive alternatives are available can one argue that the child is selectively interested or attentive to the infant. While most investigations of behavioral interest use a laboratory playroom stiuation with toys available to the child, generally there is no attempt to ensure that noninfant stimuli in the environment are potentially of equal attraction to the child.

A final difference to be noted in behavioral measurements of interest concerns the unit of measurement employed. In some cases, the unit of measurement is a time-interval. For example, Berman and Goodman (1984) record the presence of at least one instance of various behaviors within each 10-sec interval. Similarly, Feldman and Nash in their studies use a 6-sec interval and record no more than one instance of each category occuring within each interval. By contrast, Melson & Fogel in their work (1982; Mistry, Fogel, & Melson, in press; Fogel et al., this volume) measure behaviors continuously from videotaped records of sessions and derive frequency and duration scores. The latter method appears to be a more sensitive indicator of differences in interest and for that reason, may reveal individual variation more readily.

The Contribution of the Infant

When children are observed in situations including a live infant, the potential for infant characteristics and behavior to affect the child is of course, much greater than when children's interest in infants is assessed pictorially.

Berman et al. (1977) observed the behavior of preschool children in a daycare center toward a 13-month-old toddler in a playpen. They noted that the toddler often attempted to initiate interaction with the older children by reaching out of the playpen to touch them. Children with whom the toddler initiated interaction were more likely to respond than were children who did not experience toddler initiatives. Melson and Fogel (1982) also noted that in their observations of preschoolers in a laboratory playroom with a 6- 8- month-old infant, the infants appeared to be highly interested in the children.

These two studies are typical of other investigations of young children's responsiveness to infants in that the behaviors of the infants or toddlers are either not measured at all (for example, Berman & Goodman, 1984) or are given cursory attention. For example, in a study by Feldman and Nash (1977), one of the behaviors observed in a waiting room situation containing an older child and a 5- 9-month-old-infant and its mother is *ignores baby*. This category assesses behaviors directed at the baby within 6 sec following infant noise. Melson and Fogel (1982) showed that perceived gender of the infant affected preschoolers' responsiveness. With the exception of older preschool boys, children were more responsive to infants whom they perceived as "like them" in sex (the sex of the infants being experimentally manipulated in instructions to the child). Four-to-five year-old-boys, however, were more interested in an "opposite-sex" infant.

In none of studies cited above was the full behavioral repertoire of the infant or toddler measured and its possible impact on the child noted. Most of the studies in the responsiveness to infants literature observed children with infants who could crawl or walk. Thus, they would be capable of following the child and making active bids for attention and interaction. In general, infants possess a wide range of motoric and affective behaviors that could function as signals to the child.

It is particularly surprising that the role of the infant in nurturant interactions has been largely ignored when numerous studies point out that children appear to be affected by individual differences in infant characteristics and behavior (Berman & Goodman, 1984). However, this is usually viewed as a possible source of error in measuring children's responsiveness, rather than a direction for further inquiry and is "corrected" by employing a larger number of infants as participants.

One reason the infant's contribution has received little attention may be because nurturance has been conceptualized not as a characteristic of the interaction, but as a set of behaviors exhibited by the child (or adult) under varying circumstances. Within this view, the infant is seen as one of the many situational variables that might affect the frequency, duration, and intensity of nurturant behaviors. Thus, if the research question is directed at the impact of other variables (e.g., age or sex), attempts are made to control for the behavior of the infant participants in the study.

By shifting attention to the interaction rather than the individual child as actor and the infant as object, questions concerning the determinants of infant behavior within the interaction arise. For example, what variables are predictive of an infant's responsiveness to a particular child? If infants and toddlers do vary widely in responsiveness, to what extent is such individual variability consistent across situations? In other words, is it valid to think in terms of generally "friendly" and "unfriendly" or aloof infants? If an infant's behavior is situationally responsive, to what characteristics and behaviors of the child does the infant respond?

In order to assess how infants responded to various children, we conducted an analysis of infant behavior toward children in 71 videotaped sessions in which a preschoolage child was observed for 10 min in a laboratory playroom containing a 6- 8-month-old infant and the infant's mother, who was instructed to be uninvolved with either infant or child unless necessary for the infant's welfare. (See Mistry et al., in press). An array of novel and attractive age-appropriate toys was available for the child, as well as a selection of infant toys scattered on the floor just out of reach of the infant. The experimental situation is depicted in Fig. 4.2.

The children were 37 boys and 34 girls, at two age levels (Ms = 37 mos, 54 mos). Approximately one third of the children were singletons, one-third had younger siblings, and one-third were the youngest of two or more children. All the children were attending a university child development laboratory preschool.

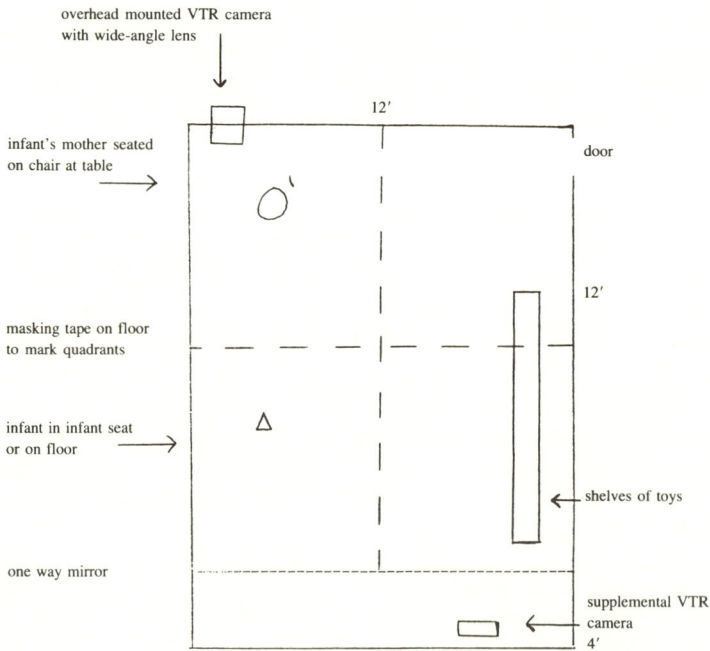

FIG. 4.2. Experimental playroom layout (from Melson & Fogel, 1982).

Twenty-six mother-infant pairs also participated. Both mothers and children were drawn from a largely white, middle-class population of intact families.

From the videotapes, child and infant behaviors were coded independently. The following categories, in mean duration, were derived: *responsiveness to mother,* (looks, vocalizations or verbalizations, approaches, etc.) *responses to toys,* (not involving an interactant), *negative responses* (fuss, whine, cry, frown) and *no directed interest* (time spent staring around room, wandering, etc.). In addition, for the infant, *responsiveness to child* was coded when the infant looked at the child. This was often accompanied by smiling, pointing, vocalizations, and in the case of crawling infants, approach. For the child, *responsiveness to infant* was coded when the child approached or remained in proximity to the baby, vocalized to the infant, or engaged in toy play.

As Table 4.2 indicates, when measures for infant and child are compared, it is evident that the infants in our sample showed considerably more interest in the children than the latter did in them. In addition, infants were less likely to exhibit negative responses or to show no directed interest than did children.

Influences on Infant Responsiveness

Do infants exhibit the same heightened level of interest toward all children? Examination of infant responsiveness by age and sex of the child indicated a significant age $\times$ sex interaction ($F = 3.73, p < .06$). Infants responded least to older males ($M = 26\%$), most to older females ($M = 44\%$) and about the same to younger children of either sex ($M = 37\%$).

Since most infants participated in more than one session, it was possible to compare the behavior of the same infant in interaction with different children. No evidence of systematic consistency was obtained. A comparison of dependent measures across sessions for the same infant revealed few significant correlations. Moreover, in general, sex or sibling status differences among infants were not strongly predictive of variations in responses to the children. Male infants

TABLE 4.2
Mean Duration (as Proportion of Total Interaction Time) and Standard Deviation (in parenthesis) for Children's and Infants' Behavior (n = 71)

Measure	Child	Infant	Wilcoxin	P
Response to other	.17(.21)	.36(.20)	5.17	.0001
Response to mother	.06(.15)	.09(.11)	3.18	.001
Response to toys	.36(.33)	.36(.32)	.56	ns
Negative response	.25(.29)	.13(.20)	2.55	.01
No direct interest	.18(.22)	.01(.02)	5.69	.0001

were somewhat more interested in toys than were female infants ($F = 2.91$, $p < .10$; M = 42% males, 27% females). Infants with siblings were somewhat less interested in the child ($M = 29\%$) than those without siblings ($M = 39\%$) ($F = 3.30$, $p < .08$). Thus, infants were responding primarily to the individual child within the context of the immediate situation.

In order to develop a better understanding of the particular behaviors infants exhibit toward unfamiliar children, we next conducted a more detailed analysis of infant and child behaviors of 26 of the above sessions. We chose those sessions that included the most evidence of interaction by selecting only the ones in which each individual displayed at least three bouts of responsiveness. (A bout was defined as one continuous period in which one individual responded to the other).

In this subsample, 9 of the pairs had male children and 17 had female children. There were 12 male and 14 female infants. Eight of the children were older preschoolers and 18 were younger. Finally, 10 pairs were same-sex dyads, while 16 were opposite-sex. None of these differences were significant (binomial sign test, two-tailed).

In this analysis, frequency of the following infant and child behaviors was coded: *initiates interaction, looks at partner, bids for attention, explores objects, positive expression, checks back to mother,* and *negative responses* to partner (intrude, reject). Table 4.3 presents a comparison of infant and child behavior.

As inspection of the mean differences between infant and child indicates, infants showed a wider range of affect, being both more negative and more positive in their expression than were the children. While infants focused most of

TABLE 4.3
Comparison of Total Frequencies of Infant and Child Behaviors
(n = 26 Dyads)[a]

Measure	Child	Infant	Wilcoxin	P
Bids for interaction	119	73	1.59	ns
Checks back to mother	129	37	3.00	.01
Looks at other	241	245	.20	ns
Negative expression	1	85	3.59	.001
Explore objects	226	219	.14	ns
Positive behavior	35	80	2.18	.05
Negative responses to partner (intrude, reject)	21	56	2.00	.05

[a] From Mistry, Fogel, and Melson, in press.

their attention on the children, the children were more likely to use the mother as a source of information about the baby (by asking questions, etc.) and they frequently checked back with the mother, perhaps for reassurance or permission.

The results from both our complete sample and the supplementary analysis performed on the subsample confirm the general impression, noted in many investigations, of strong infant interest in young children. Indeed, inspection of our videotapes reveal many instances in which infants made repeated and urgent bids for the attention of the older child who may have been involved in playing with toys or who resolutely ignored the baby's efforts.

These impressions suggest that although they have a smaller repertoire of social skills, infants may not only be more responsive in an overall sense to young children than the latter are to them, but also that infants may be more likely to initiate bids for interaction and once the child responds, less likely than the child to terminate the interaction. In other words, the mean differences in overall behavioral interest raise the possibility that the infant is more active an interactive partner in initiating and maintaining interactive sequences. An hypothesis of this sort requires one to shift analysis from the level of the individual to that of the contingencies of interaction at the level of the dyad.

CONTINGENT RESPONSIVENESS

From the point of view of the older child, while behavioral interest is seen as basic to nurturance, measures of *contingent responsiveness* tap a child's ability to be responsive to specific aspects of the infant's behavior. Thus, contingent responsiveness is a class of behaviors that incorporate more aspects of nurturance than interest or attraction. The term indicates that the child's behavior is regulated in some way by the infant's behavior.

One might expect the child's interest in infants to be a necessary, but not a sufficient, condition for contingent responsiveness, in that maintaining interest in the infant is essential to a determination of appropriate contingencies. To the extent that this question has been investigated, results are in accordance with this prediction. For example, Nash and Feldman (1981) reported a negative correlation between "ignores baby," defined as extent of responsiveness to infant noise within 6 sec, and measures of positive interest.

Although there is some evidence that young children are contingently responsive to infants, at least when infant signals are clear and unmistakable—cries, noises—the evidence we presented earlier concerning the high level of interest infants express toward children suggests that infants may also be contingently responsive toward children in dyadic encounters between them.

To tell us more about the actual sequencing of behavior when infant and child are together, we dischotomized the infants' and children's behaviors in the 26 sessions into states of responsive vs. unresponsive, or more simply ON and OFF.

84 MELSON, FOGEL, AND MISTRY

At any given moment, the pair will be in one of four possible dyadic states: child ON-infant ON, child OFF-infant ON, child ON-infant OFF, and child OFF-infant OFF.

In Fig. 4.3, we show the probabilities of transitions between each state. In principle, any given state could change to any of the other three dyadic states. In practice, it was very unlikely that both infant and child would change at exactly the same moment (these would be the transitions between states going vertically or horizontally). Because of coder time error limitations, transitions of less than 1 sec were included in this category.

The eight transitions presented in Fig. 4.3 were computed by summing the number of transitions from the target state to either of two destination states and dividing each by the total number of instances of the target state (given in parentheses in each box). Differences between transitions were tested using a Wilcoxon matched-pairs signed-ranks test.

One should note first, by inspecting the boxes in Fig. 4.3, that the state, child OFF–infant ON, was about twice as likely as the state child ON–infant OFF, again showing the relatively greater responsiveness of the infant to the child than vice versa.

Second, to see who was more likely to initiate an interaction, one can compare the probability of the infant shifting to ON while the child is still OFF (.651) with the probability of the child shifting to ON while the infant is OFF (.225) (z = 3.54, $p < .0001$). Thus, we see that infants are not only greater in overall

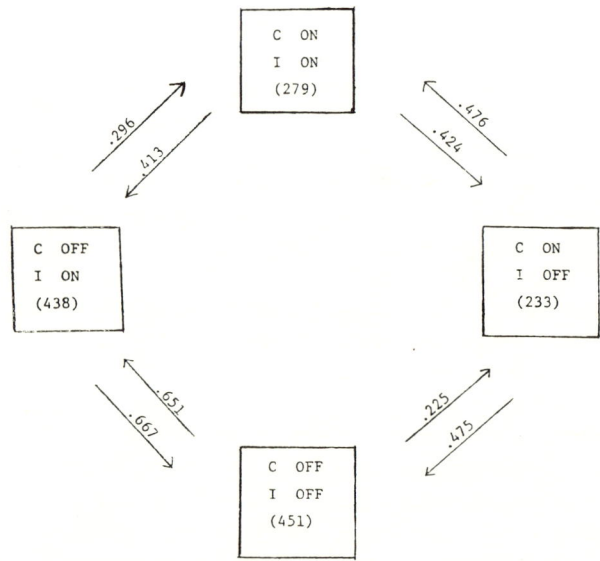

FIG. 4.3. Child-infant response contingencies.

responsiveness, but they are also significantly more likely to initiate an interaction.

Who is more likely to respond once the other has taken the initiative? To answer this question, one can compare the probability of the infant changing to ON once the child is ON (.476) with the probability of the child changing to ON once the infant is ON (.296). ($z = 4.11, p < .0001$). Again, it is evident that the infant is more responsive to initiatives of the other than is the child.

Who is more likely to terminate an interaction? A comparison of the probability of the child going OFF vs. the infant going OFF from the state where both are ON (.413 vs. .424) indicates no significant difference between child and infant in this regard. Both are equally likely to terminate a state of mutual responsiveness.

However, a somewhat different picture emerges when we take into account the amount of time elapsing before a state change. Most transitions occurred in the first five seconds following the onset of a dyadic state. The only exception to this general rule occurred for infant transitions when the child was OFF. In comparison to child transitions when the infant was OFF, we found that the infant was more likely to continue to remain ON, following the child's shift to OFF. (z-test for independent proportions, Glass & Stanley, 1970; $p < .001$, using a Bonferroni correction for total number of tests). Thus, while child and infant were equally likely to terminate an interaction, once the child had ceased to respond to the infant, the infant was likely to persist in trying to elicit a response from the child.

Responsiveness of the child to the infant and vice-versa can also be tested by looking at differences in the likelihood that each will make any kind of change, as a function of the state of the other. Are infants more likely to shift either to ON or to OFF when the child is ON or when the child is OFF? Infants are more likely to shift to ON when the child is OFF (.651) rather than when the child is ON (.476) ($z = 2.00, p < .05$) and they are more likely also to shift to OFF when the child is OFF (.667) rather than when the child is ON (.424) ($z = 3.78, p < .0001$). The infant is less likely to change state while the child is ON, suggesting that there is a reluctance either to begin or end an interaction once the child has started to interact. If the young child begins to engage the infant while the infant is looking away, the child's chances of getting the infant to look and continue looking at the child are less than if the child starts the interaction when the infant is already looking.

Overall, there were no differences in these transitional probabilities between groups based on age of child, sex of child, sex of infant, or sex composition of the child-infant pair (t-tests, two-tailed).

This analysis of the transitional probabilities between interactive states provides rather clear documentation concerning the contingent responsiveness of the infant. Infants as compared with preschoolers were more likely to initiate interactions, respond to the initiatives of their partner and persist in interacting.

In order to find out more about the kinds of behaviors infants and children used in initiating, maintaining, and terminating interactions, we examined specific child and infant behaviors as antecedent states, rather than the ON–OFF dichotomy presented above. We performed a series of multiple event lag analyses (Sackett et al., 1978) in which the probability of any given multievent sequence is compared to others, and it adjusts for the total number of events and event lags.

To determine the degree to which infants are contingently responsive to unfamiliar children, we can take the child's behavior as the criterion and examine what infant behaviors, if any, have a significant probability of following within a few seconds of a particular child behavior. Similarly, to assess the extent to which children are contingently responsive to infants, infant behaviors are considered the criterion and the probability of certain child behaviors following the criterion are examined.

As Table 4.4 indicates, the kinds of contingent behaviors infants exhibited consisted primarily of looks at the child, explorations of objects, and demands from the child for attention. For example, if the child looked at the infant, the infant was likely to look back. If the child tried to initiate interaction with the infant or distract the infant, usually by offering an "infant" toy such as a rattle, the infant responded by exploring the object. In cases where the child rejected the infant by turning away, the infant "demanded" interaction by reaching out toward the child while looking and attempting to touch.

TABLE 4.4
Event Sequence Analysis: Child Behavior as Criterion[a]

	Child Behavior	Frequency	Lagged Behavior	Observed Probability	Z
Positive Interest	Initiate	119	Infant explore object	.227	3.68***
	Complement	62			NS
	Distract	18	Infant explore object	.059	2.34**
	Looking	241	Infant looking	.183	2.34**
	Direct Interest		Child check back to mother	.167	2.09*
	Indirect Interest		Child positive expression	.130	3.43***
	Hesitant Interest		Child complement	.094	2.68**
Negative Interest	Ignore	226			NS
	Intrude	22			NS
	Reject	9	Infant demand	.222	4.27***

*$p < .05$
**$p < .01$
***$p < .001$
[a]From Mistry et al., in press.

In what ways did the child respond contingently to the infant? In Table 4.5, we examine those events that followed when infant behaviors were considered the criterion. This analysis showed that children, too, were contingently responsive but only to infant distress or demand. When the infant was fussy or cried, children sometimes tried to distract the baby. Sometimes, the infant calmed down on its own or the mother intervened. In addition, when infants "demanded" the child's attention by reaching, looking and touching, the children generally tried to distract the babies, usually by offering toys, or "complemented" the infants' behaviors. The latter refers to behaviors that encourage or support the infant's behavior by verbal encouragement, mirroring or imitation, recovering a fallen object, etc.

Although children tried to alleviate infant distress and satisfy infant demands, they were not responsive to more subtle signals, such as infant looks or positive expression. It appears that when infant signals are clear and unmistakable—cries, for example—even young preschoolers appropriately and successfully can meet infant needs. An episode we observed frequently in our videotapes illustrates this: an infant is straining for a rattle just beyond reach. Soon the infant begins to fuss and whine. The child picks up the rattle and offers it to the infant who immediately quiets, eagerly grabs the toy, and quietly begins to suck on it.

However, when infant signals are more subtle and unclear—infant looks, for example—the preschoolers in our sample were not very responsive to them. This suggests that for young children, the ability to nurture by satisfying the immediate needs of the infant is dependent upon the child's ability to read the infant's signals.

TABLE 4.5
Event Sequence Analysis: Infant Behavior as Criterion[a]

	Infant Behavior	Frequency	Lagged Behavior	Observed Probability	z
Positive Responses	Positive expression	80			NS
	Looking	245			NS
	Demand	38	Child complement	.263	7.88***
			Child distract		2.70**
Negative Responses	Fail to reach goal	35	Infant discontent	.251	6.81***
	Discontent	70	Child distract	.118	9.08***
	Distress	15	Child distract	.071	2.36*
			Infant calms	.143	5.85***
			Mother mediates	.071	2.54**
	Reject	56			NS

*$p < .05$
**$p < .01$
***$p < .001$
[a]From Mistry et al., in press.

Even when signals are clear, children may interact inappropriately with the infants, because they are not aware of the appropriate responses, cannot execute them, or are not motivated to do so. In our videotapes of preschoolers with 6- 8-month-old infants and their mothers, it was common to find that children who expressed interest in the infants attempted to interact with them inappropriately. These children attempted to play with the infant as if he or she were a peer. One child, for example, trying to have a "tea party" with a baby, became upset when the infant wanted only to bang the cups and saucers together. Berman (this volume) has noted that among her sample of 8- 9-year-olds interacting with toddlers, girls who showed strong interest in the younger children were often insensitive to their needs, restricting them and 'smothering' them with affection.

The skills required for appropriate contingent responsiveness are complex. A child must be aware that the infant has expressed a need and be able to identify what that need is. This is difficult for young children who are often at a loss to understand the infant's behavior. In our videotapes of preschool children with infants, a typical reaction to infant distress is to first look searchingly around the room and at the mother whom the children recognize as ultimately responsible for satisfying the infant's needs.

SUMMARY

A hierarchy of expressions of nurturance has been examined and data bearing on the contribution of the infant have been presented. The most limited assessment perhaps is through preference measures in response to visual stimuli, an approach used with older children and adults, but one about which we know little concerning young children's responses. Although the possible impact of infant characteristics is limited in picture preference assessments, we presented evidence that perceived gender and age of the infant are salient to children as young as three years of age. Moreover, children ascribe differential characteristics to infants based on their perceived age (but not gender). These findings raise the possibility that interest in infants, as measured by picture preferences, may also be affected by infant characteristics such as age, gender, or physical attractiveness.

Behaviorally expressed interest allows for a wider range of infant characteristics to affect the child. Here, a number of studies concur that children who show interest in an infant by looking, approaching, touching, verbalizing, etc. also tend to respond in some way to infant cries or noises. A detailed analysis of child behaviors contingent upon various infant behaviors revealed that when toys are available, preschoolers react to infant distress or infant demands by attempting to distract the infant by offering toys or helping the infant retrieve fallen toys.

Although children show considerable skill in responding appropriately to these infant behaviors, they are less responsive when more subtle infant signals are emitted. Thus, when infants gaze at the child and make positive bids for interaction, children often ignore them or respond inappropriately.

Infants, on the other hand, appear to be highly responsive to young children. At least in settings in which their mothers remain in sight and which contain a variety of interesting toys, infants between 6- and 8-months-of-age showed heightened interest in unfamiliar preschoolers, gazing at them, making repeated bids for their attention and signaling demand for response by reaching, vocalizing, and touching the child. They are relatively uninterested in their own mothers. There is evidence from other studies (Berman, this volume) that older infants and toddlers also show a similar pattern of interest in children.

Using a data base of 71 videotaped child-infant dyads, we presented several analyses designed to show the extent to which infants are important contributors to any interaction with a young child. Not only are infants more interested in children than the reverse, but analysis of interactive sequences shows that infants are more likely to initiate, maintain, and respond to the child's initiative than the child is to them.

These data, taken together, suggest that we can best understand children's interest in and responsiveness toward infants within the context of *interactions*. Here, both infant and child play a role in initiating, maintaining, and terminating interactive sequences. The contribution of the infant at each point is considerable.

REFERENCES

Bell, R. Q. (1968). A reinterpretation of the direction of effects in studies of socialization. *Psychological Review, 75,* 81–95.

Berman, P. (1980). Are women more responsive than men to the young? A review of developmental and situational variables. *Psychological Bulletin, 58,* 668–695.

Berman, P. W., & Goodman, V. (1984). Age and sex differences in children's responses to babies: Effects of adults' caretaking requests and instructions. *Child Development, 55,* 1071–1077.

Berman, P. W., Goodman, V., Sloan, V. L., & Fernander, L. (1978). Preferences for infants among black and white children: Sex and age differences. *Child Development, 49,* 917–919.

Berman, P. W., Monda, L. D., & Meyercough, R. P. (1977). Sex differences in young children's responses to an infant: An observation within a day-care setting. *Child Development, 48,* 711–715.

Brooks, J., & Lewis, M. (1976). Infants' responses to strangers: Midget, adult, and child. *Child Development, 47,* 323–333.

Edwards, C. P. (1984). The age group labels and categories of preschool children. *Child Development, 55,* 440–452.

Feldman, S. S., & Nash, S. C. (1979). Changes in responsiveness to babies during adolescence. *Child Development, 50,* 942–949.

Feldman, S. S., Nash, S. C., & Cutrona, C. (1977). The influence of age and sex on responsiveness to babies. *Developmental Psychology, 13,* 675–676.

Field, T. F. (1979). Infant behaviors directed toward peers and adults in the presence and absence of mother. *Infant Behavior and Development, 2,* 47–54.

Fogel, A. (1979). Peer versus mother directed behavior in 1- 3-month old infants. *Infant Behavior and Development, 2,* 215–226.

Fullard, W., & Reiling, A. M. (1976). An investigation of Lorenz's "babyishness." *Child Development, 49,* 1182–1188.

Glass, G. V., & Stanley, J. C. (1970). *Statistical methods in education and society.* New York: Prentice-Hall.

Intans-Peterson, M. J., & Reddel, M. (1984). What do people ask about a neonate? *Development Psychology, 20,* 358–359.

Lamb, M. E. (1978). Development of sibling relations in infancy: A short-term longitudinal study. *Child Development, 49,* 1189–1196.

Lerner, R., & Busch-Rossnagel, N. (1981). (Eds.). *Individuals as producers of their own development.* New York: Academic Press.

Lewis, M., & Brooks-Gunn, J. (1979). *Social cognition and acquisition of self.* New York: Plenum Press.

Lewis, M., & Rosenblum, L. (1975). (Eds.). *Freindship and peer relations.* New York: Wiley.

Lorenz, K. (1943). Die angebornen Formen moglicher Erfahrung. *Zeitscrift fur Tierpsychologie, 5,* 235–282.

Melson, G. F., & Fogel, A. (1982). Young children's interest in unfamiliar infants. *Child Development, 53,* 693–700.

Melson, G. F., Fogel, A., & Toda, S. (in preparation) *Children's ideas about infants and their care.* Unpublished manuscript, Purdue University.

Mistry, J., Fogel, A., & Melson, G. F. (in press). Interactions of six-month-olds with preschool-aged children. *Acta Paedologica.*

Nash, S. C., & Feldman, S. S. (1981). Sex-related differences in the relationship between sibling status and responsivity to babies. *Sex Roles, 7,* 1035–1042.

Whiting, B. B., & Whiting, J. W. M. (1975). *Children of six cultures: A psycho-cultural analysis.* Cambridge, MA: Harvard University Press.

Zahn-Waxler, C., Friedman, S. L., & Cummings, E. M. (1983). Children's emotions and behaviors in response to infants' cries. *Child Development, 54,* 1522.-1528.

PERSPECTIVES ON THE DEVELOPMENT OF NURTURANCE: CULTURE, BIOLOGY, AND RISK

In this section, factors influencing the developmental course of nurturance are examined. In particular, the following chapters focus on the role of cultural variation, biological determinants, and environmental contexts posing risks to the nurture of the young.

Part II begins with Chapter 5, "Another style of competence: The caregiving child" by Carolyn Pope Edwards. Using ethnographic descriptions from Kenya and the Philippines of children engaged in the care or supervision of younger children, Edwards demonstrates how such contexts may promote children's social learning. Specifically, she shows that when children are assigned responsibility for those younger than themselves, they often engage in reasoning about the rights and duties of others. As a result of participating in multiage groups, both older and younger children show evidence of learning about moral rules involving care, reciprocity and harm as well as important social conventions concerning proper etiquette, address, and behavior. Edwards effectively demonstrates how cultural variations in the assignment of children to caregiving tasks may have important developmental consequences for both caregiving children as well as those younger children in their charge.

Hideo Kojima, in "Becoming Nurturant in Japan" (Chapter 6), draws on both historical documents and contemporary observations to discuss stresses on parenting in rapidly changing Japanese society. Traditional emphasis on the adult female role as dedicated to the nurture of children is described as under attack from a variety of social forces. Kojima shows how increased female employment, emerging redefinitions of the maternal role, declining birth rate, privatization of child care within the home, and changing attitudes toward the value of life all may affect the quality of parental caregiving. Although the consequences for the development of nurturance are not explicitly treated, Kojima's analysis suggests that the social changes affecting contemporary Japanese parenting are also likely to influence the developing child's understanding of and experiences with nurturance.

While the chapters by Edwards and Kojima address cultural influences on nurturance, Fleming and Orpen, in chapter 7, "Psychobiology of maternal behavior in rats, selected other species and humans," examine what is known about the role of hormones in eliciting and maintaining maternal behavior in the rat and other species and assess the implications of this knowledge for our understanding of maternal behavior in humans. Their review demonstrates how hormonal influences interact with infant characteristics and other environmental aspects to predict maternal responding in a variety of animal species. Thus, while the complex interplay of hormones may act to reduce timidity and increase interest in rat pups, maternal responding is also affected by the behavior of the infants themselves. Fleming and Orpen point out the difficulties of generalizing from such evidence of hormone-environment interaction in rats and other species to humans. Both methodological flaws of existing studies as well as the much greater complexity of determinants of human maternal responding make extrapolations to the human species very difficult.

Another route toward understanding human parenting is suggested in Chapter 8, "Antecedents of early parenting" by Feldman and Nash. They survey what is known about the mediators of parenting in fathers and mothers during the first year of the child's life. This examination of predictors of initial parenting reveals that influences on parenting often differ for men and for women. Moreover, the caregiving of each spouse is affected not only by the marital relationship, but by many characteristics of the other adult. What emerges is a picture of a number of complex, alternative pathways to early parenting.

While Feldman and Nash examine determinants of parenting when significant risk factors are not present, chapters 9 and 10 address issues raised by parental nurturance under stress. A population in which optimal nurture of children is thought to be at risk is that of adolescent parents. Brooks-Gunn and Furstenberg, in Chapter 9, "Antecedents and consequences of parenting: The case of adolescent mothering," examine what is known and not known about adolescent mothers' parenting behavior, knowledge, and attitudes. The authors point out that while both the adolescent mother's and her child's life opportunities are often truncated by early child-bearing, little evidence exists concerning the process of parent-child interaction among adolescents and their children. Brooks-

Gunn and Furstenberg review the state of existing knowledge concerning predictors of parenting among adolescents and call attention to areas of needed research.

Goldberg and Marcovitch, in Chapter 10, "Nurturing under stress: The care of preterm infants and developmentally delayed preschoolers," review evidence concerning the responses of parents to children who are preterm, Down's syndrome and developmentally delayed from other causes. They show that the particular type of risk factor involved in early parenting is an important predictor of the kinds of parental stresses and supports likely to be present, and hence, may affect the quality of parental nurturing. For example, mothers of Down's syndrome children whose condition may be identified soon after birth appear to be less stressed and more relaxed when observed with their children than are mothers of children whose developmental delays were less promptly identified. In their analysis, Goldberg and Marcovitch assess the kinds of parental adjustments that appear to be associated with more effective nurturing of developmentally delayed children.

5 Another Style of Competence: The Caregiving Child

Carolyn Pope Edwards
University of Massachusetts—Amherst

"Play is the business of childhood."
Read, 1971, p. 169.

"Play is how preschool children spend most of their working hours."
Clarke-Stewart and Koch, 1983, p. 190.

". . . play among primates is preparation for adult life . . ."
Rudolph and Cohen, 1984, p. 93.

"I have to play, that's my job."
American child quoted in Fein, 1978, p. 268.

These are statements of cultural values. One thing upon which most psychologists and early educators in North America currently agree is the necessity for children to play. *Play* can be defined as nonserious self-motivated activity performed for the satisfaction it brings, not for the end it accomplishes. *Work*, in contrast, may or may not be enjoyable, but is primarily performed to accomplish a useful end.

Although exactly what play accomplishes for the developing child is still not fully understood (Christie & Johnson, 1983), nevertheless authorities seem confident in asserting that play provides unique and irreplaceable opportunities for cognitive and social development. The playing child is seen as the *thinking* child.

The child-rearing folk wisdom of many other cultures, in contrast, puts much less stress on play. Although it is true that play is common to children of all cultures, nevertheless the time that children in different societies have allotted for free, uninterrupted play varies enormously (Whiting et al., in preparation). For example, parents in many parts of the developing world routinely recruit their children to help with child care and subsistence tasks. Ethnographers have established that parents in traditional, subsistence economies are especially apt to put strong pressure on children to be responsible, obedient, and competent assistants in the household economy (Barry, Child, & Bacon, 1959; B. Whiting, 1974; Whiting & Whiting, 1975). Because their livelihoods depend on group effort and the accumulation of valuable resorces (such as livestock, land, cultivated produce), they teach their children to attend carefully to responsibilities assigned to them. Far from believing that they are thereby depriving their children of valuable learning time, these parents believe that they are ensuring that their children acquire the capacity for productive and reproductive success in maturity.

Does the experience of caring for others provide cognitive or emotional benefits to the developing child, or merely specific skills? Recently, psychologists and anthropologists have begun to ask systematic questions about competencies that children might acquire during task performance, for example, during caretaking. Not surprisingly, much less theory and data presently exist concerning the developmental effects of caretaking—or other types of task performance—than of play (see Ember, 1973; Gallimore, Tharp & Speidel, 1978; Nerlove & Snipper, 1981; Snipper, 1978; Weisner & Gallimore, 1977; Wenger, 1983; Whiting, 1983; Whiting et al., in preparation).

This paper discusses child and sibling caretaking as an opportunity for the learning of nurturance and responsibility. The focus is on the social-cognitive underpinnings of nurturance, specifically, the *reasoning about "rational" and "conventional" moral rules,* that is given a developmental impetus in the caretaking experience. In other words, the focus is on the cognitive-structural nature of the development of nurturant capacities, and its relationship to particular dimensions of interpersonal interaction.

I shall argue, using case examples from ethnographic material, that children in multiage dyads or groupings negotiate constantly with one another the rights and wrongs of acts and who should do what when. The children's discussions and conflicts focus on types of acts and transgressions that U.S. children in school settings have also been found to frequently discuss—aggression, harmdoing, sharing, justice. These are acts that seem to the American mind to lie close to the heart of morality and ethics. Just as interestingly, however, the children's discussions also frequently focus on types of rules and related transgressions that U.S. children in school settings *do not* as frequently recognize and/or defend, namely, conventional role expectations and setting-specific regulations (Nucci & Turiel, 1978). These are acts from what Elliot Turiel (1975, 1978a) has labeled the "social-conventional" rule domain, regulating interactions within social groups and institutions, including the domestic unit. They concern such matters as sexual modesty, dress codes, etiquette and rules of respectful address, task assignment and the chain of command, rules regulating the use of social space and property, and age and gender behavior codes.

Thus, the multiage, caretaking situation will be seen to provide exceptionally rich possibilities for the child to develop an understanding of a broad range of rules: not only those having to do with harm-doing, welfare, and justice, but also those related to conformity to other norms of society and the domestic group. Piaget (1932) in his classic study of moral judgment development, argued that peer interaction (occurring primarily in *play,* he naturally assumed) provides the optimal experience of conflict and reciprocity that children need to develop moral autonomy and a sense of justice. Piaget's lead in focusing on peer play has been followed up to the present time by researchers interested in the naturalistic study of moral development. Apparently, it seems intuitively "right" to us American researchers that conscience development should be observed by looking at school children at play (for examples, see Much & Shweder, 1978; Nucci & Nucci, 1982; Nucci & Turiel, 1978). Yet why not look at a broader range of daily experiences? For it would appear that the peer relations of same-age playmates may constitute a severely limited developmental context for fostering conventional reasoning, in particular. Among these playmates there is typically no formal differentiation in authority roles, responsibility, or privileges based on assigned status or marked differences in developmental level. Therefore, an adult is often needed to help the child mediate disputes. No one peer clearly "has the right" or the responsibility to "shape up" the others' social behavior. Furthermore, when peer relations take place at school, the surrounding social system is typically large, complex, and multilayered (relative to the home). Children, especially young ones, may have some difficulty in comprehending and identifying with the goals and rules of school authorities. They may be less inclined to take these goals as their own and seek to help teachers enforce them.

In contrast, the cross-age interactions of caretaking—typical of domestic or neighborhood groupings that contain children of multiple ages and stages—may provide a more optimal environment for understanding conventional rules and norms. In the family setting, especially, sibling order provides a natural hierarchy of authority and competance. Family rules and customary procedures are handed down by persons with whom the children naturally and easily identify— the parents. In the family setting, because of its small size, simple organization, and thorough familiarity to the child, the child may more easily understand the group perspective on problems of social coordination. There, as we shall see, even the youngest child can sometimes be seen to vigorously assert and defend conventional rules and norms. The caretaking child does not focus on moral issues mostly (or only) concerning harm, justice, and welfare, as does the young U.S. child at school.

We shall see, furthermore, that this learning of rules and prosocial norms by the caretaking child is not an automatic, mindless process. Rather it is an active process, in which the child participates in conversational routines and negotiations and thereby gains a basis for learning and understanding her society's basic rules. The child's rule knowledge is partly self-constructed out of experiences in social interaction, and partly learned (socially-transmitted) by others' "powerful suggestions and occasional correction" (see Shweder, 1982, p. 55). The child constructs and continually revises an understanding of how rules and roles function to constrain and coordinate social action and social life. The responsible, nurturant child becomes not merely a caring and feeling child, but also a thinking child, acquiring his or her own distinctive brand of social-cognitive competence.

RATIONAL VERSUS CONVENTIONAL MORAL RULES AND REASONING

Elliot Turiel (1975, 1978a, 1978b) has made provocative claims concerning the development of social/moral understanding, and we must describe them briefly. Our main concern is with their cross-cultural validity.

First, Turiel has argued that not all rules are of the same type and that even very young children can intuitively appreciate this fact. Rules centered for U.S. children on concepts of harm, justice, and welfare, are called by Turiel "moral" because they are seen as more *important, obligatory, unalterable,* and *universally generalizable* than other rules. The obligatoriness of rules proscribing physical harm is seen, for example, when children say that hitting other children at school is wrong, regardless of whether there is a specific school rule about it, "because hitting hurts" (Nucci & Turiel, 1978). What Turiel calls "conventional" rules, in contrast, are seen as less important and binding, and more subject to contextual considerations. The relativity of conventional rules is seen when children say that it would *not* be wrong to disobey a school regulation (such as carrying snack food away from the snack table) if there were no specific rule against it (Nucci & Turiel, 1978). The relativity is also seen when children, accused of violating a conventional rule, try to justify themselves by referring to contextual considerations that might disqualify the rule (saying, for example, "It's okay to take my apple away from the snack table because it's not crumbly.") This kind of excusing or accounting occurs much less often with justice or harm-related transgressions (Much & Shweder, 1978).

Empirical studies have supported the hypothesis that American children from preschool age onward differentiate rules along dimensions of importance, obligatoriness, and generalizability (Much & Shweder, 1978; Nucci & Nucci, 1982; Nucci & Turiel, 1978; Smetana, 1981; Smetana, Bridgeman, & Turiel, 1983; Turiel, 1978b; Weston & Turiel, 1980). However, Shweder (1982) has put forward a strong case that both of Turiel's categories have to do with morality. Shweder re-labels Turiel's moral domain as "rational morality." Following

Shweder's criticism, I shall refer to the two domains as *rational morality* versus *conventional morality*.

Furthermore, Pool, Shweder, and Much (1983) have suggested that the cultural domains underlying rules may be more complex and heterogeneous than imagined. Some rules may not be clearly identifiable as rational moral versus conventional, because the domain boundaries may not be clearcut. Moreover, the specific content of rational versus conventional moral categories may vary cross-culturally. For example, sexuality, dress codes, dietary customs, and marriage rules may vary in their moral meaning and status from society to society (Shweder, Turiel, & Much, 1981). Turiel and Smetana (1983; Smetana 1983) have countered this argument with the explanation that specific rules may be supported by both moral and conventional rationales simultaneously. In their view, moral and conventional domains are distinct and nonoverlapping, but particular rules may merge considerations from both sides.

Turiel, Nucci, Smetana, and colleagues make a second claim. They say that rational and conventional moral rules are learned in distinctively different kinds of social interactions. Rational moral rules are thought to be rationally self-constructed from the experience of social interactions involving direct and visible harm to persons, violations of trust and rights, or the distribution of scarce resources. These transgressions tend to be followed by responses that highlight the unfortunate consequences of the transgression (for example, the distress or harm it causes). "The individual's view of the events as transgressions and his formulation of prescriptions can originate from the events themselves" (Turiel, 1978a, p. 10). Conventional rules, in contrast, are thought to be learned through construction of knowledge not about acts' inherent consequences but rather their normative status. They are learned in social interactions in which someone representing the point-of-view of the group or the society (e.g., an adult or older child), focuses the child's attention on (arbitrary) social definitions of situations. In American school settings, for example, conventional transgressions usually lead to reprimands, sanctions, threats of sanctions, commands, and rule-statements. These utterances are said by Turiel and colleagues to call children's attention to social order and regularity, to appropriate role behavior, to sanctions following misbehavior, and to the rules themselves as structuring mechanisms or "rules of this place." Such considerations are said to be not obvious and intrinsic, but rather important only insofar as one learns "society's" arbitrarily defined point of view. Empirical studies in American schools and preschools do appear to find, in fact, that children rarely command or enforce school regulations before they reach age 10 or so, whereas they enforce rational moral rules at early ages.

Turiel and colleagues' theory makes a most interesting starting point for a cross-cultural study of social reasoning-in-action because it is put forward as culturally universal or generalizable. It suggests certain specific ways of looking at social interactions as stimulators of development. Rational moral rules are said to be learned in one way, conventional moral rules in another. The wrongness of rational moral rules is said to be obvious and intrinsic to the situation—requiring no authority figures to "stand in" for the victim and say the act is wrong. Young children are expected to more readily grasp the wrongness of rational moral transgressions, whose consequences are intrinsic, than the wrongness of conventional transgressions, whose normative status derives from society's arbitrary rules for coordinating people and groups.

Can this theory be used to describe the development of children in all cultural settings? If not, why not? As we shall see, the theory is in fact culturally limited, but understanding the reason why will lead us to a deeper appreciation of the caretaking situation as a context for social-cognitive development.

NURTURANCE AND PROSOCIAL RESPONSIBILITY AS ASPECTS OF INTERCHILD BEHAVIOR

To begin to form a theory of how the caretaking situation relates to the development of moral and conventional reasoning, we must lay out the social-cognitive demands of interchild nurturance and responsibility. "Nurturance" and "prosocial responsibility," as defined by Beatrice and John Whiting (1975), are different but complementary behavior systems. When described in some detail it becomes strikingly evident that nurturance revolves more around the "rational" moral considerations of harm-doing and welfare, whereas prosocial responsibility revolves more around "conventional" moral considerations.

Nurturance is "offering" behavior, the giving of physical or emotional resources by one person to another perceived to be in a state of need or desire. In contrast, prosocial responsibility, as an interpersonal behavior, occurs when one person attempts to influence another to conform to the rules of family or society, either for the other's own good or for the good of the group as a whole. The distinction between nurturance and prosocial responsibility can be vividly illustrated by contrasting the behavior typically elicited by infants to that typically elicited by toddlers and young preschoolers. Beatrice Whiting has conceptualized this distinction from a comparative cultural perspective.[1]

The infant (child under about 15-months-of-age) is a relatively helpless, vulnerable, and fragile social partner. Yet this infant is not powerless, for it seems to have the power to call forth or "elicit" caretaking behavior and entertaining play from the social surround, including other children. Observations of infants in a wide variety of cultural settings (Edwards & Whiting, 1980; Whiting, 1983; Whiting & Edwards, 1973; Whiting et al., in preparation; Whiting & Whiting, 1975) demonstrate that the profile of behaviors directed to infants by children is

---

[1]The following section of this paper draws heavily on Whiting (1983) and Whiting et al. (in preparation). The interested reader may consult these sources for empirical documentation.

highly similar cross-culturally. The positive aspects of the nurturant profile include behaviors intended to *promote the pleasure and welfare, reduce the distress,* and *prevent from harm* the other. In all societies studied, even the youngest children, aged 2 or 3, respond in a generally nurturant way to infants. They smile, imitate, and make faces to entertain them; they pat, caress, and seek to hold them; they give them objects, tickle them, and play peek-a-boo; and they seek to alleviate their distress by guessing their needs for food, warmth, or maternal intervention. Infants seem to be able to elicit some nurturance even from tired, bored, or reluctant child caregivers. In fact, both Konrad Lorenz (1943) and John Bowlby (1969) have argued that infants are born biologically equipped with physical features and behaviors that serve to inhibit aggression and elicit and maintain proximity and nurturant involvement. Lorenz has claimed that the "babyish" character of infants' appearance triggers the inhibition of aggression and release of nurturance: their relatively large heads, predominance of brain capsule, large and low lying eyes, bulging cheeks, short and thick arms and legs, and springy, elastic bodies. Bowlby has focused on their attractive and appealing "attachment" behavior—their gazing, smiling, vocalizing, clinging, and following of the caretaker.

The distinctive profile of "nurturant" behavior elicited in children by infants is seen in the following example, drawn from Ann Snipper's (1978) study of child caretaking in a rural area near Mexico City:

Yolanda [age 9½] is expected to wash dishes and sweep two rooms, but she seems to enjoy child care more than these chores. On two occasions she only relinquished Pablito's care to an aunt with reluctance after repeated requests from her mother. The following incidents give a flavor of Yolanda's interactional style. On one occasion, Yolanda and the infant [age 13½ months] were in her aunt's house. The older cousins were playing records on a record player. Yolanda would alternately bounce or pat Pablito in time to the music or hold him on her lap, watching him, handing him a toy and giving him quick kisses on the top of his head. She remained in physical contact with the baby until the mother asked her to perform another chore. A diapering session was also marked by a variety of physical contact beyond the routine cleaning required, including kissing, tickling and massaging. On two occasions when Pablito was fussy, her tactics to calm him included picking him up, shifting his position, jiggling him in her arms and standing him on the ground encouraging him to walk. (Snipper, 1978, pp. 109–110).

Yolanda behaved nurturantly, in the Whitings' terms, in that she was responsive to the succorant demands of Pablito and anticipated his desires. These behaviors required that she *perceive and attend to his needs and desires,* as she understood them. Her nurturant acts included a variety of specific "offering" behaviors; she gave both physical and emotional resources, including diapering care, toys, comfort, affection, entertaining play, and motor practice.

Of course, not everything that children do to infants can be called nurturant. Children also overexcite infants, leading to tears, hurt them while exploring their bodies too roughly, become impatient and aggressive with infants, and even abandon them or take their food away when their own competing needs interfere. Thus, an equally important part of learning consistent and successful nurturance involves gaining self-control over aggressive impulses, that is, acquiring the ability to *inhibit or dampen behavior that distresses or harms the other.*

This learning by the older child to mute and curtail his aggressive impulses toward a baby can be aptly illustrated by the following example. The observation was made in Tarong, Philippines (cf. Nydegger & Nydegger, 1963) of a 7-year-old boy with his 1-year-old brother. The brothers were sitting on a sled in a courtyard. Crescencio, the elder, bored and yawning, was watching other children play tag. To elicit Crescencio's flagging attention, the baby repeatedly dropped his stick and cried for it to be retrieved. Crescencio, in turn hit, insulted, and shouted at the baby, but always to an inhibited degree. In the end, the baby's desires won out and Crescencio was forced to pick up the child to soothe his escalating distress.

> Baby Pico starts to fuss. Crescencio turns to look at him, apparently surprised by the fussing, and picks up the stick Pico has dropped.
>
> "This is your toy," says Crescencio, then turns away to watch the other children. He notices Pico crying again and says (annoyed but not yet angry), "Stupid! You keep dropping it! And then you let me pick it up!"
>
> Crescencio picks up the stick and hands it to Pico, who immediately throws it to the ground.
>
> "No! Do not!" Crescencio angrily shouts, and lightly slaps his brother's bottom. Then he breaks into a smile and returns the stick to Pico, who starts to throw it yet again.
>
> "You want me to put you there in the manure pile? I'll slap you, huh?" says Crescencio, lightly slapping Pico's bottom again. Pico starts to cry, dropping the stick.
>
> Crescencio, looking resigned but a little concerned over Pico's crying, hands Pico the stick. Then Crescencio settles himself to look over the yard. Pico again drops the stick.
>
> Crescencio sees the stick fall but does not move to get it. Pico starts to whimper and Crescencio imitates his whimpering sound, "Uh, uh, uh." Then Crescencio pushes Pico the stick with his foot. Pico now fusses loudly and Crescencio resignedly picks up the baby and walks off with him toward the older children.

Toddlers (children aged approximately 15 months to 3 years) differ from infants in being much less vulnerable, helpless, and fragile. Now beginning to walk securely and to understand language, they begin to elicit a distinctive pattern of behavior from both adults and children. Of course, they still receive much nurturance, too, but now this nurturance is tempered by pressure for more mature behavior on the part of the toddler. The core of this pressuring pattern is commands, reprimands or suggestions to socialize the toddler in appropriate forms of behavior and to control his behavior to coordinate it with the (legitimate) needs of the group. This pattern can be considered "responsible" or "prosocial," in Whitings' terms—akin to nurturance, but more dominant in form, *focused on long-term training and short-term control* of the exploratory, unruly, and self-centered small child.

For example, consider this case example from Snipper's (1978) study, focused on Hilda Y. (age 9). Hilda fires many commands and suggestions at Eloy (age 2), and she is most responsive and friendly to him when he seeks to learn from her and help her with her work.

> [Hilda's] interactions with Eloy [age 2] were primarily verbal, telling him to get out of the way, suggesting he play with a certain toy, asking him brief questions. He played by himself frequently. . . . There were two instances of prolonged contact between the two. Once when Hilda was washing dishes, he hung at her side, watching every move. She explained every step to him and then enlisted him to carry the clean dishes from the outside tap into the house. On the other occasion, Eloy sat in a toy car and Hilda pushed him around the yard. She did this with an air of duty, talking only to give short commands—"Wait," "Hang on," "Get out of the car," or to complain—"Ay, ay, ay," "You're too heavy," etc. (Snipper, 1978, pp. 110–111).

Thus, a toddler is pushed by its elders out of the protected and privileged cocoon of infancy. As Nydegger and Nydegger (1963) say of the Tarong, Philippines toddler at weaning: "He who was master of the household is now but a beggar at the gates" (p. 827). In every culture the child as either a toddler or preschool-aged child is expected to modulate some of its demands for constant help and attention and to behave in more mature and appropriate ways. It is expected to begin to *learn and respect certain rules of appropriate behavior,* although which ones and how early depends on the cultural context and the folk theory about what toddlers can reasonably understand and do. In return it can expect its culturally-defined "legitimate" needs to be met and "rights" to be respected, although not necessarily immediately. In all of the cultural communities we have studied (Whiting et al., in preparation; Whiting, 1983), older children are usually stopped by others from physically abusing or harming toddlers, from allowing them to cry inconsolably for long periods when they want to join in or have a turn, and from abandoning them when they move to a new location of play. The young child's desire and needs are respected by older children, but in a way that involves coordination with the desires and needs of the others.

> Irritable, pushy children do not exist in Taira, [Okinawa]. Those who try to get things by "walking over others" do not get far, for children ostracize and avoid

them. One 4-year-old, observed over a period of months, altered his methods of acquiring goals from pushing and bullying to socially sanctioned techniques, such as asking, waiting his turn, and sharing. The change was startling (Maretski & Maretski, 1963, p. 494).

In sum, the two profiles, nurturance and prosocial responsibility should not be considered to be mutually exclusive nor only directed to infants and toddlers. Quite the contrary, they are two complementary and overlapping patterns, frequent in all interchild behavior, but especially frequent in multiage dyads or groups where one or more older children are expected to look after or look out for one or more younger children.

THE MATERIAL FOR THIS STUDY

This study attempts to show how rich cross-cultural observations of children's behavior can be as a source of data on social-cognitive development. In what follows, observations of East African children are systematically examined to see what conclusions might be most reasonable to draw concerning nurturant and prosocial reasoning in comparative cultural perspective.

The observational material is drawn from the work of Carol R. Ember, who studied children in a Luo community of about 250 people in the South Nyanza district of Kenya (Ember, 1970, 1973). This community, which shall be referred to as Oyugis (actually the name of the market town 2.5 miles away), is one in which task-assignment is a prominent feature of the daily lives of children. The community that Ember studied was a set of dispersed homesteads whose heads had descended from a common ancestor two to five generations back. Although these dispersed households could not be distinguished as a separate unit from an aerial photograph (because homesteads just dot the countrysides), the people from these homesteads interact frequently and think of themselves as a unit. Households were large, averaging about 10 members each (Bookman & Ember, in press). The women were responsible for most of the agricultural work (except ploughing), and also for the housework, food preparation, and child care. Mothers of necessity delegated a great deal of work to children over about the age of 5. The amount of work assigned to a particular child depended upon his or her age, sex, sibling position, and school attendance. Most girls over age 6 were found to do a great deal of child care and household tasks. Boys without older siblings at home also were seen to do much *feminine* work, whereas boys with available older siblings did far less (Ember, 1973).

Ember studied 28 children aged 7½ to 16 years, to explore the influence of feminine task assignment on the social behavior of boys. Her trained observers (educated Luo-speakers) collected nine 15-min-long running record protocols on each child's behavior and interaction, using a randomizing procedure to ensure that the observations were representative of the children's daytime experience.

The observations were taken in the form of descriptive sentences (including the children's speech to one another), and later coded into social-behavior categories using an adaptation of the Six Cultures code (Whiting & Whiting, 1975). Because Ember trained her observers to catch as much of the children's exact speech to one another as possible, Ember's observations provide an unusual corpus of naturalistic, cross-cultural data on children's social reasoning-in-action.

My method has been to analyze the observational material in order to construct an ethnographic description of the children's reasoning-in-action. Most of the reasoning involves moral conflicts or transgressions (actual or potential). We can tell a conflict or transgression has taken place (or was about to) because one person intervenes with a criticism or suggestion toward the other. The transgressor (or potential transgressor) in turn sometimes offers an account or excuse, or he refuses or ignores the suggestion, or he obeys.

My analysis is based on 109 episodes excerpted from the main body of the observations because they were seen as somehow relevent to moral development, considered broadly.[2] The episodes were coded according to the age and kinship relationship of the enforcing authority (i.e., the person defending the rule or norm) and the person being commanded or corrected. Each episode was further coded for (a) presence or absence of resistance to the commander's authority, by refusing, ignoring, or counter-command; and (b) use of sanctions (or threats of sanctions) by the enforcing authority(ies) to prevent or punish deviance. Finally, each episode was systematically classified according to the nature of the rule or cultural norm at issue, as follows: (1) commands concerning aggression towards small children; (2) commands concerning aggression towards animals; (3) suggestions related to meeting the needs of others; (4) conflicts over turn-taking and sharing; (5) discussions about task assignment; and (6) commands concerning proper social behavior. (See Table 5.1.)

The first three of the categories relate closely to nurturance, as the Whitings conceive it, even though they do not involve direct caretaking acts. Commands seeking to prohibit or stop agression toward defenseless victims are nurturant in that they are motivated by an intention to protect someone from physical harm. Similarly, suggestions related to meeting the needs of others exemplify indirect nurturance in which children ask or tell others to perform caretaking actions or give others advice as how best to take care of someone else. While these three categories of behavior thus involve only indirect acts of nurturance, nevertheless they are particularly interesting to us because they involve explicitly stated rules or rationales for compliance. Thus, they provide a window into the moral underpinnings of the children's nurturance.

---

[2]The excerpting was done by myself over 10 years ago for an entirely different purpose. Recently returning to the excerpted material, I was struck by how it elucidates the problem of the social-cognitive basis of nurturance and prosocial responsibility.

TABLE 5.1
Classification of 109 Moral Episodes (Oyugis, Kenyan Children)[a]

Type of Rule/Norm at Issue	No. Episodes	Age of Enforcing Authorities	Authority Meets Resistance/Questions	Authority Uses Threats/Sanctions
1. Aggression toward children	20	3½ to grandparent	6 (30%)	13 (65%)
2. Aggression toward animals	8	3 to parent	3 (38%)	2 (25%)
3. Positive action to meet needs of others	26	2½ to parent	9 (35%)	4 (15%)
4. Conflicts over turns or sharing	7	4 to parent	4 (57%)	2 (29%)
5. Task assignment	34	2½ to parent	18 (53%)	3 (9%)
6. Proper social behavior	14	2½ to parent	8 (57%)	5 (36%)

[a] Drawn from the observational data of Carol Ember

AGGRESSION TOWARDS SMALL CHILDREN

Turiel and colleagues have claimed that rational moral rules about aggression are constructed by children on the basis of social interactions in which one person harms another. They suggest that the most important information for the cognizing child is the victim's response, which suggests the intrinsic wrongness of hurting. The theory assumes that human beings are naturally emphathic and distressed by injury to others.

Without wishing to discount the role that early empathy may play in moral development, nevertheless, I would suggest on the basis on the Oyugis material that the victim's response is not the main, and certainly not the only, source of information for Oyugis children. To judge from the observations, Oyugis community values include strong prohibitions against the striking of infants and toddlers by older children. Adults clearly communicate to children, first, that infants and toddlers are too little to be beaten no matter what, and, second, that hurting or striking small children is a punishable offence. (Wenger, 1983, has described similar values for a community on the Eastern coast of Kenya.)

Two examples were found that suggest that Oyugis mothers sometimes take the time to carefully explain to their children the importance of inhibiting aggression to babies. These maternal responses would be expected to help children to focus on the intrinsic wrongness of aggression toward infants.

> J. (Boy, 3½) to Mother: "I can beat the infant."   (1)
> Mother: "Never do it, father" (Note to reader: By addressing her small son as "father," she flatters him in a culturally appropriate way and thereby appeals to his most mature self).
> J.:   "Why is he destroying my book?"
> Mother: "I'll buy you a new one."

> Infant (8 months old) urinates on the dress of W. (Sister, 6), holding   (2)
> him. W. takes a stick and hits him.
> Mother to W.: "Don't beat him. He does not know."
> Moments later, infant urinates again and this time W. simply reports it to mother.

Many other examples, however, suggest that adults typically use sanctions and threats of santions on older children who hurt small children. The cries or "tattling" of a small child almost invariably draw a most undesirable form of adult attention.

> Grandfather to J. (Boy, 3½, crying): "Who has beaten you?" (3)
> J.: "It was G. (Boy, 5)."
> Grandfather: "Stop crying. I'll beat him in turn." J. stops.
>
> J. (Boy, 3½): "Father N. has hit me." Father whips N. (Boy, 8). (4)

Oyugis children themselves become early and strong defenders of these rules about aggression. J., 3½, in the example above demonstrated his early "commitment" to the rules by speaking to his mother *before* striking the baby, as well as by informing on his brother. In other observations, older children past the age of about eight enforce the rules on behalf of others, not just themselves. They become protectors of young children, and enforce the rules in the role of sanctioning agents—a role considered culturally desirable for Oyugis children. Other children accept the moral authority of their peers when it comes to acts and transgressions concerning physical aggression (as clearly seen in excerpts (6) to (8) below).

> I. (Boy, 16) to J. (Brother, 4): "If anybody plays about with you (5) [i.e., hurts you], tell me and I'll beat him."
>
> E. (Girl, 8) to S. (Brother, 2½): "Stop hitting the infant." (6)
> Later, J. (Brother, 6) beats S., and S. cries. Now E. protects little S. She says to J., "Stop beating that boy." J. stops.
>
> B. (Girl, 6) hits G. (Brother, 2½) on the head for no apparent reason. (7)
> G. cries. J. (Brother, 8) hits B. as a punishment. B. suppresses a tear.
>
> J. (Boy, 13) to R. (Brother, 8): "It's bad to hit people with grass." (8)
> R. stops hitting.

It is striking in the above excerpts that the offender almost always "accepts" the punishment or correction of the intervener without demur. This suggests that intervenor and transgressor agree that the aggressive act is wrong and that others "have a right" to intervene.

AGGRESSION TOWARDS ANIMALS

Aggression toward animals is probably regarded differently in Oyugis from aggression toward human beings. The people of many parts of Kenya do not consider that animals should necessarily be treated with the same kind of consideration as people (B. Whiting, personal communication). While some roughness by children toward animals is expected and tolerated, it appears that needless cruelty to animals is not considered desirable by the people of Oyugis. The observations suggest that children are not left to construct moral rules concerning cruelty to animals on their own, simply from observing the victim's responses. Rather, aggressive children are assisted in inhibiting action by intervening adults and children.

In eight observational episodes, interveners invariably used commands or threats of sanctions to stop agressive behavior. These are the kinds of responses that Nucci and Turiel (1978) say typify responses to conventional moral transgressions not rational moral ones. Here are some typical examples:

J. (Boy, 13) and JW. (Nephew, 19) hit a lizard crawling on the (9) roof. W. (Nephew, 22) to others: "Stop killing that innocent creature." They stop.

J. (Boy, 4) tries to throw a stone at the dog. (10)
M. (Brother, 7½): "Stop, or I'll beat you." J. stops.

B. (Girl, 6) pulls cat by the tail. G. (Brother, 3): "Stop that or I'll (11) beat you." (Instead, the older sister picks up a stick and chases younger brother away).

G. (Boy, 3) responds to an observed transgression of sister by (12) informing to older brother: "L. is killing your grasshoppers."
J. (Boy, 9) to L.: "Don't do that. I want to see them alive."
L. (Girl, 4): "G. is lying. I'm only touching them, not killing them."

What do the commands, sanctions and threats mean to the children of Oyugis? What information do they convey? Turiel suggests, for U.S. children that commands, sanctions, and threats of sanctions are part of what children think about in constructing the arbitrariness of conventional rules. For Oyugis children, however, commands, sanctions, and threats of sanctions probably convey a different kind of information. In the Oyugis cultural context, these strong responses convey information about the basic *importance* and *unconditionality* of rules prohibiting aggression. "These rules are not to be taken lightly. Obey them whether I am there or not," is the message conveyed by Oyugis parents.

POSITIVE ACTION TO MEET THE NEEDS OF OTHERS

Positive action to meet the needs of others is, of course, the essence of nurturance. The Whitings believe that children learn to be nurturant primarily by being assigned to settings where they are close to mothers and infants. There they can imitate the nurturant behavior of caretaking models. Further, when they themselves are put in charge of babies, they automatically become subject to the intrinsic reinforcements of cries and smiles that teach or shape them toward successful and consistent nurturance.

By now this argument has a familiar ring to it. It precisely parallels Turiel's argument about how children construct rational moral rules. The Whitings' and Turiel's theories converge in suggesting that the most important social encounters for helping children to construct norms of positive nurturance are those of direct interaction between children.

Without wishing to dispute the idea that there is something intrinsically "informational" about the cries and smiles of others, nevertheless I doubt that this information by itself is a sufficient basis for the construction of norms of nurturance.

In Oyugis, mothers hold children directly accountable for their care of younger children. This means that children (especially older ones) are threatened with physical punishment for neglect of their child care duties. Furthermore, children occasionally but not frequently receive praise for responsible performance. (In many parts of sub–Saharan Africa, praise is considered to spoil children; see Whiting, Edwards, et al., in preparation). Here are two excerpts that show these processes in action.

> A group of children are running along together and stop to examine (13) a hole. A small boy (age 2) tries to look in too. Then J. (Brother, 13) says to him, "Don't. You'll fall in, and mother will beat me." The small boy stops looking and slowly walks away.

> E. (Girl, 7) helps her mother thresh millet. She says, "Am I not (14) doing well?"
> Mother: "Yes, my daughter. Nowadays, I'll be leaving this work for you to do in my stead. You are fit."

Furthermore, not only mothers but other children play an active role in the teaching of nurturance, in Oyugis as in many other communities around the world that rely on child caretaking. One of the best descriptions of this process I have seen comes from Tarong, Philippines (Nydegger & Nydegger, 1963). In this example, several people, including a baby, behave in a way to impress upon a child caretaker, age 7½, the positive value of nurturance. Three school-aged children spontaneously come to help the caretaker with the crying baby. Their concern surely underlines to Simeon the importance of the moral norm.

> One of our most amusing observations involved such training of a 7½-year-old boy, Simeon, at an informal late-afternoon candy party. Almost all the members of three households were present, among them Simeon's tired, cranky, teething baby brother Pico. Pico was being soothed and rocked by his mother, Marina, who suddenly called to Simeon, "Here, put him to sleep," in a challenging tone. Simeon smiled and swaggered over, took the baby and went into the next room where a hammock was strung up. The eldest girl of the household ran after him, saw to it that the baby was laid down properly in the hammock, and cautioned

Simeon to rock it gently. As she left the room, Simeon began to sing a rousing march in rhythm with his rocking.

In the next room all the adults were grinning. Marina, requesting conspiratorial conversational cover-up by pantomine, sat next to the door where she could hear but not be seen. Despite the singing and rocking, Pico was soon roaring again. Simeon rocked more violently and sang still louder, his voice drowning Pico's wails. At this, a younger cousin, Jose, left the group to join Simeon.

After some consultation with the equally inexperienced Jose, Simeon cradled and patted Pico in his arms as he himself sat in the hammock. Jose pushed the hammock as one would push a swing, both he and Simeon singing loudly while Pico's wails rose above the din. Marina was now peering through the door crack, convulsed with laughter, and the other women joined her, giggling at the peephole. Jose's older brother went to the door where he stood watching critically, finally bursting into laughter too. He then replaced Jose and convinced Simeon, by example, that gentle patting, cooing, and rocking were more effective (Nydegger & Nydegger, 1963, p. 852).

An example, of course, is not proof of anything. It is at most suggestive. Yet the example from Tarong, Philippines, is similar to many of the Oyugis excerpts. Oyugis children also frequently intervene in a supporting or commanding way with one child to indirectly benefit a third, younger child. The conversational discourse that takes place in these scenarios reveal a characteristic persistence on the part of the intervening moralist child. The intervener uses a variety of response types. He may use threats, helpful suggestions, repeated commands, or angry reprimands to make his point, but make it he does. Notice that in excerpt (20), the intervener is only 3-year-old, yet still his older brother feels compelled to respond to his question, even if in a somewhat sarcastic fashion.

J. (Girl, 11) to T. (Brother, 5): "Go and take that baby because he's (15) crying." T. laughs but doesn't go. "I'm telling you to go and you are just playing around with me. Go or else I'll beat you." T. runs to pick up the baby.

J. (Girl, 8, visiting) to E., who is holding her baby sister: "Why is (16) she crying?"
E. (Girl, 7): "I do not know."
J.: "Tie her on your back and she will be all right." E. does so. "Let us go and sit away from your mother. I think that will help the infant stop crying." E. does so.

An infant picks up a tin can being played with by G. (Brother, 3). (17) G. tells the infant, "Stop that." B. (Visitor Girl, 6) to G.: "Give the baby one." G. does not comply. P. (Sister, 5½) to G.: "Give the baby a tin." G. does not. "Please give her one, my father." G. complies.

M. (Boy, 7½) and E. (Brother, 9½) are walking along a path together. (18)

M.: "We better go home. The baby will cry." E., the elder, ignores. M. repeats the command. E. still ignores.

Y. (Girl, 13) goes to fetch water from the waterhole with kids (19) following near her. S. (Boy, 15), reprimands her angrily, "Why have you taken those kids with you there?" Y. does not answer.

S. (Boy, 5) holds a crying infant. L. (Brother, 3½): "Why is she (20) crying?"
S.: "I do not know."
L.: "Does she want food?"
S.: "I do not know because she doesn't talk."

CONFLICTS OVER TURN-TAKING AND SHARING (POSITIVE JUSTICE)

It is a striking fact that few conflicts over turn-taking and sharing occur in the Oyugis excerpts. To the U.S. observer this seems puzzling because we are so used to seeing fairness as a constant topic of dispute among children.

Are the people of Oyugis simply unaware of fairness concerns? That is unlikely to be the case. The few relevant Oyugis episodes sound too "familiar" to us, as if the reasoning behind them is similar rather than dissimilar to our own. Here are three examples.

Children are playing hopscotch. Mother says to daughter, 7½: "Don't (21) interfere with another person's turn." Daughter stops.

J. (Boy, 6) asks E. (Sister, 8) for a lemon. (22)
She tells J. to go bring a knife. He goes. S. (Brother, 2½) asks sister for a piece.
E. to youngest, S.: "It's J.'s turn now. You've had some."
S.: "I haven't." (He has).
E.: "All right." But she does not ever give him any.

E. (Boy, 9½) pulls J. (Brother, 4) around on a "car" (really a wagon). (23) E. to J.: "Get off. It is the baby's turn." J. does not heed. "Then I won't let you ride again." J. gets off, and E. pulls the infant in the "car."
J. to elder E.: "You come and pull me. It's my turn." E. does not heed. J. charges him with a stick, but E. runs away.

Because so few quarrels about fairness in sharing and turn-taking seem to occur among the Oyugis children, one might wonder whether another issue is of greater concern to them. Task assignment does appear to be that issue.

CHILDREN'S DISCUSSIONS ABOUT TASK ASSIGNMENT

Task assignment—and issues about authority in commanding—are frequently discussed and sometimes hotly disputed among Oyugis children. The same zest that U.S. children show in talking among themselves about sharing and turn-taking is shown by Oyugis children in talking about tasks. There is certainly little evidence that they consider these conventional moral matters to be less "important" than issues related to welfare, harm, and justice. The excerpts reveal further the Oyugis children are active reasoners, though they may not engage in as prolonged verbal arguments as U.S. children commonly do. Before running off to do someone else's bidding, Oyugis children seem to want to establish two things: first, that the task really needs doing; and second, that the commander has the legitimate right to command. Oyugis children are anything but slavishly obedient to other children. If anything, they seem to enjoy occasional testing of each other. The observations illustrate how cross-age social relations inspire children to become legal experts on the rights and wrongs of prosocial responsibility.

Oyugis children do not question or test adults about these same matters. Oyugis adults definitely do not encourage such questioning by children. Children are expected to simply obey adults. Young children who question the legitimacy of their parents' commands receive a rude awakening, and such conversations as the one below between a mother and her 3-year-old are simply not found with older children.

>Mother: "Get me a chair." (24)
>G. (Boy, 3): "It concerns you."
>Mother: "I'll tell father to beat you." Child runs and fetches chair.

We have all the more reason, then, to believe that the conversational discourses among children represent true learning encounters for them, that is, opportunities to construct knowledge about prosocial responsibility.

Consider the following examples. We focus on the learner as the younger child in the interaction. When the "learner" is forced to change her strategy of suggesting or to provide a rationale, or when she argues with the commander's right to command and receives either an acceptance or rebuttal of her argument, she is provided with food for thought.

Many episodes suggest that Oyugis children receiving task commands try to extract rationales for why the task needs to be done. They seem more likely to comply if genuinely convinced that their job is a necessary service or will protect or preserve family property. Compare the resistance of children in the following four excerpts. They put up no resistance in the first two, perhaps because they are provided convincing rationales. They put up strong, more or less successful, resistance in the second two cases.

>Two brothers are washing clothes. S. (Boy, 13½): "Draw some (25)
>more water."
>T. (Brother, 5½): "Why?"

S.: "For the final washing." T. fetches the water.

J. (Boy, 6): "Why do you leave soap in the water? Don't you know (26) it gets used up faster that way?"
S. (Brother, 2½): "I never knew." He takes bar of soap out.

B. (Elder sister): "Go home and find out whether the hens are feeding (27) on the corn spread out in the sun." (L., Girl, 10) doesn't take heed but goes on playing. "What are you doing? Do you mean to say you haven't heard my words? Go quickly, otherwise I'll cane you." She picks up a stick. L. runs away, then stands by watching elder sister and looking at her angrily.
B.: "I'll be satisfied in only you'll go where I've sent you."

S. (Boy, 14) is making rope for weaving a mat. He tells brother to (28) divide the sisal in little pieces for him.
M. (Brother, 8): "Certainly not. Don't think I've come here to work for you."
S. backs down, doesn't reply.

Related episodes suggest that children receiving task commands need to be persuaded not only that the task is necessary, but that it is necessary to be done *now*. The child in the first episode below apparently is so persuaded, but the child in the second successfully refuses his brother's command by questioning its urgency.

Y. (Girl, 13): "Collect the firewood and shelter it under the eaves (29) before it rains."
T. (Brother, 8) complies. Sister stands by the door and examines the [threatening] weather.

L. (Boy, 11): "What are you still doing? Come quickly and help me do this (30) cloth, quickly." (He has been waiting 4 min).
A. (Brother, 9 rudely): "You have no right to hurry me up."

The expected chain of command in Oyugis is elder child to younger child. Once a child graduates from the priviledged state of infancy, he is expected to accept the benevolent domination of his elders.

K. (Boy, 3): "G., swing me." (31)
G. (Brother, 5, humorously): "I'm not your employee."

Younger children must therefore phrase their requests to older ones politely or submissively if they are not to violate Oyugis norms. In the following observations, both younger children must modify their initial styles of commanding before they meet with success.

J. (Boy, 4): "Hold this dish for me so I can sit down." (32)
M. (Brother, 7½): "You can do it yourself."

J. (pleadingly): "Please." M. takes the dish.

Two children are playing together. G. (Boy, 5): "Run quickly to the (33) pond and fetch water."
N. (Sister, 8): "You've no right to tell me that. If you keep playing with me that way, I'll beat you." G. is now silent. N. walks to the pond carrying the tin can in her hand.

It is apparent, finally, that certain kinds of reciprocity considerations figure into children's cooperation or noncooperation with each other's task commands. This might be called the interaction of "nurturance" issues with "authority" issues. In the following excerpt, a boy who refuses his elder sister's command receives the same rude treatment in kind, even though he has a legitimate need for help.

Two children are bathing at home. L. (Girl, 10): "Get me some water (34) to wash my leg."
R. (Boy, 7½): "That's not my concern." Later he requests, "Get me water to wash the soap off my face before it hurts my eye."
L.: "That's for you to do. I did not hold you and force you to put soap on your face."

In his elder sister's remarks, the boy has actually heard in capsule form a theory of respect that I heard espoused by Africans from all parts of Kenya when I conducted research on moral reasoning of university students and local community moral leaders (Edwards, 1974). This theory is that authorities should be obeyed (respected) because of the concrete help (nurturance) they provide those under their command. Elders who are obeyed *should* be nurturant in appropriate ways. Not only do young Oyugis children hear this concept, but apparently they also can articulate it themselves. In one telling episode, a very young boy (5-years-old) actually was seen to manipulate this concept to his advantage against an older cousin. This example is one of the clearest for showing how conflicts concerning nurturance and responsibility can challenge cognitively and morally the children involved.

I. (Girl, 10, visiting the household) calls O. (Boy, 8) to come get the (35) baby because it's crying. O. tries to come but on the way is deliberately blocked by his little brother, G. (5). The girl canes G. to let O. go by.
G. (complaining, wittily): "Can't you remember what I've done for you? I brought the baby from the other house for you, and now you're caning me!"
N. (Sister, 8) offers comfort to G.: "If she can't remember what you did for her, then never help her anymore." The cousin leaves G. alone and withdraws into the house.

Another episode shows an even younger girl, only 4-years-old, demonstrating her working knowledge of the same concept. This girl tells her mother to give her a potato (i.e., maternal nurturance) because she cared for the baby (i.e., obeyed her mother). When her mother stalls on the potato, the daughter seeks and receives nurturance of another sort, namely, praise. This child, like the 5-year-old boy above, shows herself as an active and successful moral reasoner and persuader.

> L. (Girl, 4) to Mother: "Give me a potato to eat because I've cared for the infant long enough." (36)
> Mother: "What if I don't have any?"
> L: "But you promised me." (Mother doesn't reply). "You see, Pamela doesn't know how to handle the baby. She didn't cry when I was taking care of her."
> Mother: "You know [how to do] it pretty well, my daughter."

COMMANDS CONCERNING PROPER SOCIAL BEHAVIOR

The last aspect of prosocial development we consider concerns proper social behavior. Most African cultures, those of Kenya included, put a great deal of stress on proper social forms—etiquette, address, bearing, cleanliness, and other matters related to good manners and presentation. African cultures, in general, emphasize age and sex hierarchies in interpersonal relations (LeVine, 1973). Respectful terms of address, appropriate greetings and blessings, deferential displays, and various kinds of restraint and avoidance are widespread cultural forms that serve to emphasize interpersonal differences in rank, status, or power.

Americans, of course, emphasize the equality of persons and tend to think of manners and related matters as "mere conventions." Turiel (1975) believes conventional rules are usually seen as less important than rational moral rules. To his mind, conventions are not part of the true moral domain. Shweder (1982), on the other hand, considers conventions to be symbolic expressions of the moral order.

We cannot resolve that debate here, but we can examine the conventional discourse among Oyugis children related to conventions of proper behavior, to see what they tell us. They do suggest that Oyugis children early construct a working knowledge of their society's social conventions.

Very young children in Oyugis stoutly assert conventional norms of etiquette, modesty, and protection of property. In most cases, the offenders accept the etiquette and modesty corrections of even younger children without dispute. Never, in fact, do they engage in the kind of legalistic argumentation about conventional rules (whether in this situation they apply, whether an exception should not be made, etc.) that American children seem so ready to use (Much & Shweder, 1978).

> Two girls, aged 4 and 4½, examine the observer's raincoat. G. (Boy, 3) to sister, "Stop touching the visitor's possessions." She stops. (37)

> K. (Boy, 3, domineeringly): "Get off my father's chair." J. (Boy, 3½) ignores him. (38)

> P. (Girl, 5½): "Ogodo is coming here. Don't come outside unless you put on your dress." B. (Girl cousin, 6) doesn't answer. She does not dress but sits in the bedroom. (39)

> J. (Boy, 6) to S. (Brother, 10): "Go and greet the visitor." S. goes. (40)

As with other types of rules, Oyugis children readily resort to physical sanctions to back up their commands. In three episodes found, punishment flows from elder to younger, and is accepted by the younger child.

> A. (Boy, 9) hits N. (Niece, 8) for letting the infant defecate on his mother's bed. N. cries. (41)

> N. (Girl, 8): "Clean your nose." K. (Brother, 3) ignores. N. repeats command, picking up a cane. K. still ignores. N. repeats, trying to hit him. K. goes off unwillingly and comes back. "It's not very clean," says N. Again K. goes to clean and comes back. A few minutes later, sister N. tells little brother to go wash his face. He refuses by mimicking her rudely. (42)

> J. (Boy, 3) tries to uproot a pumpkin in the family garden. P. (Sister, 11½): "Don't or I'll beat you." J. runs away. (43)

Addressing people respectfully and by the proper titles is an important Oyugis value. Although preschool children receive much correction on such matters, none of the Oyugis excerpts show preschoolers in the act of correcting others. Perhaps these rules are too complex for young children to have mastered. Beyond about the age of 8, however, children are observed doing something rather subtle with the rules of address. In a culturally appropriate manner, they use age/kinship terms as status terms and address age-inferiors with age-superior titles, to flatter them into mature cooperation (also confer excerpts (14) and (17):

> J. (Girl, 9½) to P. (Sister, 2½, who had burst into tears for no obvious reason): "What do you want, my mother?" (44)

> I. (Boy, 12½) to K. (Brother, 3): "Come, mzee [senior man]." K. runs over. (45)

By age 8, of course, most Oyugis children have spent countless hours in the company of children younger than themselves. They have experienced innumerable occasions on which it was desirable to influence the behavior of a bothersome or out-of-control small child. Having been on both the giving and receiving end of much rude and improper behavior, Oyugis children have had many opportunities to observe how the rules of respect, modesty, and hygiene facilitate pleasant and smooth relations within the group. This process has possibly been facilitated by the fact that the typical Oyugis household is large compared with the typical American household, although still a small enough social system for a child to comprehend. In short, they have many chances to see how conventional rules coordinate the flow of group life.

SUMMARY AND CONCLUSION

In considering the social-cognitive base of nurturant and prosocial behavior, this chapter has focused on *rules* that children learn about in everyday social encounters. Children in all societies discuss and negotiate with one another about right and wrong, of course, but the content or focus of their discussions may vary greatly. In traditional rural communities, such as those of sub-Saharan Africa, children spend a great deal of time in multiage groups. In these settings, older children are given much formal or informal authority and responsibility over small children. The focus of children's moral commands and accountings to one another in this setting appears to be "conventional" moral rules at least as much as "rational" moral rules of justice, harm, and welfare.

This paper has attempted to defend form claims.

1. First, because toddlers and young children require so much behavioral guidance and elicit so many prosocial commands, they help their caretakers construct knowledge about "conventional" moral rules of respect and propriety. Infants (and animals), on the other hand, mainly require positive nurturance and inhibition of aggression. Caring for them especially helps children construct knowledge about "rational" moral rules of harm and welfare. The multiage caretaking situation, composed of infants, toddlers, and older children, may represent a more broadly stimulating environment for reasoning about morality than does the school peer group, where children may have less stimulation to exercise conventional than rational moral reasoning.

2. Because North American children typically spend so much time in extrafamilial settings with same-age peers, and so little time caring for infants and toddlers, their social/moral development may be lopsided, biased on the side of "rational" morality (focused on justice, harm, and welfare). Thus, the findings of American researchers concerning children's moral development may be culturally limited, not universal as is claimed. In particular, the finding that Ameri-

can children consider conventional moral rules to be more trivial and negotiable than rational moral rules appears a good candidate for the culturally-specific.

3. Turiel's theory can be considered a valuable contribution to understanding the development of nurturance and prosocial responsibility because of its delineation of multiple rules domains. Furthermore, by hypothesing what kinds of social encounters lead the child to construct rules about each domain, it has focused our attention in a most useful way on children's everyday social interactions. However, I would state on the basis of material I have studied on Kenyan children (including the Oyugis data of Carol Ember considered in detail here) that rational moral rules, on the one hand, and conventional moral rules, on the other, are not necessarily learned in different kinds of social encounters. Rather, I believe that both rational and conventional moral rules are based on knowledge of the consequences of acts and their normative status. Just as a child who receives a hit or kick can "see" for himself the purpose of rules prohibiting aggression, so a child who tries to manage and control her occasionally rude and uncooperative younger siblings can see for herself the purpose of conventional rules. Furthermore, just as conventional moral rules are "taught" to children through the powerful suggestions and corrections of their elders, so too rational moral rules require similar enforcing by sanctioning agents to convince children which rules are serious and not to be forgotten. Children pay attention to the distress cries and needs of others not only because it is intrinsically satisfying to do so but also because they have been told that they are accountable for their actions (Zahn-Waxler, Radke-Yarrow, & King, 1979). They obey and enforce conventional norms not only because society defines these norms as right, but also because they can see for themselves that the norms relate to desirable consequences for themselves, others, and the family group as a whole.

4. Finally, this paper has sought to at least convince the reader that cross-cultural observations of nurturant and prosocial behavior offer potentially rich insights into social-cognitive development. Becoming nurturant and responsible involves much more than learning specific skills of caretaking and acquiring role-taking and empathic capacities. Rather, the caretaking child must also develop abilities to *think about* certain kinds of social situations and to *influence and convince others* when necessary. Therefore, we can learn much about the origins of nurturance from the close study of the reasoning-in-action of children "at work," trying their best to satisfy the needs of self and others in multiage, familial groups.

ACKNOWLEDGMENT

I wish to express my deep appreciation to Carol R. Ember, Professor of Anthropology, Hunter College, for her generous permission to use her observational data as a source of insight and illustrations. Carol Ember, Elliot Turiel, Judith Smetana, Richard Shweder, and Edward Tronick provided thoughtful criticisms to an earlier draft of this paper. I am indebted to Beatrice and John Whiting for help over the years in constructing a cultural perspective on the development of nurturance and prosocial concern.

REFERENCES

Barry, H. H., Child, I. L., & Bacon, M. K. (1959). Relation of child rearing to subsistence economy. *American Antrhopologist, 61,* 51–63.
Bookman, A., & Ember, C. (in press). *Luo Child and Family Life.* New Haven, CT: Human Relations Area Files.
Bowlby, J. (1969). *Attachment and Loss (Vol. I). Attachment.* New York: Basic Books.
Christie, J. F., & Johnsen, E. P. (1983). The role of play in social-intellectual development. *Review of Educational Research, 53,* 93–115.
Clarke-Stewart, A., & Koch, J. B. (1983). *Children: Development through adolescence.* New York: Wiley.
Edwards, C. P. (1974). *The effects of experience on moral development: Results from Kenya.* Unpublished doctoral dissertation, Harvard University.
Edwards, C. P., & Whiting, B. B. (1980). Differential socialization of girls and boys in light of cross-cultural research. In C. M. Super & S. Harkness (Eds.), *Anthropological perspectives on child development (New directions for child development,* No. 8). San Francisco: Jossey-Bass.
Ember, C. R. (1970). *Effects of feminine task-assignment on the social behavior of boys.* Unpublished doctoral dissertation, Harvard University.
Ember, C. R. (1973). Feminine task assignment and social behavior of boys. *Ethos, 1,* 424–439.
Fein, G. G. (1978). *Child development.* Englewood Cliffs, NJ: Prentice-Hall.
Gallimore, R., Tharp, R. G., & Speidel, G. E. (1978). The relationship of sibling caretaking and attentiveness to a peer tutor. *American Educational Research Journal, 15,* 267–273.
LeVine, R. A. (1973). Patterns of personality in Africa. *Ethos, 1,* 123–152.
Lorenz, K. Z. (1943). Die angeborenen Formen moeglicher Erfahrung. *Zeitschrift fuer Tierpsychologie, 5.*
Maretski, T. W., & Maretski, H. (1963). Taira: An Okinawan village. In B. B. Whiting (Ed.), *Six cultures: Studies of child rearing.* New York: Wiley.
Much, N., & Shweder, R. A. (1978). Speaking of rules: The analysis of culture in breach. In W. Damon (Ed.), *Moral development (New directions for child development, Vol. 2).* San Francisco: Jossey-Bass.
Nerlove, S. B., & Snipper, A. S. (1981). Cognitive consequences of cultural opportunity. In R. H. Munroe, R. L. Munroe, & B. B. Whiting (Eds.), *Handbook of cross-cultural human development.* New York: Garland STPM Press.
Nucci, L., & Nucci, M. (1982). Children's social interactions in the context of moral and conventional transgressions. *Child Development, 53,* 403–412.
Nucci, L., & Turiel, E. (1978). Social interactions and the development of social concepts in preschool children. *Child Development, 49,* 400–407.
Nydegger, W. F., & Nydegger, C. (1963). Tarong: An Ilocos barrio in the Philippines. In B. Whiting (Ed.), *Six cultures: Studies in child rearing.* New York: Wiley.
Piaget, J. (1932). *The moral judgment of the child.* (Reprint: New York: Free Press, 1965).
Pool, D. L., Shweder, R. A., & Much, N. C. (1983). Culture as a cognitive system: Differentiated rule understandings in children and other savages. In E. T. Higgins, D. N. Ruble, & W. W. Hartup, *Social cognition and social development. A sociocultural perspective.* New York: Cambridge University Press.

Read, K. H. (1971). *The nursery school: A human relations laboratory.* Philadelphia: W. B. Saunders.

Rudolph, M., & Cohen, D. H. (1984). *Kindergarten and early schooling.* Englewood Cliffs, NJ: Prentice-Hall.

Shweder, R. A. (1982). Beyond self-constructed knowledge: The study of culture and morality. *Merrill-Palmer Quarterly, 28,* 41–69.

Shweder, R. A., Turiel, E., & Much, N. C. (1981). The moral intuitions of the child. In J. H. Flavell & L. Ross (Eds.), *Social cognitive development: Frontiers and possible futures.* New York: Cambridge University Press.

Smetana, J. G. (1981). Preschool children's conceptions of moral and social rules. *Child Development, 52,* 1333–1336.

Smetana, J. G. (1983). Social cognitive development: Domain distinctions and coordinations. *Developmental Review, 3,* 131–147.

Smetana, J. G., Bridgeman, D. L., & Turiel, E. (1983). Differentiations of domains and prosocial behavior. In D. L. Bridgeman (Ed.), *The nature of prosocial development: Interdisciplinary theories and strategies.* New York: Academic Press.

Snipper, A. S. (1978). *Child-caretaking in Mexico: An observational study.* Unpublished doctoral dissertation, Cornell University.

Turiel, E. (1975). The development of social concepts: Mores, customs and conventions. In D. J. De Palma & J. M. Foley (Eds.), *Contemporary issues in moral development.* Hillsdale, NJ: Lawrence Erlbaum Associates.

Turiel, E. (1978a). The development of concepts of social structure: social convention. In J. Glick & A. Clarke-Stewart (Eds.), *The development of social understanding.* New York: Gardner Press.

Turiel, E. (1978b). Social regulations and domains of social concepts. In W. Damon (Ed.), *Social cognition (New direction in child development, Vol. 1).* New York: Jossey-Bass.

Turiel, E., & Smetana, J. G. (1983). Social knowledge and action: The coordination of domains. In W. M. Kurtines & J. L. Gewirtz (Eds.), *Morality, Moral Behavior, and Moral Development.* New York: Wiley.

Weisner, T. S., & Gallimore, R. (1977). Child and sibling caretaking. *Current Anthropology, 18,* 169–180.

Wenger, M. (1983, June). *Gender role socialization in an East African community: Social interaction between 2-3-year-olds and older children in social ecological perspective.* Unpublished doctoral dissertation, Harvard University.

Weston, D. R., & Turiel, E. (1980). Act-rule relations: Children's concepts of social rules. *Developmental Psychology, 16,* 417–425.

Whiting, B. B. (1974). Folk wisdom and child rearing. *Merrill-Palmer Quarterly of Behavior and Development, 20,* 9–19.

Whiting, B. B. (1980). Culture and social behavior: A model for the development of social behavior. *Ethos, 2,* 95–116.

Whiting, B. B. (1983). The genesis of prosocial behavior. In D. Bridgeman (Ed.), *The nature of prosocial development: Interdisciplinary theories and strategies.* New York: Academic Press.

Whiting, B. B., & Edwards, C. P. (1973). A cross-cultural analysis of sex differences in the behavior of children aged 3-11. *Journal of Social Psychology, 91,* 171–188.

Whiting, B. B., Edwards, C. P., Ember, C., Erchak, G., Harkness, S., Munroe, R., Munroe, R. L., Seymour, S., Super, C., & Weisner, T. (in prep.). *The company they keep: The genesis of gender role behavior.*

Whiting, B. B., & Whiting, J. W. M. (1975). *Children of six cultures: A psycho-cultural analysis.* Cambridge, MA: Harvard University Press.

Zahn-Waxler, C., Radke-Yarrow, M., & King, R. A. (1979). Child-rearing and children's prosocial initiations toward victims in distress. *Child Development, 50,* 319–330.

6 Becoming Nurturant in Japan: Past and Present

Hideo Kojima
Nagoya University

INTRODUCTION

In this chapter problems in the process of becoming nurturant in Japanese society are discussed. First, as a historical background, Japanese traditional attitudes and sentiments related to the young are reviewed. Many Japanese believe that the Japanese attitude and sentiments with regard to children have traditionally been very nurturant. Several literary works, a diary, descriptions by Western visitors, and ethnographers' descriptions are referred to in order to construct the traditional attitudes.

Nowadays many Japanese are concerned that Japan has diverged greatly from its traditional, nurturant ways of treating children. During the past 2 or 3 decades, many changes occurred in Japanese child-rearing. In the second section, problems in the process of nurturing children in present-day Japan are discussed. Beginning with clinical cases of so-called child-rearing neurosis in young mothers, I review more pervasive background problems. Immediate and situational factors are discussed first. Then, changing ecological factors related to problems of child-rearing are reviewed from several aspects. Finally, the changing Japanese conceptualization of living things, which, in my view, is very relevant to development of nurturance, is briefly discussed. It is the writer's hope that by discussing problems encountered in Japan, we may increase our understanding of the process of becoming nurturant in any society.

JAPANESE TRADITIONAL ATTITUDES TOWARD CHILDREN: HISTORICAL BACKGROUND

Japanese attitudes toward children have been characterized traditionally as follows.

Literary Works

Since ancient times, children have been valued not only instrumentally but also sentimentally and romantically. Some examples are in order.

1. *Man'yo-shu,* the first Japanese anthology of poets compiled in about 753A.D., includes many poems about children. One poet wrote, for example, "As a treasure which excels everything else, could there be anything equal to children!" From the same poet, there are included three poems of bitter mourning by a father who lost his son in infancy. A similar kind of mourning for a lost daughter also appeared in *Tosa nikki* (934-5).

2. *Ryojin hisho,* a collection of popular songs compiled in the 12th century, includes songs which describe, with a sympathetic tone, naïveté of children. For example, children were characterized as the beings who were born in nature to play. They were also characterized as innocent. A song describes how a rich father induced his child to get out of a burning house by saying, "Why don't you come out to go for a ride on a sheep carriage, or on a deer carriage?"

3. *Kashiwazaki nikki,* a family diary written by a low-ranked warrior (Watanabe, 1971) over a period of 10 years in the first half of the 19th century, includes many descriptions concerning the mother's deep affection for her son living apart. Also described in this diary was the parents' interest in developmental changes in children. The parents were keen to recognize and enjoy the childlike acts of their children and the emergence of new skills. For example, all the adults in the family laughed at the sight of Oroku's deferred imitation of hunting lice in her cloths. She was 13-months-old at that time. In addition to those mentioned, many more poems describing children were compiled by Takashima (1910).

Records by Western Visitors

Western visitors to Japan were generally impressed by the mild, patient, and nurturant child treatment they observed. During the second half of the 16th century and the early 17th century, European missionaries, largely Jesuits and Franciscans, visited Japan. They were shocked by the frequent abortions and infanticides seen there. To their eyes, however, the Japanese child-rearing method was much milder and was done with more reason than the contemporary European method.

Jesuit missionary Luis Frois (Eden & Willes, 1577) wrote in his letter of February, 1565 in Kyoto, "In bringing up their children they use words only to rebuke them, admonishing as diligently and advisedly boys of six or seven years age, as though they were old men" (p. 255). Another Jesuit, Jean Crasset (1705) published a French book in 1689 based on correspondence from the missionaries abroad. As to Japanese child-rearing, he summarized as follows:

> The great happiness of a kingdom depends chiefly on the education of youth, in which the *Japonians* properly excel. First they use altogether sweetness for fear of

cowing their spirits, and never either threaten and chastise them, be they never so untoward; but seeing the Holy Ghost commands parents to correct and chastise their children, to make them governable; we cannot much admire this piece of conduct. At the same time, they live in sufficient awe, being under parents that are impowered to take away their lives. (1705, p. 15)

Christianity had been introduced into Japan in 1549, and Christian missionaries were rather successful in western and central Japan. The feudal ruler's fear of Christian influence led Japan to isolate herself from European countries around 1640, and the Chinese and Dutch trading post located on a small island in Nagasaki was the only official window to foreign countries other than Korea during the next 2 centuries.

Morse (1917), an American zoologist who lived in Japan for a few years soon after the Meiji Restoration in 1867, often described Japanese children and their treatment in those days. Thus, for example, he wrote, "A rare thing is to hear a baby cry, and thus far I have never seen the slightest sign of impatience on the part of the mother. I believe Japan is the only nation in the world that yields much to the babies, or in which babies are so good" (Vol. 1, p. 10). He also wrote, "There is one subject, among many subjects, that foreign writers are unanimously agreed upon, and that is that Japan is the paradise for children. Not only are they kindly treated, but they have more liberty, take less liberty with their liberties, and have a greater variety of delightful experiences than the children of any other people" (Vol. 1, p. 41). A summary comment of his is, "The Japanese have certainly solved the children problem, and no better behaved, kinder children exist, and no more patient, affectionate and devoted mothers are found. However, this is all trite, as every book on Japan has said the same thing again and again" (Vol. 1, pp. 351–352).

No doubt the information obtained by these writers was not adequately sampled across various settings and within-group variations of child-rearing in those days. We also should take into account the cultural background of these writers. Probably, Jesuits had experienced strict child treatment in their home countries. It is also said that Morse himself was exposed to strict disciplines in his home in 19th century New England. However, it is worth noting that these writers, even though separated by a few hundred years, shared the same kind of judgment of Japanese child-rearing just before and after the Edo period (1600-1867).

Ethnographic Descriptions

The above-mentioned impressions held by Western visitors were endorsed at least partly by some Japanese sources. Yanagita (1932), a pioneering ethnographer in Japan, wrote, "Since old times, Japan has been a country where children have been loved by gods." As reflected in a series of rituals beginning at the 5th month of pregnancy, childbirth and child-rearing have been the common concern of the whole community (Ohtoh, 1969). Though abortion and infanticide were not infrequent, especially in the latter half of the Edo period, once a child was accepted to be brought up he or she was welcomed and incorporated into the network of community living. In a society like Japan, where interdependent relationships between related persons were of the utmost importance, it was natural that the rearing of children was the common concern of the community members.

In traditional village living, children grew to adulthood step-by-step through several stages. The crucial points in development were ascertained and celebrated by community members in the form of feasts or rituals that usually began at the 5th month of pregnancy when pregnant woman wore a special belt (*iwata-obi*) around the abdomen, and under the kimono. This has been interpreted by Japanese ethnographers (e.g., Ohtoh, 1969) as a ritual of preparation for introducing a coming baby to the human world through collaboration of many related persons surrounding him. The day of birth, the 3rd day, and the 7th day—which were thought to be critical days for baby's survival—were celebrated with feasts by related people. Normally the baby was named on the 7th day. At about 1 month, the baby was taken to the community shinto shrine as a first step in becoming a parishioner. At about 100 days, the baby was fed a grain of rice as a ritual, and the first birthday was celebrated happily.

Children went through the milestone ages of 3, 5, and 7 with accompanying ceremonies. Children under 7-years-of-age were mainly reared by family members. In some districts children under 7 were believed to be deities; Japanese ethnographers maintain that children under that age were thought to be beings that have not yet become completely human.

Until age 7 when children began to be assigned tasks and boys and girls were treated differently, adults were permissive, or even indulgent to children. This can be inferred from the descriptions by ethnographers, from descriptions in *Kashiwazaki nikki* (Watanabe, 1971), and from novels (e.g., Eiseido, 1773) and *senryu* (short humorous verse).

For example, Watanabe (1971) often described in his diary that he and his wife were annoyed, but at the same time amused, with their children who asked peevishly for the impossible. Both parents and a resident baby-sitter seemed to find any opportunity to take their young children to various places in their small town to entertain them. Not simply that children could mingle with adults' activities, but a considerable part of adults' daily life was devoted to child-centered activity. Eiseido's (1773) novel satirically illustrated typical, indulgent child-rearing practices in rich merchant families.

Incidence of Infanticide

Of course we cannot deny a dark side of child treatment in past Japan. Abortion and infanticide soon after birth (*mabiki*, i.e., thinning or weeding) were rather frequent, as can be inferred from demographic data and descriptions by ethnographers. Recently, however, a claim was made that thinning was actually not so prevalent in the Edo period (1600-1867) as has been generally believed (Chiba & Ohtsu, 1983). Records of famines in the Edo period also tell us that the rate of starvation was lower among children than among male adults.

In a word, evidence suggests that the Japanese attitude to children has traditionally been very nurturant. Japanese adults acknowledged the importance of the young for the family and community. Not only did they treat children with much care, they also recognized special characteristics of children and adjusted their ways of treating children accordingly.

PROBLEMS OF NURTURING CHILDREN IN PRESENT-DAY JAPAN

The present status of Japanese child-rearing is believed by many concerned people (mainly male) to have diverged from the traditional ways as described earlier. They feel threatened by the rapid change of society's attitude and values of child-rearing. However, in my view, Japan in the past could not simply be regarded as a golden age of child nurturance. In some respects, we have lost traditional attitudes and practices, and in others, their functions still remain in different forms. In this section we analyze some current problems related to child nurturance.

Problems in Becoming Nurturant as Reflected in Clinical Cases

One of the biggest problems of child-rearing in present-day Japan is called *ikuji Neurose* (child-rearing neurosis) among young mothers. This phenomenon began to attract attention around the middle of the 1960s, several years after rapid economic growth began in postwar Japan. It was also the time when competition for entrance examinations in high school and college levels began to intensify, and school achievement became an extremely dominant dimension for evaluating children. At the same time, popular child-care books in Japan changed their contents from routine and medical care to include the intellectual and personality development of infants. For example, in the preface to a handbook of baby care (Hoken Dojin-sha, 1967), the author wrote: "Most of the past books on infant care have been concerned with medical care. They dealt with the methods of how to prevent illness and injury of infants, but not with the psychological development of infants. The present book, however, is concerned to a great measure with the psychological aspects of infants and their development." This shift in emphasis may reflect the social trends of those days, when parents began to believe that children do not develop naturally, but that active participation by parents is indispensable to development. Parents also began to view child-rearing and child development as a kind of competition between each other to create the most successful child.

Child-rearing neurosis is a symptom prevalent among young mothers who rear their babies in urban areas isolated from their relatives, and without psychological support from their husbands, close friends, and neighbors. These mothers are also overly sensitive to the evaluative responses of others and to the comparison of their babies with others'. Though in its extreme form mothers go so far as to kill their infants, child-rearing neurosis is different from child abuse. Incidentally, there are no reliable nation-wide statistics related to incidence of child abuse (physical and sexual abuse and neglect). However, generally speaking, their incidence in Japan (Ikeda, 1982) is estimated to be much lower than in the United States. On the other hand, according to Wagatsuma (1981), Japanese parents are more likely than other cultural groups to abandon or kill their children.

The chief characteristics of mothers suffering from child-rearing neurosis are the following. First, they cannot enjoy child-rearing but regard it a serious business to be executed correctly. Second, they feel that they are inadequate mothers and lose self-confidence not only as a mother, but also as a person. In addition, they are overly concerned about the physical and psychological development of their children, and they believe that *their* children are not growing well compared to other children. Actually their children fall well within the developmental age norms for Japanese children. However, these mothers try hard to rear infants in order for them to meet the criterion of normal, or in some cases, ideal infants. Needless to say, many more factors that include the mother's personality, her health conditions, and the degree of her *ittaikan* (feeling of oneness) with her infant, as well as interpersonal relations involving the mother, are related to the development of child-rearing neurosis in a mother.

In their desperate suffering to be perfect in child-rearing, some of them, but only the visible tip of an iceberg comprising the total cases of maternal neuroticism, commit suicide and infanticide, that is, so-called *oyako shinju* (parent-child joint suicide). This type of suicide may very well be a uniquely Japanese phenomenon (Wagatsuma, 1981). Typical cases of mother-child suicide are committed by mothers between 25 and 34 years old, and over 40% of children are under 2 years old. Out of 133 mother-child suicides that occurred in Tokyo from 1966 to 1975, about 40% of their causes involved neurosis in mothers (Koshinaga, Takahashi, & Shimamura, 1975). The major reasons for committing mother-child suicide included, "lost self-confidence as caretaker," "tired of child-rearing," and "fallen into neurosis after child birth." With the exception of families with severely handicapped children, it is almost always mothers, not fathers, who suffer from child-rearing neurosis, since it is still the mother who assumes all the responsibility of child-care and education in Japan. Though we have no formal statistics for the incidence of child-rearing neurosis, there has been an increase in these cases reported in newspapers, and recently a paperback book titled *Child-Rearing Neurosis* has been published (Sasaki, Takano, Ohinata, Jimba, & Serizawa, 1982).

Background Problems of Child-Rearing

Although mother-child suicide and clinical cases of child-rearing neurosis represent only a small proportion of mothers, there is an increasing amount of difficulty encountered by most young parents in present-day Japan. In the next three sections we discuss the background problems of child-rearing in present-day Japan. These problems are related to: (1) immediate and situational factors that surround the family, (2) changing ecological factors in Japan as reflected in the life history of the parents, and (3) the changing cultural concept of human life. Explanations of these three factors are in order.

1. Problems related to immediate and situational factors

Isolation of the nuclear family is the most important factor to be examined. In present-day Japan, about 60% of all households consist of nuclear families. Imagine young parents who are going to rear their first-born child in an environment where they have almost no acquaintances around them. Typically, expectant mothers will travel to their own mother's home to give birth in hospitals in their home town, surrounded by their mothers and other relatives. Taken good care of by these people, the new mothers, novices in child-rearing, can overcome the psychological transition accompanying child birth. However, after the mothers come back from their home town, they inevitably face many difficult problems of child-rearing. As is explained in the next section, many of them are not well prepared for rearing their children. Mothers become overly worried, even about the child's minor sickness. Wrestling with many child-care books, they try hard to do what's best for their babies. Because many of the mothers have not acquired attitudes that enable them to select suitable information out the flood of available books, often containing mutually contradictory information, they are at the mercy of inconsistent advice or admonition.

A high incidence of mothers' anxiety over baby care was revealed by a questionnaire study at a public health center *(hoken-jo)* in Nagoya. Suzuki (1980) found that even just after the health examination of the babies at 3-months-of-age, 48.7% of the mothers with normal babies still had some misgivings about baby-care. The main context of their misgivings were feeding and weaning problems and apprehension over possible illness in the future. Although the birth order of the babies was not significantly related to maternal anxiety (52.9% of the mothers with first born babies versus 45.6% of them with later borns), significantly more (65.7%) mothers with higher educational level (more than 14 years completed) had misgivings as compared to the other two groups (46.3% for the education level of 12 years; 39.3% for that of 9 years).

Many nuclear families in urban districts, especially those with first-borns, are isolated from other members in the community. If they have no relatives around them to seek advice on child-rearing, it is often the case that young parents have difficulty in coping with problems. Especially when the mother is suffering from chronic anxiety because of her personality, because the baby is not growing well, or because of her own ill health, the situation will be very difficult. While advice and guidance by veterans of child-rearing may not always be the best solution, they can still serve as a kind of safety valve to prevent the mother from making urgent, and often inappropriate responses to the problem. Assuring is comforting to the mother who is upset and cannot put things in perspective.

These young mothers need a viable support system for performing the parental role. According to a survey conducted with the readers of a Japanese baby-care magazine (Niwa, 1980), they resorted to child-care books and magazines as well as to their own mothers and friends to seek advice on child-care. They were satisfied with the magazine primarily because it provided them with information about how other mothers were treating their babies. Readers also expressed their interest in contributing to the magazine in order to impart their own experiences with babies to other mothers, especially as to how they solved the problems of child-care. Indeed, 64% of the mothers reported that they had helped others (largely their friends) by making use of their knowledge of child-care. It is true that this is not a representative sample of the present-day Japanese mothers, but their need to establish a communication network with other mothers seems to be strong. This network is a kind of *meso-system* that is an important environmental system for human development (Bronfenbrenner, 1979). Unfortunately, mothers' needs have not yet been satisfied in their communities due to lack of organized activity both in governmental and voluntary sectors.

What about fathers, who we might expect to be key persons in the support system for mothers? Japanese fathers in the young generations are much more cooperative with their wives than the former generations. For example, they bathe babies and play with them, and willingly accompany their wives when they take babies to the clinic. Some fathers take over household chores so that wives may have time to interact with babies. According to Miura (1981), Japanese fathers participated with their 3- to 4-month-old babies in various kinds of baby care activities at home. For example, 91% of them tried to mollify crying babies, 90% played with babies, 72% bathed, and 52% changed diapers, at least once or twice a week. However, these busy fathers had contact with babies (care and play) only for short periods of time, especially on week days. More than 50% of the fathers had contact with babies only up to 20 min a day, and only 16% of them had contact with their babies more than an hour a day. That these fathers' reports were reliable was supported by the fact that the mothers' rating of the fathers' helpfulness correlated significantly with the fathers' self-report of the number of hours they spent with babies. Incidentally, it is of interest to note that in Miura's sample, maternal and paternal attachments to babies significantly correlated with each other ($r = .32$, $p < .05$). In addition, fathers with high attachment scores were, according to their own report, quick to respond to mollify crying babies ($p < .01$).

In this way, young fathers, though their time is rather limited, support wives in ordinary life through both direct and indirect measures so that the mothers can fulfill their maternal roles. Unfortunately, however, these fathers cannot be depended upon when it comes to more serious problems of child-rearing or sickness.

Fathers, and mothers alike, are not prepared for serious child-rearing practices due to lack of child-care experience in their formative years. In many prefectures in Japan only girls learn domestic sciences in junior and senior high schools. In addition, there is a more fundamental problem. In many families wives are assigned the maternal role after the child is born, and their role as wives becomes deemphasized. Furthermore, in many Japanese homes, the framework for family role naming is based on the youngest member of the family. For example, soon after the first child is born, husband and wife often call each other "mother" and "father," instead of using first names or personal pronouns. Besides, many Japanese fathers, instrumentally and psychologically dependent on their wives, themselves seem to demand "maternal care" from their mates. Many Japanese males have not been trained throughout their formative years to take care of themselves independently. In a comparative research study between Japan and the United States, only 30.2% of Japanese boys in junior and senior high schools, as compared to 88.5% of American boys, participated in housework such as cooking, shopping, and sweeping (the Prime Minister's Office of Japan, 1976).

Japanese male adults expect that they will be cared for by someone; their mother, wife, or some other female. These extra burdens placed on the young Japanese wife by her husband may contribute to the difficulty they experience in child-rearing. Hence, fathers, potentially the most important social support for mothers, cannot perform that role when their wives need it.

A discrepancy of role expectation exists between fathers and mothers. While 68% of mothers wish the fathers to support them psychologically, rather than to play with babies, 87% of the fathers thought they should have direct contact with babies, rather than to provide psychological support to their wives (Miura, 1981).

In addition, fathers, who may have been helpful to mothers in child-care duties when the children were young, begin to be bound up with demands from their jobs. They begin to feel that problems of child-rearing and education are burdens to them. Mothers who feel that their husbands do not share responsibility in these matters become dissatisfied with, and psychologically detached from their husbands. Thus, mothers who are forced to become so involved in child-rearing become guilty of failure, and proud of successes in child-rearing. Their self-evaluation is based on success or failure of their children. In this way, many mothers who have been denied *direct* self-realization in society begin to take the route of *vicarious* self-realization. For them, children are extension of themselves.

2. Problems related to changing ecological factors

Throughout the formative years of an individual in present-day Japan, there are several factors in his or her socialization that may cause problems in handling nurturant roles. All problems are related to a lack of experience in caring for the young in family and society. In my view, the following three factors are outstanding:

Number of siblings in a household. During the past 3 decades, the number of children in a household has been decreasing. For more than 10 years, the average (about 55% in 1982) has been the two-child family. It was estimated that for a household with children under the age of 18, the average number of children was 1.84 in 1983. In the past, when the average number of children born to a woman was about 5 (5.04 in 1940 and 4.93 in 1952 as contrasted with 2.20 in 1972 and 2.23 in 1982), elder siblings took care of younger siblings. After the marriage of elder siblings, it was often the case that younger siblings took care of nephews and nieces. In this way both elder and younger siblings had the experience of taking care of, or observing the care of the younger under the supervision of experienced caretakers. In the typical present-day family, on the other hand, the elder sibling is only a few years older than the second-born. Neither has a chance to care for the young, nor to model themselves after mothers who are caring for the young. It is true that, as we found in our ongoing research, children as young as 2-years-of-age are interested in assisting mothers take care of younger siblings, but this type of behavior is primarily motivated by a desire to help an adult, and without more systematic experience it does not transfer to nurturant behavior toward the young when there is no adult around them.

Child-rearing in isolated places. Children in present-day Japan have only a limited chance to care for or to observe young children in the community. This is because child-rearing is done within a closed, private family, or in more or less age-segregated day care centers by a specially trained staff. According to Morioka (in press), one direction of change in Japanese families after World War II is characterized as privatization. In addition, an increase in the number of working mothers has necessitated an increase in day care centers for infants.

Lack of baby-sitting experience. Baby-sitting is unpopular in present-day Japan for several reasons. First, as was explained earlier, the elder sibling is not old enough to care for the younger sibling, unlike the past when baby-sitting by siblings was prevalent. Elder children with a young sibling on their back was a sight often described by foreign visitors to Japan soon after the Meiji Restoration (e.g., Morse, 1917). According to a recollection by a woman who was born in a peasant family around 1905 (Kobayashi, 1974), she had barely been 4-years-old when she began to baby-sit for her sister, strapped to her back (so-called *Ombu*).

According to Watanabe (1971), his daughter Oroku baby-sat her 1-year-old brother when she was 9-years-of-age. However, when she wished to help her mother arrange dolls used in the Girls' Festival, Watanabe himself took over the duty of baby-sitting.

Second, present-day Japanese high school children, too busy by the demands of schooling and examinations, are excused from doing housework by protective, and education-minded parents. Indeed, Japanese and French children at the ages of 10 and 15 were ranked the lowest in their time spent in housework in a comparative study of six countries (the Prime Minister's Office of Japan, 1981). Other countries were the United States, Britain, Thailand, and Korea. According to the report, only 8.0% of boys and 8.7% of girls in Japan, as compared to 15.1 and 27.1% of American boys and girls respectively, took care of their younger siblings. Especially in the 15-year-olds, only 2.2% of girls and virtually none of boys baby-sat in Japan.

Third, the Japanese have a negative attitude toward hiring resident and part-time baby-sitters. In the past, perhaps from the middle of the Edo period (1600-1867) to the prewar period, resident baby-sitters *(komori)* were prevalent in Japan not only among townsmen but also among rich farmers. Many of them served under indentures for several years. Around the age of 8, girls of poor peasants left their home mainly in order to save families' food. As was reflected in folk nursery songs (Matsunaga, 1964), resident baby-sitters in those days had a hard time.

As can be seen from the experts' advice on child-rearing in the Edo period, they were concerned about the quality of care by wet- and dry-nurses. Since the Japanese traditional concept of child-rearing was that the baby was deeply influenced by his caretakers (Kojima, in press), parents were advised to carefully select the proper caretakers for their children. In the late 1870s, the concern about the possible ill effect of unsupervised baby-sitters led people to establish training institutions for baby-sitters *(komori renshu-jo),* and in the 1880s, schools for baby-sitters *(komori gakko).* The komori gakko was established in order to give baby-sitters who could not attend ordinary elementary school a chance to have an elementary education. According to the curricula in those days, baby-sitters also had lessons about manners and infant care, and cultivation of sentiments was intended, too (Shinano Kyoiku-kai, 1900; Watanabe, 1884). Still, the concerned educators in those days appeared not to be satisfied with the quality of baby-sitting (Kurahashi, 1937). The *komori gakko,* once prevalent, disappeared around 1940. In my view, this history is related to the Japanese negative attitude toward the practice of baby-sitting.

The fourth reason why baby-sitters are lacking in present-day Japan, though many parents badly need this kind of relief, is the following. Especially in urban districts, houses are small and they have no room for resident or part-time baby-sitters. The more important factor is the change of the Japanese family toward privatization (Morioka, in press). The Japanese do not want part-time baby-sitters, unrelated persons, to come into their homes, which are meant to be private sectors that exclude outsiders.

Finally, though the situation is gradually changing, there still remains a traditional family ideology which dictates that parents, especially mothers, should devote themselves to children. If a husband and a wife spend their own time alone together, or if a wife goes out on her own to meet with friends or to go to a concert, leaving children in the care of a sibling or nonfamily baby-sitter, not only the wife but also the husband may be accused of neglect. As can be inferred from the accusing tone of newspaper reports on accidents suffered by young children who have been left by themselves while their parents are out, many Japanese still feel that the role of parent should have priority over that of husband and wife.

These five factors have prevented Japan from developing the kind of baby-sitting practice by children and youth that is popular in America. The baby-sitting system, when it works well and has necessary provisions for training, may contribute to fostering nurturance in baby-sitters. Not only does baby-sitting provide children and youth with direct experience in child care, it also makes sitters aware that they are given charge of a child by his/her parents. And, to play an important part in the child's wellbeing, though only for a limited time, may be a good experience that makes baby-sitters realize their potential for nurturance.

In this section, I have stressed the importance for the developing individual the experience of caring for the young. There are some empirical studies showing that early experience in child care was related to females' interest and attachment to young children.

For example, Kosugi (1980) found that unmarried female college students who had positive images of babies (as revealed by the semantic differential scales) tended to recollect more experiences of caring for the young, and also to make positive evaluations of their own mothers. Hirai (1976) conducted a questionnaire study on maternal affection and its background factors. The mothers in this sample had first-born children who were either 1-, 3-, or 5-years-of-age at the time of testing. He found, for example, that mothers who had a positive attachment to children had more experience caring for the young in their own childhood and adolescence. They also reported that they felt happy soon after the birth of their first children.

Both of these studies relied on retrospective reports of the respondents about early experience of caring for the young. Correlations between current interest and affection for young children and past experience may partly be an artifact arising from using the same data source to obtain the two measures to be correlated. However, these results suggest that attachment to children may have been formed through one's life history, i.e., from childhood to young adulthood. Theoretically, it is plausible that by direct experience of caring for young children, one's attitude to them becomes more favorable. This may be the case not only for females who have a positive attitude to children from the beginning, but also for those whose attitude to them is neutral. Their caretaking activity may be reinforced by young children's positive responses (e.g., smile, vocalization or speech, and dependent behavior), and this effect may spread to an attitude level.

In addition to past experience, the current emotional state of mothers may also be related to their attitude to babies. In a short-term prospective interview study, Ohinata (1978) found group differences in several indices of maternal attachment among three groups of mothers. These groups were mothers who felt (1) very happy, (2) somewhat happy, and (3) embarrassed, when they were informed of their pregnancy. For example, compared to groups 2 and 3, group 1 mothers tended to report that at 6- to 7-months-of-pregnancy, they were very fond of children in general, they were moved by the quickening of the fetus, they were proud of the changes in their body due to pregnancy, they were not envious of other nonpregnant women who enjoyed their lives, and they felt happy. Four or 5 months after child birth, these mothers reported that they were happy to have babies, were attached to babies soon after birth, and didn't feel child-care to be a troublesome job.

Several factors may contribute to make mothers feel happy during pregnancy. Among them are their basic attitude to children in general, and current family relationships surrounding them. Their past experience, positive and nurturant attitudes to the young, and current supportive environment may form a group of interrelated factors that influence the mothers' current feeling and behavior toward young children.

3. Problems related to the changing conception of human life

In this section I discuss an important background factor of nurturance, i.e., the cultural concept of the meaning of human life. Under the heading of "need Nurturance," Murray (1938) described various aspects of the need. For example, the desire and effect of the need is "to give sympathy and gratify the needs of a helpless object" (p. 184). As for feelings and emotions, he mentioned pity, compassion, and tenderness. With regard to the action (general), he wrote as follows: "To be particularly attracted to the young, the unfortunate, the sorrowing. To enjoy the company of children and animals. To be liberal with time, energy and money when compassion is aroused. To be moved by the distress of others. To feel more affectionate when an object exhibits a weakness. To be moved by tears. To inhibit narcistic needs in the presence of an inferior object. To be lenient and indulgent. To give freedom. To condone. To become indignant when children are maltreated" (p. 184).

According to another definition of nurturance (see Fogel, Melson, & Mistry, this volume), the essential quality underlying Murray's descriptions is empathy and altruism for the less competent. But, his concept of nurturance reminded me of a stereotyped Japanese sentiment and attitude about living things in general, and about human beings and animals in particular. Perhaps due to the Buddhist precept against killing animals, a traditional Japanese conception was that human beings and other living things were basically similar to each other, and the Japanese were led to have a sympathetic attitude toward all living things, for each of us was a member of them. However, in order to live, the Japanese did fishing and hunting. To make amends for the sin, professional fish dealers and cooks held, and still hold, a special ceremony once a year. Of course the human fetus and newborn baby were not exceptions. Special tombs for aborted fetuses and "thinned" babies were sometimes constructed.

However, as time passed, the special ceremony by the fish dealers and cooks was almost stripped of its original meaning. Almost all Japanese lost the Buddhist view that both men and animals were the same living things, and the ceremony has become a ritual without much content. In Japan, abortion was legalized in 1948. Besides other birth control methods to prevent unwanted conception, abortion became very prevalent, and it may have influenced the Japanese concept of human life. Several decades ago, the child was considered as a gift from Heaven, but recently, a child is thought of as something to be "made." On the other hand, as is certain from the recent revival of *mizuko jizo* (a guardian deity of aborted or miscarried fetuses and of stillborn babies, babies who died shortly after birth, and victims of infanticide) in Japan (Brooks, 1981), guilt feelings on the part of parents has not been considerably reduced. However, after purchasing an expensive *jizo* figure to be placed in the temple yard and/or paying cash tribute to an often commercialized temple to pray for the lost life, many adults feel relieved of the guilty feeling caused by abortion.

A related issue is teen-age pregnancy and abortion. Though pregnancy among unmarried teen-agers is not uncommon in present-day Japan, "children bearing children" has not become a major problem since abortion has prevented them from giving birth. In Japan, in contrast to the general decreasing trend of the total incidence of abortion, the past several years have witnessed a sharp increase in the number of abortions in teen-agers. In 1979, it was about 17,000, and in 1984, it was estimated to be over 25,000.

According to a report on incidence of unmarried teen-age pregnancy in northern part of Japan (Katagiri & Shinagawa, 1980), 86.8% of them had abortions and only 7.5% gave birth to babies (natural miscarriages and abnormal pregnancies comprised the residual cases). In addition, most of the girls who gave birth did not want to do so, but it was too late for an abortion. In the small proportion of cases where pregnant girls wanted to give birth to their babies, their parents strongly persuaded them to have an abortion. These parents believed that abortion was the best solution to the problem from the point-of-view of the daughters' best interests. Shinagawa (1981) attributed a high incidence of abortion to the society's negative attitudes toward unmarried teen-age prenancy. In addition to social sanction to these girls and expulsion from senior high schools, parents tend to lose face with the world, and even their siblings are sometimes socially handicapped in their later lives, especially in time of their own marriage.

Although, except for a few clinical cases, no data are available as to the psychological consequences of this practice for girls, the experience of abortion under social pressure may have negative consequences for the development of nurturant feelings and behavior in individual girls. Katagiri and Shinagawa (1980) reported that all of the 160 cases of unmarried teen-age pregnancies were unplanned ones and only 10 of them felt happy when they were informed of their pregnancy. In addition, 81% of them had guilty feelings toward fetuses or children.

However, the effects of widespread practice of abortion on the cultural concept of human life may be more consequential, and may deeply influence the process of developing nurturance in each individual. Some Japanese are deeply concerned about recent reports of cruel abuse of living things (e.g., goldfish in a basin and swans in the pond), by Japanese, from preschool children to young adults. They are also concerned about a recent increase in physically and psychologically abusive acts by children directed toward peers, and sometimes toward homeless people sleeping in parks and stadia, on the one hand. According to a recent report (Aoki, 1984), ten children between the ages of 14 and 16 attacked homeless people and killed three of them. These boys were not aggressive at home or school. They talked about their homicide as if it were other people's affairs, and had no recognition that they had committed murder. The interviewer Aoki was shocked by their lack of sympathy toward human beings. On the other hand, some adolescents appear not to put much value on their own lives (e.g., drug addiction and reckless driving). We do not fully understand the network of causal factors that might explain the occurrence of these incidences. However, it seems certain that changing cultural concepts of the meaning and value of living things is a basic factor that must be examined further.

ACKNOWLEDGMENT

I am indebted to Alan Fogel for his editing work, comments, and suggestions, and to Kyoko Murakami for her comments, regarding an earlier draft of this article.

REFERENCES

Aoki, E. (1984). *Yatto miete-kita kodomo-tachi* [At long last, I began to understand children's inner world]. Tokyo: Asunaro Shobo. (in Japanese)

Bronfenbrenner, U. (1979). *The ecology of human development.* Cambridge, MA: Harvard University Press.

Brooks, A. P. (1981). *Mizuko kuyo* and Japanese Buddhism. *Japanese Journal of Religious Studies, 8,* 119–147.

Chiba, T., & Ohtsu, T. (1983). *Mabiki to mizuko* [Thinning and unborn fetus]. Tokyo: Nohsangyo-son Bunka Kyokai. (in Japanese)

Crasset, J. (1705). *The history of the church of Japan.* Vol. 1. (N. N. Webb, Trans.). London: Unknown. (Original work published 1689)

Eden, R., & Willes, R. (Eds.). (1577). *The history of travayle.* London: Richarde Jugge.

Eiseido, K. (1773). *Shoni sodate katagi* [Characteristic ways of child-rearing]. (Compiled in M. Yamazumi & K. Nakae (Eds.), *Kosodate no sho.* Vol. 2. [Books on child-rearing]. Tokyo: Heibon-sha, 1976.) (in Japanese)

Hirai, N. (Ed.). (1976). *Bosei-ai no kenkyu* [A study on maternal love]. Tokyo: Dobun Shoin. (in Japanese)

Hoken Dojin-sha. (1967). *Akachan no sodate-kata hyakka* [Handbook of baby-care]. Tokyo: Author. (in Japanese)

Ikeda, Y. (1982). A short introduction to child abuse in Japan. *Child Abuse and Neglect, 6,* 487–490.

Katagiri, S., & Shinagawa, N. (1980). Sanfujinka-i kara mita Aomori-ken ni okeru jakunen mikonsha no ninshin no jittai [Unmarried teen-age pregnancies in Aomori Prefecture: Views of obstetrics and gynecology]. In Nippon Kazoku Keikaku Kyokai (Ed.), *Shishun-ki to ninshin* [Pregnancy in adolescence]. Tokyo: Author. (in Japanese)

Kobayashi, H. (1974). *Onna san-dai* [Three generations of women in a peasant family]. Tokyo: Asahi Shimbun-sha. (in Japanese)

Kojima, H. (in press). Child-rearing concepts as a belief-value system of the society and the individual. In H. W. Stevenson, H. Azuma, & K. Hakuta (Eds.), *Child development and education in Japan.* San Francisco: Freeman.

Koshinaga, J., Takahashi, S., & Shimamura, T. (1975). Sengo ni okeru oyako shinju no jittai [Parent-child suicide in post-war Japan]. *Kosei no Shihyo, 22*(14), 8–17. (in Japanese)

Kosugi, K. (1980). *Images of the baby in unmarried, female college students.* Unpublished graduation thesis, Nagoya University, Nagoya. (in Japanese)

Kurahashi, S. (1937). Komori [Baby-sitter]. In S. Abe et al. (Eds.), *Kyoiku-gaku jiten* [Dictionary of Education]. Tokyo: Iwanami Shoten. (in Japanese)

Matsunaga, G. (1964). *Nippon no komori-uta* [Folk nursery songs in Japan]. Tokyo: Kinokuniya Shoten. (in Japanese)

Miura, K. (1981). *Chichioya no yoiku eno sanka* [Fathers' participation in caring for their three-month olds]. Unpublished graduation thesis, Nagoya University, Nagoya. (in Japanese)

Morioka, K. (in press). Privatization of the family life. In H. W. Stevenson, H. Azuma & K. Hakuta (Eds.), *Child development and education in Japan.* San Francisco: Freeman.

Morse, E. S. (1917). *Japan day by day.* 2 vols. Boston: Houghton Mifflin.

Murray, H. A. (1938). *Explorations in personality.* New York: Oxford University Press.

Niwa, Y. (1980, October). Baby Age dokusha enquete yori [A questionnaire study with subscribers of the Baby Age, a magazine for young mothers]. In T. Yamashita (Chair), *Developmental research and society II.* Symposium conducted at the 22th Annual Convention of the Japanese Society of Educational Psychology, Tokyo. (in Japanese)

Ohinata, M. (1978, September). Bosei-ishiki no hattatsu ni kansuru kenkyu 2 [Development of maternal consciouness and attitudes 2]. *Proceedings of the 20th Annual Convention of the Japanese Society of Educational Psychology* (pp. 140–141). Yokohama: Yokohama Kokuritsu Daigaku. (in Japanese)

Ohtoh, Y. (1969). *Koyarai* (2nd ed.) [Child-rearing]. Tokyo: Iwasaki Bijutsu Shuppan. (in Japanese)

Prime Minister's Office. (1976). *Katei to sei-shonen chosa* [A survey on family and children]. Tokyo: Author. (in Japanese)

Prime Minister's Office. (1981). *Kokusai hikaku: Nippon no kodomo to hahaoya* [Japanese children and their mothers: International comparison]. Tokyo: Ohkura-sho Printing Office. (in Japanese)

Sasaki, Y., Takano, A., Ohinata, M., Jimba, Y., & Serizawa, M. (1982). *Ikuji Neurose* [Child-rearing neurosis]. Tokyo: Yuhikaku. (in Japanese)

Shinagawa, N. (1981). Waga-kuni ni okeru 10-dai no mikonsha no ninshin to kongo no mondai-ten [Current status of unmarried teen-age pregnancy in Japan and its problems]. *Sexual Medicine, 8*(3), 12–17. (in Japanese)

Shinano Kyoiku-kai. (1900). *Komori kyoiku-ho* [Training method of baby-sitters]. Tokyo: Kinko-do. (in Japanese)

Suzuki, T. (1980). 3 kagetsu-ji o motsu hahaoya no ikuji fuan ni tsuite [Anxieties about baby-care among mothers with 3-month-age babies]. *Shoni Hoken Kenkyu, 38,* 493–499. (in Japanese)

Takashima, H. (1910). *Jido o utaeru bungaku* [Literary works on children]. Tokyo: Rakuyo-do. (in Japanese)

Wagatsuma, H. (1981). Child abandonment and infanticide: A Japanese case. In J. E. Korbin (Ed.), *Child abuse and neglect: Cross-cultural perspective.* Berkeley: University of California Press.

Watanabe, K. (1971). *Kashiwazaki nikki* (abridged) [Diaries written at Kashiwazaki]. In K. Tanigawa et al. (Eds.), *Nippon shomin seikatsu shiryo shusei* (Vol. 15). [Collections of records of Japanese folk life]. Kyoto: San'ichi Shobo. (Originally written between 1839-1848) (in Japanese)

Watanabe, Y. (1884). *Komori kyoiku-ho* [Training method of baby-sitters]. Tokyo: Fukyu-sha. (in Japanese)

Yanagita, K. (1932). *Nippon no densetsu* [Japanese legends]. Tokyo: Shun'yo-do. (in Japanese)

7 Psychobiology of Maternal Behavior in Rats, Selected Other Species and Humans

Alison Fleming
Gail Orpen
Erindale College, University of Toronto

All mammalian species require some form of parental behavior to insure the growth, development and survival of the offspring. The type of parental behavior shown will depend on the type of social unit into which the young are born, on the mobility and developmental maturity of the young at birth, and the number of offspring born at one time (see Gubernick, 1981). The present chapter discusses the maternal behavior of only a few mammalian groups. In fact, as the vast majority of studies of the physiology of parental behavior—including our own work--have used laboratory rodents, the primary focus of this review is on mechanisms controlling maternal behavior in the rat.

Despite the clear limitations in generalizing mechanisms from one species to another, use of animals in the study of the physiology of behavior has many obvious advantages over the use of humans. For one, it permits experimental and causal analyses. For example, rather than simply determining the correlation between levels of hormones and levels of some behavior, as one can do in humans, use of animals permits one to establish the direct involvement of particular hormones in behavior, by observing the changes in behavior after first surgically removing the endocrine organ or organs which secrete the hormone and then by replacing or injecting the suspected hormone back into the animal. Moreover, if one is interested in the role of different parts of the brain in mediating a particular behavior one does not have to rely on studying individuals sustaining accidental brain damage or devise ingenious, but indirect, methods to determine, for instance, which side of the brain is doing the processing; instead one can actually assess changes in behavior after the production of localized damage or electrical or chemical stimulation of specific brain regions. In order to determine the importance of different brain regions in ongoing behavior, one can also monitor different brain regions for ongoing electrical activity, blood flow patterns or uptake patterns of radioactively labeled sugars. Use of animals rather than humans also permits greater control over a variety of environmental variables which could mask the role of particular factors in the control of behavior. Thus, it is possible to vary one parameter, like the duration of postpartum exposure to offspring, while controlling for other environmental, social and/or developmental factors.

For these sorts of experimental analyses to have any general relevance, however, it is necessary to study a wide variety of species and note and attempt to account for areas of similarity and difference among them. While generalizability from lower mammals to humans should be done with caution, there are a number of areas, as we shall see, where the animal work has given us valuable hints for a fruitful direction to pursue in our analyses of human behavior.

The first three sections of this review are concerned with hormonal, sensory, and neural mechanisms which control rat maternal behavior. However, where appropriate, we also point out similarities and differences between rats and other mammals. In the final section we describe selected studies which grapple with issues relating to the physiological basis of maternal behavior in humans.

This review includes considerably more of our own work than would be warranted in a balanced review of the literature. We have, however, attempted to at least cite most of the relevant studies by other investigators. For those we have omitted or have given short shrift to, we apologize.

FUNCTIONAL FEATURES OF MATERNAL BEHAVIOR IN THE RAT

The maternal behavior of the laboratory rat involves quite a complicated sequence of behaviors which change as the young develop (Weisner & Sheard, 1933). Rat young are born in an altricial state, in litters of 10 to 15 pups, and are cared for exclusively by the mother. At birth young are hairless and unable to hear or see. They do, however, use contact stimuli, thermal cues and odors when orienting to the mother and attaching to the nipples for sucking (Blass & Teicher, 1980; Hall, Cramer, & Blass, 1977; Porter, 1983). As soon as the young are born, the mother tears off the membranes surrounding the fetuses, eats the placentae and licks off the pups. She retrieves the pups into the nest, reconstructs the nest and eventually adopts a nursing position over the pups (Dollinger, Holloway, & Denenberg, 1980; Rosenblatt & Lehrman, 1963). During the first 10–15 days the mother spends a great deal of time in contact with the pups. After about 2 weeks, when the young are more mobile and begin to eat some solid food, the mother spends more and more time away from the nest (Galef, 1981; Grota & Ader, 1969; Rosenblatt, 1965, 1970; Rosenblatt & Lehrman, 1963) .

Throughout the maternity cycle the mother engages in behaviors that are beneficial both to herself and the young. For instance, during the first 16- to 18-days, rat mothers spend a considerable amount of time licking the pups and, in particular the anogenital region of the pups (Fleming & Rosenblatt, 1974a; Reisbick, Rosenblatt, & Mayer, 1975). This behavior affects the young in a number of ways (Gubernick & Alberts, 1983). Licking by the mother functions to reflexively elicit urination in the pups (Capek & Jelinek, 1956; Ewer, 1968). Without such licking pups will die. Mothers lick male pups more than female pups, which apparently contributes to the differentiation of male sex characteristics (Moore, 1983; Moore & Morelli, 1979). Licking by the mother also provides tactile stimulation to the pups which may facilitate the maturation of the pituitary-adrenal neuroendocrine axis as well as general growth, metabolism and peripheral blood flow (see Gubernick & Alberts, 1983). The mother, in turn, derives considerable benefit by licking pups. The urine contains needed electrolytes (Na^+ and K^+) as well as water and is used to supplement the large fluid intake necessary to maintain the large fluid output associated with lactation (Friedman & Bruno, 1976; Gubernick & Alberts, 1983).

When the pups are displaced from the nest and become cooled, they emit ultrasonic vocalizations that alert the mother, causing her to orient to them and leave the nest in search of them (Allin & Banks, 1970, 1972; Brewster & Leon, 1980a, 1980b). Once she locates the pups she retrieves them back into the nest and reconstructs the nest around them. The nest and pup huddle created by the mother helps the pups retain their body heat and reduce oxygen consumption by exposing less body surface to the ambient temperature (Alberts, 1978a, 1978b). In addition, by placing pups together in the nest, mothers can nurse all the young at the same time.

When mothers initiate a nursing bout, they enter the nest and adopt a crouch posture over pups, lowering the nipple line onto the pup huddle. Once stimulated into activity pups readily attach to suckle. On occasion the mother actively helps pups to attach by pulling them towards her ventrum and exposing more of the ventral surface to them. The mother's nursing behavior occurs in bouts whose duration seems to be regulated by changes in the mother's own body temperature (Jans & Leon, 1983; Leon, Croskerry, & Smith, 1978; Woodside & Leon, 1980; Woodside, Pelchat, & Leon, 1980). When the mother is on the pups, her core temperature rises. When body temperature reaches a certain point, she leaves the nest site and returns only when cooled down. By means of such a behavioral mechanism, the mother is able to regulate her own body temperature as well as provide warmth and nutrients to the pups.

Finally, with the birth of a litter, the mother rat undergoes changes in her responses to other animals. A formerly docile female rat can become quite aggressive to other rats introduced into her home cage (Fleming & Luebke, 1981), and especially if the pups are present at the time (Erskine, Barfield, & Goldman, 1978b; Erskine, Denenberg, & Goldman, 1978a). This increased aggressiveness seems to last for a limited period during the early postpartum days and probably functions to protect the young from predators when the young are most vulnerable. When strange rats are permitted access to the nest containing a litter of young pups they frequently attack and kill the pups (Erskine et al., 1978a; for species comparisons see Svare, 1981, and Ostermeyer, 1983).

As can be seen by these few examples, the rat mother's behavior is well adapted to the needs of her young as well as her own needs. In order to promote health and survival of the young, the mother must be appropriately attuned to her pups (their odor, temperature changes, vocalizations, and movements); she must have access to the maternal response repertoire and finally, she must be motivated to express this pattern when pups first appear at parturition.

In the following review of the literature, we describe the variety of mechanisms which are involved in promoting these characteristics. We discuss the role of the different pregnancy and parturitional hormones, where in the brain they act and how they influence the female's responsiveness to different sensory cues from the pups.

SENSITIZATION OF MATERNAL BEHAVIOR IN THE VIRGIN RAT

In contrast to the behavior of the new mother, the virgin female who has not undergone pregnancy and parturition does not respond maternally when provided with newborn pups. Instead, she engages in a pattern of approach-sniff and withdrawal sequences which suggest a certain ambivalence towards the pups (Rosenblatt, 1967). After a number of such approaches, the female either stays at a distance from the pups or, on occasion, conceals them under nesting material or cannibalizes them (Fleming & Luebke, 1981). However, the intact virgin female can be induced to respond maternally if presented daily with a newly fed litter of foster pups and left in their continuous presence (Rosenblatt, 1967). Although initially somewhat hesitant and timid (Stern, 1977; Stern & MacKinnon, 1976), after a number of days of maternal experience the behavior of the intact virgin is in many respects quite similar to the behavior of the newly parturient female (Fleming & Rosenblatt, 1974a). She retrieves displaced pups into the nest site, licks them, and eventually builds a nest. Although she does not lactate, she adopts a nursing posture over the pups.

This procedure, known as pup-induction or sensitization (Noirot, 1972) has been used as a way of determining the effects of different manipulations on maternal responsiveness. Thus, the number of days of exposure to pups required for a virgin animal to begin showing pup-retrieval, pup-licking, and nursing behavior reflects the degree of underlying maternal responsiveness in that animal. For example, the new mother has a latency of zero days to become maternal (less than 1 day) while virgin animals have an average latency of between 5 and 15 days in different laboratories, depending on the strain, cage size, pup age, sensitization procedure, etc. Manipulations (hormonal, neural, environmental, etc.) applied to virgin animals which increase or decrease their latencies to respond maternally may be thought of as agents which decrease or increase the sensitivity of the maternal substrate and thus the maternal motivation or responsiveness. Accordingly, as the underlying responsivity increases, the animal requires less stimulation by pups before it will express the behavior. With decreasing responsivity, the duration of necessary pup exposure increases.

HORMONAL CONTROL OF MATERNAL BEHAVIOR IN THE NEW MOTHER

Hormones and Maternal Behavior in Rats

Although the behavior of the new mother and of the virgin who has been sensitized to respond maternally through pup stimulation looks quite similar (Fleming & Rosenblatt, 1974a), the underlying mechanisms differ. While hormones are not involved in the virgin sensitization (Rosenblatt, 1967), it is clear that the rapid appearance of maternal behavior at the time of the birth is mediated by the pattern of hormonal changes occurring pregnancy and, especially, during the last few days before parturition.

During the first 2 weeks of the rat's 22-day pregnancy, progesterone from the ovary is the predominant hormone, rising gradually and peaking on day 16 (Morishige, Pepe, & Rothchild, 1973; Orpen, Fleming, & Wong, in preparation; Pepe & Rothchild, 1974); during the last week preceding the birth and the first appearance of maternal responding, progesterone declines and ovarian estradiol rises, peaking near parturition (Shaikh, 1971; Orpen, Fleming, & Wong, in preparation). At this point the ratio of estrogen to progesterone undergoes a reversal. Pituitary prolactin and oxytocin also rise at the end of pregnancy (Pepe & Rothchild, 1974). The relative contributions of these different hormones in initiating the heightened responsiveness at birth has been thoroughly investigated and reviewed elsewhere (Rosenblatt & Siegel, 1981; Rosenblatt, Siegel, & Mayer, 1979). In discussing the role of hormones, we will, therefore, not be exhaustive, but will only describe representative studies which demonstrate the involvement or lack of involvement of a particular hormone or pattern of hormones.

Hormones and the Onset of Maternal Behavior in the New Mother

Role of Estrogen and Progesterone. The first clear demonstration that blood borne factors are involved in the onset of maternal behavior in the rat was made by Terkel and Rosenblatt (1968, 1972). Different groups of virgin rats whose ovaries had been removed (a procedure called ovariectomy or OVX) were tested with foster pups after being cross-transfused with blood from females who were either 24 hours prepartum, 30 minutes postpartum, or 24 hours postpartum. These groups were compared to groups of virgins receiving blood from other virgin females. Virgins exposed to blood taken within 30 minutes of parturition, became maternal more rapidly than all the other groups (in general, within 15 hours), indicating that the hormonal milieu close to the time of parturition is sufficient to stimulate rapid maternal behavior and that the prior pregnancy changes are not essential. It should be noted, however, that these animals did not respond *immediately* (with zero latency), indicating that their physiological condition was somewhat less effective than that found normally in parturient animals.

Two subsequent studies by Moltz, Lubin, Leon, and Numan (1970) and Zarrow, Gandelman, and Denenberg (1971) indicated that estrogen, progesterone, and prolactin may be the relevant hormones in this end-of-pregnancy effect. These two studies used the same basic strategy of injecting OVX virgin female rats with a regimen of hormones designed to simulate the hormonal events of pregnancy. Animals received a series of daily estrogen and progesterone injections, with progesterone terminating two days prior to estrogen termination, (thereby mimicking the end-of-pregnancy shift in the estrogen/progesterone ratio) and with prolactin introduced at the end of the series. Both groups of investigators found that, in comparison to rats receiving a variety of control injections, females receiving this temporal sequence of hormones responded maternally to foster pups significantly more rapidly, usually within 35 to 40 hours of pup exposure.

In order to determine which of the three hormones is essential to the facilitation of maternal responding, Moltz et al. (1970) studied additional groups of females who received various combinations of the hormones. They found that the groups receiving estrogen and progesterone, omitting the prolactin, also showed a facilitation, although the effect was not as strong as when prolactin was included. Omitting either estrogen or progesterone blocked the facilitation almost entirely.

Most of the research concerned with the role of estrogen and progesterone in the initiation of maternal behavior at term has been concerned with separating out the effects of the end of pregnancy progesterone decline or withdrawal from those of the estrogen rise in stimulating maternal responsiveness. To summarize this rather complicated series of studies done primarily at the Institute of Animal

Behavior, Rutgers, by Harold Siegel, Robert Bridges, Jay Rosenblatt, and their colleagues, there is good evidence that (1) estrogen alone can be effective in stimulating a short latency maternal behavior (Siegel & Rosenblatt, 1975b), but that (2) the effectiveness of this steroid is considerably enhanced following a period when progesterone has been high and has subsequently declined (Bridges, 1981, 1984; Doerr et al., 1981; Krehbiel & LeRoy, 1979; Siegel & Rosenblatt, 1975a, 1977, 1978a). However, a period of progesterone stimulation alone followed by its withdrawal, without a subsequent estrogen rise, has either no effect (Doerr et al., 1981), or only small effects (Moretto, personal communication). In contrast, a period of combined estrogen and progesterone stimulation followed by their withdrawal does produce some facilitation (Bridges et al., 1978; Bridges, 1984). Finally, progesterone, at elevated levels, may inhibit maternal behavior produced by estrogen alone or by the withdrawal of estrogen and progesterone (Bridges, Rosenblatt, & Feder, 1978; Moltz, Levin, & Leon, 1969; Siegel & Rosenblatt, 1975c, 1978a).

These findings indicate that short latency maternal responding witnessed shortly after birth in the new mother is due primarily to the elevated levels of estrogen occurring on the last few days of pregnancy, against a background of declining progesterone. As we shall see, however, the changes associated with earlier stages of pregnancy seem both to increase the underlying maternal responsiveness of the female and to prime the animal to become more responsive to the shift in the progesterone to estrogen ratio which occurs right at the end of pregnancy.

Role of Prolactin and Oxytocin. Although estrogen and progesterone are able to influence other endocrine hormones, their effects on maternal behavior are probably direct and not mediated via other hormones. It is known, for instance, that estrogen stimulates endogenous prolactin release from the pituitary gland (which probably explains the prolactin rise immediately prepartum, Blake et al., 1972; Kalra et al., 1973; Vermouth & Deis, 1974) and that it produces an increase in sensitivity to oxytocin by inducing the production of oxytocin receptors in the uterus (Soloff et al., 1979). A number of studies have been done to assess the role of these hormones in the rapid induction of maternal behavior postpartum. With the exception of a recent study by Bridges (1984), most of the evidence suggested that prolactin plays no role (Lott & Fuchs, 1962; Numan et al., 1977; Rodriquez-Sierra & Rosenblatt, 1977; Stern, 1977). However, Bridges (1984) has recently found that the estradiol and progesterone silastic regimen which is effective in stimulating maternal behavior in the ovariectomized animal, loses its effectiveness if the pituitary is also removed, suggesting that the exogenous estradiol is stimulating the release of prolactin from the pituitary. Replacement with prolactin in this homonally primed hypophysectomized preparation also restores short latency maternal behavior.

The evidence for oxytocin is also conflicting. Using a very responsive strain of rat, Pederson and his colleagues (1979, 1982) found that infusion of oxytocin into the cerebral ventricles in estrogen-primed ovariectomized females induces maternal behavior within 2 hours of exposure to pups in a dose-dependent fashion. Pederson et al. (1979) postulate that normally at the end of the pregnancy, the estrogen rise stimulates the production of oxytocin receptors in the brain and that the oxytocin rise which occurs at the time of parturition is able to act on these receptors to stimulate rapid maternal responding. Using a less sensitive strain, with latencies of 2 to 5 days, as opposed to a matter of hours, Rubin, Menniti, and Bridges (1983) were unable to produce an oxytocin facilitation of maternal behavior. Clearly the role of oxytocin has yet to be resolved.

As to other neuropeptides, a strong case has also been made for a role in maternal behavior for the opioids (for a further discussion of these agents, see Bridges & Grimm, 1982; Bridges & Ronsheim, 1983). The role of other neurotransmitters is less well established (see Bridges, Clifton, & Sawyer, 1982; Hansen, Kohler, & Ross, 1982; Moltz et al., 1975; Steele et al., 1979).

Development of Maternal Responsiveness Across Pregnancy

Although end of pregnancy hormonal changes are able to produce immediate maternal behavior at birth, the underlying state of maternal responsiveness does not come on suddenly (Lott & Rosenblatt, 1969); responsiveness to pups and pup-related cues along with increases in self-licking (Roth & Rosenblatt, 1967), attraction to placenta (Kristal et al., 1981), and nest-building seem to develop gradually over the pregnancy, peak at the time of birth, are maintained for a period after the parturition (even in the absence of pup stimulation) and then decline (Koranyi, Lissak, Tomasu, & Kamaras, 1976; Rosenblatt & Siegel, 1975). This pattern of changing responsiveness is also hormonally mediated.

If pups are presented to females at different stages of pregnancy, starting well before the steep elevations in progesterone and estrogen, one finds that as pregnancy advances, animals become increasingly responsive to pups (Rosenblatt & Siegel, 1975), showing immediate responding 2–14 hours prior to parturition (Slotnick, 1973). In one study done in our laboratory, we presented foster pups to virgins or to animals on days 1, 8, 12, 14, 16 and 22 of gestation. As shown in Fig. 7.1, animals showed somewhat elevated latencies, as compared to virgins, on days 1, 8 and 12 and decreased latencies between days 14 and 22. The reduced responsiveness on days 1, 8 and 12 of pregnancy may be due to the inhibitory effects of the high progesterone levels which characterize this period. Subsequent latency declines over the latter half of pregnancy probably reflect a combination of the cumulative priming effects of the combined estrogen and progesterone stimulation and declining progesterone to estrogen ratios which begins after day 16. Siegel and Rosenblatt (1977) found a similar but more striking pattern when the pregnancy was terminated by hysterectomy (HYST) at

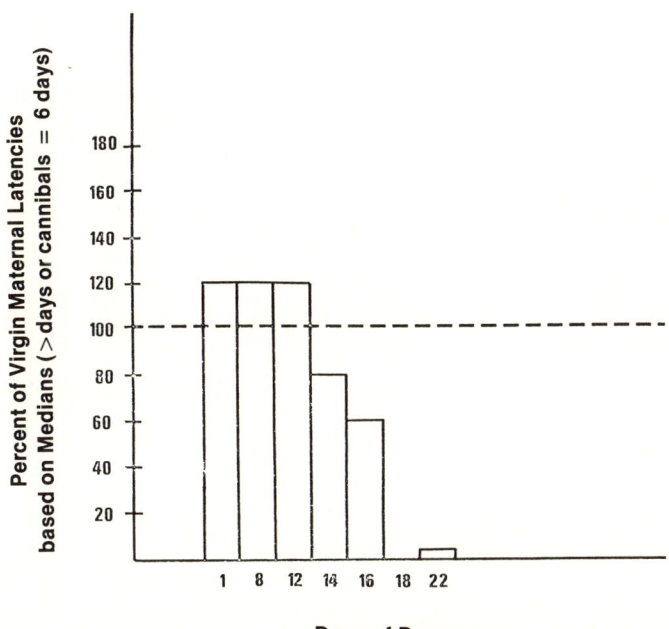

FIG. 7.1. Changes in maternal responsiveness across pregnancy. Groups tested at different stages of pregnancy. Latencies to maternal behavior expressed as percent of virgin baseline latencies. Latencies of 6 days were given to females who did not become maternal during the 5 day test or who cannibalized pups.

different stages. Depending on the stage of pregnancy, this procedure (which involves removing pups along with the uteri) mimics to different extents the hormonal changes normally associated with parturition—a decline in ovarian progesterone, due to the removal of progesterone-stimulating placental factors and a subsequent rise in ovarian estrogen. Pregnancy termination on days 13, 16, and 19 clearly stimulated more rapid maternal responding than that seen in virgins, but termination on days 8 and 10 did not. In an attempt to simulate these same pregnancy and pregnancy-termination effects by exogenous means, Bridges (1984) found that ovariectomized virgin females implanted with silastic capsules containing estradiol and progesterone showed different maternal latencies depending on the length of the period of hormonal stimulation. Durations of 5, 9, 13 and 21 days yielded latencies of 4, 3, 1, and 1 days, respectively.

Although we now have considerable experimental evidence that hormones are important in augmenting maternal responsiveness, in a series of radioimmunoassay studies in which we measured circulating levels of estradiol and progesterone, we have not been able to find a direct correlation within groups between plasma levels of the different hormones and individual latencies to become maternal (Orpen, Fleming, & Wong, in preparation). Thus, animals with shorter onset latencies do not have consistently higher levels of estrogen or estrogen to progesterone ratios than do animals with long onset latencies. These results are not surprising given that each animal was assayed at only one point in time, and it is unlikely that the differences across animals in the level of maternal responsiveness would be reflected in the instantaneous levels of any particular hormone or set of hormones.

Taken together these studies indicate that the effect of the shift in the progesterone to estrogen ratio which occurs normally at the end of pregnancy as well as after surgically produced pregnancy-termination (by HYST), is influenced by the duration of prior hormonal stimulation (Bridges et al., 1977;Siegel & Rosenblatt, 1978a; Stern & MacKinnon, 1976). This steroidal priming seems to involve the cumulative effects of both estrogen and progesterone (see Bridges, 1984; also Doerr et al., 1981) and is reflected in the increasing maternal responsiveness which occurs over the pregnancy prior to parturition. Thus, responsiveness seems to grow during the pregnancy when estrogen levels are not particularly high, to peak at parturition following the decline in progesterone and rise in estrogen and, if pups are removed at parturition, to decline following parturition.

Hormones and the Continuance of Maternal Responsiveness Postpartum

In a study designed to determine how long animals remain maternally responsive following birth if they are prevented from interacting with their pups, we pregnancy-terminated (by hysterectomy, HYST) different groups of rats at the end of pregnancy (a procedure called day 22 HYST), thereby preventing any contact between the female and her pups, and tested for maternal behavior to foster pups 1, 2, 3, 5, 7, 8, 9 or 10 days later. As can be seen in Fig. 7.2, maternal responsiveness remained high (and, therefore, latencies low) during the first 7 days, decreased significantly between days 7 and 9 and reached virgin levels by day 10. If one looks at the proportion of animals retrieving pups on first exposure to pups (as normally occurs at the time or parturition) in the different groups, one finds again that responsiveness is markedly reduced by the 8th day. The percentage of animals retrieving young within the first hour of exposure to pups in groups tested in days 1, 2, 3, 5, 7, 8, 9 and 10 postsurgery are 60, 90, 50, 40, 60, 23, 11 and 6% respectively. Since in this study 13% of control virgin females retrieved on first exposure to pups, an increase in the percentage responding in pregnant groups above that on virgin groups may be interpreted as being due to effects of the prior pregnancy and its termination.

These data indicate that although animals are not immediately as responsive postpartum as they are at parturition, they remain quite responsive to pups for up to a week after the hormonal changes associated with pregnancy-termination; responsiveness begins to wane more substantially by day 8 and is at virgin control levels by day 10. Apparently, responsiveness to pups in the absence of

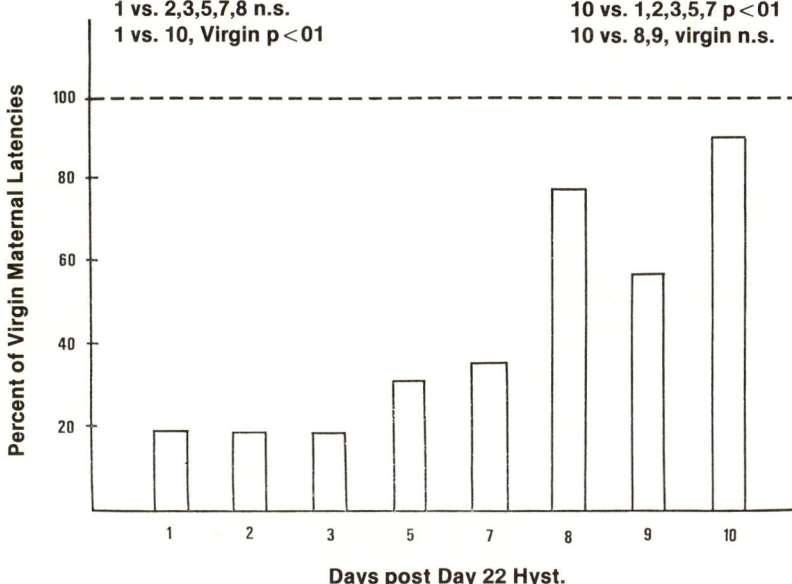

FIG. 7.2. Changes in maternal responsiveness during the postpartum period in different groups pregnancy-terminated (by hysterectomy) on day 22 of pregnancy and tested on different post-hysterectomy days. Latencies to maternal behavior expressed as percent of virgin baseline latencies.

pup stimulation is retained much longer in our strain of rats (Wistars) than in the Sprague-Dawley strain used in an earlier study by Rosenblatt and Lehrman (1963). It should be pointed out, however, that probably different aspects of the maternal pattern are retained for different lengths of time. Smotherman, Bell, Hershberger, and Coover (1978) report, for instance, that a mother rat's normal strong responsiveness to pup ultrasounds drops out as soon as pups are removed, even if she has had some postpartum exposure to the vocalization.

In order to determine whether the sustained maternal behavior is due to the secretion of ovarian hormones following birth or pregnancy termination, we repeated our separation study described above but removed the ovary at the same time as pregnancy-termination on day 22 (day 22 OVX-HYST) and tested animals 7 days later. As can be seen in Fig. 7.3 (hysterectomy day 22 = day 22 HYST), removing the ovary on day 22 at the time of hysterectomy did not prevent a short-latency maternal behavior 7 days later. Both intact and ovariectomized groups had latencies of between 3 and 4 days, which were significantly shorter than control virgins tested 7 days after hysterectomy. These data suggest that ovarian changes following pregnancy termination are not the cause of the elevated responsiveness which persists for 7 days. To support these conclusions, in a recent study in which we measured levels of estradiol and progesterone 2, 7,

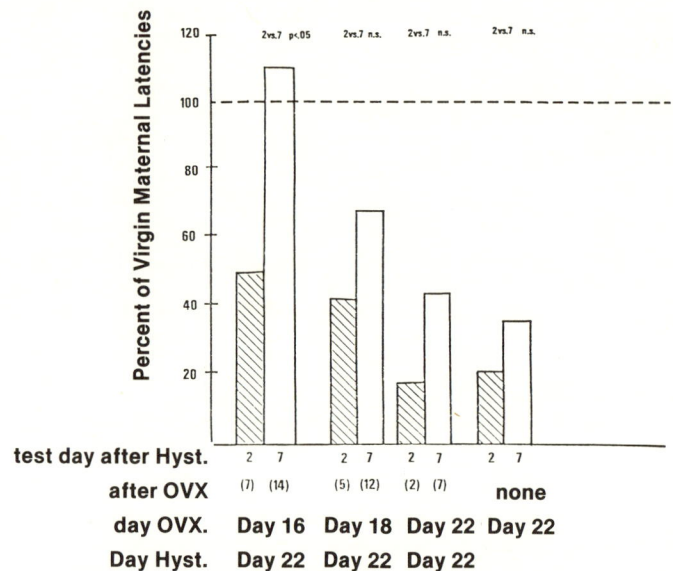

FIG. 7.3. Maternal responsiveness 2 and 7 days after pregnancy termination (by hysterectomy) on day 22 of pregnancy in groups in which the ovary is removed at different stages of pregnancy (on days 16, 18, or 22). Latencies to maternal behavior expressed as the percent of virgin baseline latencies. Hatched bars are animals tested 2 days after HYST. Open bars are animals tested 7 days after HYST.

and 10 days after pregnancy termination (leaving the ovary *in situ*), we found that plasma estrogen and progesterone levels have returned to premating baseline levels by day 7 (Orpen, Fleming, & Wong, in preparation).

In order to determine whether the *pre*partum rise in ovarian estrogen, which we know facilitates the immediate onset of maternal behavior at birth, is involved in the continued responsiveness 7 days after the end of pregnancy, we then removed the ovary on day 16 of pregnancy prior to the rise in estrogen or, in another set of studies, we removed the ovary at the same time as pregnancy termination (by HYST) performed at various points earlier in the pregnancy (on days 8, 12, 14, or 16 of pregnancy). In all cases tests for maternal behavior with foster pups were done either 2 days or 7 days after pregnancy termination.

To briefly summarize our results, and as shown in Fig. 7.3, we found that (1) in contrast to the earlier results of Siegel & Rosenblatt (1977), all groups, *including the early pregnancy groups*, responded maternally 2 days after pregnancy termination more rapidly than did virgins, but only the group which was pregnancy-terminated after the full 22 days of pregnancy (day 22 HYST) responded maternally *immediately*, and (2) the heightened maternal responsiveness witnessed 7 days after pregnancy-termination was seen only in the day 22 HYST group. Groups tested 7 days after pregnancy-termination on day 16 of pregnancy or at earlier stages of pregnancy did not show elevated responsiveness. These data reinforce the earlier findings that two days after pregnancy-termination some facilitation of responsiveness can occur, without a rise in estrogen, but that for *immediate* maternal responding the animal requires a rise in estrogen against a background of declining progesterone. However, 7 days after pregnancy-termination by HYST, only animals hysterectomized on day 22 who had experienced a prolonged 22-day period of combined estrogen and progesterone followed by a progesterone withdrawal and an estrogen rise showed the sustained maternal responsiveness.

In order to confirm that the facilitated responding observed 7 days after pregnancy termination requires more prolonged stimulation by estrogen and progesterone than does responding at the time of hormone termination, we implanted groups of (OVX) virgins with silastic capsules containing estrogen and progesterone or control substances for either 15 or 20 days, and tested for maternal behavior either immediately or 7 days after the end of hormone treatment. In all hormone treated groups the end of the hormone regimen involved a shift in the estrogen to progesterone ratio as normally occurs at the end of pregnancy. At present we have only completed the group receiving 15 days of hormone stimulation.

As shown in Fig. 7.4, the group that showed the shortest onset latencies was the hormone group tested immediately at the end of the hormone period. In contrast, the group which was tested 7 days after hormone termination was no different from control groups. These results confirm our previous observations that the absence of elevated responsiveness seen 7 days after pregnancy termination on day 16 of pregnancy may be due to the absence of a period of combined stimulation by estrogen and progesterone which is greater than 16 days. Confirmation of this hypothesis awaits the results of groups who received silastic capsules for the full 20 days and who were tested 7 days later.

Hormones and Maternal Behavior in Other Mammals

Although the vast majority of studies on the hormonal control of maternal behavior have been done using the rat, other rodent species have also been studied. Despite wide differences in gestation length and hormonal state, most of these species undergo an increase in maternal responsiveness across pregnancy. Both hamsters and gerbils who in the nulliparous state normally cannibalize young, show sharp decreases in cannibalism during late pregnancy (Elwood, 1977; Richards, 1966; Siegel, Clark & Rosenblatt, 1983; Wallace et al., 1973). Hamsters and mice also show a late pregnancy increase in maternal responding (Noirot & Goyens, 1971; Richards, 1966; Siegel, Clark & Rosenblatt, 1983; Siegel & Greenwald, 1975). A similar pattern of augmented maternal responsiveness has also been found in rabbits (Zarrow, Sawin, Ross, & Dennenberg, 1962b), ewes (Poindron & Le Neindre, 1979, 1980), as well as two primate

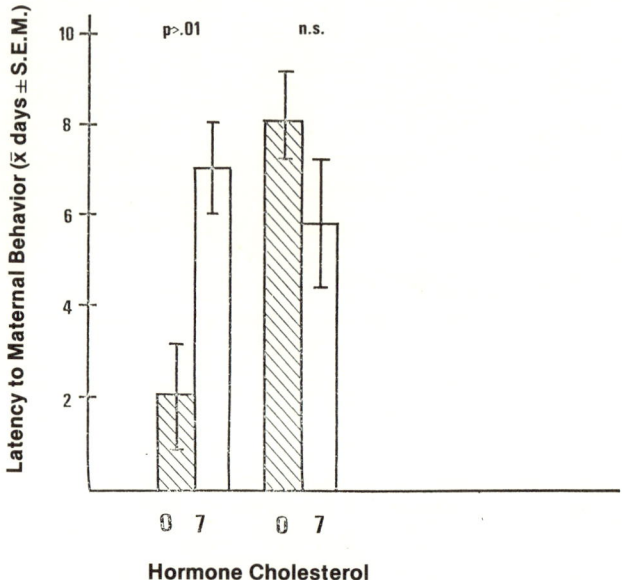

FIG. 7.4. Maternal responsiveness 0 and 7 days after termination of hormone silastic treatment in virgin groups receiving 15 or 22 days of hormone stimulation. Cholesterol is the control condition. Hatched and open bars represent animals tested 0 and 7 days after HYST, respectively.

species, the rhesus monkey (Tinkelpaugh & Hartman, 1932) and the squirrel monkey (Rosenblum, 1972).

Despite the cross-species similarity in the gestational development of maternal responsiveness, the hormonal mechanisms mediating these changes as well as the onset of responsiveness postpartum are probably quite different. Hamsters, for instance, have a short (16 day) gestation period and do not undergo a shift in the P/E ratio near term. Instead levels of both hormones decline with parturition (Baranczuk & Greenwald, 1974). It has not been possible to induce maternal behavior in the hamster by means of injections of E and P and there is some evidence that the decline in these hormones is not necessary for the appearance of the behavior. Administration of E and P starting on the day before parturition does not block parturition or maternal behavior postpartum (Siegel & Greenwald, 1975). Similarly, in the gerbil, who has a longer pregnancy, injections of progesterone initiated preterm and extended 7 days after pregnancy termination do not block maternal behavior (Wallace, 1973). In the rabbit, pregnancy termination after the midpoint of pregnancy (Ross, Sawin Zarrow, & Denenberg, 1963; Zarrow, Farooq, & Denenberg, 1962a; Zarrow, Sawin, Ross, & Denenberg, 1962b; Zarrow, Sawin, Ross, Denenberg, Crary, Wilson, & Farooq, 1961) or prolonged exogenous treatment with progesterone followed by a shift in the E to P ratio (Zarrow et al., 1962a, 1962b) produces rapid onset of hair loosening and nest building, suggestive of the pattern in rats, but not in hamsters and gerbils. With the exception of 1 or 2 brief nursing bouts (each approximately 5 minutes in duration) this maternal nestbuilding behavior is the normal maternal response shown in rabbits. However, the stimulatory effects of E (Zarrow et al., 1961, 1962a, 1962b) on nestbuilding in the rabbit are probably mediated by estrogen-induced release of prolactin (Anderson et al., 1971; Zarrow et al., 1971). To date, no one has induced the maternal nursing posture in rabbits with hormones.

In mice, who have a pregnancy hormone profile similar to rats but who are normally very maternally responsive without hormones, low levels of estrogen in connection with high levels of progesterone synergize to stimulate augmented nestbuilding (Lisk, 1971; Lisk et al., 1969). Voci and Carlson (1973) found prolactin implanted directly into the brain also stimulates nestbuilding, as well as retrieval responses. Taken together these results with rodents suggest that the ovarian progesterone either alone or in connection with E, may play a role in maternal nestbuilding. For most of these rodent species the role of hormones in the pup-directed maternal behaviors have not yet been worked out.

The hormonal mechanisms regulating maternal behavior have also been extensively investigated in the ewe. Interestingly, this species shows a pregnancy hormone profile which is similar to the rat, with declining levels of P and rising levels of E prepartum. Poindron and Le Neindre (1980) found, for instance, that both a long (36 day) or short (7 day) term regimen of P and EB injected into nonpregnant nulliparous ewes produced maternal licking, bleating, vocalization, and acceptance of suckling by young in over ½ the ewes tested. Although single injections of both P & E are effective in facilitating responsiveness in young, estradiol seems to be most effective.

Ungulates, like the rat and some other rodent species, have a postpartum sensitive period. If the ewe does not have contact with her lamb immediately after parturition, she will reject its advances to her. If, on the other hand, she has a very short period of contact with the lamb within the first few hours, she will continue to accept her lamb and will reject alien young (see section below). In the case of ungulates the postpartum period of heightened sensitivity is very short but can be extended by hormone stimulation. If ewes are separated from their lambs at parturition and tested for responsiveness after 0, 4, 12, or 24 hours, one finds that by 12 hours only 25% of the females will accept lambs. If ewes are induced to lamb by being injected with estradiol, 60–75% are willing to accept lambs at 12 and even 24 hours, suggesting that estrogen not only initiates responsiveness but can extend the period of responsiveness. Estrogen-induced prolactin does not seem to be involved in the effect since E, in combination with a prolactin-blocker, does not prevent the extension of the period of sensitivity.

SENSORY CONTROL OF MATERNAL BEHAVIOR IN THE NEW MOTHER

Taken together, the studies reviewed in the previous section indicate that females become maternally responsive to young at the time of parturition and sustain a certain level of responsiveness for a short period after the birth, as a result of hormonal changes which occur over the pregnancy and near term. However, it is clear that mothers continue to care for their young long after the hormonally induced responsiveness is known to have waned, indicating that some other mechanism assumes control of the behavior. We now know that experiences acquired while interacting with pups during the hormonally mediated period of heightened sensitivity function to maintain and modulate the female's subsequent responsiveness to pups throughout the lactation period.

In order to discuss which aspects of the mother-young interaction are important for maintaining and modulating maternal responding during the lactation period, it may help to first define the classes of stimulus effects involved. These can be divided into three groups. In the first are the sensory stimuli emanating from the pups which directly activate or guide the female's behavior. In the second group are varieties of pup stimulation, such as suckling, which affect the mother's physiology. In the third group are what might be termed psychological stimuli—the actual performance of the behaviors (physically and cognitively) and the satisfying of a motivational drive (cf. Gallistel, 1980).

Changes in Mothers and Pups During Lactation

The quality of the different pup stimuli changes during the lactation period as the young develop. For instance, newborn rat pups are pink and hairless; they move very little and at that, mostly by wiggling in one place. They emit audible squeaks if disturbed, and make ultrasonic calls when they are cold, out of the nest, or being handled by their mothers (Bell, 1974; Noirot, 1972). They respond to the mother if she is nearby, burrowing under her, searching for nipples and suckling, but they do not seem to perceive her from a distance. The pups grow very rapidly and become more mobile, so that by day 5 they can rapidly crawl across the cage. However, their movements are not yet fully co-ordinated or directed. Ultrasonic calling in response to cold stress increases in the first few days after birth and then declines as the pups develop homeothermic control (Noirot, 1968); tactually elicited ultrasonic signals are highest right after birth and decline over the first 10 days (Bell, 1974).

By the end of the first 2 weeks, the pups have a full coat of hair, are well co-ordinated and directed in their movements and approach the mother efficiently. In addition, they stop making the ultrasonic calls, and leave the nest to explore and to eat and drink. By weaning, around day 21 postpartum, the pups are fully capable of independent existence.

Thus, over the lactation period the auditory, visual and tactile characteristics of the pups change drastically. The changes in pup behaviors (as well as in sensory characteristics) during the postpartum period clearly result in changes in the kind of care they require. Associated with changes in the pups are changes in the mother's behavior. In the first few days after parturition, the female is very attentive to her young, spending as much as 80% of her time in the nest with them. The number of times the mother approaches her pups in a 24 hour period remains constant for the first 15 days of lactation, but the length of time she remains with them gradually decreases (Leon, Croskerry, & Smith, 1978). Furthermore, the amount of time the mother spends in licking, retrieving, and nursing the pups in the first 15 minutes after the return of her pups, following a brief separation also remains constant for the first 12 days of the lactation period (Fleming & Rosenblatt, 1974a). After day 12, however, she begins to spend less and less of this 15 minute period retrieving and nursing the pups, although the time spent ano-genital licking remains high (Reisbick et al., 1975). She also begins to withdraw from the pups and to actively reject them after day 12 (Reisbick et al., 1975). An added feature, seen in hamsters (Richards, 1966) and gerbils (Elwood, 1981) is the suppression of their usual tendency to cannibalize during the first ten days of the postpartum period, and its subsequent reappearance after day 11.

Proximal Influences on Behavior

The question that we, and many others, have been trying to answer is to what extent the changes that we have just described in maternal behavior during the postpartum period are inherent and internal to the female, and to what extent they follow changes in the young. We will discuss in more detail the evidence concerning the influence of young on maternal responding during two segments of the postpartum period—during the first two weeks, and during the subsequent period of decline of maternal responding.

First Two Postpartum Weeks

The intense attention which a newly parturient female directs to her young is in sharp contrast to the attitude of a virgin female (in rats, Weisner & Sheard, 1933; hamsters, Rowell, 1960; Siegel, Giordano, Mallafre, & Rosenblatt, 1983; gerbils, Elwood, 1981; and sheep, Alexander, 1960). We have seen that these differences in behavior are the result of hormonal differences between the two types of animal. However, in addition to the hormonal influences, stimulation by the young also influences the behavior of the new mother. Numerous studies suggest that this influence is multi-sensory; that no single sensory system is necessary for the expression of maternal behavior, but that each may be, to some extent, unique in its influence. We will consider the role of each sensory system separately.

Olfaction. Herrenkohl and Rosenberg (1972) and Fleming and Rosenblatt (1974b) both found that naive primiparous females who had their olfactory bulbs removed prior to parturition were still able to retrieve and care for their pups. A quantitative comparison with intact control animals revealed that the bulbectomized females differed from the controls in only two behaviors. The bulbectomized females spent less time licking and nursing the pups, although they spent the same amount of time in the nest (Fleming & Rosenblatt, 1974b). Similarly, Beach and Jaynes (1956) found that lactating female rats, made anosmic after several days of experience with pups retrieved as rapidly as intact females. However, if the pups were confined in wire mesh cages which allowed olfactory, and presumably auditory, cues only, the anosmic females were much less able than intact females to discriminate between empty cages and cages containing pups. Furthermore, intact lactating females showed altered behavior toward pups which had altered olfactory (as well as tactile, thermal and auditory) characteristics. Pups coated with oil of lavender were retrieved, but only after the nontreated pups. These perfumed pups also were cannibalized more than the normal pups. In contrast, freshly killed pups (which smell normal, but have altered auditory and visual characteristics) were retrieved only slightly more slowly than intact pups, and were less subject to cannibalism. Pups completely coated in vasoline were more slowly and less completely (64%) retrieved, and stimulated much more cannibalism than did untreated or perfumed pups. Chilled, freshly killed pups were even less effective as a retrieval stimulus and were more likely to stimulate cannibalism—72% of them being eaten and only 7% being retrieved. It seems that increasing loss of olfactory, thermal and tactile stimulation from the pups results in increasing deficits in retrieving pups, but it is difficult to separate these three factors in these studies.

Smotherman et al. (1978), testing in a Y-maze on days 6–15 of lactation, found that although the females showed no preference for pup odor vs. no odor, the preference which they showed for ultrasounds over no sounds (discussed in the next section) was enhanced when pup odor was also present. Thus, even though mothers do not show a preference for pup odors when odors are presented in the absence of other cues, the odors are able to modulate the female's responsiveness when other cues are present.

In contrast to effects in primiparous animals, removal of olfactory function in virgins has quite striking effects. Following olfactory deafferentiation, cannibalistic virgin hamsters or avoidant virgin rats actually begin to carry and retrieve pups (Marques, 1979; Fleming & Rosenblatt, 1974b, 1974c; Fleming, Vaccarino, Tambosso, & Chee, 1979). Thus, in naive rat and hamster virgins, pup odors initially elicit avoidance or cannibalism, effects which are prevented by events during pregnancy. The fact that both late-pregnant rats and hamsters become responsive to foster pups before their own pups are born suggests that one way hormones may be acting is to change the female's olfactory response to pups (see below, p. 34).

Unlike rats and hamsters, in mice pup odors seem to be an important facilitating influence on maternal responding. Virgin mice are very responsive to pups and about 80% of them will begin to care for pups within 5 minutes of first exposure (Noirot, 1969a) and in this sense, they resemble newly parturient rats. Removal of the olfactory bulbs in virgin or in naive pregnant mice causes them to either cannibalize their young or not to care for them (Gandelman, Zarrow, Denenberg, & Myers, 1971). However, fewer mice exhibited cannibalism after bulbectomy at later stages of lactation, suggesting that odor loses its importance as a motivating stimulus (Gandelman, Zarrow, Denenberg, 1971). In summary, the odor of young continues to modulate the female's behavior for up to day 15 of lactation, even when she does not show a specific preference for those odors.

Audition. It appears that, like olfaction, in the rat audition is not essential for the initiation of maternal behavior. Herrenkohl and Rosenberg (1972) found that pregnant female rats who were deafened shortly before delivery cared for their pups, although they were slower to retrieve and sniff the pups. The results reported by Beach and Jaynes (1956) on retrieval of warm freshly killed pups also suggest that auditory stimulation is not essential for maternal responding.

However vocalizations do modulate the quality of the mother's response. Allin and Banks (1972) showed that 50% of lactating females would leave the nest and their pups in response to the playing of a recording of pup ultrasounds. As mentioned earlier, in studies by Smotherman et al. (1978), lactating females showed a marked preference for ultrasounds from a 10 day old pup when these were paired, in a Y-maze, with either no sounds or with pup odors. This preference for the pup ultrasounds remained fairly constant from day 6–15 of the lactation period, when the Y-maze alternative was an "empty" goalbox, although this may have been an artifact of having used ultrasound from pups of only one age. When odor was the Y-maze alternative to ultrasound, the females showed an even greater preference for ultrasound. This preference decreased gradually over the 10-day test period, suggesting that the influence of pup odor in augmenting the female's response to ultrasound is greater earlier in the lactating period. Because the ultrasound stimulus used in these experiments was always the same regardless of the stage of lactation at which the tests were done, it is more difficult to discuss changes in the effects of ultrasounds over the lactation period.

Bell et al. (1973) varied the strengths of ultrasonic calling by varying the duration of cold exposure in neonatal pups and observed females' responses to these ultrasounds. The differences in stress level produced provided three groups of pups which emitted the different levels of ultrasonic calling. The handled controls did not vocalize; moderately cold stressed pups vocalized very intensely in the initial few minutes and then quieted down; the severely cold stressed group of pups called less initially but continued calling for much longer. The mothers of the moderately stressed group of pups began to attend to the pups after the initial, intense calling had declined, and then nursed more than did either the controls or the mothers of the severely stressed pups. The mothers of the severely stressed pups spent less time grooming and nursing the pups than did the mothers of the moderately stressed pups, but did not differ from the handled controls. However, these mothers showed greater agitation and avoidance of the pups, which may have been due to the longer duration of the ultrasonic calling.

From these data, it appears that pup vocalizations function to attract and alert the female to the presence of the pups and so facilitate retrieval, but that intense ultrasonic calling inhibits maternal responding in which case the behavior is only initiated after the calling has begun to decline.

Vision. Vision is also not essential for the appearance of maternal behavior. Herrenkohl and Rosenberg (1972) found that blinded female rats were able to retrieve and care for their pups. In fact, they spent more time licking their pups than did the corresponding control animals, and more time nursing than did either deafened or anosmic animals, suggesting that vision may actually interfere with maternal responding. Similarly, Beach and Jaynes (1956) found that blinded females were more attracted to pups in the wire cages than were intact animals. One aspect of the visual stimulus, movement of the pups, is only an influence on day 5 of lactation. Smith and Berkson (1973) offered mothers a mixed group of four awake and four anaesthetized pups for retrieval on days 2, 5, 10 and 15 of lactation. They played a background of white noise to mask any vocalizations. The mothers showed a preference for the active pups on day 5 only.

Touch. Beach and Jaynes (1956) showed that anaptic female rats still retrieved their pups as quickly as did controls; but they also found that a number of treatments which one would expect to interfere with the tactile and thermal (as well as olfactory) properties of the pups also seriously interfered with retrieval. As mentioned before, females showed impaired responses to pups coated with vaseline or collodion, or killed and chilled. Kenyon, Cronin and Keeble (1981) found that perioral anaesthesia, which rendered the snout anaptic, impaired retrieving for one hour. These investigators noted that the females often attempted to retrieve the pups by pushing them with their noses, indicating that the retrieval impairment probably resulted from motor difficulties rather than any deficits in the female's motivation to respond.

We have been discussing the sensory factors which influence the female's initial behavior with her young at the onset of maternal responding and for the following 10 days. The evidence suggests that, in rodents, odor and vocalizations from the young attract the female's attention. Once she has approached them, the thermal and tactile qualities of the pups also influence her willingness to retrieve them. Vision, on the other hand, seems to interfere with approach and retrieval. Since the female initiates pup-caring bouts at a constant rate over this period, it appears that the stimuli which she receives and their effect on her form an integrated, constant response. Since pup ultrasonic calling is known to decline during this time, and both the attraction to pup odors and the potentiation of ultrasound effects by pup odors also declines, one might speculate that the basic responsiveness of the female to pup stimuli increases during this time.

In the next section, we discuss the gradual fading of maternal behaviors in the last week before weaning.

The Response Decline

After about postpartum day 12, females begin to be less responsive to their pups. This is shown by a decrease in the nurturant behaviors shown and an increase in rejecting behaviors (Reisbick, Rosenblatt, & Mayer, 1975). These changes seem to be related to changes in the pups as they grow and develop. Reisbick et al. (1975) found that if the females were given younger pups (4–8 days), they continued to demonstrate a high level of responsiveness, even though their responsiveness to the older pups, that they were living with, was fading.

Rowell (1960) and Swanson and Campbell (1981) found a similar phenomenon in the hamster. Late in lactation the performance of maternal behavior also declines; however, given an appropriate stimulus, the motivation to behave maternally can be demonstrated to still be present. Thus, Swanson and Campbell (1981) left 3-day-old pups with female hamsters who were 13 days postpartum. These females continued nursing and caring for their foster young until day 38 of their lactation period, when the pups were 28 days old. A control group of females stopped nursing their own litter at 28 days. The investigators found that both behavioral weaning and estrous cycling were dependent on the age of the pups, but that milk and prolactin release were dependent on the stage of the lactation period. Similarly, using gerbils, Elwood (1979) found that replacing older pups with younger ones prolonged the pup caring period and prevented the return to cannibalism usually seen in gerbils after day 11. This suggests that the older pups have either lost the stimulus characteristics which elicit maternal responding or have developed characteristics which inhibit maternal responding or which promote cannibalism. Whichever of these is the case, it is clear that although the actual caring behaviors have faded away, the underlying basic responsiveness is still present. We discuss this phenomenon and some of the factors involved in it in the next section.

Enduring Sensory Influences on the Maintenance of Maternal Behavior

Influences in Rats

Effects of Maternal Experience. In the previous section, we discussed the importance of experience with pups for continued maternal responding. However, it is not necessary for animals to be with pups throughout the postpartum period to maintain maternal responsiveness. In fact, a relatively brief period of contact with young results in a prolongation of maternal responsiveness without further pup contact. This has been demonstrated most clearly by a number of studies of postpartum separation of the dam from her pups. Thus, Rosenblatt and Lehrman (1963) found that females who were separated from their young for 4 days, immediately after parturition, responded at virgin levels when their pups were returned. However, maternal responding remained at high levels following a similar 4-day separation given after several days of experience with the pups. Fleming (1972) and Fleming and Rosenblatt (1974a) found that postpartum females allowed 1½ days of pup contact were more responsive, 2 weeks later, than females allowed no contact with their pups.

Bridges has done a series of studies to define more closely the nature and timing of the necessary pup experience in rats. In his first study, Bridges (1975) found that as little as 1–1½ hours of pup contact was sufficient to maintain the female's responsiveness 25 days later and this was true even when the ovaries were removed or the nipples cauterized to prevent milk removal. Bridges (1977) also found that parturition itself was not necessary for this maintenance of responsiveness, since females who had their young removed by Caesarian section and were then given a short exposure to pups, were still responsive 25 days later. In a third study, Bridges (1978) determined that this re-establishment of maternal behavior is not subject to progesterone inhibition as is the initial hormonal induction of maternal responsiveness. He tested the response of females to pups during a second pregnancy, 30–36 days after their last contact with their first litter, at a time during pregnancy when progesterone is high, and found them to be rapidly maternal.

From these studies, it appears that during the initial contact with young the mother undergoes permanent or semipermanent changes in her responsiveness to young, a process which we refer to as "consolidation."

We were interested in extending these studies to more precisely define both the nature and the necessary duration of the female's experience with her young. We removed pups by Caesarian section on day 22 of pregnancy (day 22 HYST), and allowed the females varying amounts of exposure to four 0–1 day old foster pups, presented on the day following surgery. The six exposure conditions given were (1) *NE*—no exposure, (2) *NR*—no retrieval, (3) *R*—exposure to pups until retrieval only, (4) *R+15*—retrieval and 15 minutes of interaction with pups, (5) *R+30*—retrieval and 30 minutes of interaction with pups, and (6) *FE*—full exposure and interaction with pups for a full 24 hours. All groups were tested 9 days later (10 days after HYST) for maternal behavior toward foster pups.

As shown in Table 7.1, the two groups interacting most with the pups—Groups *FE* and *R+30*—both had significantly shorter median latencies and a smaller proportion of females who failed to respond to the pups within 10 days of

TABLE 7.1
Effects of Limited Maternal Experience During the First Postpartum Day on Maternal Behavior Ten Days Later

Groups	N	Latency to Maternal Behavior [Median (IQR)]	% Maternal in 24 Hrs	% Not Maternal in 10 Days
No Exposure	25	8(3.25-10)†	6	35
Exposure but no Retrieval	11	7(1.75-9.25)Δ	18	36
Retrieval Only	9	6(1.25-10)≡	22	33
Retrieval + 15 min	9	4(0.25-8.25)ϕ	44	33
Retrieval + 30 min	11	1(0-2)†Δ≡ϕ	64	0
Full Exposure	17	.1(0-1)†Δ≡ϕ	76	6

†Δ≡ϕ = $p < .05$

testing, than did all other groups and did not differ from one another. On these two measures, the other four groups also did not differ from one another.

Groups *FE* and *R+30* also had a higher proportion of females responding to the pups within 24 hours of the beginning of testing than did Groups *NE* and *NR*, the two groups with least interactive experience. However, neither Groups *FE* and *R+30*, nor Groups *NE* and *NR*, differ from the two intermediate groups given exposure, Groups *R* and *R+15*.

These results suggest that 15 minutes of caring for pups is not sufficient to maintain the female's postpartum responsiveness for 10 days but 30 minutes is, and an increase to 24 hours of contact does not further increase her responsiveness. The percentage of animals in each group becoming maternal within 24 hours of the presentation of pups seems to be graded across groups, with increasing amounts of exposure resulting in increasing numbers of animals behaving maternally within 24 hours of pup presentation.

Effects of Exposure to Distal Pup Cues. To follow up these initial studies we then went on to determine whether distal sensory stimuli, in the absence of an actual interaction, is able to maintain long term responsiveness. In our first study we compared the effectiveness of varying kinds of experience with distal and proximal stimulation from the pups on the maintenance of maternal behavior (Cummings & Fleming, 1974). We removed pups by Caesarian section on day 22 of pregnancy (day 22 HYST) and for 7 days exposed females to pups enclosed in small boxes which were placed in the female's cage. Pups were rotated daily and replaced by a freshly-fed litter. For different groups boxes differed in opaqueness and in presence or absence of perforations such that some females were exposed to (1) a 2-cue condition—pup vocalization and odor but no visual or tactile cues, (2) a 3-cue condition—pup vocalization, odor, and visual cues but no tactile cues, (3) an all-cue condition—pups in cage but not in box so female could interact with them, and (4) a no-cue condition—no pups but an empty box. In tests for maternal behavior undertaken at the end of the preexposure phase on day 8, we found no significant differences in overall induction latencies among the no-cue, 2-cue and 3-cue conditions, while the all-cue animals who interacted with pups were maternal immediately. Although an analysis of overall latencies indicated that simple exposure to distal cues has no enduring effects on maternal responsiveness when one looks at the proportion of animals in each group responding maternally on each day, there is some indication of an effect of distal cues. For instance, there was a tendency for the 3-cue condition to produce a bimodal response. When compared to the no-cue or 2-cue conditions, a significantly higher proportion of the 3-cue animals responded maternally within 5 days. However, animals in the 3-cue condition who didn't respond rapidly had exceedingly long latencies of up to 32 days.

These data suggest that actual interaction with pups, in which the female is able to perform behaviors and receive multiple input from the pups, is considerably more effective in sustaining maternal behavior than is mere exposure to distal cues from pups. However being exposed for a prolonged period to pups without actually interacting with them can facilitate subsequent responding in some animals but seems also to inhibit it in others. An explanation for these paradoxical effects may be that the prolonged 8-day pre-exposure during the postpartum period was acting to stimulate the release of prolactin and progesterone which, as indicated earlier, can, in fact, be exerting inhibitory effects on the behavior (Jakubowski & Terkel, 1980; Koranyi, Phelps, & Sawyer, 1977; Stern & Siegel, 1978).

According to this formulation, in animals who start out with a higher level of responsiveness prior to pup exposure, the progesterone-mediated inhibitory effects of preexposure and the few days of induction exposure are not sufficient to counteract the facilitatory 'sensitization' effects of the exposure. However in less sensitive animals who require considerably more days of induction exposure to become maternal, progesterone is released in greater quantities thus intensifying the inhibitory effects, and consequently animals take considerably longer than controls to become maternal. Tests of this hypothesis using ovariectomized (and adrenalectomized) animals (and thus non progesterone-producing animals) are presently underway. Using a somewhat different preexposure paradigm, Stern (1983) found effects consistent with ours: a strong long term effect of prior interactive experience and, if one looks at the proportion of animals responding early in the induction phase, a weak effect of distal stimulation.

To get a better handle on what being preexposed to distal cues from pups does to females who are not able to retrieve, lick, or contact pups, we undertook another study in which females received only 24 hours of preexposure to pups which would not be long enough to produce significant elevations of progesterone or, at the very least, would permit an interval between exposure and testing sufficient for progesterone levels to decline. Also, rather than placing pups in boxes, in this study pups were placed underneath a perforated plastic mound in the female's nest area so she could smell, see and hear pups and even lie over them on top of the mound, but not touch, lick or nurse them.

Pregnant females were Caesarian delivered on day 22 of pregnancy (day 22 HYST). Three groups of day 22 HYST were subjected to different pup exposure schedules. The exposure conditions were: (1) *NE*—No pup exposure; (2) *PE*—Partial pup exposure: Four 0–1 day old pups were placed in a cluster under a perforated plastic mound in the bottom of the female's cage for 24 hours beginning 24 hours after Caesarian section; and (3) *FE*—Full pup exposure: Four 0–1 day old pups were placed in a cluster in the front of the female's cage and she had full access to them for 24 hours, beginning 24 hours after Caesarian section. During the exposure period, pups were put into the appropriate cages in the morning and the female's behavior toward them was recorded in spotchecks during the day and on the following morning before the pups were removed. On the 10th day after Caesarian section, all females were tested for maternal responding to foster pups.

As shown in Table 7.2, we found that the no exposure (NE) and partial exposure (PE) groups had longer latencies to respond maternally than did the full exposure (FE) group, but did not differ from each other. These latency data agree with results reported by Stern (1983), and seem to suggest that exteroceptive sensory stimuli play no role in consolidating maternal responsiveness. However, if one compares the percentage of females in each group becoming maternal within 24 hours of initial presentation of pups, quite a different picture emerges. When compared to the no exposure condition, partial exposure to pups significantly increased the proportion of females responding to pups within 24 hours in tests undertaken 10 days after Caesarian delivery, although full exposure resulted in a still greater proportion of short latency responders. Partial exposure also decreased the rate of cannibalism from 32% (in the nonexposed group) to 5%. Thus, it appears that sensory exposure by itself can promote consolidation of maternal responsiveness in some animals, although full exposure to pups with the opportunity to care for them is considerably more effective.

Collectively, the results from these experiments answer some of our questions concerning the role of the pups in maintaining the level of responsiveness in their mothers. It is clear that a very short period of full interaction with pups (Group FE) is sufficient for maintained maternal responding for 10 days and much longer, but that distal sensory stimuli (Group PE) must be present for much longer. However, if distal stimuli are present for too long in animals prevented from responding maternally when hormonally prepared to do so, an inhibition of responsiveness can occur.

Hormone-Experience Interactions. As we have seen certain kinds of experience with pups during the period of hormonally-mediated elevated sensitivity can promote long term retention of responsiveness. However, the amount or kind of experience necessary to produce maintenance probably depends on whether the experience is acquired under hormonal priming or not.

In an early study Fleming (1972) compared reinduction latencies 2 weeks after acquiring maternal experience in primiparous females and in pup-induced virgins. In the experience phase, both groups had 1 to 2 days during which they responded maternally. On reinduction both groups took approximately 3–4 days to respond maternally. However, virgin reinduction latencies were shorter than initial induction latencies.

These data suggested to us that experience effects are equivalent regardless of the reproductive state during which the experience was acquired. However, in a more recent study, in which groups were reinduced 25 (rather than 14) days after the initial experience, (and in which, unfortunately, the highly responsive virgins were excluded from the analyses), Cohen and Bridges (1981) report that maternal experience during the postpartum period (of either 1, 4, or 9 days duration)

TABLE 7.2
Effects of Distal Exposure to Pups During the First Postpartum Day on Maternal Behavior Ten Days Later

Groups	N	Latency to Maternal Behavior [Median (IQR)]	% Maternal in 24 hrs	% Not Maternal in 10 Days	% Cannabalizing
Full Exposure (24 hrs with pups)	17	1(0-1)†,Δ	76	6	—
Partial Exposure (24 hrs under platform)	20	5(1-10)†	42	21	5
No Exposure	25	8(3,25-10)Δ	6	29	32

†,Δ = p<.05

produces a more profound retention at 25 days than comparable experience obtained by virgin rats following pup-sensitization. In both groups, one day of maternal experience was as effective as 4 or 9 days of experience. However in all experience conditions, primiparous animals had shorter reinduction latencies than did virgins.

In a series of studies we are now doing to follow up these results using ovariectomized virgins, we are also finding that 30 to 45 minutes of maternal experience obtained following a period of priming by exogenous P and E (by the silastic route) results in greater facilitation of maternal behavior 10 days later than does the same amount of maternal experience acquired under nonhormonal control conditions. Based on preliminary findings such as these, it seems that hormones not only exert direct effects on the onset of maternal responsiveness but that they may also heighten the long term retention of that maternal experience.

Although hormones may act to facilitate experience effects, as we have seen, experiences obtained over longer periods of time which are not acquired under hormones may also have enduring effects. In fact, in a recently completed study we have found that 20 days of exposure in the breeding room to lactating females and their pups occurring between days 1 and 20 of life but not between days 45 and 65 facilitated the onset of a number of maternal behaviors during sensitization tests in the adult virgin (Moretto, Paclik, & Fleming, in preparation). The fact that a similar exposure regimen in the adult animal is without substantial effect suggests that like the hormonally primed animal, the infant and adolescent animal may be especially susceptible to being influenced by early odor and/or social experiences.

Influences in Other Species

Work in mice and sheep suggests that sensory stimuli may also be important in these animals. Noirot (1969a, 1970) showed that exposing virgin female mice, which are already highly responsive, to auditory and olfactory stimuli (a live pup in a perforated metal box) increased maternal responding to a dead pup, a suboptimal stimulus. In a second study, Noirot (1969b) showed that not only were distal sensory stimuli from the pups able to increase the subsequent responsiveness of the mice, but that different sensory modalities augmented different components of the maternal behavioral response. Thus, female mice exposed to pup vocalizations only spent more time nest-building, while those exposed to pup odors only spent more time licking pups. In rodent species which cannibalize pups in the nonpregnant or lactating state, experience being maternal does not permanently suppress pup cannibalism. Elwood (1980) reports, for instance, that female gerbils return to cannibalizing pups after their own pups reach 11- to 29-days-of-age. Also, in the hamster, 24 hours of maternal experience is not sufficient to suppress cannibalism and sustain maternal responsiveness for 10 days (Siegel & Greenwald, 1978).

In sheep and goats, distal sensory stimulation does play a role in the consolidation of maternal responsiveness (Hersher, Moore, & Richmond, 1958; Poindron & Le Neindre, 1980; Poindron, Martin, & Hooley, 1979). Poindron and Le Neindre (1980) allowed different groups of parturient ewes different kinds of experience with lambs for the first twelve hours postpartum. In the subsequent testing, all groups which had been able to smell the lambs during the first twelve hours accepted them, while those ewes which had not been able to smell the lambs rejected them regardless of the presence or absence of other distal stimuli such as sight and sound from the lambs. Thus, the lamb odor appeared to be necessary for the maintenance of the ewe's responsiveness, but since odor was never the only stimulus presented it may not be sufficient. The rejection of alien lambs by ewes has been found to result from an olfactory label on these lambs that is acquired from their own mother (Gubernick, 1980). However, the lambs in Poindron and LeNeindre's study had not been with a ewe and so presumably were unlabelled. Thus, perhaps the odor of the lamb itself influenced the basic responsiveness of the ewe while the odors acquired in association with a ewe result in a specificity of the expression of that responsiveness. Of interest in the light of these findings on odor is a recent study showing that human mothers are able to identify clothing from their own baby by odor, within 20 to 40 hours of delivery, in a situation where the authors felt there was little transfer of odors from the mother to the baby (Porter, Cernoch, & McLaughlin, 1983).

WHAT HORMONES MAY BE DOING TO PROMOTE MATERNAL RESPONSIVENESS

In the first four sections of this chapter we have discussed work that we and others have done which attempts to unravel the contributions of hormonal and sensory factors in the regulation of maternal behavior. In this next section we discuss the variety of ways in which hormones may be acting to promote maternal responsiveness at birth, by reducing the animal's natural timidity in new situations and by increasing the animal's attraction to pup related odors.

Hormonal Effects on Fear-Mediated Responses

In order to determine the variety of ways hormones may be acting to promote maternal behavior at the time of parturition we undertook a series of studies designed to assess other ways in which parturient and virgin animals may differ which could contribute to the differences in their initial responses to pups. The maternal aggression literature shows that a formerly docile and timid animal can become quite aggressive to intruders which threaten the nest site (Erskine et al., 1978b) and that this difference in agonistic tendency between the postpartum and virgin animal suggests a more general difference in emotionality between the two types of animals.

Our first indication that such a difference exists was in our observations of differences in avoidance responding in virgin and postpartum females, when exposed to pups. If pups are placed into the nest site of the virgin female, initially she will actively move her nest site, preferring to sleep in a quadrant removed from the pups. Over successive days she comes to avoid pups less, until one day she stops avoiding pups, and within a day or so she starts to respond maternally to them. The new mother, in contrast, never avoids pups (Fleming & Luebke, 1981).

In order to demonstrate that this difference in avoidance reflects a more general difference in emotionality between the virgin and postpartum animal, we then went on to compare the two types of animal on a variety of non pup-related tasks designed to measure timidity or fear in a novel environment (Fleming & Luebke, 1981). As shown in Table 7.3, on all these tests the postpartum animal was less timid than the virgin animal. She emerged more rapidly from a familiar area into the open field, she ambulated more while in the field, she ambulated more in central as opposed to peripheral squares, and she investigated more.

These differences between virgin and parturient females in their fear-mediated responses is very likely due to hormonal differences between the two kinds of animal and, as with maternal behavior, estradiol is probably a primary contributor. A number of investigators have reported that animals who were in estrus and who, therefore, have elevated levels of estrogen, show less fear on a number of different tasks than do animals in other stages of the estrous cycle (Archer, 1973; Gray, 1971; Ikard et al., 1972; Quadagno et al., 1972).

To determine whether the hormonal regimen which facilitates maternal responsiveness also reduces emotionality and, furthermore, whether these same hormones also produce heightened interest and responsiveness to the odors of pups, we implanted ovariectomized-hysterectomized virgin female rats with silastic capsules containing the Bridges (1984) 15 day hormone regimen, described earlier. Animals were tested on days 15 and 16, 48, and 72 hours after the removal of P and also 7 days later (when, under this hormonal regimen, animals are no longer maternally responsive). All animals received two test periods daily on two consecutive days. Each test period consisted of an emergence test followed by an open field test. On one test period each day nest material taken from the nest of a 2–4 day postpartum lactating female and her pups was placed into a jar which was placed close to the opening into the field; on the other test, clean shavings were presented. As shown in Fig. 7.5, animals receiving the hormone regimen (at both 0 and 7 post-hormone) had a significantly reduced latency to emerge into the open field, ambulated more while in the field, and ambulated more in the central, as opposed to the peripheral, squares.

Using these traditional measures of emotionality, animals treated with hormones were, then, less timid than control animals. The fact that hormone depen-

TABLE 7.3
Performance of Nulliparous and Parturient Female Rats on a Number of Fear-Mediated Tasks

Groups	N	Emergence Latencies (sec) (Mean+SEM)	Squares Crossed in Open-Field in 8 min period (Mean+SEM)	Proportion of Squares Crossed, Located in Middle of the Field (Mean+SEM)	Rearing Frequency (Mean+SEM)	Frequency of Defecations and Urinations (Mean+SEM)
Nulliparous females	24	645.8 ± 62.0*	87.9 ± 10.9*	7.2 ± 1.5*	13.7 ± 2.2*	1.8 ± 0.4
Parturient females	9	224.3 ± 78.6*	137.3 ± 10.2*	13.5 ± 2.6*	24.6 ± 2.8*	1.9 ± 0.9

*Differences between Nulliparous and Parturient groups significant ($p < 0.05$).

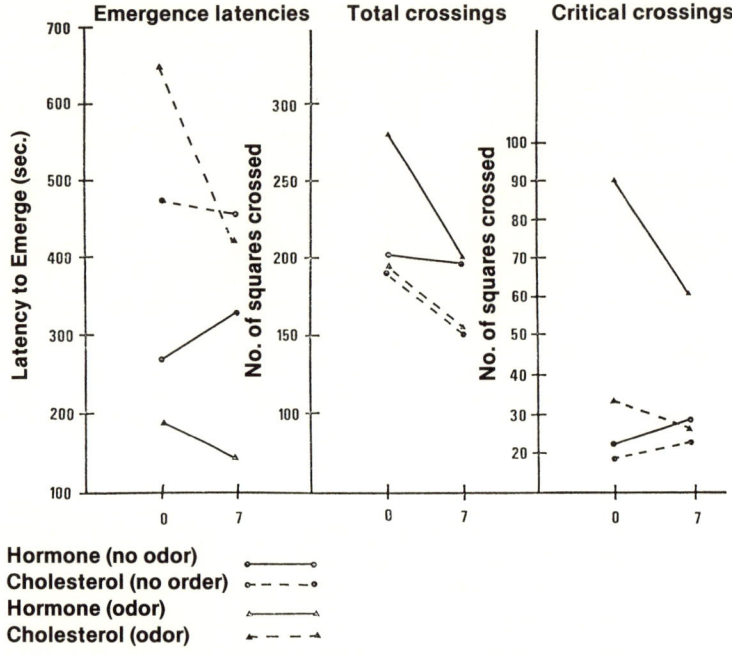

FIG. 7.5. Latency to emerge, total number of crossings and total number of crossings into critical area around odor source in hormonally treated groups tested 0 and 7 days after termination of 15-day silastic hormone regimen.

dent differences were not found for the number of critical squares traversed or frequency of grooming, contacts with the nest material or rearings indicates that group differences were not simply because the hormone-treated animals were more active in general.

Hormonal Effects on Responses to Pup Odors

In addition to promoting decreased emotional behavior and increased maternal responsiveness to pups, combined stimulation by estrogen and progesterone also seems to produce a greater responsiveness to the odor of pups (as shown in Fig. 7.5). In our open field study we found very strong odor and odor x hormone interaction effects. Animals in the pup odor condition crossed more total squares, more central squares and proportionately more squares in the critical area around the nest material than did those in the neutral odor condition. During odor trials animals also showed a high frequency of rearings and contacts with the nest material. Thus, odor of pups stimulated more activity and more investigatory behavior in all groups. However, in all cases, the odor effects were stronger in the hormone treated groups, yielding highly significant odor x hormone interactions for most of the ambulation measures indicated above, as well as emergence latencies. Of still greater interest are the findings that although no differences between 0 and 7 were found for many of these behaviors when odors were not present, when pup odors were present, hormone-treated animals tested on day 0 ambulated more into the area containing the odorants and into the center of the field than did hormone-treated animals tested on day 7. In these analyses, cholesterol groups either showed no differences, or showed the opposite pattern, yielding significant odor x hormone x interval interactions.

Based on these results it seems that hormones (1) reduce the animal's timidity and (2) increase the animal's interest in pup, as opposed to neutral, odors. Unlike our findings for maternal behavior, hormone-treated animals are equally responsive in the open field 0 and 7 days after hormone treatment when pup odors are not present. However, when pup-odors are present, hormone treated animals are much more responsive on day 0 than on day 7, suggesting that although hormones are able to sustain for a 7-day period, reduced levels of overall timidity (as reflected in emergence and open field scores), they are not able to maintain the markedly elevated levels of responsiveness to the odor of pups. Although reactivity to pups is still higher on day 7 in hormone than in cholesterol animals, it has declined considerably from the day 0 levels. Our findings are consistent with the findings reported by Bauer (1983), in which both late pregnant and postpartum primiparous females, but not virgins, show an elevated attraction to lactating nest odors, an effect which Bauer believes is hormonally mediated.

Why the Virgin is Not Immediately Maternal

Taken together, the emotionality and odor attraction results suggest that one of the possible reasons that the maternally inexperienced virgin animals take so long to respond maternally to foster pups is because they find the pups and other associated odors, which are new and unfamiliar, to be quite aversive and, being quite neophobic, they thus avoid pups for a period. This avoidance permits distance between the female and the pups and thus prolongs the period of contact required for sensitization of the behavior to occur. According to this view one of the effects that hormones may be having in the new mother is to decrease the female's fear of the pups as well as to make the pups more attractive, so that animals do not go through an avoidant phase and can therefore be sensitized to be maternal more rapidly. This hypothesis is consistent with Terkel and Rosenblatt's findings of a direct relationship between the size of the cage in which virgins are tested and their onset latencies (Terkel & Rosenblatt, 1971). Females placed with pups in a small cage such that they could not avoid pups become maternal considerbly more rapidly than those housed with pups in a very large cage.

NEURAL CONTROL OF MATERNAL BEHAVIOR

Where in the brain do these sensory influences exert their effects? Are brain sites which respond to sensory cues the same or different from sites which are activated by hormones? In this next section we review the evidence which suggests that the same neural systems are involved in sensitization in virgins and in the hormonal induction in postpartum females.

Many different brain areas and pathways have been shown to have an influence on maternal behavior in the rat. In comparing studies on the role of a particular neural structure or system in the control of maternal behavior, attention should be paid to (1) mode of induction of the behavior (whether hormonally mediated in the parturient animal or through sensitization in the virgin), (2) the stage of the maternal behavior cycle the animal is in (whether in the early stages at the time of first onset of the behavior or after a number of days of experience, during the maintenance phase), (3) the parity of the animal (whether the animal has had prior experience being maternal with prior litters), and (4) what aspect or feature of the behavior is affected.

Structures which have been implicated in the control of maternal behavior may be divided into 3 groups based in part on their anatomical proximity to one another and in part on their functional similarities (see Fig. 7.6). Included among the limbic system structures are (1) the cingulate cortex-hippocampal-septal group, which are interconnected with one another via the fimbria/fornix and dorsal fornix fiber systems, (2) the olfactory-amygdala-bed nucleus/stria terminalis-medial preoptic (MPOA) group, which are interconnected primarily by the lateral olfactory tracts (main and accessory) and the stria terminalis (ST), and (3) a third group of structures consisting of the medial preoptic area-anterior hypothalamus (MPOA-AH) and the midbrain, including the medial forebrain bundle (MFB) and more lateral fiber systems.

Cingulate-Hippocampal-Septal Control of Behavioral Sequencing

The first group of structures, the cingulate cortex, hippocampus and septum are similar in that they are located in a dorsal position in the forebrain, they lie in close proximity to one another, are interconnected and they do not show sensitivity to, or contain receptors for, any of the steroids (estradiol or progesterone) or neuropeptides (opioids or oxytocin) which are believed to activate maternal behavior. Thus, one would not expect these structures to influence the hormonally-mediated onset of behavior. Lesions of the cingulate cortex (Slotnick, 1967; Stamm, 1955), the dorsal hippocampus (Kimble et al., 1967) and the septum (Fleischer & Slotnick, 1978) produce similar effects on the maternal behavior seen at parturition in the postpartum rat. In each case animals have normal

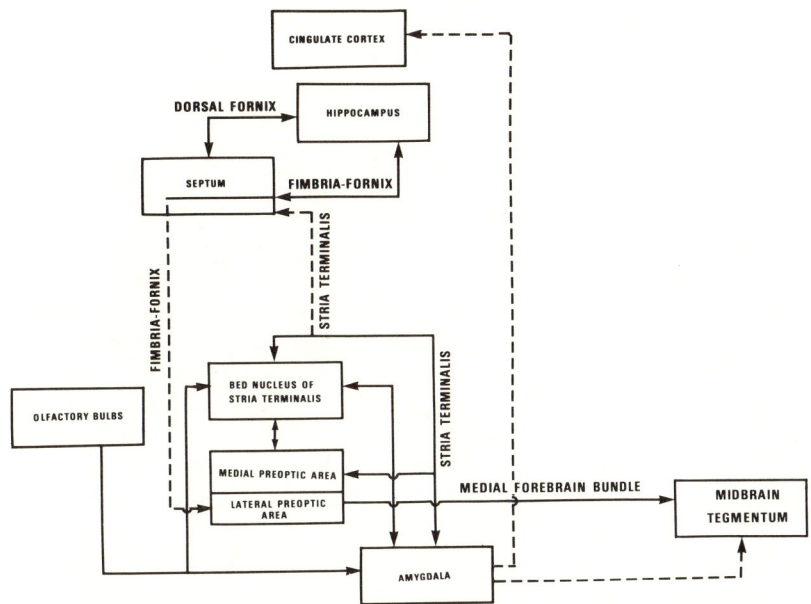

FIG. 7.6. Schematic diagram of the anatomy relevant to the expression of maternal behavior in rats. Three distinct groups are emphasized: (1) the cingulate—hippocampal—septal group, (2) the medial preoptic MFB-tegmental group, and (3) the olfactory—amygdala bed nucleus—medial preoptic group.

pregnancies and give birth normally to healthy litters. Moreover, animals seem quite interested in the pups and motivated to respond to them; they care for the pups in appropriate ways, but the performance is disorganized. Thus, they retrieve pups, but deposit them at multiple sites and fail to group them. Nestbuilding and nursing behaviors are also disorganized or absent. A similar disruption results from these lesions in sensitized virgin females who still become maternal through pup exposure, but once maternal, show disorganized responses.

These data suggest that following cingulate, hippocampus and/or septal lesions, the "motivational" onset mechanisms are intact and can be influenced by hormonal or by sensory stimulation, but some aspect of the spatial or sequential execution of the behavior once it appears is disrupted. Whatever the nature of the deficit, there is some, albeit disputed, evidence that the same behavioral deficits can also be produced by leaving the septum and the hippocampus intact, but deafferenting them by means of damage to the pathways which interconnect the dorsal hippocampus and the septum (Terlecki & Sainsbury, 1978). However, considerably more severe deficits have been found following complete transection of the fimbria/fornix (Steele & McCann, 1980; Steele, Rowland, & Moltz, 1979). Whether the discrepancy between the two fimbria studies results from differences in the two studies in the degree of damage sustained by the fimbria or in the precise location of the damage or in some other design differences between the two studies is not known.

Medial Preoptic Control of Maternal Responsiveness

In contrast to the structures described above, the medial preoptic area and its interconnections seem to be critical to both the onset and maintenance of maternal behavior; damage to the medial preoptic area bordering on the anterior hypothalamus (MPOA-AH) prevents the hormonally-induced onset of complete maternal behavior in the parturient female, prevents the sensory-induced onset in the virgin female and eliminates the maintenance of the behavior in the experienced lactating animal (Jacobson et al., 1980; Miceli, Fleming, & Moretto, 1983; Numan, 1974).

Although the MPOA is clearly critical to the full expression of maternal behavior (and, as we shall see, can be activated to produce the behavior by estradiol), the effects of lesions to this area can also be produced by the disruption of fiber systems interconnecting the MPOA with extra-hypothalamic structures. Knife-cuts above, in front of, or immediately behind, the MPOA which transect fiber systems interconnecting the MPOA and other limbic and forebrain structures do not severely disrupt the expression of maternal behavior in the postpartum animal. However, parasagittal knife-cuts between the MPOA and the LPOA which transect medial-lateral connections between the MPOA, the medial forebrain bundle (MFB) and more lateral projecting pathways disrupt the onset and the maintenance of maternal behavior in the postpartum animal (Franz, 1981; Miceli, Fleming, & Malsbury, 1983; Numan & Callahan, 1980; Numan et al., 1977) as well as the onset in the virgin animal (Miceli, Fleming, & Malsbury, 1983). Parasagittal knife cuts situated more laterally, leaving intact connections between the MPOA and the MFB but transecting laterally projecting pathways, disrupt the initiation of maternal behavior and retrieval in virgin and postpartum animals, although some postpartum animals still engage in nursing, pup licking and nestbuilding (Miceli, Fleming, & Malsbury, 1983).

These data are consistent with the findings of Franz (1981), which suggest that the connections between the MPOA and the MFB are essential for nestbuilding and may be involved in nursing behavior but that retrieval behavior is mediated by pathways which do not project through the medial forebrain bundle (MFB). Although there is ample evidence that lesions of the MPOA and knife cuts lateral to the MPOA disrupt the onset of the complete pattern of maternal behavior in both hormonally-primed parturient females and sensitized virgin females, some interesting differences do emerge, which may be due to differences in the hormonal condition of the two types of animal. A number of studies report that lesions or knife cuts to the parturient female completely eliminate retrieval responses but in some animals nursing responses continue to occur (Jacobson et al., 1980; Numan & Callahan, 1980) when the pups initiate them by crawling to the mother's nest site and pushing themselves under the female. This pattern is in marked contrast to the virgin animal who rarely shows crouchng behavior following MPOA lesions or mediolateral knife cuts (Fleming & Miceli, 1983; Miceli, Fleming, & Malsbury, 1983). While it is possible that these differences are due to differences in the precise lesion location or size in the different studies, it may also be that progesterone withdrawal and/or estrogen present in the parturient or hormonally primed hysterectomized animal also function to promote a greater willingness on the part of the female to be in contact with pups. Once in contact, they passively adopt a nursing or crouch posture, if sufficient pup stimulation is present. As indicated previously, virgins, on the other hand, are rarely willing to permit such contact, but instead move away from pups (Fleming & Luebke, 1981).

Brainstem Structures and Motor Control

Efferents from the MPOA project either directly or via synapses in the lateral hypothalamus to the substantia nigra (SN), the ventral tegmental area (VTA), and to lower brainstem structures (Conrad & Pfaff, 1976; Maeda & Mogenson, 1980; Phillipson, 1979, Swanson, 1976). The SN and VTA are both associated with motor and sensorimotor function and may well be involved in the execution of the active components of maternal behavior, retrieval and nestbuilding (see Numan & Nagel, 1983). Numan and Nagel (1983) found that bilateral lesions of the substantia nigra on day 4 postpartum disrupt all components of maternal behavior for a 4 day period, as well as producing abnormal levels of stereotyped behaviors. Based on a number of follow-up experiments, these investigators believe that the deficits are due to a disruption of a maternal behavior system mediated by MPOA-SN pathways, rather than due to a general motor disability mediated by connections of the SN with other motor sites. Although projections to (or through) the SN seem to be involved in the expression of maternal behavior, bilateral lesions of these nuclear groups do not mimic entirely the effects of MPOA lesions. Animals with MPOA lesions do not show recovery of function, as do animals with SN lesions. As Numan and Nagel (1983) point out this discrepancy may occur because some of the relevant fibers are spared and can take over the function of the destroyed fibers or that the control of the behavior may involve other projections from the MPOA to sites deeper in the brainstem. This interpretation is consistent with the observation that lesions of the ventral mesencephalic tegmentum (Gaffori & LeMoal, 1979) induce cannibalism in postpartum animals. This in fact, seems to be the case. In a recent paper, Numan and Smith (1984) found that bilateral lesions to the VTA or unilateral lesions to the VTA and contralateral knife cuts transecting connections between the MPOA and VTA completely and permanently disrupted maternal retrieving and nestbuilding in postpartum lactating animals.

Alternately, as suggested by Miceli and Malsbury (1982), the MPOA fibers projecting laterally into the substantia innominata or the amygdala, and not descending in the MFB, may be involved. This latter interpretation is supported by the studies of Franz (1981), which also found a recovery of function in primiparous females sustaining unilateral MPOA cuts and contralateral MFB cuts, which again suggests the relevant MPOA output may entail more than its descending MFB projections.

Olfactory-Amygdala and Inhibition of Maternal Responding in Virgin Animals

While the MPOA system may be involved in the animal's motivation to respond maternally and the brainstem in the translation of that motivation into motor responses, another system seems to be implicated, through its inhibitory influences, in preventing the virgin animal from expressing maternal behavior when it encounters foster pups.

This system, which functions to interconnect olfactory-limbic- and MPOA systems involves the main and accessory olfactory bulbs, the cortical and medial nuclei of the amygdala, the stria terminalis, the bed nucleus of the stria terminalis, and the final projection sites in the MPOA (see Fig. 7.6).

In a series of studies done in our laboratory over the past few years we have been studying the functional neuroanatomy of this system. A number of aspects of this circuit make it a good candidate for an involvement in the regulation of maternal behavior in the rat. First, it can be directly influenced by odor input from the pups, which, as discussed above, may be important for the initiation and/or expression of maternal behavior in the rat and in a wide variety of other mammalian species. Also, it has been implicated in the control of other hormone-dependent species-characteristic behaviors (e.g., sexual behavior in the male hamster; Lehman et al., 1980; Powers & Winans, 1975; Winans & Powers, 1977), as well as in the modulation of affect, which can influence the expression of these species-characteristic behaviors. It is made up of nuclear groups which take up and bind estradiol (Pfaff & Keiner, 1973) and groups which synthesize the opioids (Uhl, Kuhar, & Snyder, 1978; Wardlaw, Thoron, & Frantz, 1982). Finally, each structure within this circuit is reciprocally interconnected with the MPOA and with brainstem mechanisms (Baras & Pay, 1980; Berk & Finkelstein, 1981; Conrad & Pfaff, 1976a; Hopkins, 1975; Krettek & Price, 1978; Turner & Knapp, 1976).

In the first set of studies in the series, we assessed the effects on the onset of maternal behavior in postpartum and virgin animals of removing the olfactory function (by olfactory bulb removal or by temporary disruption of olfactory receptors), and thus, the animal's ability to smell the odor of the pups. Since virgins require considerable sensory input to respond maternally, while the hormonally-primed animal does not, we predicted that the postpartum animal would be minimally affected by the procedure, while the virgin would show either prolonged latencies or a complete absence of maternal responsiveness to pups.

While our predictions with regard to the postpartum animal were borne out, our predictions regarding the virgin were completely incorrect. Instead of taking longer to become maternal, virgins became excessively responsive to pups, responding maternally in a matter of hours in some animals and by 2 to 3 days in others. Moreover, these animals seemed less avoidant of the pups, more willing to remain in their proximity and to sniff, lick, and mouth the pups, prior to the onset of retrieval and the other maternal behaviors. These data suggested to us that the odor of the pups may be in some way aversive to the virgin animal, causing avoidant responses and thereby precluding close contact and a rapid sensitization.

To determine where odors were acting in the brain to suppress the rapid expression of maternal behavior in the virgin, we did lesions and knife cuts of structures which receive olfactory projections and which project to the MPOA. The two primary chemosensory systems which are activated when the female sniffs or mouthes/licks pups, respectively are the olfactory system which responds to odor molecules which are airborne and the vomeronasal system which responds to odor molecules in a liquid medium, as when licking occurs. Receptors of both systems reside in the nasal cavity and project to the main (airborne) and accessory (liquid) olfactory bulbs. Axons of cells in the olfactory bulbs project to a number of sites. We have concentrated primarily on those sites described in our original circuit, which project to the MPOA. The bed nucleus of the stria terminalis and the medial nucleus of the amygdala receive input from the vomeronasal or accessory olfactory system while the cortical and posteriormedial nucleus (C3) amygdaloid nuclei receive primarily main olfactory input (Scalia & Winans, 1975; Winans & Scalia, 1970).

We were therefore interested in determining what the effect would be on maternal behavior in the virgin animal of lesions in the medial and cortical nuclei of the amygdala, which receive chemosensory input. We compared latencies to become maternal in groups of virgin females sustaining lesions of the corticomedial amygdala which receives olfactory and vomeronasal input, the basolateral amygdala, which does not, and a variety of control sites. As shown in Table 7.4, we found that lesions of the corticomedial, but not the basolateral regions, resulted in a rapid onset of maternal behavior. Controls and the basolateral group did not differ from one another.

To determine whether facilitation was due to the destruction of olfactory axon terminals which project to these sites or to cells which integrate the olfactory information, we undertook to transect pathways projecting away from the amygdala into the MPOA or the Bed nucleus of the stria terminalis. Lesions and knife cuts of the stria terminalis, which projects dorsally from the corticomedial amygdala into the BST and into the MPOA (Berk & Finkelstein, 1981; de Olmos & Ingram, 1974) produced a facilitation of maternal behavior in the virgin animal

TABLE 7.4
Effects of Lesions of the Olfactory-Amygdala-Preoptic Circuit
on Maternal Behavior in the Nulliparous Female Rat

Groups	N	Latency in Days to Become Maternal ($\bar{x}$ days SD$\pm$)
INTACT		
Nulliparous	8	8.13$\pm$2.62
Parturient	8	0
OLFACTORY SYSTEM		
Olfactory bulbs	7	2.67$\pm$1.86^a
Lateral olfactory tract	10	2.10$\pm$0.49^b
Internal controls	12	7.00$\pm$2.83^{a,b}
AMYGDALA		
Corticomodial	16,11	4.73$\pm$4.04^{a,b,c}, 3.18$\pm$3.60^d
Basolateral	7	10.42$\pm$1.51^a
Implant controls	9	10.67$\pm$0.71^b
Lesion controls	6,10	8.83$\pm$2.79^c, 8.71$\pm$1.97^d
STRIA TERMINALIS		
Dorsal stria terminalis	5,6	3.00$\pm$3.08^a, 3.4$\pm$3.9^b
Lesion controls	15,9	8.53$\pm$3.05^a, 7.2$\pm$3.3^b
PREOPTIC-AMYGDALA		
Amygdale	9	2.67$\pm$3.46^{a,b,c}
Preoptic	6	8.67$\pm$3.72^a
Preoptic-Amygdala	5	11.00$\pm$0
Lesion controls	12	7.09$\pm$4.35^c

a,b,c,d differences significant by a Mann-Whitney U test, $p \leq .05$.

(Fleming, Miceli, & Vaccarino, in preparation), Knifecuts of the ventral amygdala pathway which may project ventrally from the medial nucleus of the amygdala into the BNST (Lehman & Winans, 1983; Weller & Smith, 1982) had no effect (Fleming, Miceli, & Vaccarino, in preparation). These results suggested that the facilitatory effects of the amygdaloid lesions on maternal behavior in the virgin is not due directly to damage of the olfactory fibers, but to a disruption of functions mediated at the level of the amygdala and transmitted to the diencephalon through its major efferent pathway, the stria terminalis. Since lesions of the MPOA abolish maternal behavior (and the ST projects directly into the MPOA), we assumed that the inhibition normally exerted by the stria terminalis is directly on MPOA cells. However, the stria terminalis also projects to the BNST which is located directly above the MPOA and the BNST projects down into the MPOA (Conrad & Pfaff, 1976b). To determine whether the inhibitory amygdaloid input reaches the MPOA through the direct ST projection or the indirect ST projection through the BNST, we tested groups of ovariectomized virgin female rats who sustained lesions of the MPOA, the BNST, the AMYG and the AMYG in combination with either the MPOA or cortical control sites. These results show that the BNST mimics the facilitatory effects of the amygdaloid lesions, suggesting either that amygdaloid input does project through this indirect pathway or that the BNST lesions also disrupted the direct stria terminalis pathways from the amygdala to the MPOA. We believe the latter interpretation to be correct, since knife cuts between the BNST and the MPOA-AH which should transect fibers connecting these two regions do not produce a rapid onset of maternal behavior in the virgin animal. Moreover, we found that the facilitation of maternal behavior produced by amygdaloid lesions could be blocked by simultaneous MPOA lesions, but not be lesions at other sites, which further supports the notion that the amygdaloid inhibition is probably acting directly on the MPOA.

Taken together, these neural studies suggest that activation of the olfactory systems by pup stimulation sustains activity in the corticomedial amygdala which, in turn, exerts a direct inhibition on the MPOA through its primary efferent system, the stria terminalis.

Amygdala and Pup Avoidance in the Virgin Female Rat

Although these studies indicate a neural circuit which acts on the MPOA and which may function to prevent the virgin from behaving maternally with pups, we feel that this inhibition is not being exerted on the maternal behavior system directly, but is being accomplished indirectly by the activation of behaviors and functions which preclude the expression of maternal behavior. One observation we repeatedly made in groups sustaining damage to the olfactory and amygdaloid systems was the females seemed less timid in general and less avoidant with pups, in particular. This observation is concordant with one known function of the amygdala, which is in the mediation of emotional or affective responses. A number of studies have shown that bilateral lesions of both the corticomedial and basolateral amygdala produce decreased timidity and emotionality in a variety of paradigms designed to assess fear responses to aversive, novel or threatening stimuli (Blanchard & Blanchard, 1972; ; Coover, Ursin, & Levine, 1973; Galef, 1970; Nachman & Ashe, 1974; White & Weingarten, 1976).

Based on these studies we predicted that virgin females sustaining lesions to different portions of the amygdala would differ from control animals in their avoidant responses to pups, specifically, and in their responses in a variety of other non pup-related, but emotion-provoking, situations.

In one study, we placed pups into the established nest site in the cage and determined over the next 6-hour period, whether the female continued using her nest site or whether she moved to a new quadrant of the cage. A female was said to have changed her preferred nest site if over the next six spotchecks she was observed to be spending the majority of her time in a quadrant different from the quadrant in which pups were placed. As predicted, we found that animals with lesions of the amygdala (of either corticomedial or basolateral regions) avoided pups less than intact or control-lesioned animals. In general, these animals did not move away from the pups; instead, they remained in the quadrant, often permitting the pups to push under them while sleeping. Within 1–2 days of such contact these females were usually also showing active nursing, retrieval and licking responses.

To determine whether this apparent reduced timidity in the presence of pups was specific to pups, or reflected, instead, a more general change in affect, we then tested animals sustaining lesions of the amygdala on a variety of tasks traditionally used to assess "fear" in rats (Archer, 1973). As shown in Table 7.5 we found that animals with lesions to either the basolateral or the corticomedial nuclear groups of the amygdala were less timid than control groups. They ambulated more in the open field apparatus, spent proportionately more time in the center, as opposed to the periphery, of the field, emerged more rapidly from a dark familiar box into a bright unfamiliar arena, and were more inclined to investigate the field. Based on these data we conclude that under normal circumstances, the amygdala and its projections control the animal's emotional responsivity and promote appropriately avoidant responses if the presenting stimulus is strong and unfamiliar.

Amygdaloid Lesions May Accelerate Maternal Responding in the Virgin by Reducing Fear

In the virgin animal, the strong and strange odor of the pups act on the substrate and cause the animal to initially move away from and avoid the pups. With repeated exposure, however, the pup becomes more familiar and thus, less aversive; the female is then willing to tolerate contact with the pups. The subsequent sensory exposure then acts in some cumulative fashion to activate the MPOA and related substrates of maternal behavior. Lesions of the amygdala eliminate this process and preclude the avoidant phase so that maternal behavior can be expressed more rapidly. Whether or not the animal shows maternal behavior would, however, be dependent on the integrity of the MPOA. If this area is lesioned along with bilateral lesions of the amygdala, animals are willing to be in contact with pups and not avoid pups, but they will not show retrieval and crouch responses (Fleming, Miceli, & Moretto, 1983).

WHERE IN THE BRAIN DO HORMONES ACT?

Hormones act in a number of different ways to promote appropriately directed maternal responsiveness at birth, and may accomplish these separate functions by acting on a number of different neural sites. The hormone (or hormones)

TABLE 7.5
Effects of Lesions in the Amygdala on Fear-Mediated Behaviors in the Rat

		Emergency Tests		Open-Field Activity	
		Latency to Emerge into the Open Field $\bar{X} \pm SD$ (in sec)	Latency to Emerge into the Y Maze $\bar{X} \pm SD$ (in sec)	Squares Crossed ($\bar{X} \pm SD$)	
Groups	N			Prestimulus	Poststimulus
Basolat	7	112.8 ± 67.4	113.2 ± 112.7	182.0 ± 55.2	157.9 ± 27.6*
Cortmed-small	9	131.0 ± 128.9	107.8 ± 86.9#	198.7 ± 79.9	137.3 ± 60.9§
Cortmed-large	7	106.4 ± 47.8¶	68.2 ± 77.4†‡	178.1 ± 74.3	140.3 ± 52.5‡
Implant control	9	570.3 ± 764.5¶	206.1 ± 108.7†	154.4 ± 60.2	71.9 ± 65.1†§*

†*Differences significant by a Mann-Whitney U test, $p \leq 0.05$, 2-tailed.
†§¶#Differences significant by a Mann-Whitney U test, $p < 0.05$ 1-tailed.

could act directly on the substrate controlling maternal behavior such that pup stimulation could easily elicit the pattern; the steroids could act on the olfactory system and alter the strength, character, salience or liking for the perceived odor complex emanating from the pups and mediated through the olfactory system; the hormones could act on other neural structures to alter the animal's affective state and reduce its neophobic responses.

For the hormones to be able to alter activity of the different neural sites these sites must contain receptors which bind the hormones and the implantation of the hormones at these sites should affect the animal's behavior in a specific way. As indicated earlier, all the primary structures in this circuit—the amygdala, the BNST, the MPOA—contain receptors for estradiol (McEwen, Davis, Parsons, & Pfaff, 1979; Pfaff & Keiner, 1973). They do not, however, contain receptors for P. In line with these observations, estrogen implants in a number of these sites have been effective in altering maternal responding in animals. However, in all cases researched to date, the effectiveness of E has required prior priming with progesterone.

Numan (1974) and Numan et al. (1977) found, for instance, that estradiol implanted into the MPOA in animals pregnancy-terminated and ovariectomized on day 16 of pregnancy (day OVX-HYST) induced immediate maternal behavior in most animals. Longer latencies were found for estradiol implants into the VMH or control sites. It seems then that estradiol can act on the MPOA to facilitate maternal behavior in the female rat which has been primed by a prior pregnancy and high levels of progesterone.

We were interested in determining the effects of estradiol on other neural sites known to bind estrogens. Using the same paradigm as Numan, we, therefore, investigated the effects of estradiol implanted in the amygdala, the BNST, the hippocampus and other control sites in day 16OVX-HYST females (Fleming & Orpen, in preparation). In this study we found that estradiol implants in the corticomedial amygdala, which is the area which binds estradiol, produced more rapid maternal responding than did estrogen in the basolateral amygdala, in other sites which do not bind estradiol, or than did control cholesterol implants in the amygdala. Estrogen in the BNST had no such facilitatory effects. However, estrogen in the ventricles, which permits diffusion all over the brain produced a facilitation comparable to the one produced by amygdala implants.

We were also interested in determining whether estrogen in the amygdala reduces fear-mediated responding. However, we found that all pregnancy-terminated groups regardless of hormone condition, showed similar short latencies to emergence and high ambulation scores, when compared to nonoperated controls. We felt the series of operations and associated anaesthetics, handling, etc. may have the effect of reducing fear in a nonspecific way and that prior hormonal priming associated with pregnancy may have already had an influence on the animal's level of emotionality prior to our day 16 surgeries. We, therefore, undertook a hormone implant study using nonprimed ovariectomized virgin females. Our initial results indicate that when compared to cholesterol controls, animals with estradiol in the amygdala emerge into the open field significantly more rapidly. However, no open field activity differences are apparent. We are presently following up these initial findings.

Taken together these studies suggest that among the ways hormones may be acting to promote maternal responding to pups is by acting in a number of different brain sites to reduce the animals overall neophobia and to increase her attraction to pup odors, thereby increasing the likelihood that she will stay in contact with pups.

BIOLOGICAL CONTROL OF MATERNAL BEHAVIOR IN HUMAN MOTHERS

Although this review has focused primarily on the hormonal, sensory and neural mechanisms of maternal behavior in the rat, an attempt has been made to point out similarities and differences between the rat and selected other species for which information is available. The fact that there are considerable species differences in the role of the different hormones or in the role of experiential factors in maternal behavior, indicates that the rat is just one among a number of possible models for an understanding of the mechanism present in humans, and perhaps not the best one. However, since most of this work has been done using the rat, human researchers have tended to structure their studies and ask many of the same questions of humans as have been asked with respect to the rat.

In the following, we briefly review some of the studies which attempt to assess the biological basis of maternal behavior in human mothers and discuss some of the problems peculiar to the study of humans which are associated with such an endeavor. Studies which either directly or indirectly address the biological/physiological control of maternal behavior fall into a number of different categories. Some studies are concerned with demonstrating the existence of some species-characteristic behaviors in the mother. Others tackle the problem of determining whether or not humans have a period of elevated sensitivity to infants following the birth. In the final category of studies are those which compare affective responses to babies or pictures/films of babies, in men and women in different stages of their lives or reproductive cycles.

Methodological Constraints

Not surprisingly, there are no data which directly assess the hormonal control of maternal behavior in human mothers. Given the complexity, obvious methodological constraints and variability of human behavior as well as the clear importance in its control of/experiential and social factors, the problems associated with such as endeavor are considerable.

How to Define Maternal Behavior in Mothers

The issue of how to characterize or define maternal responsiveness or maternal attachment in humans is a very real one. Unlike most nonprimate mammals who show very little variance in responsiveness and whose behavior is often quite stereotyped and predictable, human mothers have a wide range of attitudes relating to babies and motherhood and are able to adequately care for their babies physical (and emotional?) needs using a wide variety of mothering styles. Excepting the extremes, when abuse and/or neglect occur, what constitutes poor or good maternal behavior is not altogether obvious and may vary widely in different cultures, religious groups, economic classes, etc. (see Feldman & Nash, this volume).

Different studies have used different measures to demonstrate maternal attachment during the puerperium and later months. For instance, in the early/extended contact literature, measures of bonding which have been used include

1. frequency or time spent engaged in holding, affectionate touching, smiling or kissing the baby (Carlsson et al., 1978; deChateau & Wiberg, 1977; Hales et al., 1977),
2. time spent in the "en face" position (deChateau & Wiberg, 1977, Kennell et al., 1974),
3. duration of nursing (Sosa et al., 1976),
4. frequency or time spent in ventral holds,
5. holding baby on the heart side (deChateau et al., 1976),
6. willingness to leave baby with a babysitter (Kennell et al., 1974; Klaus & Kennell, 1976)
7. interest exhibited during a pediatric examination (Kennell et al., 1975; Klaus et al., 1972), and
8. complexity of verbal exchanges with the baby (Ringler et al., 1975).

As will become evident, in different studies the early/extended contact manipulations seem to influence different behaviors, although in each case an effect on maternal bonding was assumed to have occurred.

In a longitudinal study we are in the process of completing, we (Fleming & Ruble, in preparation) used a variety of different self-report and behavioral measures to assess material attachment and found remarkably little intercorrelation among the measures. Women were observed nursing and playing with their babies at different time points postpartum (36 hr, 1, 3, and 18 months) and also responded to a series of attitude items concerning (1) what kind of attributes they feel they, as mothers, have (2) how attached or "bonded" they feel to their babies, (3) how well they like caretaking activities, and (4) how adequate they feel in the mothering role, to name a few. Behaviors were recorded on a computer-based event recorder and grouped into different conceptual categories such as (1) noninstrumental 'contact' touching, (2) instrumental, caretaking activities, (3) talking to the baby, (4) looking away from the baby, and (5) orienting to the baby or in "en face." In our preliminary observations we found that although there were high intercorrelations among many of the self-report attitude clusters, only the caretaking attitude cluster correlated with the behavioral measures of "attachment." We found that if we divided our 3-month population into those who like and those that do not like caretaking activities (caretaking cluster scores divided into high and low by a median split), the two groups behaved differently while nursing their babies; the high caretaking group engaged in more noninstrumental contact "affectionate" behaviors. Not only did we find poor intercorrelations between self report of attachment and measures of attachment behavior, we also found that women differed markedly from one another in their mothering styles. While nursing their babies, some mothers remained very quiet, but maintained steady 'en face' position; others were very active and playful, but not maintaining a steady gaze; some touched and fondled their babies frequently; others did not, but instead, talked or sang continuously to them. Some mothers seemed very engaged with their babies and expressed concern for the health and wellbeing of their babies; however in some of these cases mothers tended not to be sensitive to infant cues and frequently responded in a noncontingent fashion. Since all the mothers reported feeling quite bonded to their babies and since so many behavioral styles were apparent we were not at all convinced that there is a set of behaviors which exclusively signals attachment, although it is quite likely that an analysis of behavioral contingencies rather than of durations or frequencies of particular behaviors might be a more fruitful way of discriminating mothers who are attuned or sensitive to their babies and those that are less so.

However, Klaus et al. (1970) argue that there do exist some similarities across cultures in attachment behaviors and that, in fact, there exist some behaviors which all mothers in all cultures show. Klaus et al. (1970) filmed the first contacts between 12 mothers and their full-term infants within ½ to 13 hours after delivery. They report that although mothers varies widely in background, socioeconomic status and parity they were similar in that they showed "an orderly and predictable pattern of behavior . . . commencing hesitantly with fingertip contact on the extremities, within 4 to 5 minutes (the mother) began caressing the trunk with her palm, simultaneously showing progressively heightened excitement, which continued for several minutes." They also report a striking increase over the first 10 minutes of contact in the amount of time mothers spent in the 'en face' position. Mothers often indicated that once eye-to-eye contact was established they felt closer to their babies. Based on these findings, Klaus et al. (1970) suggest that the "en face" position, the contact behavior and very likely, actual nursing behavior, constitute important species-characteristic patterns which, if permitted to occur soon after birth of the baby, may contribute to or hasten the mother's subsequent feelings of attachment to her baby during the first postpartum weeks. While these data indicate some stereotype in the initial touching responses of these mothers to their newborns, attempts to replicate even these findings using a Guatemalan population have not been successful (Klaus, Trause, & Kennell, 1975).

How to Assess the Role of Hormones in Women

In addition to the definitional problems, it is obviously not possible in humans to undertake endocrinological, surgical or other manipulations for research purposes. Thus, in order to establish the relationships between behavior and hormones one either has to test different populations which have experienced spontaneously-occurring gynecological or obstetrical dysfunctions—which is exceedingly difficult to do—or do studies correlating hormone levels and behavior. Assuming we knew what behaviors to look at in humans, we do not know what hormones to measure. Moreover, assuming we knew what hormones to assay, it is highly unlikely that we would find a relationship between the configuration of hormones or hormone levels at any single point in time and intensity of maternal behavior shown at that time.

Even in rats, where we have a much better handle on both the behavior of interest and the relevant hormones, we have yet to find a meaningful correlational relationship between the two in postpartum animals. In a study we recently completed in which we measured plasma levels of estradiol and progesterone we found no relationship between levels of any of those hormones and latencies to show maternal behavior during pregnancy or at 2, 7, or 10 days postpartum.

A similar problem is presently confounding researchers investigating the endocrine bases of the postpartum "blues" syndrome. This mood state is a considerably easier phenomenon to investigate than is maternal behavior. By self-report, approximately 50 to 75% of women undergo periods of elevated lability, heightened reactivity and tearfulness between 3 and 10 days postpartum (Pitt, 1973; Stein, 1982). This phenomenon, entitled, "the moody blues" is widely believed to be hormonally mediated. Despite many correlational studies investigating a relationship between the different hormones and the "blues" or single symptoms of the "blues," few have unequivocally demonstrated a relationship (Stein, 1982). Candidates for hormonal causes of the blues include (1) a progesterone decline (Nott et al., 1976), (2) elevated levels of prolactin (George et al., 1980), (3) cortisol (Handley et al., 1977, 1980), (4) decreases in thyroid output (How & Brewsher, 1978), and (5) decreases in endogenous endorphins (Newnham et al., 1984). In short, despite the relative ease of measuring the symptoms of the "blues," the relative similarity of the phenomenon across women, the high incidence and the accessibility of the suffering population, we still cannot find hormonal correlates of the condition, despite the clear belief that some/one such exists. One clear problem in all such hormone-behavior studies with humans is the difficulty in obtaining repeated assays from single individuals. Unless we can trace patterns over time in the hormones and behaviors, we are not likely to ever be able to demonstrate a relationship.

Perhaps if we reframed our question we would have a better handle on how hormones might influence maternal behavior in humans. One could, for instance, imagine a situation in which variations in hormones would account for differences in intensity of a women's reaction but that hormones essentially have equivalent qualitative effects in all women—that of causing an increase in lability and reactivity; in this situation the behavioral differences would come about as a result of a combination of past differences (personality structure/past experiences, etc.) and present environmental differences. According to this formulation, the hormones predispose the individual to have a very intense and, possibly, chaneable reaction—say, to the new baby—but that whether the reaction will be positive or negative, whether mood will be elation or dysphoria, will depend on personality and situational factors (baby's health, separation from the baby, presence of a supporting father, financial stressors, relationship with parents, etc.) This is a testable proposition.

Postpartum Sensitive Period in Women

Although the relationship between hormones and maternal behavior in humans has not been directly demonstrated, the substantial literature concerned with the effects of early and/or extended contact with babies in the hospital on the development of bonding in the mother has, as a guiding premise, the belief that in humans—as in the rat and some ungulates—there exists a postpartum sensitive period during which mothers are particularly sensitive and responsive to their babies and during which experiences interacting with babies can most easily become consolidated. The underlying assumption of these studies is that, in humans as in rats and ungulates, the sensitive period is hormonally mediated and that in the absence of interactive experience with the baby during this perinatal period, the bonding process will become disrupted or retarded.

Over the past 10 years an intensive research effort has been directed at establishing the long and short term effects on maternal behavior of providing new mothers with contact with their babies, either for a short period immediately after the birth (early contact) and/or for a more extended period, starting somewhat later (extended contact). The early studies seemed to suggest the existence of a sensitive period and argued for the idea of both long and short term beneficial effects of early and/or extended contact.

If mothers experienced skin-to-skin contact with their newborns during the first hour after delivery they spent more time holding (deChateau & Wiberg, 1977), rubbing, patting and touching (Carlsson et al., 1978) or being affectionate with (Hales et al., 1977) their babies during the postpartum lying-in period than if they experienced the usual hospital regime of being separated from their babies immediately after delivery. At three months mothers who received extended/

early contact postpartum spent more time in the "en face" position and kissing their infants than did control mothers (deChateau & Wiberg, 1977). Moreover, their infants were more visually alert, cried less and laughed more than control babies—which may in part account for the behavioral differences in the mothers. If mothers are permitted more extensive postpartum contact during the first three postpartum days they show altered responsiveness to their babies for up to 2 years after delivery, when compared to control mothers who experienced the usual hospital regimen, (Klaus & Kennell, 1983); and at 2 years, when talking to their children, these mothers asked more questions and engaged in a more complex, richer verbal exchange (Ringler et al., 1975; Klaus & Kennell, 1983).

However, in a very thorough reveiw of the more recent literature, Lamb points out the extensive methodological problems associated with these studies and describes other recent, better controlled studies which fail to replicate these initial results (Svejda, Campos, & Emde, 1980). For instance, most of the studies use an extensive battery of behavioral measures, but find differences in only a small proportion of measures—about as many as one might expect by chance (deChateau & Wiberg, 1977; Hopkins & Vietze, 1977; Klaus et al., 1972). Moreover in the various studies, different measures are found to significantly differentiate extra-contact and non extra-contact groups (Hales et al., 1977; deChateau & Wiberg, 1977) and in some, the relevant measures do not seem to reflect maternal responsiveness at all (mother's posture while lying in bed, deChateau & Wiberg, 1977). Also, even in cases where effects are replicable, it is often not clear to what to attribute the effects. In a number of studies the medical staff was aware of which women were included in which group and may well have given experimental women more attention (Klaus et al., 1972); moreover, mothers in extra-contact conditions were sometimes rooming with mothers not receiving extra-contact and so may have realized their special status (Klaus et al., 1972; Hales et al., 1977). Finally, as indicated earlier, many of the effects have not been replicated.

Based on his review of the literature, Lamb therefore concludes that there is no convincing evidence that extended contact with babies after birth has either short-term or long-term effects on maternal behavior or claims relating to incidence of child abuse, marriage break-up, etc. As to the effects of early contact with the baby, there is some suggestion that early contact may have positive short-term effects on the behavior (up to the first 2 observations in the hospital) but no long-term effects (see Grossman, Thane, & Grossman, 1981).

Although there is very little good evidence that early or extended contact has enduring effects on maternal behavior in women, there is some evidence to suggest that separation from the baby during the perinatal period influences the mother's self-confidence and feelings of adequacy. In one study, Sostek, Scanlon, and Abramson (1982) report that mothers who were separated from their babies for medical reasons, when compared to mothers rooming in with their babies, exhibited less self-confidence 2–3 days after delivery and were more anxious at 1 month (see also Greenburg, Rosenberg, & Lind, 1973; Seashore et al., 1973).

In our study (Fleming & Ruble, in preparation) we also noticed that mothers whose babies had high bilirubin counts and whose babies had to spend much of the time under the ultraviolet lights, tended to experience more anxiety while in the hospital and feel less confident with their babies when left alone with them at home. These effects of separation on anxiety and maternal confidence probably reflect the very real situation that these first time mothers are inexperienced and have not had the same opportunity as mothers not separated from their babies to practice and become familiar with basic caretaking skills.

Effect of Mother's Mood on her Maternal Behavior

Taken together, the above studies do not support the idea that there exists a sensitive period in women during which they become most-easily bonded to their babies. However, experiences during this period can affect the mothers in a variety of other ways which could then indirectly effect maternal behavior (see Feldman & Nash, this volume). First time mothers are initially clearly insecure with their babies and an extended separation from the baby during the first days may well influence their mood, feelings of confidence, etc. These feelings in turn may influence how the mother responds to the baby.

In the preliminary analyses of our longitudinal study, we, in fact, find a relationship between the mother's mood and her maternal behavior (Fleming & Ruble, in preparation), but only at certain times. The amount of time the mother spends with her baby during the first 24 hours significantly predicts her mood, but not her maternal behavior, during the puerperium. However the mother's mood during the puerperium does predict her mood state at 1 and 3 months postpartum and differences in mood at these time points is predictive of differences in maternal behavior at these same time points. As shown in Table 7.6 women who score as more dysphoric at either one or three months postpartum also feel less adequate in their role as mothers and engage in significantly less affectionate touching of their babies, than do the happier mothers; the two groups do not differ on the talking or caretaking measures, nor on their expressed attitudes and feelings towards their babies.

These data suggest that alterations in maternal responding which may result from being separated from the baby may not reflect the absence, during a period of heightened sensitivity, of a crucial experience or exposure to the baby per se (as one finds in some ungulates); rather it may come about as a result of an effect of separation and attendant experiences on the mother's mood and self confidence which *indirectly* affects her maternal behavior as we discussed. An inverse relationship between anxiety and/or depression during pregnancy and postpartum mothering has also been reported by Feldman and Nash (1982) and Gross-

TABLE 7.6
Maternal Behaviors and Attitudes During One and Three Months Postpartum in Women Experiencing High and Low Mood ($\bar{X}$ and SEM)

	1 Month Postpartum						3 Months Postpartum			
	High		Low		Intermediate		High		Low	
Behaviors	$\bar{X}$	SEM	$\bar{X}$	SEM	$\bar{X}$	SEM	$\bar{X}$	SEM	$\bar{X}$	SEM
AFFECTIONATE										
with bottle	128.5	29.3X	54.5	12.7X	105.9	27.4	137.9	26.1*	81.1	22.0*
without bottle	141.7	28.2X	63.8	15.4X			160.4	25.3X	99.4	25.9X
TALK TO BABY	53.4	13.8	77.9	20.1	74.7	24.3	97.7	17.6	84.0	24.9
ORIENT TO BABY	425.8	21.0X	318.3	47.8X	343.8	44.0	493.3	43.5	456.8	42.9
CARETAKING	172.8	39.6	109.1	24.2	116.2	31.0	115.1	20.4*	82.8	21.0*
LOOK AWAY	76.2	11.6	101.6	20.5	137.0	44.3	55.2	18.5	119.8	38.2
Attitudes										
ADMOM	28.2	.7X	20.9	1.8≡	26.2	1.5≡	27.9	1.1*	24.5	2.0*
BOND	27.2	1.5	25.8	1.2	25.4	1.2	28.1	1.1	25.7	1.2
CARETAKING	26.4	1.2X	19.3	.7X	18.3	.8	18.9	.6	17.2	.9
ANXFET	6.2	.7	6.4	.8	6.5	.7	4.8	.6	6.2	.9
RELHUS	13.8	1.3X	25.1	1.6X	18.3	2.2	15.0	1.6*	21.0	2.4*

X Hi vs. Lo, $p < .05$, 2T
≡ Lo vs. Int, $p < .05$, 2T
* Hi vs. Lo, $p < .05$, 1T

man et al. (1980). As indicated earlier, a positive relationship between elevated mood (e.g., reduced timidity) and maternal responsiveness is also seen in rats.

Maternal Responsiveness During Pregnancy

If bonding is not restricted to a circumscribed sensitive period postpartum, when does it occur? Although the definitive longitudinal study has not been done, there is some evidence that the process of maternal attachment can be quite gradual, starting in some cases during the pregnancy and for others extending through the first postpartum year. Most notable in the studies described below are the large individual differences in the pattern shown.

While many studies have looked at the early postpartum development of maternal attachment in woman, surprisingly few have attempted to systematically trace changes in maternal feelings towards the fetus during pregnancy and to look at prepartum maternal behavior towards other infants. Such studies could be quite informative as pregnancy responses are possibly less influenced by situational factors and thus more amenable to a more strictly biological interpretation. Most studies on the normal psychological changes of pregnancy have been psychoanalytic in orientation and have been based primarily on clinical impressions and case histories (e.g., Benedek, 1959; Bibring, 1961; Deutsch, 1945). For example, Benedek (1959) analyzed reported fantasies and dreams in women during different phases of their reproductive cycle and reports that pregnant women and women in the luteal phase of their menstrual cycle both experience "an intensification of the receptive-retentive tendencies" and "an increased integrative capacity of the ego." Benedek attributes the emergence of these qualities—which she interprets to be the psychodynamic correlates of a biologic need for motherhood—to the elevated levels of progesterone characterizing both these phases. She asserts,

> Pregnancy is a biologically normal, but exceptional period in the life of women. At conception a biologic 'symbiosis' begins that steers the woman between happy fulfillment of her biologic destiny and its menacing failures. The heightened hormonal and metabolic processes which are necessary to maintain the normal growth of fetus augment the vital energies of the mother. It is the interlocking psychologic processes between mother and fetus that makes the pregnant woman's body abound with libidinous feelings. As metabolic and emotional processes replenish the libido reservoir of the pregnant woman, this supply of primary narcissism becomes a well-spring of her motherliness. Self centered as it may appear, it increases her pleasure in bearing her child, stimulates her hopeful fantasies, diminishes her anxieties (p. 138).

Although these clinical approaches have suggested hypotheses about the possible psychological impact of pregnancy, they have been limited by psychoanalytic preconceptions of what pregnancy *should* represent psychologically. They have also tended to lack the empirical orientation necessary to provide a normative description of changes and reactions to pregnancy.

One exception to this predominantly clinical approach is a recent study by Leifer (1980), who provides a detailed description of the development of maternal feelings in 19 healthy middle class white, primipara. These descriptions were based on 4-hour open-ended interviews with the mothers-to-be and an attachment-to-baby checklist administered during each trimester. While Leifer (1980) did not statistically analyze her data, she reports that most women in her sample underwent an orderly sequence in the development of maternal attachment, which is consistent with what has been reported in other species. Most women experience no strong maternal feelings during the first trimester. However, with "quickening" and fetal movements during the second trimester maternal feelings usually deepened and the woman would engage in lengthy imaginative conversations with her baby. During this second period women also frequently expressed anxiety about the health and well-being of the fetus. By the last trimester of pregnancy most women expressed strong attachment to the fetus. At this time they would also engage in a variety of "nesting" behaviors, in preparation for the baby. These observations are consistent with anecdotal descriptions of maternal feelings during pregnancy given by Taylor and Hall (1979) who report " . . . affiliation with and investment in the fetus as a separate and unique being . . . begins at about the time of quickening and increases for the duration of the pregnancy. Investment in the fetus is reflected by active, practical, preparation for the new baby, or 'nesting behavior.' Throughout the gestation, but more notably, during the final weeks, women actively fantasize about the fetus . . . Most of the conscious fantasies deal with the expected, hoped-for infant" (p. 74).

Whether these feelings of attachment to the fetus during pregnancy actually translate into heightened responsiveness to babies is not known. In the only study analogous to our rat studies which looked at the reactions of expectant mothers to 6- to 10-month-old-infants, Feldman and Nash (1978) report the interesting finding that pregnant women were not different from childless nonpregnant women in level of responsiveness to babies in a waiting room situation but they were less responsive in this situation than mothers of infants. Responsiveness was assessed by the combined one-zero scores for looks, smiles, funny faces/ gestures, talks, shows/gives object and touches. These behavioral findings were confirmed on a subsequent perceptual task in which groups were compared for the percent of time they spent looking at slides depicting babies versus those showing objects and adults.

While these results suggest no change in responsiveness to babies prior to the actual birth of the baby, such a conclusion seems premature. Women were observed only once during their pregnancies and no information was given

Relationship of Postpartum Feelings and Postpartum Adaptation

Although it is generally assumed that the attitudes and expectations of the prospective mother will influence her ability subsequently to adapt to her new role, there have been only a few systematic examinations of such relationships. While not specifically looking for changes in maternal responsiveness over pregnancy, Shershefsky and Yarrow (1973) interviewed 60 couples at 3 and 7 months of pregnancy and at 1, 3, and 6 months postpartum. Following these semistructured interviews the members of the psychiatric team rated each subject on a number of variables. Factor analysis of 700 such rated items yielded 46 initial factor scales, nine of which were related to womens' feelings about her infant or about her role as mother. These investigators report that women who had no trouble visualizing themselves as mothers or who showed an interest in children early in pregnancy tended to make a good maternal adaptation postpartum.

These findings are consistent with Leifer's (1977) observation of a "high association between attachment to the fetus during pregnancy and maternal feelings toward the baby." She found that most women in her sample who were negative or indifferent to the fetus at the beginning of pregnancy became attached to it by the end of pregnancy. However, some did not and these were the women who, in general, experienced greater difficulties feeling close to their babies during the postpartum period.

For both these studies it would be of considerable interest to know whether feelings experienced during early pregnancy reflect the woman's prepregnancy feelings, as assumed by Leifer (1980) or whether these feelings developed during the pregnancy. It is unfortunate that neither of these studies included a control group of nonpregnant women or a group of women whose first assessment took place before conception. In contrast to Leifer's results, Robson and Moss (1970) did not find a relationship between feelings during the last trimester of pregnancy and 3 months postpartum. Based on interviews of 54 primiparous mothers Robson and Moss (1970) report that maternal feelings tended not to be present at birth, but they clearly developed over the first 6 weeks. At birth and through the first 4 to 6 weeks postpartum mothers reported feeling somewhat aloof from the baby, regarding it as an anonymous nonsocial object. Between 4 and 6 weeks after the baby began to show smiles, eye-to-eye contact and following the eyes, mothers began for the first time to articulate feelings of attachment to the baby. By 3 months the mothers were all strongly bonded. In general, as reviewed in the chapter by Feldman & Nash (in this volume), good postpartum maternal adaptation has been reported to be fostered by a variety of factors during the pregnancy as well as during the postpartum period. Pregnancy factors include such personality variables as ego-strength and maturity, an elevated mood, an interest in or experience with babies, reduced self-directed interests as reflected in fewer psychosomatic complaints, a commitment to career, and overall, a generally good adaptation to pregnancy (see also Leifer, 1980; Sherefesky & Yarrow, 1973). Postpartum factors which have been reported to predict a good maternal adaptation include a healthy, responsive baby (Magnus, 1980; Moss, 1967), and a sympathetic and supportive home environment. Other postpartum factors which probably also affect the course of the mother's attachment to her baby are the child's sex, birth order, probability of survival (Klaus & Kennell, 1976; Mead & Newton, 1967) and quality of postpartum interaction with the baby.

In short, many social and psychological factors, not of relevance in other animals, take precedence during the postpartum period in human mothers.

REFERENCES

Alberts, J. R. (1978a). Huddling by rat pups: Multisensory control of contact behavior. *Journal of Comparative and Physiological Psychology, 92,* 220–230.

Alberts, J. R. (1978b). Huddling by rat pups: Group behavioral mechanisms of temperature regulation and energy conservation. *Journal of Comparative and Physiological Psychology, 92,* 231–245.

Alexander, G. (1960). Maternal behavior in the Merino ewe. *Proceedings of the Australian Sociaty of Animal Production, 3,* 105–114.

Allin, J. T., & Banks, E. M. (1970). Effects of temperature on ultrasound production by infant albino rats. *Developmental Psychobiology., 4,* 149–156.

Allin, J. T., & Banks, E. M. (1972). Functional aspects of ultrasound production by infant albino rats (*Rattus norvegicus*). *Animal Behavior, 20,* 175–185.

Anderson, C. O., Zarrow, M. X., Fuller, G. B., & Denenberg, V. H. (1971). Pituitary involvement in maternal nest-building in the rabbit. *Hormones & Behavior, 2,* 183–189.

Archer, J. (1973). Tests for emotionality in rats and mice: A review. *Animal Behavior, 21,* 205–235.

Baranczuk, R., & Greenwald, G. S. (1974). Plasma levels of oestrogen and progesterone in pregnant and lactating hamsters. *Journal of Endocrinology, 63,* 125–135.

Baras, S., & Pay, S. (1980). *Neuroscience Letters, 17,* 265–269.

Bauer, J. H. (1983). Effects of maternal state on the responsiveness to nest odors of hooded rats. *Physiology & Behavior, 30,* 229–232.

Beach, F. A., & Jaynes, J. J. (1956). Studies of maternal retrieving in rats. III. Sensory cues involved in the lactating female's response to her young. *Behavior, 10,* 104–125.

Bell, R. W. (1974). Ultrasounds in small rodents: Arousal-produced and arousal-producing. *Developmental Psychobiology, 7,* 39–42.

Bell, R. W., Nitschke, W., Bell, N. J., & Zachman, T. A. (1973). Early experience, ultrasonic vocalizations and maternal responsiveness in rats. *Developmental Psychobiology, 7,* 235–242.

Benedek, T. (1959). Parenthood as a developmental phase. *American Psychoanalytic Association., 78,* 389–417.

Berk, M. L., & Finkelstein, J. A. (1981). Afferent projections to the preoptic area and hypothalamic regions in the rat brain. *Neuroscience, 6,* 1601–1624.

Bibring, G. L. (1961). A study of the psychological processes in pregnancy and the earliest mother-child relationship. *Psychoanalytic Studies Child, 16,* 9–44.

Blake, C. A., Norman, R. L., & Sawyer, C. H. (1972). Effects of estrogen and/or progesterone on serum and pituitary gonadotropin levels in ovariectomized rats. *Proceedings of the Society of Experimental Biology and Medicine, 141*, 1100–1103.

Blanchard, D. C., & Blanchard, R. J. (1972). Innate and conditioned reactions to threat in rats with amygdaloid lesions. *Journal of Comparative & Physiological Psychology, 81,– 281–290.*

Blass, E. M., & Teicher, M. H. (1980). Suckling. *Science, 210*, 15–22.

Brewster, J., & Leon, M. (1980a). Relocation of the site of mother-young contact: Maternal transport behavior in Norway rats: Maternal transport behavior. *Journal of Comparative and Physiological Psychology, 94*, 69–79.

Brewster, J., & Leon, M. (1980b). Facilitation of maternal transport by Norway rat pups. *Journal of Comparative and Physiological Psychology, 94*, 80–88.

Bridges, R. S. (1975). Long-term effects of pregnancy and parturition upon maternal responsiveness in the rat. *Physiology & Behavior, 14*, 245–249.

Bridges, R. S. (1977). Parturition: Its role in the long term retention of maternal behavior in the rat. *Physiology & Behavior, 18*, 487–490.

Bridges, R. S. (1978). Retention of rapid onset of maternal behavior during pregnancy in primiparous rats. *Behavioral Biology, 24*, 113–117.

Bridges, R. S. (1981, June). *A new and reliable preparation for examination of the hormonal regulation of maternal behavior in the rat* (Abstract). Conference on Reproductive Behavior, Nashville, Tennessee.

Bridges, R. S. (1984). A quantitative analysis of the roles of estradiol and progesterone in the regulation of maternal behavior in the rat. *Endocrinology, 114*, 930–940.

Bridges, R. S. (1984). Abstract. Institute of Animal Behavior—J. S. Rosenblatt Conference, Newark, New Jersey.

Bridges, R. S., Clifton, D. K., & Sawyer, C. H. (1982). Postpartum luteinizing hormone release and maternal behavior in the rat after late-gestational depletion of hypothalamic norepinephrine. *Neuroendocrinology, 34*, 286–291.

Bridges, R. S., Feder, H. H., & Rosenblatt, J. S. (1977). Induction of maternal behaviors in primigravid rats by ovariectomy, hysterectomy, or ovariectomy plus hysterectomy: Effect on length of gestation. *Hormones & Behavior, 9*, 156–169.

Bridges, R. S., & Grimm, C. T. (1982). Reversal of morphine disruption of maternal behavior by concurrent treatment with the opiate antagonist naloxone. *Science, 218*, 166–168.

Bridges, R. S., & Ronsheim, P. M. (1983, November). *Changes in B-endorphin concentrations in the medial preoptic area during pregnancy in the rat* (Abstract). Society for the Neurosciences, Boston, Massachusetts.

Bridges, R. S., Rosenblatt, J. S., & Feder, H. H. (1978). Serum progesterone concentrations and maternal behavior in rats after pregnancy termination: Behavioral stimulation following progesterone withdrawal and inhibition by progesterone maintenance. *Endocrinology, 102*, 258–267.

Bridges, R. S., Rosenblatt, J. S., & Feder, H. H. (1978). Stimulation of maternal responsiveness after pregnancy termination in rats: Effect of time of onset of behavioral testing. *Hormones & Behavior, 10*, 235–245.

Capek, K., & Jelinek, J. (1956). The development of the control of water metabolism. I. The excretion of urine by young rats. *Phsiol. Bohemoslov., 5*, 91–96.

Carlsson, S. G., Fagerberg, H., Horneman, G., Hwang, C. P., Larsson, K., Rodholm, M., Schaller, J., Danielsson, B., & Gundewall, C. (1978). Effects of various amounts of contact between mother and child on the mother's nursing behavior. *Developmental Psychology, 11*, 143–150.

Cohen, J., & Bridges, R. S. (1981). Retention of maternal behavior in nulliparous and primiparous rats: Effects of duration of previous maternal experience. *JCPP, 95*, 450–459.

Conrad, L. C. A., & Pfaff, D. W. (1976a). Efferents from medial basal forebrain and hypothalamus in the rat: I. An autogradiographic study of the medial preoptic area. *Journal of Comparative Neurology, 169*, 185–220.

Conrad, L. C. A., & Pfaff, D. W. (1976b). Efferents from medial basal forebrain and hypothalamus in the rat: II. An autoradiographic study of the anterior hypothalamus. *Journal of Comparative Neurology, 169,* 221-262.

Coover, G., Ursin, H., & Levine, S. (1973). Corticosterone and avoidance in rats with basolateral amygdala lesions. *Journal of Comparative and Physiological Psychology, 85,* 111-122.

Cummings, L. A., Fleming, A. S. (1974). *The effects of distal sensory stimulation from neonatal pups on the maintenance of maternal responsiveness in Caesarian-delivered rats.* Unpublished undergraduate B.Sc. thesis, University of Toronto.

deChateau, P., Holmberg, H., & Winberg, J. (1976). *Left-side preference in holding and carrying newborn infants during the first week of life.* Unpublished manuscript, University of Umea.

deChateau, P., & Wiberg, B. (1977). Long-term effect on mother-infant behavior of extra contact during the first hour postpartum: I. First observations at 36 hours. *Acta Paediatrica Scandinavica, 66,* 137-143.

deChateau, P., & Wiberg, B. (1977). Long-term effect on mother-infant behavior of extra contact during the first hour postpartum: II. Follow-up at three months. *Acta Paediatrica Scandinavica, 66,* 145-151.

de Olmos, J. S., & Ingram, W. R. (1974). The projection field of the stria terminalis in the rat brain: An experimental study. *Journal of Comparative Neurology, 146,* 303-334.

Deutsch, H. (1945). *Psychology of women,* Vol. II. New York: Grune and Stratton.

Doerr, H. K., Siegel, H. I., & Rosenblatt, J. S. (1981). Effects of progesterone withdrawal and estrogen on maternal behavior in nulliparous rats. *Behavioral and Neural Biology, 32,* 35-44.

Dollinger, M. J., Holloway, W. R., & Denenberg, V. H. (1980). Parturition in the rat (*Rattus norvegicus*): Normative aspects and the temporal patterning of behaviors. *Behavioral Processes, 5,* 21-37.

Elwood, R. W. (1977). Changes in the responses of male and female gerbils (*Meriones unguiculatus*) towards test pups during the pregnancy of the female. *Animal Behavior, 25,* 46-51.

Elwood, R. W. (1979). Maternal and paternal behavior of the Mongolian gerbil: A correlational study. *Behavioral and Neural Biology, 25,* 555-562.

Elwood, R. W. (1980). The development, inhibition, and disinhibition of pup-cannibalism in the Mongolian gerbil. *Animal Behavior, 28,* 1188-1194.

Elwood, R. W. (1981). Postparturitional reestablishment of pup cannibalism in female gerbils. *Developmental Psychobiology, 14,* 209-212.

Erskine, M., Barfield, R. J., & Goldman, B. D. (1978b). Intraspecific fighting during late pregnancy and lactation in rats and effects of litter removal. *Behavioral Biology, 23,* 206-218.

Erskine, M., Denenberg, V. H., & Goldman, B. D. (1978a). Aggression in the lactating rat: Effects of intruder age and test arena. *Behavioral Biology, 23,* 52-66.

Ewer, R. F. (1968). *Ethology of mammals.* London: Elek Science.

Feldman, S. S., & Nash, S. C. (1978). Interest in babies during young adulthood. *Child Development, 49,* 617-622.

Feldman, S. S., & Nash, S. C. (1982). *Prediction of mothering behavior from pregnancy.* Unpublished manuscript, Stanford University.

Fleischer, S., & Slotnick, B. M. (1978). Disruption of maternal behavior in rats with lesions of the septal area. *Physiology & Behavior, 21,* 189-200.

Fleming, A. S. (1972). *Olfactory and experential factors underlying maternal behavior in the lactating and cycling female rat.* Unpublished doctoral dissertation, Rutgers University, Newark, New Jersey.

Fleming, A. S., & Luebke, C. (1981). Timidity prevents the virgin female rat from being a good mother: Emotionality differences between nulliparous and parturient females. *Physiology & Behavior, 27,* 863-868.

Fleming, A. S., Moretto, D., & Miceli, M. O. (1983). Lesions of the Medial Preoptic Area prevent the facilitation of maternal behavior produced by amygdaloid lesions. *Physiology & Behavior, 31,* 503-510.

Fleming, A. S., Miceli, M. O., & Vaccarino, A. (in preparation). Effects on maternal behavior following knife cuts to amygdala-BNST-MPOA projections.

Fleming, A. S., & Orpen, B. G. (in preparation). Effects of estradiol implants in the brain on maternal behavior in rats.

Fleming, A. S., & Rosenblatt, J. S. (1974a). Maternal behavior in the virgin and lactating rat. *Journal of Comparative and Physiological Psychology, 86,* 957–972.

Fleming, A. S., & Rosenblatt, J. S. (1974b). Olfactory regulation of maternal behavior in rats: I. Effects of olfactory bulb removal in experienced and inexperienced lactating and cycling females. *Journal of Comparative and Physiological Psychology, 86,* 221–232.

Fleming, A. S., & Rosenblatt, J. S. (1974c). Olfactory regulation of maternal behavior in rats: II. Effects of peripherally induced anosmia and lesions of the lateral olfactory tract in pup-induced virgins. *Journal of Comparative and Physiological Psychology, 86,* 233–246.

Fleming, A. S., & Ruble, D. (in preparation). The development of maternal responsiveness and mood during pregnancy and the postpartum period in women.

Fleming, A. S., Vaccarino, F., Tambosso, L., & Chee, P. (1979). Vomeronasal and olfactory system modulation of maternal behavior in the rat. *Science, 203,* 372–374.

Franz, J. (1981). *Effects of hypothalamic knife cuts and experience on components of periparturitional behavior in the rat.* Unpublished doctoral dissertation. S. U. N. Y., Buffalo.

Friedman, M. I., & Bruno, J. P. (1976). Exchange of water during lactation. *Science, 191,* 409–410.

Gaffori, O., & Le Moal, M. (1979). Disruption of maternal behavior and appearance of cannibalism after ventral mesencephalic tegmentum lesions. *Physiology & Behavior, 23,* 317–323.

Galef, B. G., Jr. (1970). Aggression and timidity responses to novelty in feral norway rats. *Journal of Comparative and Physiological Psychology, 70,* 370–381.

Galef, B. G. (1981). The ecology of weaning—Parasitism and the achievement of independence by altricial mammals. In D. J. Gubernick & P. H. Klopfer (Eds.), *Parental care in mammals.* New York: Plenum Press.

Gallistel, C. R. (1980). *The organization of action: a new synthesis.* Hillsdale, NJ: Lawrence Erlbaum Associates.

Gandelman, R. (1973). Maternal behavior in the mouse: Effect of estrogen and progesterone. *Physiology & Behavior, 10,* 153–155.

Gandelman, R., Zarrow, M. X., & Denenberg, V. H. (1971). Stimulus control of cannibalism and maternal behavior in anosmic mice. *Physiology & Behavior, 7,* 583–586.

Gandelman, R., Zarrow, M. X., Denenberg, V. H., & Myers, M. (1971). Olfactory bulb removal eliminates maternal behavior in the mouse. *Science, 171,* 210–211.

George, A. J., Copeland, J. R. M., & Wilson, K. C. M. (1980). Prolactin in the maternity blues. *British Journal of Pharmacology, 70,* 102–103.

Gray, J. A. (1971). Sex differences in emotional behavior in mammals including man: endocrine bases. *Acta Psychologica, 34,* 29–46.

Greenberg, M., Rosenberg, I., & Lind, J. (1973). First mothers rooming-in with their newborns: Its impact on the mother. *American Journal of Orthopsychiatry, 43,* 783–788.

Grossman, F., Eichler, L., & Winickoff, S. (1980). *Pregnancy, birth, and parenthood: Adaptations of mothers, fathers, and infants.* San Francisco: Jossey-Bass.

Grossman, K., Thane, K., & Grossman, K. E. (1981). Maternal tactual contact of the newborn after various postpartum conditons of mother-infant contact. *Developmental Psychology, 17,* 159–169.

Grota, L. J., & Ader, R. (1969). Continuous recording of maternal behavior in *Rattus norvegicus.* *Animal Behavior, 17,* 722–729.

Gubernick, D. J. (1980). Maternal "imprinting" or maternal "labelling" in goats? *Animal Behavior, 28,* 124–129.

Gubernick, D. J. (1981). Parent and infant attachment in mammals. In D. J. Gubernick and P. H. Klopfer (Eds.), *Parental care in mammals*. New York: Plenum Press.

Gubernick, D. J., & Alberts, J. R. (1983). Maternal licking of young: Resource exchange and proximate controls. *Physiology & Behavior, 31*, 593–601.

Hales, D. J., Lozoff, B., Sosa, R., & Kennell, J. H. (1977). Defining the limits of the maternal sensitive period. *Developmental Medicine and Child Neurology, 19*, 454–461.

Hall, W. G., Cramer, C. P., & Blass, E. M. (1977). Ontogeny of suckling in rats: Transitions toward adult ingestion. *Journal of Comparative and Physiological Psychology, 91*, 1141–1155.

Handley, S. L., Dunn, T. L., Baker, J. M., Cockshott, C., & Goulds, S. (1977). Mood changes in the puerperium and plasma tryptophan and cortisol. *British Medical Journal, 2*, 18–22.

Handley, S. L., Dunn, T. L., Waldron, S., & Baker, J. M. (1980). Tryptophan, cortisol and puerperal mood. *British Journal of Psychiatry, 136*, 498–508.

Hansen, S., Kohler, C. H., & Ross, S. B. (1982). On the role of the dorsal mesencephalic tegmentum in the control of sexual behavior in the rat: Effects of electrolytic lesions, ibotenic acid and DSP4. *Brain Research, 240*, 311–320.

Herrenkohl, L., R., & Rosenberg, P. A. (1972). Exteroceptive stimulation of maternal behavior in the naive rat. *Physiology & Behavior, 8*, 595–598.

Hersher, L., Moore, A. U., & Richmond, J. B. (1958). Effects of postpartum separation of mother and kid on maternal care in the domestic goat. *Science, 128*, 1342–1343.

Hopkins, J. B., & Vietze, P. M. (1977, March). *Postpartum early and extended contact: Quality, quantity or both?* Paper presented to the Society for Research in Child Development, New Orleans.

How, J., & Brewsher, P. D. (1978). Thyroid disease in pregnancy. *British Medical Journal, 2*, 1568–1569.

Ikard, W. L., Bennett, W. C., Lundino, R. W., & Trost, R. C. (1972). Acquisition and extinction of the conditioned avoidance response. A comparison between male rats and estrus and nonestrus female rats. *Psychol. Rec., 22*, 249–254.

Jacobson, C. D., Terkel, J., Gorski, R. A., & Sawyer, C. H. (1980). Effects of small medial preoptic lesions on maternal behavior: Retrieving and nest building in the rat. *Brain Research, 125*, 471–478.

Jakubowski, H., & Terkel, J. (1980). Induction by young of prolonged diestrus in virgin rats behaving maternally. *Journal of Reproduction and Fertility, 58*, 55–60.

Jans, E. J., & Leon, M. (1983). Determinants of mother-young contact in Norway rats. *Physiology & Behavior, 30*, 919–935.

Kalra, P. S., Fawcett, C. P., Krulich, L., & McCann, S. M. (1973). The effects of gonadal steroids on plasma gonadotropins and prolactin in the rat. *Endocrinology, 92*, 1256–1268.

Kennell, J. H., Jerauld, R., Wolfe, H., Chesler, D., Kreger, N. C., McAlpine, W., Steffa, M., & Klaus, M. H. (1974). Maternal behavior one year after early and extended post-partum contact. *Developmental Medicine and Child Neurology, 16*, 172–179.

Kennell, J. H., Trause, M. A., & Klaus, M. H. (1975). In *Parent-infant interaction*, CIBA Foundation Symposium 33. Amsterdam: Elsevier Publishing Co.

Kenyon, P., Cronin, P., & Keeble, S. (1981). Disruption of maternal retrieving by perioral anaesthesia. *Physiology & Behavior, 27*, 313–321.

Kimble, D. P., Rogers, L., & Hendrickson, C. W. (1967). Hippocampal lesions disrupt maternal, not sexual behavior in the albino rat. *Journal of Comparative and Physiological Psychology, 63*, 401–405.

Klaus, M. H., Jerauld, R., Kreger, N. C., McAlpine, W., Steffa, M., & Kennell, J. H. (1972). Maternal attachment: Importance of the first postpartum days. *New England Journal of Medicine, 286*, 460–463.

Klaus, M., & Kennell, J. H. (1976). Human maternal and paternal behavior. In M. H. Klaus J. H. Kennell (Eds.), *Maternal-infant bonding*. St. Louis: Mosby.

Klaus, M., & Kennell, J. H. (1983). In A. Hamilton (Ed.), *Bonding: The beginnings of parent-infant attachment.*

Klaus, M. H., Kennell, J. H., Plumb, N., & Zuehlke, S. (1970). Human maternal behavior at first contact with her young. *Pediatrics, 46,* 187–192.

Klaus, M. H., Trause, M. A., & Kennell, J. H. (1975). Does human maternal behavior after delivery show a characteristic pattern? In *Parent-Infant Interaction,* Ciba Foundation Symposium #33. Amsterdam: Elsevier.

Koranyi, L., Lissak, K., Tomasu, V., & Kamaras, L. (1976). Behavioral and electrophysiological attempts to elucidate central nervous system mechanisms responsible for maternal behavior. *Archives of Sexual Behavior, 5,* 503–510.

Koranyi, L., Phelps, C. P., & Sawyer, C. H. (1977). Changes in serum prolactin and corticosterone in induced maternal behavior in rats. *Physiology & Behavior, 18,* 287–292.

Krehbiel, D. A., & Le Roy, L. M. (1979). The quality of hormonally stimulated maternal behavior in ovariectomized rats. *Hormones & Behavior, 12,* 243–252.

Krettek, J. E., & Price, J. L. (1978). Amygdaloid projections to subcortical structures within the basal forebrain and brainstem in the rat and cat. *Journal of Comparative Neurology, 178,* 225–254.

Kristal, M. B., Peters, L. C., Franz, J. R., Whitney, J. F., Nishita, J. K., & Steven, M. A. (1981). The effect of pregnancy and stress on the onset of placentophagia in Long-Evans rats. *Physiology & Behavior, 27,* 591–595.

Lehman, M. N., Winans, S. S., & Powers, J. B. (1980). Medial nucleus of the amygdala mediates chemosensory control of male hamster sexual behavior. *Science, 210,* 557–560.

Lehman, M. N., & Winans, S. S. (1983). Evidence for a ventral non-strial pathway from the amygdala to the bed nucleus of the stria terminalis in the male golden hamster. *Brain Research, 268,* 139–146.

Leifer, M. (1977). Psychological changes accompanying pregnancy and motherhood. *Genet. Psych. Monog., 95,* 55–96.

Leifer, M. (1980). *Psychological effects of motherhood. A study of first pregnancy.* New York: Praeger Science.

Leon, M., Croskerry, P. G., & Smith, G. K. (1978). Thermal control of mother-young contact in rats. *Physiology & Behavior, 21,* 793–811.

Lisk, R. D. (1971). Oestrogen and progesterone synergism and elicitation of maternal nest-building in the mouse *(Mus musculus). Animal Behavior, 19,* 606–610.

Lisk, R. D., Pretlow, R. A. 3rd, & Friedman, S. M. (1969). Hormonal stimulation necessary for elicitation of maternal nest-building in the mouse *(Mus musculus). Animal Behavior, 17,* 730–737.

Lott, D., & Fuchs, S. (1962). Failure to induce retrieving by sensitization or the injection of prolactin. *Journal of Comparative and Physiological Psychology, 55,* 1111–1113.

Lott, D. F., & Rosenblatt, J. S. (1969). Development of maternal responsiveness during pregnancy in the rat. In B. M. Foss (Ed.), *Determinants of infant behavior,* Vol. IV. London: Methuen.

Maeda, H., & Mogenson, G. J. (1980). An electrophysiologic study of inputs to neurons of the ventral tegmental area from the nucleus accumuens and medial preoptic-anterior hypothalamic areas. *Brain Research, 197,* 365–377.

Magnus, E. M. (1980). Sources of maternal stress in the postpartum period: a review of the literature and an alternative view. In J. E. Parsons (Ed.), *Psychobiology of sex differences and sex roles.* New York: McGraw Hill.

Marques, D. M. (1979). Role of the main olfactory and vomeronasal systems in the response of the female hamster to young. *Behavioral & Neural Biology, 26,* 311–329.

McEwen, B. S., Davis, P. G., Parsons, B., & Pfaff, D. W. (1979). The brain as a target for steroid hormone action. *Annual Review of Neuroscience, 2,* 65–112.

Mead, M., & Newton, N. (1967). Cultural patterning of perinatal behavior. In S. A. Richareson &

A. F. Guttmacher. *Child bearing: Its social and psychological aspects.* Baltimore: Williams and Wilkins.

Miceli, M. O., Fleming, A. S., & Malsbury, C. W. (1983). Disruption of maternal behavior in virgin and postparturient rats following sagittal plane knife cuts in the preoptic area-hypothalamus. *Behavioral Brain Research, 9,* 337–360.

Miceli, M. O., Fleming, A. S., & Moretto, D. (1983). Lesions of the medial preoptic area prevent the facilitation of maternal behavior produced by amygdala lesions. *Physiology & Behavior, 31,* 503.–510.

Miceli, M. O., & Malsbury, C. W. (1982). Sagittal knife cuts in the near and far lateral preoptic-area hypothalamus disrupt maternal behavior in female hamsters. *Physiology & Behavior, 28,* 857–867.

Moltz, H., Levin, R., & Leon, M. (1969). Differential effects of progesterone on the maternal behavior of primiparous and multiparous rats. *Journal of Comparative and Physiological Psychology, 67,* 36–40.

Moltz, H., Lubin, M., Leon, M., & Numan, M. (1979). Hormonal induction of maternal behavior in the ovariectomized nulliparous rat. *Physiology & Behavior, 5,* 1373–1377.

Moltz, H., Rowland, D., Steele, M., & Halaris, A. (1975). Hypothalamic norepinephrine: Concentration and metabolism during pregnancy and lactation in the rat. *Neuroendocrinology, 19,* 252–258.

Moore, C. (1983). *Accounting for sex differences.* Paper presented at the Winter Animal Behavior Conference V, Park City, Utah.

Moore, C. L., & Morelli, G. A. (1970). Mother rats interact differently with male and female offspring. *Journal of Comparative and Physiological Psychology, 93,* 677–684.

Moretto, D., Paclik, L., & Fleming, A. (1984). Effects of early rearing environments on maternal behavior in juvenile and adult female rats. Manuscript submitted for publication.

Morishige, W. K., Pepe, G. J., & Rothchild, I. (1973). Serum luteinizing hormone (LH), prolactin and progesterone levels during pregnancy in the rat. *Endocrinology, 92,* 1527–1530.

Moss, H. A. (1967). Sex, age and state as determinants of mother-infant interaction. *Merrill-Palmer Quarterly.*

Nachman, M., & Ashe, J. H. (1974). Effects of basolateral amygdala lesions on neophobia, learned taste aversions and sodium appetite in rats. *Journal of Comparative and Physiological Psychology, 87,* 622–643.

Newnham, J. P., Dennett, P. M., Ferron, S. A., Tomlin, S., Legg, C., Bourne, G. L., & Rees, L. H. (1984). A study of the relationship between circulating B-endorphin-like immunoreactivity and post partum 'blues'. *Clinical Endocrinology, 20,* 169–177.

Noirot, E. (1968). Ultrasounds in young rodents. II. Changes with age in albino rats. *Animal Behavior, 16,* 129–134.

Noirot, E. (1969a). Serial order of maternal response in mice. *Animal Behavior, 17,* 547–550.

Noirot, E. (1969b). Changes in responsiveness to young in the adult mouse: V. Priming. *Animal Behavior, 17,* 542–546.

Noirot, E. (1970). Selective priming of maternal responses by auditory and olfactory cues from mouse pups. *Developmental Psychobiology, 2,* 273–276.

Noirot, E. (1972). The onset of maternal behavior in rats, hamsters and mice. In D. S. Lehrman, R. A. Hinde, & E. Shaw (Eds.), *Advances in the study of behavior,* Vol. 4. New York: Academic Press.

Noirot, E., & Goyens, J. (1971). Changes in maternal behavior during gestation in the mouse. *Hormones & Behavior, 2,* 207–215.

Nott, P. N., Franklin, M., Armitage, C., & Gelden, M. G. (1976). Hormonal changes and mood in the early puerperium. *British Journal of Psychiatry, 128,* 379–383.

Numan, M. (1974). Medial preoptic area and maternal behavior in the female rat. *Journal of Comparative and Physiological Psychology, 87,* 746–759.

Numan, M., & Callahan, E. C. (1980). The connections of the medial preoptic area and maternal behavior in the rat. *Physiology & Behavior, 25,* 653–665.

Numan, M., & Nagel, D. S. (1983). Preoptic area and substantia nigra interact in the control of maternal behavior in the rat. *Behavioral Neuroscience, 97,* 120–139.

Numan, M., Rosenblatt, J. S., & Komisaruk, B. R. (1977). Medial preoptic area and onset of maternal behavior in the rat. *Journal of Comparative and Physiological Psychology, 91,* 146–164.

Numan, M., & Smith, H. G. (1984). Maternal behavior in rats: Evidence for the involvement of preoptic projections to the ventral tegmental area. *Behavioral Neuroscience, 98,* 712–727.

Orpen, B. G., Fleming, A. S., & Wong, P. Y. (in preparation). Maternal behavior is not correlated with plasma levels of hormones.

Ostermeyer, M. C. (1983). Maternal aggression. In R. W. Elwood (Ed.), *Parental behavior of rodents.* New York: Wiley.

Pederson, C. A., Ascher, J. A., Monroe, Y. L., & Prange, A. J. (1982). Oxytocin induces maternal behavior in virgin female rats. *Science, 216,* 648–650.

Pederson, C. A., & Prange, A. J. (1979). Induction of maternal behavior in virgin rats after intracerebroventricular administration of oxytocin. *Proceedings of the National Academy of Science, U.S.A., 76,* 6661–6665.

Pepe, G., & Rothchild, I. (1974). A comparative study of serum progesterone levels in pregnancy and various types of pseudopregnancy in the rat. *Endocrinology, 95,* 275–279.

Pfaff, D., & Keiner, M. (1973). Atlas of estradiol-concentrating cells in the central nervous system of the female rat. *Journal of Comparative Neurology, 151,* 121–158.

Phillipson, D. T. (1979). Afferent projections to the ventral tegmental area of Tsai and interfasacular nucleus: A horseradish peroxidose study in the rat. *Journal of Comparative Neurology, 187,* 117–144.

Pitt, B. (1973). Maternity blues. *British Journal of Psychiatry, 122,* 431–435.

Poindron, P., & Le Neindre, P. (1979). Hormonal and behavioral basis for establishing maternal behavior in sheep. In L. Zichella & P. Pancheri (Eds.), *Psychoneuroendocrinolgy in reproduction.* Amsterdam: North-Holland Biomedical Press.

Poindron, P., & Le Neindre, P. (1980). Endocrine and sensory regulation of maternal behavior in the ewe. In J. S. Rosenblatt, R. A. Hinde, C. Beer, & M. C. Busnel (Eds.), *Advances in the study of behavior,* Vol. II. New York: Academic Press.

Poindron, P., Martin, G. B., & Hooley, R. D. (1979). Effects of lambing induction on the sensitive period for the establishment of maternal behavior in sheep. *Physiology & Behavior, 23,* 1081–1087.

Porter, R. H. (1983). Communication in rodents: Adults to infants. In R. W. Elwood (Ed.), *Parental behavior of rodents.* New York: Wiley.

Porter, R. H., Cernoch, J. M., & McLaughlin, F. J. (1983). Maternal recognition of neonates through olfactory cues. *Physiology & Behavior, 30,* 151–154.

Powers, J. B., & Winans, S. S. (1975). Vomeronasal organ: Critical role in mediating sexual behavior of the male hamster. *Science, 187,* 961–963.

Quadagno, D. M., Shryne, J., Anderson, A., & Gorski, R. A. (1972). Influences of gonadal hormones on social, sexual, emergence and openfield behavior in the rat (*Rattus norvegicus*). *Animal Behavior, 20,* 732–740.

Reisbick, S., Rosenblatt, J. S., & Mayer, A. D. (1975). Decline of maternal behavior in the virgin and lactating rat. *Journal of Comparative and Physiological Psychology 89,* 722–732.

Richards, M. P. M. (1966). Maternal behavior in virgin female golden hamsters (Mesocricetus auratus Waterhouse): The role of the age of the test pup. *Animal Behavior, 14,* 303–309.

Richards, M. P. M. (1966). Maternal behavior in the golden hamster: Responsiveness to young in virgin, pregnant, and lactating females. *Animal Behavior, 14,* 310–313.

Ringler, N. M., Kennell, J. H., Jarvella, R., Navojosky, B. H., & Klaus, M. H. (1975). Mother-to-child speech at 2 years - effects of early postnatal contact. *Behavioral Pediatrics, 86,* 141–144.

Robson, & Moss (1970.

Rodriquez-Sierra, J., & Rosenblatt, J. S. (1977). Does prolactin play a role in estrogen-induced maternal behavior in rats: Apomorphine reduction of prolactin release. *Hormones & Behavior, 9,* 1–7.

Rosenblatt, J. S. (1965). The basis of synchrony in the behavioral interaction between the mother and her offspring in the laboratory nest. In B. Foss (Ed.), *Determinants of infant behavior,* Vol. III. London: Methuen.

Rosenblatt, J. S. (1967). Nonhormonal basis of maternal behavior in the rat. *Science, 156,* 1512–1514.

Rosenblatt, J. S. (1970). Views on the onset and maintenance of maternal behavior in the rat. In L. R. Aronson, E. Tobach, D. S. Lehrman, & J. S. Rosenblatt (Eds.), *Development and evolution of behavior: Essays in memory of T. C. Schneirla.* San Francisco: Freeman.

Rosenblatt, J. S., & Lehrman, D. S. (1963). Maternal behavior of the laboratory rat. In H. L. Rheingold (Ed.), *Maternal behavior in mammals.* New York: Wiley.

Rosenblatt, J. S., & Siegel, H. I. (1975). Hysterectomy-induced maternal behavior during pregnancy in the rat. *Journal of Comparative and Physiological Psychology, 89,* 685–700.

Rosenblatt, J. S., & Siegel, H. I. (1981). Factors governing the onset and maintenance of maternal behavior among nonprimate mammals: The role of hormonal and nonhormonal factors. In D. J. Gubernick & P. H. Klopfer (Eds.), *Parental care in mammals.* New York: Plenum Press.

Rosenblatt, J. S., Siegel, H. I., & Mayer, A. D. (1979). Progress in the study of maternal behavior in the rat: Hormonal, nonhormonal, sensory and developmental aspects. In J. S. Rosenblatt, R. A. Hinde, C. Beer, & M. C. Busnel (Eds.), *Advances in the study of behavior,* Vol. 10. New York: Academic Press.

Rosenblum, L. A. (1972). Sex and age differences in response to infant squirrel monkeys. *Brain Behavior and Evolution, 5,* 30–40.

Ross, S., Sawin, P. B., Zarrow, M. X., & Denenberg, V. H. (1963). Maternal behavior in the rabbit. In H. L. Rheingold (Ed.), *Maternal behavior in mammals.* New York: Wiley.

Roth, L. L., & Rosenblatt, J. S. (1967). Changes in self-licking during pregnancy in the rat. *Journal of Comparative and Physiological Psychology, 63,* 397–400.

Rowell, T. E. (1960). On the retrieving of young and other behaviors in lactating Golden hamsters. *Proceedings of the Zoological Society of London, 135,* 265–282.

Rubin, B. S., Menniti, F. S., & Bridges, R. S. (1983). Intra-cerebroventricular administration of oxytocin and maternal behavior in rats after prolonged and acute steroid pretreatment. *Hormones and Behavior, 17,* 45–53.

Scalia, F., & Winans, S. S. (1975). The differential projections of the olfactory bulb and accessory olfactory bulb in mammals. *Journal of Comparative Neurology, 161,* 31–56.

Seashore, M. J., Leifer, A. D., Barnett, C. R., & Leiderman, P. H. (1973). The effects of denial of early mother-infant interaction on maternal self-confidence. *Journal of Personality and Social Psychology, 26,* 369–378.

Shaikh, A. A. (1971).Estrone and estradiol levels in the ovarian venous blood from rats during the estrous cycle and pregnancy. *Biology of Reproduction, 5,* 297–307.

Shereshefsky, P., & Yarrow, L. (1973). *Psychological aspects of a first pregnancy and early postnatal adaptation.* New York: Raven Press.

Siegel, H. I., Clark, M. C., & Rosenblatt, J. S. (1983). Maternal responsiveness during pregnancy in the hamster (*Mesocricetus auratus*). *Animal Behavior, 31,* 497–502.

Siegel, H. I., Giordano, A. L., Mallafre, C. M., & Rosenblatt, J. S. (1983). Maternal aggression in hamsters: Effects of stage of lactation, presence of pups, and repeated testing. *Hormones & Behavior, 17,* 86–93.

Siegel, H. I., & Greenwald, G. S. (1975). Prepartum onset of maternal behavior in hamsters and the effects of estrogen and progesterone. *Hormones & Behavior, 6*, 237–245.

Siegel, H. I., & Greenwald, G. S. (1978). Effects of mother-litter separation on later maternal responsiveness in the hamster. *Physiology & Behavior, 21*, 147–149.

Siegel, H. I., & Rosenblatt, J. S. (1975a). Hormonal basis of hysterectomy-induced maternal behavior during pregnancy in the rat. *Hormones & Behavior, 6*, 211–222.

Siegel, H. I., & Rosenblatt, J. S. (1975b).Estrogen induced maternal behavior in hysterectomized-ovariectomized virgin rats. *Physiology & Behavior, 14*, 465–471.

Siegel, H. I., & Rosenblatt, J. S. (1975c). Progesterone inhibition of estrogen-induced maternal behavior in hysterectomized-ovariectomized virgin rats. *Hormones & Behavior, 6*, 223–230.

Siegel, H. I., & Rosenblatt, J. S. (1977, June). *Effects of pregnancy termination on maternal behavior, lordosis, ovulation and progesterone levels in the rat.* Paper presented at Eastern Conference on Reproductive Behavior, Storrs, Connecticut.

Siegel, H. I., & Rosenblatt, J. S. (1978a). Duration of estrogen stimulation and progesterone inhibition of maternal behavior in pregnancy-terminated rats. *Hormones & Behavior, 11*, 12–19.

Slotnick, B. M. (1967). Disturbances of maternal behavior in the rat following lesions of the cingulate cortex. *Behavior, 29*, 204–236.

Slotnick, B. M. (1973). Initiation of maternal behavior in pregnant nulliparous rats. *Hormones & Behavior, 4*, 53–59.

Smith, L., & Berkson, G. (1973). Litter stimulus factors in maternal retrieval (*Rattus rattus*). *Animal Behavior, 21*, 620–623.

Smotherman, W. P., Bell, R. W., Hershberger, W. A., & Coover, G. D. (1978). Orientation to rat pup cues: Effects of maternal experiential history. *Animal Behavior, 26*, 265–273.

Soloff, M., Alexandrova, M., & Fernstrom, M. (1979). Oxytocin receptors: Triggers for parturition and lactation? *Science, 204*, 1313–1315.

Sosa, R., Klaus, M., Kennell, J. H., & Urrutia, J. J. (1976). The effect of early mother-infant contact on breastfeeding, infection and growth. In *Breastfeeding and the mother*, CIBA Foundation Symposium #45. Amsterdam: Elsevier.

Sostek, A. M., Scanlon, J. W., & Abramson, D. C. (1982). Postpartum contact and maternal confidence and anxiety: A confirmation of short-term effects. *Infant Behavior and Development, 5*, 323–329.

Stamm, J. S. (1955). The function of the median cerebral cortex in maternal behavior in rats. *Journal of Comparative and Physiological Psychology, 48*, 347–356.

Steele, M., & McCann, S. M. (1980). Maternal behavior deficits and endocrine responses in fimbria-fornix lesioned post-parturient rats. *Society of Neurosciences Abstracts, 6*, 657.

Steele, M. K., Rowland, D., & Moltz, H. (1979). Initiation of maternal behavior: Possible involvement of limbic norepinephrine. *Pharmacology and Biochemistry of Behavior, 11*, 122–130.

Stein, G. (1982). The maternity blues. In I. F. Brockington & R. Kumeir (Eds.), *Motherhood and mental illness*. New York: Grune and Stratton.

Stern, J. M. (1977). Effects of ergocryptine on postpartum maternal behavior, ovarian cyclicity and food intake in rats. *Behavioral Biology, 21*, 134–140.

Stern, J. M. (1983). Maternal behavior priming in virgin and caesarian-delivered Long-Evans rats: Effects of brief contact or continuous exteroceptive pup stimulation. *Physiology & Behavior, 31*, 757–764.

Stern, J. M., & MacKinnon, D. S. (1976). Postpartum, hormonal and nonhormonal induction of maternal behavior in rats: Effects on T-maze retrieval of pups. *Hormones and Behavior, 7*, 305–316.

Stern, J. M., & Siegel, H. I. (1978). Prolactin release in lactating, primiparous and nulliparous thelectomized and maternal virgin rats exposed to pup stimuli. *Biology of Reproduction, 19*, 177–182.

Svare, B. B. (1981). Maternal aggression in mammals. In D. J. Gubernick & P. H. Klopfer (Eds.), *Parental care in mammals*. New York: Plenum Press.

Svejda, M. J., Campos, J. J., & Emde, R. N. (1980). Mother-infant "bonding": Failure to generalize. *Child Development, 51*, 775–779.

Swanson, L. W. (1976). An autoradiographic study of the efferent connections of the preoptic regions in the rat. *Journal of Comparative Neurology, 167*, 227–256.

Swanson, L. J., & Campbell, C. S. (1981). The role of the young in control of the hormonal events during lactation and behavioral weaning in the golden hamster. *Hormones & Behavior, 15*, 1–15.

Taylor, P. M., & Hall, B. L. (1970). Parent-infant bonding problems and opportunities in a prenatal center. *Seminars in Perinatology, 3*, 73–84.

Terkel, J., & Rosenblatt, J. S. (1968). Maternal behavior induced by maternal blood plasma injected into virgin rats. *Journal of Comparative and Physiological Psychology, 65*, 479–482.

Terkel, J., & Rosenblatt, J. S. (1971). Aspects of nonhormonal maternal behavior in the rat. *Hormones & Behavior, 2*, 161–171.

Terkel, J., & Rosenblatt, J. S. (1972). Humoral factors underlying maternal behavior at parturition: Cross transfusion between freely moving rats. *Journal of Comparative and Physiological Psychology, 80*, 365–371.

Terlecki, L. J., & Sainsbury, R. S. (1978). Effects of fimbria lesions on maternal behavior in the rat. *Physiology & Behavior, 21*, 89–97.

Tinkelpaugh, O. L., & Hartman, C. G. (1932). Behavior and maternal care of the newborn monkey (*macaca mulatta*—M. rhesus). *Journal of Genetic Psychology, 40*, 257–286.

Turner, B. H., & Knapp, M. E. (1976). Projections of the nucleus and tracts of the stria terminalis following lesions at the level of the anterior commissure. *Experimental Neurology, 51*, 468–479.

Uhl, G., Kuhar, M., & Snyder, S. (1978). Enkephalin-containing pathway: Amygdaloid efferents in the stria terminalis. *Brain Research, 149*, 223–228.

Vermouth, N. T., & Deis, R. P. (1974). Prolactin release and lactogenesis after ovariectomy in pregnant rats: Effect of ovarian hormones. *Journal of Endocrinology, 63*, 13–20.

Voci, V. E., & Carlson, N. R. (1973). Enhancement of maternal behavior and nest building following systemic and diencephalic administration of prolactin and progesterone in the mouse. *Journal of Comparative and Physiological Psychology, 83*, 388–393.

Wallace, P. (1973). *Hormonal influences on maternal behavior in the female Mongolian gerbil (Meriones unguiculatus)*. Unpublished doctoral dissertation, University of Texas at Austin.

Wallace, P., Owen, P., & Thiessen, D. D. (1973). The control and function of maternal scent marking in the Mongolian gerbil. *Physiology & Behavior, 10*, 463–466.

Wardlaw, A. E., Thoron, L., & Frantz, A. G. (1982). Effects of sex steroids on known B-endorphins. *Brain Research, 245*, 327–331.

Weisner, B. P., & Sheard, N. M. (1933). *Maternal behavior in the rat*. London: Oliver and Boyd.

Weller, K. L., & Smith, D. A. (1982). Afferent connections to the bed nucleus of the stria terminalis. *Brain Research, 232*, 255–270.

White, N., & Weingarten, H. (1976). Effects of amygdaloid lesions on exploration by rats. *Physiology & Behavior, 17*, 73–79.

Winans, S. S., & Powers, J. B. (1977). Neonatal and two-stage olfactory bulbectomy: Effects on male hamster sexual behavior. *Behavioral Biology, 10*, 461–471.

Winans, S. S., & Scalia, F. (1970). Amygdaloid nucleus: New afferent input from the vomeronasal organ. *Science, 170*, 330–332.

Woodside, B., & Leon, M. (1980). Thermoendocrine influences on nesting behavior in rats. *Journal of Comparative and Physiological Psychology, 98*, 41–60.

Woodside, B., Pelchat, R., & Leon, M. (1980). Acute elevation of heat load of mother rats curtails maternal nest bouts. *Journal of Comparative and Physiological Psychology, 93*, 61–68.

Zarrow, M. X., Farooq, A., & Denenberg, V. H. (1962a). Maternal behavior in the rabbit: Critical period for nest building following castration during pregnancy. *Proceedings of the Society for Experimental Biology and Medicine, 111*, 537–538.

Zarrow, M. X., Gandelman, R., & Deneberg, V. H. (1971). Prolactin: Is it an essential hormone for maternal behavior in the mammal? *Hormones & Behavior, 2,* 343–354.

Zarrow, M. X., Sawin, P. B., Ross, S., & Denenberg, V. H. (1962b). Maternal behavior and its endocrine basis in the rabbit. In E. L. Bliss (Ed.), *Roots of behavior.* New York: Harper and Row.

Zarrow, M. X., Sawin, P. B., Ross, S., Denenberg, V. H., Crary, D., Wilson, E. D., & Farooq, A. (1961). Maternal behavior in the rabbit: Evidence for endocrine basis of maternal nest building and additional data on maternal nest building in the Dutchbelted race. *Journal of Reproduction and Fertility, 2,* 152–162.

8 Antecedents of Early Parenting

S. Shirley Feldman
Sharon Churnin Nash
Stanford University

Over the last 3 decades, psychologists interested in studying the phenomena of parenting have largely focused on the impact of varying parental practices on the child. Comparatively few empirical studies have addressed the issue of what accounts for individual differences in parenting behavior itself.

> It is as if little interest exists within the discipline of developmental psychology for understanding the distal or 'formal' causes of child competence, and thus empirical energies are primarily concentrated on documenting the proximal or 'efficient' causes (e.g. parenting practices). While this special concern for efficient causality is understandable, the general failure to consider the causes of individual differences in patterns of parenting shows little appreciation for the fact that efficient casual explanations lie embedded within formal casual systems and remain dependent upon distal causes. (Belsky, Robins, & Gamble, 1984, p. 255).

Of the work that has been reported, it is clear that parenting is multiply determined. Belsky et al. (1984) have suggested that the three major determinants of parental functioning are the personal resources of the adult, the sources of stress and support, and ultimately, the characteristics of the child. Over recent years, an impressive body of work has been generated which addresses the last point. The major thrust of this research has been that children are not merely the products of parental practices, but rather in significant ways are producers of their own development (Lerner & Busch-Rossnagle, 1981).

The impact of the infant on the caregiver has become widely recognized by developmentalists and excellent reviews of the area are available (Belsky & Tolan, 1981; Lewis & Rosenblum, 1974). More recently it has been proposed

(Belsky, 1984) that neither temperament nor other child characteristics per se shape parenting, rather the *goodness-of-fit* between parent and child determines the nature and development of parent-child interactions (Lerner & Lerner, 1983). This body of research has done much to challenge the traditional, unidirectional, "social mold" orientation that previously dominated the field and exclusively focused attention on parental influence on child functioning. The theme of the present review, however, is more specifically focused on the antecedents of parenting, namely factors prior to the birth of the child that affect or predict parental functioning.

The process of parenting begins with the anticipation of a new life. "Conception is the beginning not only of the growing fetus but also of the family in a new form, with an additional member, and with changed relationships" especially for couples having their first child (Grossman, Eichler, & Winickoff, 1980, p. 3). Joint research on families and developing children underscores the importance of the transitions between expectancy, birth and early parenthood for all three members of the newly defined family (MacFarlane, 1977). A number of researchers have speculated that "early parent-child relationships evolve from a time starting prior to birth" (Entwisle & Doering, 1981). The question arises as to which types of prebirth parental characteristics or circumstances are most effective in predicting certain parent-child and child outcomes (Belsky, 1984; Heinicke, Diskin, Ramsey-Klee, & Given, 1983).

The challenges of reviewing this area are as numerous and broad as the definition of parenting itself. Parenting covers all the behaviors that parents (both mothers and fathers) carry out in the course of raising children. It is clear that this term is altogether too inclusive to deal with as a unitary global dependent variable. It is possible, even probable, that each aspect of the multifaceted parenting process (e.g., caretaking, play, limit-setting, sensitivity, etc.) is preceded by a unique constellation of antecedents. "To further pursue the impact of pre-birth parental characteristics on the post-natal family development, it is useful to choose a limited number of outcome measures and then to determine which pattern of antecedents anticipates variations in these criteria" (Heinicke et al., 1983, p. 3). Thus, the first undertaking of this review is to consider some of the components of parenting.

Not only is parenting defined by a number of different behaviors, the nature of these behaviors may be mediated by a variety of demographic variables. Such factors change the social context in which the behavior is to be understood. For example, socioeconomic status, race or ethnic-cultural differences modify the value or appropriateness of a given parental behavior, and most likely, redefine the antecedents of the same behavior (Entwisle & Doering, 1981). The complexity of the situation is increased by the probability that these mediators interact with each other in complicated ways. Since most of the available data is based on samples of convenience, i.e., mainstream middle class Caucasian subjects, it is not possible at this time to tease apart the intricate picture created by these mediating factors. However, caution is advised in extrapolating results derived from one demographic group of subjects to another.

One of the most compelling mediators of parenting behavior, and similarly, of the antecedents of these behaviors, is the sex of the adult in question. Parenting behaviors can have distinctive meanings for women in contrast to men. Despite an increased involvement of fathers in childcare, recent reviews still find play to be the major form of interaction of fathers with infants, toddlers, and young children (Parke & Tinsley, 1983; Russell & Radin, 1984). Due to limited data, it is not clear whether the antecedents of fathering are different from those of mothering. Even if a behavior is common to both mothers and fathers (e.g., nurturance) its antecedents may vary as a function of the sex-specific significance the concept has for men and women (e.g., nurturance is part of the sex-appropriate sex-typing of women but involves cross-sex-typing for men). Thus, given the fact that gender is one of the most significant differentiating mediators of parental behavior, this review deals separately with what is known about the sex-specific antecedents of mothering and fathering.

Just as the definition of parenting is related to the sex of the adult, it may also be differentially related to the sex of the child. Shereshefsky and Yarrow (1974) found that a variety of predictors of maternal behavior only held for women who had daughters but not sons. Unfortunately, few studies look separately at the antecedents of parenting girls and boys; accordingly, results for both sexes are reported together.

Parenting, whether mothering or fathering also differs as a function of the age of the child. Parenting an infant, a toddler, a verbal nursery schooler, an elementary school-aged child or a teenager differs in the amount of time it requires, the nature of the parenting activities, the amount of physical and emotional investment, and the skills it requires of parents. Thus in seeking antecedents of parenting, it is important to specify the age group of the child. This review is limited to parenting in the first year of life. Preparenting characteristics are more likely to be effective predictors during the first year of parenting than later in childhood. Subsequently, measures of interaction with the infant are apt to be better predictors of later parenting (Heinicke et al., 1983). This is not to minimize the importance of the preparenting characteristics, only to recognize that they are captured and transformed in the course of the transactions and interactions with the infant. Major developments in relationships occur in the first year of life, both in terms of the parents bonding to the infant and the infant becoming attached to the parents. These relational bonds have profound impact on subsequent parent-child relations, and child development.

Parenting a first-born child is a different experience than parenting a later-born child. Particularly during infancy, the exclusive interactions with the first-born are generally not duplicated with subsequent children, but are perhaps offset by the greater experience parents bring to interactions with later-borns. At any rate, Grossman et al. (1980) found different predictors of parenting for mothers of first- and later-borns. Since most studies have considered only primiparous women and their husbands, this chapter focuses on data for parents of firstborns. Considerably more work, however, needs to be devoted to parenting by multiparous women and their husbands.

Not surprisingly, the majority of studies that attempt to associate the adult's characteristics with parental functioning are cross-sectional in design, i.e., the presumed antecedents of parenting are measured contemporaneously with parenting behavior. As with all correlations derived in this way, inferring directionality of effects is impossible. Other studies are retrospective in design. For example, abusive mothers more often report having suffered abuse or separation from their parents than do nonabusive mothers (Parke & Collmer, 1975). While the limitations of retrospective research are well known, in seeking childhood antecedents of adult behavior there frequently is no practical alternative (other than carrying out a 30 year prospective study). Whenever possible, especially where the antecedents and outcome behavior are located closer in time, prospective research is the preferred strategy. In this review, only longitudinal studies are evaluated in order to discover and verify whether the antecedents identified and frequently cited by these other research approaches are in fact "antecedents."

The longitudinal studies reviewed in this chapter fall into two categories. The first group of studies is more selective in terms of number of antecedents of parenting evaluated (Entwisle & Doering, 1981; Lamb, Frodi, Hwang, & Frodi, 1983; McHale & Huston, 1984; and Moss & Jones, 1977). Generally these studies are better grounded in theory, i.e., they usually make predictions about findings. The second set of studies tend to be widescale, less focused studies which tend to cast their nets widely (Feldman & Nash, 1984; Feldman, Nash, & Aschenbrenner, 1983; Grossman et al., 1980; Heinicke et al., 1983; Shereshefsky & Yarrow, 1974). The latter studies generate massive data sets that have undergone a great deal of manipulation and reduction and they present summary measures based on factor analysis and other multivariate techniques. The possibility of direct replication of such research is remote, so noting convergence between different studies is particularly important.

To summarize, in this review, we limit ourselves to longitudinal studies of middle class white Americans who are parents of firstborn infants between birth and 12-months-of-age. We look at a wide diversity of parenting behaviors most of which have been observed or rated by objective, trained researchers (rather than by self-ratings). We consider the antecedents of mothering and fathering separately. By limiting our review accordingly, we hope to ascertain the "hard facts" about the prebirth antecedents of parenting.

PRENATAL ANTECEDENTS OF PARENTING: DIRECT EFFECTS

The short-term longitudinal studies reviewed here have evaluated adults during various points in the expectancy stage in an attempt to ascertain the predictive value of given variables with regard to the first year of parenting. Among the potential antecedents of parenting investigated, three basic influences have emerged. The first has to do with individual characteristics of the parent-to-be, such as age, personality, and mood states. The second involves the adjustment to and psychological preparation for the pregnancy experience itself. Finally, the remainder examines the larger social context within which parent-child dynamics exist, namely, relationships with significant others, social networks, and occupational experiences. The impact of these precursors were assessed in laboratory measures of parenting or in naturalistic home observations. At times, clinicians' ratings based on observations were compiled to create more complex, comprehensive, and subjective variables. Despite the fact that each study defined outcome measures somewhat differently, many similarities were evident. Among the most widely used dependent measures were responsiveness to the infant (which assessed the extent to which parents were attuned to the needs and signals of their infant and the promptness with which they responded to them), caregiving/childcare skills, and playful/affectionate interactions (with an aim towards initiating or prolonging social encounters).

Most longitudinal studies rely on correlational analyses (simple correlations, multiple regression analyses, or path analyses) to assess whether the presumed antecedent effectively predicted parenting. The studies are described in Table 8.1, and the results are summarized in Table 8.2 and Table 8.3.

Characteristics of the Parent-To-Be

According to the psychoanalytic view, the most significant influences on parenting are the enduring personality traits of the parents. Such an assertion has not yet received empirical confirmation since the appropriate test in which personality is assessed in the adult prior to pregnancy or parenthood remains to be done. To date, the best and most comprehensive studies have collected measures of personality during pregnancy rather than prior to it. Since pregnancy is a transitional stage, frequently accompanied by emotional upheaval and lability (Feldman & Nash, 1984; Leiffer, 1977), we should be cautious in assuming that personality measures obtained at that time reflect the prepregnant personality. However, based on the results of the longitudinal studies reviewed in Table 8.2, personality assessed during pregnancy is a valuable predictor of later parenting behavior, especially for women.

TABLE 8.1
Description of Major Longitudinal Studies of the transition From Expectancy to Parenthood for Primiparous Women and Their Husbands

Authors	Procedure	Expectancy Measures[a]	Parenting Measures
Entwisle & Doering, 1981	120 women, 60 men were studied. Half of sample was middle-class. Women were interviewed at 6th and 9th month of pregnancy, interviewed and observed at 3 weeks postpartum. Men were interviewed at 9th month of wife's pregnancy, and 4-8 weeks postpartum. (Only data from middle class sample reported in this review.)	Preparation level for birth and childcare, Plans for rooming-in and breastfeeding, Previous babycare experience.	Mothering, a composite based on type and quality of interaction with baby, feelings about holding and caring for the newborn, and response to baby's cries. Fathering, a composite based on feelings when baby was first held, feelings when baby cried, and response to baby's cries.
Feldman & Nash, 1982	30 upper middle-class women were interviewed at 7-9th month of pregnancy and interviewed and observed at 6 months postpartum.	Adaptation to pregnancy, Mood states, Sex-typing, Marital relationships, Relations with parents (past and present), Interest in unfamiliar infants, Job salience, Age.	Affectionate interactions shown by mother during an interview with both parents present. Maintaining interactive sequences with baby during play.
Feldman, Nash, & Aschenbrenner, 1983	30 upper middle-class husbands were interviewed at 7-9th month of expectancy, and interviewed and observed at 6 months postpartum.	See Feldman & Nash, 1982 (above)	Caretaking observed during play session and interview, plus reported time care-taking at home. Playfulness observed during an interview and reported playfulness at home.

Grossman, Eichler, & Winickoff, 1980	84 middle- and upper-middle class primiparous and multiparous couples were interviewed at 3rd and 8th month of pregnancy, and after delivery. Mother-infant interviews and observations were made at 2 and 12 months postpartum. Father interviews were held at 2 and 12 months, and observations were made at 2 months postpartum. (Only data for primiparous couples are reported in this review.)	Adaptation, Anxiety, Depression, Sex typing, Identification with mother, Couple preparedness, Symptoms & complications, Social support, Life change, SES	Mothering adaptations at 2 months, a composite based on observational ratings of quality of physical contact, expression of affect, sensitivity and acceptance. Reciprocity, based on ratings of observed feeding of infant. Mothering adaptation at 12 months, a composite based on observational ratings of acceptance of baby, feelings of competence and responsibility for infant. Fathering adaptation at 2 months defined as for mothering adaptation at 2 months (see above). Fathering adaptation at 12 months, an interview measure of 14 dimensions including physical contact, expression of affect, sensitivity, responsibility and acceptance.
Heinicke, Diskin, Ramsey-Klee, & Given, 1983	46 middle-class women were interviewed and tested (MMPI, IQ) at 4-5th month of pregnancy and interviewed and observed at 1, 3, 6, 12 months postpartum. Only the 12-month data are used as the outcome measure.	Adaptation/ego strength, Adaptation to pregnancy, Marital adaptation, Confidence visualizing self as mother, Experience being mothered/fathered, Experience/interest in children, MMPI scores, including ego strength, trust, warmth, hypersensitivity, persecutory ideas, family conflict, Expressive styles (12 included), SES, IQ	Responsiveness a composite measure of the appropriateness of mother's behavior to baby's needs, based on factor analysis of observations and ratings, Social stimulation of infant, Cognitive stimulation of infant,

Study	Sample	Variables
Lamb, Frodi, Hwang, & Frodi, 1982	52 middle-class Swedish couples were interviewed at 7th and 9th month of pregnancy, and at 5 months postpartum.	Value of parenthood, Value of work, Anticipated paternal involvement, Support from others regarding anticipated paternal involvement.	Amount of paternal care-taking, Father involvement with child.
McHale & Huston, 1984	34 couples in the first year of marriage were studied. All were pregnant before marriage. They were interviewed twice during pregnancy and again 2-15 months postpartum. During pregnancy and again during parenthood, 9 phone interviews were conducted.	Preference for sharing child-care role, Perceived competence at parenting, Attitudes towards women, Sex-typed personality traits.	Extent of parent involvement in child-care, assessed by proportion of parent's home activities which included the child, amount of contact with child, nature of contact (play vs. leisure).
Moss & Jones, 1977	121 lower-class and upper-middle class women were interviewed in last trimester of pregnancy. Six-hour home observations were conducted 3 months postpartum. (Only data from upper-middle class sample reported in this review.)	Depression, Anticipation of infant as positive, Interest in affectionate contact, Interest in social interaction with infant, Positive to infant/maternal role, Fearful/inadequate, Provides & seeks stimulation, Close family ties.	Caretakes, Initiates social interaction, Responds promptly to cry, Holds, Smiles, Talks, Vis-a-vis Kisses
Shereshefsky & Yarrow, 1974	60 middle-class women were interviewed at 4th, 7th, & 9th month of pregnancy, and observed with their infants at 1, 1½, 3, and 6 months postpartum.	Ego strength, Nurturance, Adaptation to pregnancy, Dealing with pregnancy fears, Visualization of self as mother, Husband's responsiveness to wife's pregnancy, Interest in children, Experience being mothered	Maternal responsiveness to infant at 3 and 6 months, based on observations and ratings.

[a] This table summarizes only those variables considered as potential antecedents of parenting. Variables included in the studies for other purposes have been omitted.

TABLE 8.2
Predicting Diverse Aspects of Mothering Behavior During the First Year of the Infant's Life From Selected Maternal Characteristics Assessed During Pregnancy

	Maturity/Ego Strength	Age	Anxiety/Depression	Feminine Traits	Masculine Traits	Marital Relations	Relations with Parents	Job Salience	Pregnancy Adaptation	Planned Pregnancy	Interest/Experience with Babies
Acceptance/sensitivity (2 mos)[b]	0	+	–	0	0	0	nd	nd	nd	0	nd
Reciprocity in feeding (2 mos)[b]	+	+	0	0	0	0	nd	nd	nd	–	nd
Caretakes (3 mos)[e]	0	nd	0	nd	nd	nd	0	nd	nd	nd	0
Initiates social interaction (3 mos)[e]	–	nd	–	nd	nd	nd	0	nd	nd	nd	+
Responds to cry (3 mos)[e]	+	nd	0	nd	nd	nd	0	nd	nd	nd	+
Responsive (1-6 mos)[f]	0	nd	–	nd	nd	0	0	nd	+	0	+
Affectionate interactions (6 mos)[a]	nd	0	–	0	0	0	0	0	0	0	+
Sustained sequences (6 mos)[a]	nd	+	–	0	+	0	+	+	0	0	+
Childcare skills (8 mos)[d]	nd	nd	nd	0	0	nd	nd	0	nd	nd	0
Distal interaction (12 mos)[c]	+	nd	nd	nd	nd	0	0	nd	0	nd	0
Responsive (12 mos)[c]	+	nd	nd	nd	nd	0	0	nd	0	nd	0
Stimulates cognitive development (12 mos)[c]	0	nd	nd	nd	nd	0	0	nd	0	nd	0
Involved/sensitive (12 mos)[b]	0	+	–	–	nd	0	nd	nd	+	0	nd

+ significant positive correlation
– significant negative correlation
0 no significant correlation
nd no data

[a] Feldman & Nash (1982)
[b] Grossman et al. (1980)
[c] Heinicke et al. (1983)
[d] McHale & Huston (1984)
[e] Moss & Jones (1977)
[f] Shereshefsky & Yarrow (1974)

TABLE 8.3
Predicting Diverse Aspects of Fathering Behavior During the First Year of the Infant's
Life From Selected Paternal Characteristics Assessed During Pregnancy

	Maturity/Ego Strength	Age	Anxiety/Depression	Feminine Traits	Masculine Traits	Marital Relations	Relations With Parents	Job Salience	Pregnancy Adaptation	Planned Pregnancy	Interest/Experience with Babies
Adaptation* (2mos)[b]	0	0	0	0	0	0	0	nd	0	nd	nd
Caretake** (5 mos)[c]	nd	nd	nd	nd	nd	nd	nd	0	nd	nd	nd
Interaction* (5 mos)[c]	nd	nd	+	0	0	+	+	0	+	nd	nd
Play (6 mos)[c]	nd	−	0	+	0	+	0	−	+	−	0
Caretake (6 mos)[a]	nd	−	0	+	0	+	0	−	+	−	0
Childcare skill** (8 mos)[d]	nd	nd	nd	nd	nd	nd	nd	0	nd	nd	0
Paternal adaptation** (12 mos)[b]	0	−	0	+	0	0	+	nd	+	nd	nd

[a]Feldman, Nash, & Aschenbrenner (1983)
[b]Grossman et al. (1980)
[c]Lamb et al. (1982)
[d]Moss & Jones (1977)

\+ significant positive association
− significant negative association
0 no significant association
nd no data

*includes first-time and experienced fathers
**interview measure

A number of investigators have speculated as to specific personality qualities which would be assets for the parenting role (Brody & Axelrod, 1978; Lamb & Easterbrooks, 1980). Heinicke (1984) has observed that global indices of personality functioning during pregnancy are the most accurate predictors of later maternal functioning. Recent longitudinal studies of at-risk populations concur that broadly defined characteristics such as "level of personal integration" are better forecasters of inadequate care than specific measures of traits (Brunnquell, Crichton, & Egeland, 1981; Sameroff, Seifer, & Zax, 1982). As indicated in Table 8.2, a number of predictive studies conclude that pregnant women who are endowed with ego strength and maturity become more effective mothers in a variety of situations. This result holds for reciprocity in a feeding situation, responsivity to crying, and for appropriateness of mother's behavior to baby's needs and temperament. It appears then, that these more molar personality antecedents reflect the extent to which the mother has the maturity and sophistication necessary for synchronous parent-child relations. Integrity and strength of ego functioning subsumes many aspects of personality, including "intellectual ability, general comprehension, and most significantly, the ability to deal effectively with the ambivalent and stressful affect inherent in a first pregnancy" and new motherhood (Brunnquell et al., 1981, p. 274).

In addition to the direct effects these general measures of personality have on maternal behavior, ego strength and maturity shape parenting indirectly by influencing the broader social context in which the mother-child relationship exists, namely marital relations, social networks, and occupational experience (Belsky, 1984). Thus, given the multifaceted impact of personality on parenting, there is convincing evidence that the well-integrated mature woman is a good candidate for coping with, and competently negotiating the new tasks of motherhood. Unfortunately, little is known about the effectiveness of men's personality characteristics as predictors of fathering behavior, in large part because the relevant studies have not been carried out.

To the extent that age is a marker for maturity, it is interesting to note that among middle-class, mostly married samples, older mothers show better maternal adaptation and more reciprocity with 2-month-olds (Grossman et al., 1980) and are better at maintaining longer interactive sequences with their 6-month-olds (Feldman & Nash, 1982). Thus for women, maturity, whether measured psychologically or chronologically, positively predicts effective parenting. In contrast, for men, age negatively predicts parental functioning. The older the expectant father the less likely it is that he will care for or play with his 6-month-old (Feldman et al., 1983), or adapt successfully to his paternal role with his 12-month-old (Grossman et al., 1980). It may be that for men between the ages of 20 and 40, the greater the length of time one goes without sharing one's spouse with a child, the more the child's arrival is perceived as an emotional dethroning. Alternatively, there may be cohort differences between the older and younger men sampled. The older fathers may have more traditional expectations concerning their participation in parenting. Younger men, having spent their teen years during a time when being an involved father was culturally sanctioned, may find it easier and more emotionally consonant to be an effective parent. This interpretation cannot be verified for a few years, until both younger and older fathers have been exposed to the current attitudes permitting a more involved fathering style. At this point in time, however, it appears that for middle class women, delaying childbearing bodes well for maternal investment, whereas for men, the longer the time without the responsibility of parenthood, the more difficult the adjustment is once it occurs.

Although there are no longitudinal data available which clearly link personality patterns evident during pregnancy to the prepregnant state, it is important to note that complex personality variables such as ego strength and maturity are not ephemeral. They evolve developmentally through gradual personal integration and are not readily amendable to change. Thus, it is reasonable to extrapolate that these more global personality descriptors predate the expectancy state when they were tapped into and studied. In contrast, mood states such as anxiety and depression tend to fluctuate (Leiffer, 1977) and it is more difficult to chart these variables over time with any confidence. This is particularly true among nonclinical populations such as the ones sampled in the studies reviewed. These were basically normal middle-class adults, functioning well in the context of their lives, who were not experiencing debilitating levels of anxiety or depression. There was no evidence to suggest their prepregnancy personalities were characterized by excessive mood states.

Given the transitory nature of moods, and the fact that emotionally lability is commonly reported among pregnant women (Feldman & Nash, 1984), it is interesting to find that both anxiety and depression are impressive (negative) predictors of mothering but not of fathering. Anxiety, whether measured first or third trimester is inversely related to mothering at 6 and 12 months postpartum (Feldman & Nash, 1982; Grossman et al., 1980). A similar picture emerges for depression (which was assessed only once, early in pregnancy). A depressed reaction to the onset of pregnancy is inversely related to maternal adaptation at 2 months (Grossman et al., 1980). Prepartum depression is also prognostic of poor maternal functioning at 12 months on self-report interview measures (Grossman et al., 1980). Thus, the results suggest that those women who are bound up with their own problems and anxieties during pregnancy are less emotionally available to their babies. What is so surprising about these results, is that longitudinal studies have indicated elevated mood states during pregnancy are commonplace (Leiffer, 1977). Nevertheless, these results suggest that elevated negative mood states during pregnancy should not be cavalierly dismissed, but rather must be considered prognostic warnings of a difficult adjustment to motherhood even among normal populations of women.

A number of studies have explored the relationship between sex-typed personality characteristics and parenting behavior. Given the absence of theoretical rationale, it is not surprising that masculinity in and of itself fails to predict parental adaptation for either women or men. However, it has been hypothesized that femininity should be linked to parenting since both are based on an expressive interpersonal orientation. In fact, motherhood is sometimes described as the ultimate expression of femininity. Consistent with studies in which mothering and sex-typed personality have been measured contemporaneously (Russell, 1978), the longitudinal data available do not indicate a positive relationship between prenatal self-ratings of femininity and good mothering. Consistent with Bem's description of the ineffectual feminine personality who did not demonstrate the instrumentality necessary to nurture a kitten (Bem, Martyna, & Watson, 1976), there is some indication that heightened femininity might even be maladaptive to sensitive mothering. Perhaps it is because the cultural definition of femininity typically includes negative characteristics such as childlike, flatterable, and gullible, which are inimical to the initiative-taking and general competence which are also essential components of good mothering. For a woman to be an effective parent, an androgynous blend of (feminine) emotional expressiveness and (masculine) instrumentality is necessary to provide the nurturant sensitivity and assertive limit-setting essential to the maternal role.

In contrast to the findings for women, femininity is predictive of good parenting among men. Self-ratings of femininity measured during expectancy are related to high-caretaking among fathers of 6-month-olds (Feldman et al., 1983), good adaptation to fathering at 12 months (Grossman et al., 1980), as well as desire to be involved with caretaking and paternal skills (McHale & Huston, 1984). There may be a threshhold phenomenon regarding the value of femininity to parenting, i.e., a certain minimum level is necessary for sensitive involved parenting, but more than that minimum prerequisite is not additionally helpful (or in extreme cases, desirable). Since most women acquire that minimum level of femininity through normal developmental socialization, femininity as a personality characteristic does not effectively differentiate women as mothers. In contrast, since fewer men in our culture acquire the minimum amount of femininity critical to effective and nurturing fathering, it becomes a more valuable parameter for differentiating men as involved/succorant fathers.

The Social Context of Parenthood

Becoming a parent typically occurs in the context of a marital or long-term interpersonal commitment. To what extent are prenatal marital variables good predictors of parenting? Four of the longitudinal studies reviewed assessed marriage during pregnancy. In each case marital measures did not predict mother-child interactions either in the laboratory or in home observations. Why the surprising absence of results for women given the importance of marriage to their emotional well-being? According to unpublished interview data collected during expectancy (Feldman & Nash, 1982), many men tried to be unusually supportive, tolerant, and flexible during their wives' pregnancies. They reported their wives to be "more moody" and worked at "not upsetting" them. Given the more tolerant atmosphere created by their husbands, women seem to express a more homogeneous, positive view of marriage during pregnancy (Feldman, 1971). Lack of variability in marital assessments may also be due to the fact that pregnancy is a period when women find it personally threatening to view their marriage as being in jeopardy. Heightened dependency needs arise due to physical limitations inherent in pregnancy, partial or full withdrawal from the work force, fears regarding bringing a child into a discordant marriage, or worse, raising a child alone. Thus, a kind of cognitive dissonance may emerge for women during pregnancy, leading them to espouse the belief that all is well with their marital relationship. For all these reasons, pregnancy (especially third trimester) may not be a particularly valid or representative time to assess marriage for women.[1] It should also be noted that among the middle-class couples that typically volunteered as subjects, those with problematic marriages were less likely to participate in the research in the first place, and when they did agree to join a study, they less often followed through. Accordingly, the studies tapped a relatively narrow range of well-adjusted marriages during a period marked by greater than usual tolerance and minimal conflict.

Although there was less variability among women in their views of their marriage (since they were given much more emotional leeway by their husbands), the men showed somewhat more diversity in their marital assessments (given the stress of putting up with their emotionally labile wives). As a result, a variety of marital variables strongly predict fathering at 2 months (Grossman et al., 1980), and at 6 months (Feldman et al., 1983), but not at 12 months (Grossman et al., 1980). It may be that a foundation of marital satisfaction predating the birth of the child, allows men to feel more secure (vis-à-vis their wives). Since their status with their mate is not threatened by the new baby, they do not develop the kinds of competitive feelings that would interfere with paternal involvement. Whatever the psychological mechanism, it appears that for men the state of the marital relationship prior to the birth of the baby is a useful predictor of paternal functioning during the first 6 months of parenthood.

Another aspect of marriage that has been investigated is sexual activity and satisfaction. Using interview measures, Grossman et al. (1980) found sexual satisfaction during the expectancy period predicts paternal adaptation at 2 months ($r = .33, p < .10$) but not at 12 months. Among women, sexual satisfaction during pregnancy was unrelated to maternal adaptation at 2 or 12 months, but correlates negatively ($r = -.41, p < .05$) with reciprocity at feeding (2 months) and with other measures of mothering when the child is older. Perhaps the reversed pattern for women indicates that focusing on sexual gratification during pregnancy is indicative of a self-focus versus a psychic investment in the coming child.

---

[1]The marital relationship assessed *after* the birth of the child is associated with diverse measures of mothering and fathering of infants, toddlers and preschool-aged children (Belsky, 1984; Cowan & Cowan, 1984; Dickie, 1984; Goldberg & Easterbrooks, 1984; Russell, 1974).

The marital relationship is one of many potential sources of social support. Social support has been defined as information which leads one to believe she/he is cared for and loved, esteemed, and a member of a network of mutual obligations (Cobb, 1976). It has been proposed that stress, especially the stress inherent in any major role transition can be ameliorated by such support (Belsky, 1984). If so, it may be that the presence or absence of social support during pregnancy may affect the adult's preparedness to cope with parenthood. Among the social support systems studied, current relationship with parents was of limited predictive value for new mothers, and somewhat more successful for new fathers. A man's relationship with his mother is related to playfulness with his baby during the first year. A positive relationship with both parents is predictive of paternal caretaking involvement (Feldman et al., 1983). Good relationship with parents indicates family orientation and/or interpersonal adaptation. Since these qualities are part of the feminine cultural stereotype, they are expected of women and thus may not be particularly useful in determining individual differences among them. In contrast, these characteristics are counterstereotypic for men and thus appear to have greater differentiating predictive value. Only one study examined relations with in-laws as a possible factor, and found no predictive connection (Feldman et al., 1983). More research is needed to clarify to what extent in-laws are part of the support system or a source of stress.

Research examining the effects of more formal social support systems reveal an inverse relationship between social supports during pregnancy and observed maternal adaptation when the infant was 12-months-old. Although the results seem counter-intuitive, they may reflect the reality that the most-stressed, least-coping pregnant women seek out social support. What is clearly needed is an experimental study which randomly assigns pregnant women to various support groups versus no formal support system to determine the short and long-term impact of prenatal support on parental adaptation.

To summarize briefly, the evidence on emotional support during pregnancy (whether it be marital, familial, or formal) suggests that women's subsequent mothering is not affected by it. Thus, it appears that for married middle-class, emotionally stable women, mothering is a "buffered" system in the sense that it is less vulnerable to the whims of social circumstances. The presence or absence of *prenatal* support has a limited impact on maternal adaptation and functioning. Support during pregnancy may ameliorate the stresses of the expectancy period itself without generalizing to the very different demands of the next stage of life. Interestingly, evidence on the presence of social support during parenthood reveals a positive relationship with more sensitive and involved parenting (Belsky, 1984; Crockenberg, 1984). Thus social support appears to be of value to pregnancy and parenthood in time-limited stage-specific ways, and does not transfer readily across stages of life.

One additional aspect of the social context within which expectant parents function is their paid occupations. Job involvement is somewhat predictive of parenting for both men and women, but in opposite directions. Among new fathers, the more important his work is to him, the less involved he is with caretaking and playing with his baby (Feldman et al., 1983). In contrast, among women, emphasis on one's career during pregnancy predicts high-sustained mother-child interactions later on. Perhaps women with high job salience are women who can commit themselves to whatever they see as their primary task. During pregnancy they are still involved with work issues. After the birth of the baby when most mothers had given up paid employment, in situations that focus on the baby they are baby-oriented, sensitive to emergent turntaking, and thus able to sustain interaction sequences. Further home observation is needed to reveal whether these women behave this way when alone with the infant in the privacy of their homes, and in particular when they return to work and experience marked job/motherhood time conflicts.

The Expectancy Experience

Many aspects of the pregnancy experience itself have been investigated. It is noteworthy that reactions to the pregnancy are more indicative of men's ultimate parental functioning than of women's. A man's adjustment to pregnancy is predictive of more caretaking and play with his 6-month-old (Feldman et al., 1983) and of paternal adaptation at 12 months (Grossman et al., 1980). For women, adaptation to pregnancy is linked to one aspect of parental functioning, more sensitive involvement with 12-month-olds (Grossman et al., 1980). Whether or not the pregnancy was planned is not related to maternal behavior since for the women sampled, the planning of the pregnancy was not correlated with acceptance of the baby. The women studied readily availed themselves of abortions for unwanted pregnancies, so unplanned pregnancies that were kept were clearly wanted. The subjective experiences of the men were somewhat different in this regard, since the final decision about the fate of pregnancy was rarely theirs. Thus for men, there may be more variability regarding the wantedness of the pregnancy. Accordingly, there is evidence that for men, there is a relationship between planning and ultimate parenting, however not in the direction one would expect. Men respond to unplanned pregnancies with greater involvement in play and caretaking of 6-month-olds (Feldman et al., 1983). This is consistent with the findings of Parke and Tinsley (1983) who concluded that men are more involved in fathering whenever there is a major stress associated with the birth of the child.

One aspect of the pregnancy itself which is of considerable value in predicting mothering is reactions to physical symptoms inherent in the 9-month span. Not surprisingly, investigations of this phenomenon have focused exclusively on the bearer of the child rather than her mate, although it could be argued that the man's reactions to the woman's physical symptoms might in fact be revealing of his fathering potential with regard to empathy, self-other orientation, etc. In any case, Zemlick and Watson (1953) followed lower socioeconomic status women over the course of their pregnancy, obtaining their obstetricians' as well as their own assessments of the number, type, and severity of physical symptoms experienced. After parturition, during the first week of life, two independent observations were made of the mother-child interaction. The investigators assessed how persistent the mothers were in feeding when the infant was disinterested; we have redefined this measure as *insensitive mothering*. They reported that the more psychosomatic symptoms manifested during pregnancy, the more insensitive mothering displayed while feeding the newborn. Similarly, Grossman et al. (1980) reported the number of physical symptoms experienced during the latter part of pregnancy predicted low reciprocity during feeding the infant and low maternal adaptation at 2 months. However, by the time the baby was 1-year-old, the numbers of physical symptoms during pregnancy was unrelated to mothering. It may be that women who are preoccupied with themselves and their physical well-being during pregnancy are revealing a more egocentric self-orientation that interferes with the other-orientation necessary for the effective mothering of a dependent other. Such women may be so attuned to their own somatic cues that their internal needs distract them from accurately tuning into the needs of the infant. As the child becomes older, somewhat more verbal, and thus clearer in expressing needs, this relationship between focusing on self prepartum and insensitivity to the infant postpartum diminishes.

In contrast to the self-orientation depicted by the women preoccupied with their personal comfort and well-being during pregnancy, women who focus on others, especially babies, during this period display far more maternal sensitivity postpartum. In fact, interest or experience with babies during pregnancy is one of the most consistent predictors of parental involvement for women, but much less so for men. Women who prenatally manifest an interest in babies and who view babies positively later initiate more social interactions with their own 3-month-olds and are more responsive to their babies' cries (Moss & Jones, 1977). Similarly, interest in unfamiliar babies positively predicts more affective and more sustained interactions between women and their own babies at 6 months (Feldman & Nash, 1982).

In addition to attitudes and behaviors during the pregnancy itself projected attitudes towards forthcoming parenthood are strongly predictive of parental functioning. For men, in particular, anticipated involvement in fatherhood is consistently demonstrated to be linked to higher levels of childcare postpartum (Entwisle & Doering, 1981; Lamb et al., 1982; McHale & Huston, 1984). Similarly, expectant fathers who described themselves as placing a high value on parenthood are ultimately more involved in caregiving to their babies. There are few comparable data on women. What is available is specific to nursing and does not generalize to other expressions of parenting, i.e., plans to breastfeed predicts breastfeeding but not mothering in general at 3 weeks (Entwisle & Doering, 1981). The clear relationship between the way men define their paternal role and the manner in which they relate to their child is due to the much wider range of choices allowed a contemporary father. It can vary from primarily a breadwinner with little or no childcare responsibilities, to assuming equal childrearing duties with the mother (to sole primary caregiving in the case of single fathers, not reviewed in these studies). Motherhood tends to be more narrowly defined since executive decision-making regarding the child is always hers regardless of how much or little childcare responsibility she delegates to others. Note also, since parenthood was only being assessed during the first year of life, motherhood was defined quite traditionally by most of the women sampled. Thus, given the diversity of self-definition allowed men (versus women) during the earliest stage of parenthood, it is not surprising that men's expectations regarding future fathering involvement are of greater predictive value than those of women.

PRENATAL ANTECEDENTS OF PARENTING: INDIRECT EFFECTS

Until now the antecedents of parenting evaluated have been typified by their clear link to the predicted behavior in question. Accordingly, interpreting the causal relationship between a given attitude or behavior during expectancy and later parental behavior was obvious at times and required creative hypothesizing at others. However, more recently, a number of studies using more intricate statistical models have discerned variables which have considerable predictive value regarding parenting, but rather than being associated with mothering or fathering directly, they are correlated with intervening variables which in turn are linked to parental behaviors. These indirect effects are of considerable statistical value in ultimately predicting parenting. However, explaining the fragmented nature of the causal links is often challenging for even the imaginative investigator.

To date, the few indirect effects related to parenting reported in the literature conveniently fall into two categories. The first involve variables that are chronologically ordered, i.e., phenomena at point 1 in time are correlated with others at point 2, which in turn are linked to point 3, in this case, parenting. Thus, the antecedents at the first point in time can indirectly predict parenting at the third point in time via each of their relationships to the connecting variable at the middle point. The other category of indirect effects involves a second person as a conduit, i.e., the behaviors or attitudes of one person (usually a significant other) is found to be of considerable value in predicting the parenting behavior of the target person.

The first category of chronologically ordered indirect effects is demonstrated most convincingly by Entwisle and Doering (1981) who assessed women at three points in time: prenatally (childbirth preparation, plans for infant care during hospitalization, plans for infant feeding), recollections of events at or shortly after birth (awareness, nature of her experience, first reactions to infant), and 3 weeks postpartum (various aspects of mothering). Based on hypotheses and earlier research, structural equations with recursive models were built, and parameters were estimated using least-squares solutions. Only a portion of their model demonstrating indirect effects is reproduced in Fig. 8.1. For example, the degree to which a woman formally prepares for childbirth does not show a *direct* association with mothering. This finding is consonant with those of other investigators (Feldman & Nash, 1982; Grossman et al., 1980; Heinicke et al., 1983; Shereshefsky & Yarrow, 1974). However, preparation for childbirth is *indirectly* associated with mothering, via birth experiences. The strength of the indirect effects is calculated by multiplying the structural (unstandardized) coefficients. In the case of preparation for childbirth, the indirect effect through awareness at birth is $.50 \times 1.00 = .50$. A second, smaller indirect effect operates through awareness at birth and birth experience ($.50 \times 1.48 \times .33 = .24$).

It is important to note that the presence of direct effects does not preclude the existence of indirect effects and vice versa. This point can be illustrated from another example provided by Entwisle and Doering (1981). The data, designed to map direct and indirect effects on fathering, are depicted in Fig. 8.2. From their findings, it appears that preparation for childbirth has a strong direct effect on fathering (.93) as well as a weaker indirect effect ($1.49 \times .35 \times .36 = .19$).

A similar phenomenon can be inferred from the data reported by Shereshefsky and Yarrow (1974). In a large scale study, they made multiple assessments of each woman's personality during pregnancy, including her ego strength, nurturance, and clarity of visualizing herself as a mother. They also took repeated measures of the woman's adaptation to pregnancy. After the infant was born, they made observations and ratings of each mother's responsiveness to her infant. A subset of their data based on simple correlations suggestive of direct and indirect effects appear in Fig. 8.3. Note, however, that simple correlations by themselves cannot *prove* indirect effects. Whereas the variables nurturance and

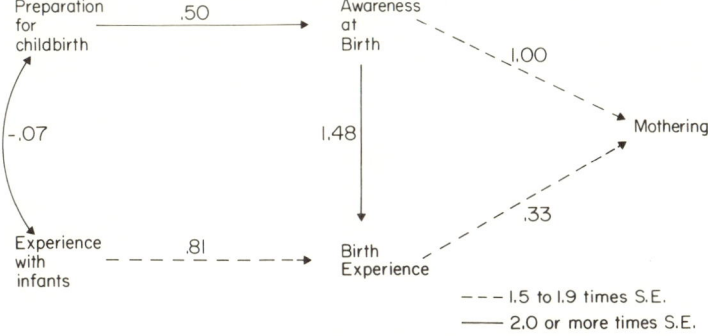

FIG. 8.1. Partial representation of model for mothering class women. Adapted from Entwisle and Doering (1981).

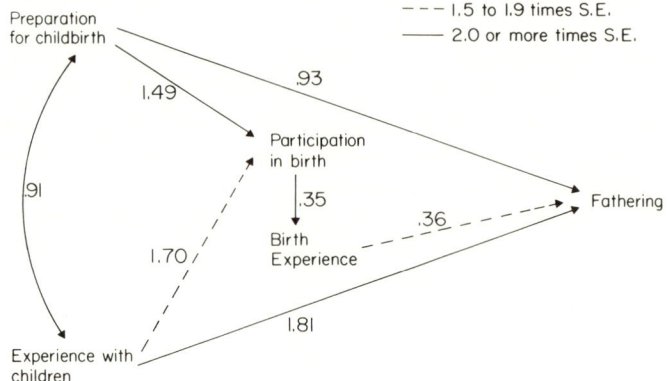

FIG. 8.2. Partial representation of model for fathering in middle class men. Adapted from Entwisle and Doering (1981).

clarity visualizing self as mother hint at both direct and indirect effects, ego-strength assessed during the third month of pregnancy suggests only indirect effects (via pregnancy adaptation) in predicting responsiveness to own infant.

These findings are of particular significance since an antecedent with both direct and indirect effects gains theoretical importance given its multifaceted impact on the outcome in question. Thus, these predictors operate in more complicated and interesting ways than had been previously documented.

The other approach to studying indirect effects has been to seek predictors of one person's behavior from another family member. Underlying this strategy is the rationale that mothering or fathering takes place within a family context. Accordingly, the feelings, attitudes and behaviors of one's spouse may have strong impact on the other's parenting behavior. In our own work (Feldman, 1984; Feldman & Nash, 1982; and Feldman, Nash, & Aschenbrenner, 1983) we

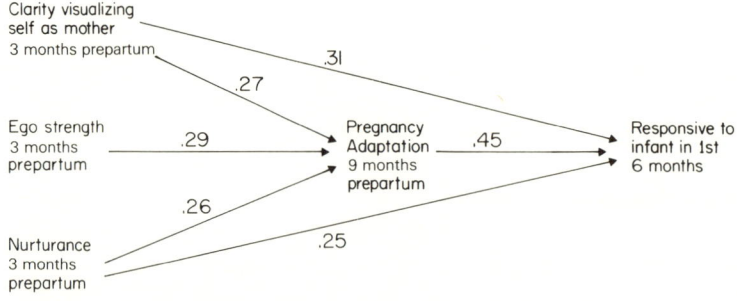

FIG. 8.3. Predicting mothers' responsiveness to her infant, based on simple correlations. Data from Shereshefsky and Yarrow (1974).

have built multiple regression models to predict diverse aspects of parenting from measures of self and spouse collected during pregnancy. For example, to predict strain during the sixth month of parenthood, three regression models were generated using measures obtained during the expectancy period. In one model the predictors were exclusively the scores from the woman, in the second the predictors were only from the man, and in the third (joint) model the predictors were derived from the couple. Whether predicting maternal or paternal strain, the joint model succeeds in accounting for most variance. Thus, information about the husband's personality and reactions to expectancy contributes to predictions of his wife's sense of strain 8 months later. Among the husband's prenatal scores that predict (or contribute to) his wife's postpartum strain are his older age, his perception of both the marriage and the expectancy period as stressful, and his preoccupation with job.

Comparably, there are data which suggest that certain characteristics of the expectant mother may predict her husband's reactions and behaviors during fatherhood. For example, when pregnant women are low in anxiety and report a happy marriage, their husbands subsequently report satisfaction with their child (Feldman et al., 1983). Additionally, younger women, those who feel negatively about their appearance during pregnancy, and those with good relationships with their parents, have husbands who subsequently become involved in caregiving to their 6-month-old.

Other researchers have also begun to look at the spouses' characteristics, attitudes, and reactions prepartum as potential indirect effects on parenting. McHale & Huston (1984) reported that the woman's mothering skill, while being unrelated to any prior measures of the woman, is predicted by her husband's prenatally expressed preference not to be involved in childcare, and by his low score of expressive (feminine) characteristics.

Indirect effects may act through different pathways. Consider for example the situation where the husband's behavior or characteristic influences his wife's subsequent mothering skill. The indirect influence can proceed either via the mother's characteristic at pregnancy, or via the father's behavior at parenthood or via both pathways simultaneously.

Clearly, the field is not yet at the point where sufficient work has been done on indirect effects to allow the listing of either the pathways of influence across time or the spouses' characteristics that influence parenting. The work cited in this section is merely illustrative of important new directions of research on predicting parenting. Additional work guided by some theoretical rationale needs to be carried out in this area.

CONCLUDING COMMENTS

"The transition to parenthood represents a normative life event and thus has the potential for restructuring the life course of individuals and families" (Belsky,

Ward, & Rovine, 1984, p. 29). Given the fact that this passage is common to each of us who are born, and again to those of us who parent, all of us as individuals and society as a whole have a vested interest in the outcome of this process.

Unfortunately, given the lack of theoretical basis on which to guide the study of this transition, the variables investigated are frequently a random assortment chosen from those found to be contemporaneously important to either pregnancy or parenthood. As was often the case, the more popularly studied variables were not always the ones with the most predictive value. For example, marriage, a favorite topic of family sociologists studying this period, was of little predictive value for women (due to the elevated levels of patience and tolerance manifested by expectant fathers). Thus, given the homogeneously positive state of the marriage (from the wives' perspective) this important variable lacks predictive value for later maternal adjustment.

One of the most compelling findings of this review is that gender is a powerful mediating factor in the determination of antecedents of parenting. Variables which successfully anticipated mothering often had little predictive value for fathering. When the same variables were significant for men and women, more often than not their effects were in opposite directions. This observation is consistent with the reality that many of the behaviors that make up parenting are traditionally viewed as sex-typed and thus have differential meanings for men and women.

Among women, various dimensions of their personalities during pregnancy were predictive of mothering. In particular, more global, broadly-defined aspects of personality such as ego-strength and maturity were precursors of positive parenting experiences. Interestingly, chronological maturity was also linked to maternal success, a hopeful prognosis given the new demographics regarding advancing age at the time of first pregnancy among married women. Another important antecedent of maternal success was a less egocentric orientation away from ones own needs (e.g., sexually or physically) and towards the needs of others (e.g., unfamiliar babies). Finally, it should be noted that even more transitory personality mood states such as anxiety or depression accurately forebodes poor adjustment to mothering at least during the early months.

Often, variables which were significant predictors for women were not systematically investigated in men (if at all). However, given the frequency with which women were used as subjects in such studies, when findings for men were indicated, clear evidence usually existed which implied no such relationship or the opposite relationship typified women. For example, a certain minimum level of femininity among expectant men was predictive of good fathering but did not differentiate women (most of whom attain that minimum level of femininity through normal socialization). Similarly, social support (whether marital or family of origin) is an asset to expectant fathers but not so for mothers-to-be. Prenatal attitudes towards expectancy and positive anticipations of fatherhood bode well for later parenting among men, but is less important for women. A heightened investment in career and advanced age are negative indicators of paternal adjustment, yet both are positively related to later maternal involvement.

A promising new direction in predicting parenting comes from the study of indirect effects. As yet, not enough data derived from this technique are available to determine convergences or extrapolate from findings. Hopefully, enough interest will be generated in this area to construct the theoretical underpinnings which are so conspicuously needed.

REFERENCES

Belsky, J. (1984) The determinants of parenting: A process model. *Child Development, 55,* 83–96.
Belsky, J., Robins, E., & Gamble, W. (1984) The determinants of parental competence: Toward a contextual theory. In M. Lewis (Ed.), *Beyond the dyad.* New York: Plenum.
Belsky, J., & Tolan, W. (1981). Infants as producers of their own development: An ecological perspective. In R. Lerner & N. Busch-Rossnagel (Eds.), *The child as producer of its own development: A lifespan perspective.* New York: Academic Press.
Belsky, J., Ward, M. J., & Rovine, M. (1984). Prenatal expectations, postnatal experiences and the transition to parenthood. In R. Ashmore & D. Brodzinsky (Eds.), *Perspectives on the family.* Hillsdale, NJ: Lawrence Erlbaum Associates.
Bem, S., Martyna, W., & Watson, C. (1976). Sex-typing and androgyny: Further explorations of the expressive domain. *Journal of Personality and Social Psychology, 34,* 1016–1023.
Brody, S., & Axelrod, S. (1978). *Mothers, fathers and children.* New York: International Universities Press.
Brunnquell, D., Crichton, L., & Egeland, B. (1981). Maternal personality and attitude in disturbances of child rearing. *American Journal of Orthopsychiatry, 51,* 680–691.
Cobb, S. (1976). Social support as a moderator of life distress. *Psychosomatic Medicine, 38,* (5), 300–314.
Cowan, C. P., & Cowan, P. A. (1984, May). *Becoming a father: Changes in self, roles and marriage.* Paper given at NICHD Conference on Men's Transition at Parenthood, Bethesda, MD.
Crockenberg, S. (1984). *Professional support and care of infants by adolescent mothers in England and the United States.* (Under review)
Dickie, J. R. (1984, May). *Intervention in the mother-father-infant triad. Why and how?* Paper given at NICHD Conference on Men's Transition at Parenthood, Bethesda, MD.
Entwisle, D., & Doering, S. (1981). *The first birth: A turning point.* Baltimore: John Hopkins University Press.
Feldman, H. (1971). The effects of children on the family. In A. Michel (Ed.), *Family issues of employed women in Europe and America.* Leiden (The Netherlands): Brill.
Feldman, S. S. (1984, May). *Predicting strain in parenthood from pre-parenting assessments.* Paper presented at NICHD Conference on Men's Transition at Parenthood, Bethesda, MD.
Feldman, S. S., & Nash, S. C. (1982). *Prediction of mothering behavior from pregnancy.* Unpublished manuscript, Stanford University.
Feldman, S. S. & Nash, S. C. (1984). The transition from expectancy to parenthood: Impact of the first born child on men and women, *Sex Roles, 11,* 61–78.
Feldman, S. S., Nash, S. C. & Aschenbrenner, B. (1983). Antecedents of fathering. *Child Development, 54,* 1628–1636.
Goldberg, W. A., & Easterbrooks, M. A. (1984). The role of marital quality in toddler development. *Development Psychology, 20,* 504–514.

Grossman, F., Eichler, L., & Winickoff, S. (1980). *Pregnancy, birth, and parenthood: Adaptations of mothers, fathers, and infants.* San Francisco: Jossey-Bass.

Heinicke, C. M. (1984) The impact of prebirth personality and marital functioning on family development: A framework and suggestions for further study. *Developmental Psychology, 20,* 1044–1053.

Heinicke, C., Diskin, S., Ramsey-Klee, D., & Given, K. (1983). Prebirth characteristics and family development in the first year of life. *Child Development, 54,* 194–208.

Lamb, M., & Easterbrooks, A. (1980). Individual differences in parental sensitivity: Some thoughts about origins, components, and consequences. In M. E. Lamb & L. R. Sherrod (Eds.), *Infant social cognition: Empiricial and theoretical considerations.* Hillsdale, NJ: Lawrence Erlbaum Associates.

Lamb, M., Frodi, A., Hwang, C., & Frodi, M. (1982). In M. E. Lamb (Ed.), *Nontraditional families: Parenting and childrearing.* Hillsdale, NJ: Lawrence, Erlbaum Associates.

Leiffer, M. (1977). Psychological changes accompanying pregnancy and motherhood. *Genetic Psychology Monographs, 95,* 55–96.

Lerner, R., & Busch-Rossnagel, N. (Eds.). (1981). *The child as producer of its own development: A life-span perspective.* New York: Academic Press.

Lerner, R., & Lerner, J. (1983). Temperament-intelligence reciprocities in early childhood: A contextual model. In M. Lewis (Ed.), *Origins of intelligence.* Second edition. New York: Plenum.

Lewis, M., & Rosenblum, L. (Eds.). (1974). *The effect of the infant on its caregiver.* New York: Wiley.

MacFarlane, A. (1977). *The psychology of childbirth.* Cambridge, MA: Harvard University Press.

McHale, S. M., & Huston, T. L. (1984). Men and women as parents: Sex role orientations, employment and parental roles with infants, *Child Development, 55,* 1349–1361.

Moss, M., & Jones, S. (1977). Relations between maternal attitudes and maternal behavior as a function of social class. In P. M. Leiderman, S. R. Tulkin, & A. Rosenfeld (Eds.), *Culture and infancy,* New York: Academic Press.

Parke, R., & Collmer, C. W. (1975). Child Abuse: An interdisciplinary analysis. In E. M. Hetherington (Ed.), *Review of Child Development Research. Vol. 5.* Chicago: University of Chicago Press.

Parke, R., & Tinsley, B. (1983). Fatherhood: Historical and comtemporary perspectives. In K. A. McCluskey & H. W. Reese (Eds.), *Life-span developmental psychology: Historical and cohort effects.* New York: Academic Press.

Russell, C. (1974). Transition to parenthood: Problems and gratifications. *Journal of Marriage and the Family, 36,* 294–301.

Russell, G. (1978). The father role and its relation to masculinity, femininity and androgyny. *Child Development, 49,* 1174–1181.

Russell, G., & Radin, N. (1984). Increased paternal participation: The fathers' perspective. In M. E. Lamb & A. Sagi (Eds.), *Fatherhood and social policy.* Hillsdale, NJ: Lawrence Erlbaum Associates.

Sameroff, A., Seifer, R., & Zax, M. (1982). Early development of children at risk for emotional disorder. *Monographs Society for Research in Child Development, 47, (No. 7).*

Shereshefsky, P., & Yarrow, L. (1974). *Psychological aspects of a first pregnancy and early postnatal adaptation.* New York: Raven Press.

Zemlick, M., & Watson, R. (1953). Maternal attitudes of acceptance and rejection during and after pregnancy. *American Journal of Orthopsychiatry, 23,* 570–584.

9 Antecedents and Consequences of Parenting: The Case of Adolescent Motherhood

J. Brooks-Gunn
Educational Testing Service

Frank F. Furstenberg, Jr.
University of Pennsylvania

Teenage parenthood is believed to cause special problems for both the mother and her children. Not only do short-term biological consequences exist, but so do long-term psychological, social, and economic difficulties. The life course of teenage mothers during their early adulthood has been extensively studied. We know, for example, that adolescent childbearers are less likely to complete high school, attend college, find stable employment, marry, or be self-supporting than later childbearers (Chilman, 1983, Furstenberg, 1976; Furstenberg, Lincoln, & Menken, 1981; Moore & Burt, 1982). In brief, the adolescent mother finds her life chances to be truncated.

What about her children's life chances? Are they limited also? With regard to the consequences of teenage parenthood for children, several issues are examined in this chapter: (1) the areas of a child's development that are affected, (2) the ages at which negative effects appear, (3) differences in negative consequences for boys and girls, and (4) the antecedents of deleterious child outcomes.

PARENTHOOD AND PARENTING

The term parenting subsumes a large, perhaps disparate number of behaviors and intentions thought to be critical to human development—behaviors in which an individual engages in the course of caring for and socializing another as well as expectancies, intentions, and attitudes related to the expression of these behaviors. A similar definition is provided by Fogel, Melson, and Mistry in this volume—"the provision of guidance, protection, and care for the purpose of fostering developmental change within the potentials of growth of the nurturance object."

Parental behaviors and intentions each are studied somewhat differently. The former is studied in terms of behaviors directed toward children or the effects of these behaviors upon the child's functioning. Parental intentions are studied in terms of knowledge of developmental milestones and implicit theories of child development, as is demonstrated in the recent work by Sameroff and Feil (1985) and Sigel (1985). Interestingly, motivation is typically not studied. Since virtually all parents wish to care for their children and to promote their development and because this is a cultural value, it is difficult to directly question parents about their motivations. Finally, aspirations and expectations for a child's development include motivations as well as awareness of a child's potential growth. Realistic expectancies are studied in a current time frame, while aspirations typically tap more long-term goals.

Individual differences in the expression of parenting can shed light on two central questions: How do parenting patterns originate, and how do parental practices affect the young child's social, physical and cognitive development? This chapter, which specifically looks at the teenage mother, addresses both these issues (research on the teenage father is not reviewed given the paucity of information; Card & Wise, 1981; Furstenberg, 1976; Parke, Power, & Fisher, 1980). First, approaches to the study of teenage parenting are considered. Then, the prevalence of teenage pregnancy is examined. Next, we review research on teenage parenting practices and their likely antecedents as well as the small literature on outcomes of teenage motherhood for children. Finally, problems with the interpretation of findings about teenage parenting are discussed.

APPROACHES TO THE STUDY OF PARENTING

Parental contributions to child outcomes have been studied using several different approaches. Most frequently, either differences in parental practices or differences in child outcomes are documented for mothers or families who differ on an interrelated set of dimensions (social, economic, educational, and marital status).

The premise underlying much of this research is that parental practices directly affect the child's cognitive and social development. However, the premise is typically examined inferentially, rather than directly. This is especially true for mothers who are believed to exhibit inadequate parenting and for children who are at risk for developmental deficits. Instead of examining the links between parenting behavior and outcome, children from groups of mothers believed to have different parental practices are compared. Thus, if children of teenage mothers have lower school performance than children of older mothers, it is assumed that the mothers' parental practices differ. However, the child outcome differences may be due to a variety of factors, with age of parent being only one. In brief, group differences either in parental practices or child outcome are typically examined rather than the patterns of relationships between practices and outcomes.

A second tradition focuses upon the origins of individual differences in parental practices, instead of child outcomes (Belsky, 1984). Again, much of this research is inferential. For example, teenage mothers are less likely to vocalize to their infants than are older mothers (Field, 1981; Sandler, Vietze, & O'Connor, 1981). And language delays are sometimes seen in preschool children of teenage mothers (Furstenberg, 1976; Marecek, 1979). Thus, inferences have been made about the origins of teenagers' vocalization patterns with their young children, rather than more direct tests of the factors that may contribute to this particular parenting pattern.

Much of this research has focused upon differences in parental practices as a function of economic and social status, the premise being that the disadvantaged mother exhibits different behavior, or inadequate parental practices, as compared to the more advantaged mother. Again, the origins of possible differences are not explicated.

It is puzzling that so little attention has been directed toward mediators which may explain links between disadvantaged status and parenting patterns. One possible reason is that developmental research has concentrated on description and prediction rather than explanation. Another more insidious reason is a possible bias toward parental patterns of disadvantaged or teenage parents. Once it has been demonstrated that parenting practices in these groups differ from the norm, the link between parenting and performance deficits of children is assumed.

Finally, research on antecedents may not be conducted because of stereotypes about the parenting practices of disadvantaged or teenage mothers. These stereotypes tend to focus on similarities rather than on diversities in teenage parents from disadvantaged backgrounds (Furstenberg, 1976). For example, Head Start originated as a program for poverty neighborhoods, and rightly so. But the fact that within neighborhoods a wide range of families exists has not been addressed. Indeed, almost 20 years after the initiation of Head Start, we do not know whether children who attended Head Start differ from those children who were eligible in their neighborhoods but did not attend. In preliminary analysis of a longitudinal study of 2,000 3-year-olds in four communities across the country who were seen in the spring prior to entrance to preschool, it seems that those who entered Head Start had lower cognitive and linguistic scores than those who did not enter Head Start programs (Schnur, Brooks-Gunn, & Shipman, in preparation). Why some mothers chose to enroll their preschoolers in Head Start and some did not, given equality of eligibility, needs to be addressed. Indeed, enrollment may be a sensitive indicator of parental goals, initiative, and access to resources.

PREVALENCE OF TEENAGE MOTHERHOOD

Teenage motherhood is believed by many to have reached epidemic proportions. Contrary to popular beliefs, fertility rates among teenagers have actually fallen over the last 25 years, as is illustrated in Fig. 9.1.

Several factors account for the tenacity of the belief. First, today's teenagers are part of the baby boom; there are, in absolute terms, a large number of teenagers. Thus, the number of adolescent births did not decline between 1960 and 1970 (as is seen in Fig. 9.2), even though the fertility rate did. The continuing decline in teenage fertility through the 1970s resulted in a small decline in the number of teenage births (see Fig. 9.2). Second, the percentage of teenage births relative to all births is relatively high; teenage births constituted 16% of all births and 29% of all first births in 1979 (National Center for Health Statistics, 1981).

Third, the birth rate increased for unmarried teenagers, especially between 1960 and 1970, as is seen in Fig. 9.3. Out-of-wedlock motherhood is a social concern since approximately 60% of unmarried mothers receive Aid for Families with Dependent Children (Moore & Caldwell, 1976). Of the out-of-wedlock births in 1979, 44% were to adolescents. Looking at the problem another way, 31% of white and 83% of nonwhite teenage births in 1979 were out-of-wedlock (National Center for Health Statistics, 1981).

Finally, the declines in fertility rates are more pronounced for older than younger teens. Unlike the 18- to 19-year-old group, no declines have occurred

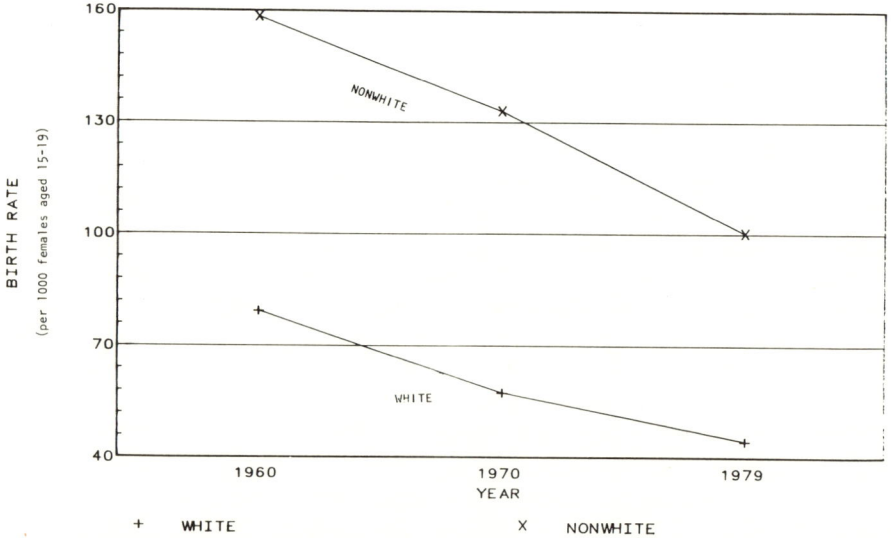

FIG. 9.1. Birth rates in the United States for 15- to 19-year-olds by race and year. (Sources: National Center for Health Statistics, Annual Volumes)

9. ADOLESCENT MOTHERHOOD   237

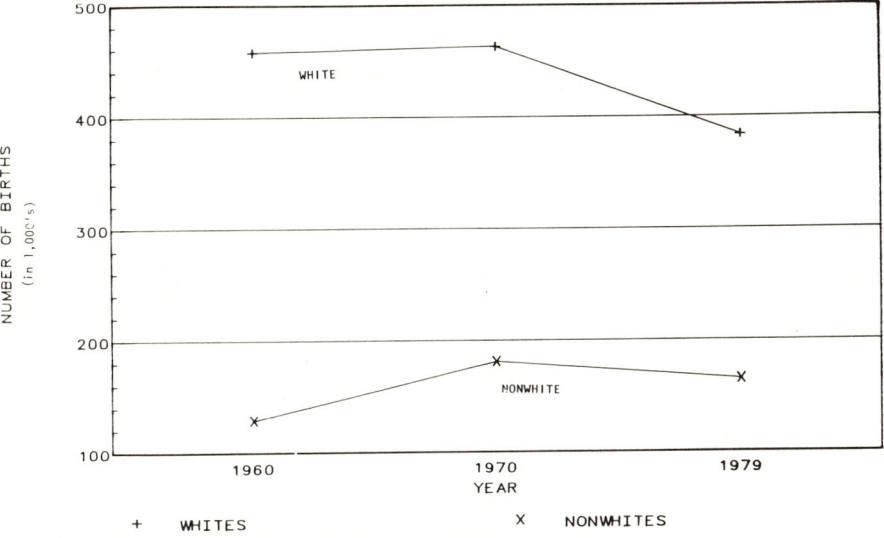

FIG. 9.2. Number of births in the United States for 15- to 19-year-olds by race and year.

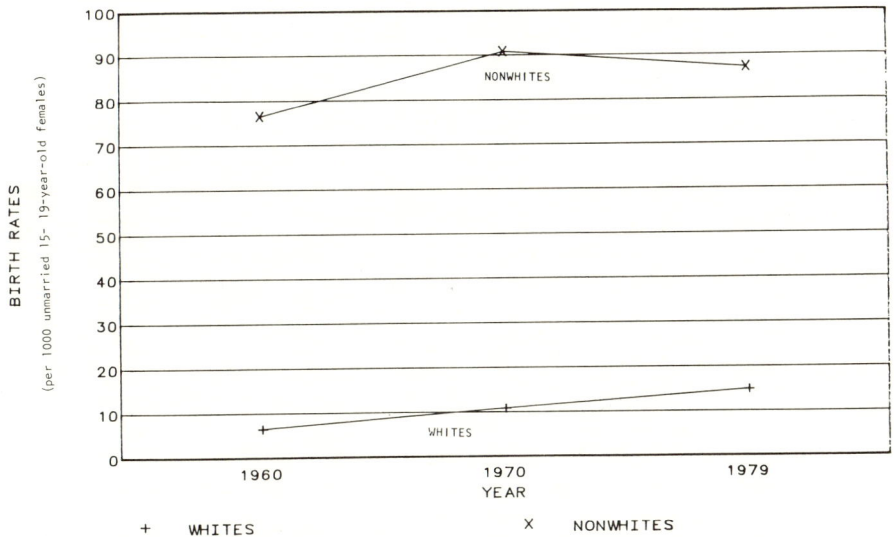

FIG 9.3. Out-of-wedlock birth rates in the United States for 15- to 19-year-old mothers by year and race. (Source: *Monthly Vital Statistics Reports;* Moore & Burt, 1981)

for the 15- to 17-year-old group. For example, for 15-year-olds, the birth rates (per 1,000 15-year-olds) were 19.2 in 1970 and 17.2 in 1979; for 16-year-olds, the birth rates were 38.8 and 32.7 for the same years (Moore & Burt, 1982). Births to females under age 15 also remained constant from 1970 to 1979.[1]

PARENTAL PRACTICES

What evidence do we have for the belief that teenage mothers exhibit different parental practices from those of older mothers? Surprisingly, few studies address this question. The meager amount of existing data to be reviewed focuses on (1) actual behavior directed toward the child, (2) knowledge of child development, and (3) attitudes toward parenting.

Several studies have examined interactions between teenage mothers and their infants, comparing them to those with older mothers and their infants. The most robust finding is that teenage mothers vocalize less to their children than do older parents (Field, 1981; Osofsky & Osofsky, 1970; Sandler et al., 1981). Field (1981) also reports that teenage mothers are more passive in their face-to-face interactions with 4-month-olds than are older mothers. However, all of the interaction studies find teenage mothers to exhibit as much warmth to their infants as do older mothers. Also, across the majority of maternal behaviors observed, differences as a function of maternal age are not found. For example, in the Nashville Comprehensive Childcare Project, 48 behaviors were observed during a mother-infant free play; only three reached significance, two being related to the vocalization finding just presented. It would appear that, with the possible exception of vocalization to infants, teenage mothers do not exhibit significant differences in parenting as compared to older mothers.

Two other studies have examined interactions with preschoolers. Using the HOME Inventory, teenage mothers were found to provide fewer opportunities for stimulation but not to be less responsive or more restrictive than older mothers who delivered in the same inner city hospital (Darabi, Graham, Namerow, Philliber, & Varga, 1984; Philliber & Graham, 1981). One study looked at 48 married couples in a semirural area rather than urban, single mothers. The adolescent couples were described as intolerant, impatient, insensitive, and irritable in interaction with their children. These observations were not based on standard interaction techniques (de Lissovey, 1973).

---

[1]Little research differentiates among different-aged teenage mothers even though becoming a mother before age 18 is more likely to be deleterious than motherhood after age 18 (Moore & Burt, 1982). For example, educational attainment may be truncated for young teens. In 1979, two-thirds of black and four-fifths of white teenage mothers were not enrolled in school 9 months after the birth of their first child (Mott & Maxwell, 1981). Since education is related to later economic and job status, teenage mothers of school age are more at risk for limited life chances than are older teenage mothers.

Teenage mothers do appear to have less realistic expectations than older mothers with regard to their young children's developmental progress. Some studies have found that teenage mothers underestimate while others have found them to overestimate the attainment of developmental milestones. In a study of 98 pregnant adolescents attending health clinics and parent education programs, the expectant mothers underestimated their infants' abilities in cognition, language, and social functioning. However, their expectations were on target for health and nutrition, motor development, and basic care—aspects of development covered in their health education classes (Epstein, 1979). It is interesting that teenage mothers expect too little, too late from infants in the areas of cognition and language, which possibly is related to the lower rates of vocalization seen in teenage mothers. Two other studies report that teenage mothers expect their children to reach developmental milestones earlier (de Lissovey, 1973; Field, 1981). In the study by Field, these unrealistic expectations were especially pronounced for teenage mothers with preterm infants; she speculates that these mothers might have less information about delays in preterm development and/or might be denying their infants' health problems. In brief, teenage mothers seem to have less knowledge about child development milestones than older mothers.

Attitudes toward parenting have been assessed in several studies. In the Nashville Project, control of children's aggressive impulses, reciprocity, closeness, acceptance of the emotional complexity of child care, and feelings of competence were assessed. No maternal age differences were seen in any of these dimensions (Sandler et al., 1981). Interestingly, the sample as a whole, which consisted of 327 women from low-income families, was likely to deny the emotional complexity of child care. In the Field study, teenage mothers' attitudes toward child rearing were more punitive than those of older mothers, a finding also reported by de Lissovey (1973).

ANTECEDENTS OF PARENTING

Three major determinants of parenting have been identified—personal resources of an adult, sources of stress and support, and characteristics of the child (Belsky, Robins, & Gamble, 1982). Historical conditions, cohort differences, cultural beliefs, and social economic status are other possible antecedents of parental practices. Parenting, in the majority of studies that are cited, is measured by behavior exhibited in parent-child interactions, including the parent's interpretation and expansion of child's signals, reciprocal interchanges or turn-taking, parental responsivity, communication patterns, conditional probabilities, and sensitivity (Bell, 1968; Field & Fogel, 1982; Lewis & Rosenblum, 1974; Osofsky, 1979; Osofsky & Connors, 1979; Wachs, 1982). In the following review, maternal attitudes, cultural beliefs, historical and cohort effects, social support, experience of life events, and child characteristics are considered as possible antecedents of parental patterns.

Endogenous Variables

Endogenous variables include maternal reactions to the birth of her child, physical health and energy level, overall mental health, and mood states.

Physical Health and Energy

Caregiving demands require a great deal of energy; the amount of available energy may affect how mothers use available supports and service systems (Lavelle & Keogh, 1980), as well as their actual parental patterns. Mothers report that fatigue is their primary symptom in the first few months after birth (Melges, 1968; Robson & Moss, 1970). In addition, such fatigue may exacerbate negative reactions to the birth of a child and ability to cope with a new child (Larsen, 1966), as has been suggested in the postpartum depression literature (Parlee, 1978). Teenage mothers, if they have adequate support, may be less likely to experience negative feelings relative to fatigue than older mothers. However, no information is available on fatigue or postpartum reactions in teenage mothers.

Ego Strength

Constructs such as ego strength and maturity have been hypothesized to contribute to effective parenting. In studies of middle-class mothers, responsivity and reciprocity directed toward infants is related to ego strength as measured during pregnancy (Feldman & Nash, this volume; Brunnquell, Crichton, & Egeland, 1981). Teenage mothers are believed to have lower levels of ego strength and to be less mature socially and emotionally, due to the necessity of negotiating the developmental tasks of adolescence (Hamburg, 1980). However, few studies directly test this hypothesis. Early case studies tend to report difficulties in psychoanalytic terms (teenage pregnancies represent "hysterical disassociation states," Kasanin & Handschin, 1941; "object losses," Greenberg, Loesch, & Lakin, 1959; "passive dependencies," Barglow et al., 1968). In studies using less clinical approaches, few differences between teenage and older pregnant subjects are found (Quay, 1981). In one of the few prospective studies, MMPI profiles taken in ninth grade were compared for girls who became pregnant later during high school and those who did not. The profiles were very similar; the only difference suggested that pregnant girls were more energetic, outgoing, and socially active (Pauker, 1969). These characteristics may be related to earlier age of first intercourse. In any case, those girls who became pregnant were not less socially mature, more passive, or less emotionally integrated than their classmates who did not become pregnant.

Lack of maturity may be inferred from indicators of self-orientation during pregnancy. In middle-class samples, women who are preoccupied with themselves, as measured by physical and sexual concerns, seem to show less effective parenting patterns in the postpartum year (Grossman, Eichler, & Winickoff, 1980). Directed inward, these mothers may not be especially sensitive to their children's needs. Whether or not this would be more true of teenage than older mothers is not known.

Mood States and Depression

Several investigators have found that moods tend to fluctuate during pregnancy (Leifer, 1977). Emotional lability during pregnancy would make it less likely that assessments of pregnancy mood states would predict later parental patterns (Feldman & Nash, this volume). However, in two studies of middle-class mothers, anxiety and depression measured during pregnancy were negatively related to effective mothering in the first year postpartum (Feldman & Nash, 1982, 1984; Grossman et al., 1980). Whether or not similar relationships would be found within disadvantaged samples or within a sample of teenage parents is unknown.

In terms of comparisons across samples, limited evidence to date suggests that teenage mothers are not more depressed than older mothers. For example, in a sample of over 500 disadvantaged women in Harlem, no differences in the incidence of depression and anxiety was found as a function of maternal age (Brooks-Gunn et al., 1984). Whether or not the incidence of depression is related to parenting and infant outcomes is currently being investigated in this sample.

Attitudes Toward Pregnancy

Even though teenage mothers may not exhibit more depressed mood states or more psychopathology than older mothers, one might expect their attitudes toward pregnancy to differ. For example, in a study of 400 teenagers who attended a prenatal clinic in Baltimore City hospitals in the late 1960s, only one adolescent in five indicated that she had been happy about becoming pregnant. And even these women qualified their responses by saying that they felt "kind of good" or "sort of happy" about getting pregnant. Another fifth of the sample reported mixed feelings about becoming pregnant, or indicated that they had not been affected much one way or the other. Three-quarters of the expectant mothers said they wished they had not become pregnant, and three-fifths stated their first reactions in unambivalently negative terms. Half of them could not bring themselves to tell their parents of the pregnancy for several months. After the first postpartum year, 70% of the teenage parents indicated they were feeling less negative about the pregnancy than they had been initially. However, fewer than one-third described themselves as "very happy" (Furstenberg, 1976, 1981).

The relationship between initial reactions to pregnancy and later adjustment to parenthood was assessed, as these mothers were seen several times during their first child's first 5 years of life. In the Baltimore Study, no relationships were found between the initial reactions to pregnancy and maternal behaviors measured 4 years after the birth of the child. However, attitudes remained consistent: Women who were initially unhappy about parenthood continued to report low interest in their children four years later. Even at the 5 year follow-up, however, attitudes about parenthood were not related to parenting behavior (Furstenberg, 1976).

Cultural Beliefs

Parenting beliefs have been shown to differ cross-culturally and within cultural subgroups in the United States (Spencer, 1982). One approach to studying cultural differences in parenting, taken by Sameroff and Feil (1985) and Sigel (1985), involves systems of measuring implicit beliefs about childrearing. How these translate into parenting behaviors is typically not studied.

A more anthropological than social-cognitive approach to beliefs about parenting also has been taken (Sears, Maccoby, & Levin, 1957). One might ask, for example, why certain behaviors are considered good parenting practices in different groups. For example, in the Harlem study of disadvantaged urban pregnant women referred to earlier, several classes on methods of discipline were conducted by the first author as part of a larger intervention program. Congruent with current child development theory, the distinction between punishment and discipline was stressed. Both community health advocates and pregnant women disagreed with this distinction. Good parenting necessitated punishment as a means of discipline; to not punish would be to not prepare the child for the realities of life in this urban community. In addition, several of the community health advocates thought that the dimensions of parenting tapped in the HOME scale were not relevant to this community. Effective parenting is clearly defined in middle class terms in the HOME Scale and similar instruments, in that behaviors considered effective or desirable are those that facilitate cognitive, linguistic, and social behaviors deemed important for schooling. Thus, the community health advocates and middle-class professionals perceive certain parental practices differently. Regardless of which perspective is correct, parent practices that are believed to promote achievement in the schools may be seen as incompatible with those that are believed to promote success in urban community survival.

Child Characteristics

Most of the literature on antecedents of behavior concentrates on infant characteristics that influence parenting (Belsky et al., 1982). A series of studies have shown that age of the child, birthweight, gender, birth order, and developmental level influence maternal behavior (Bell, 1968; Brooks-Gunn & Lewis, 1984;

Goldberg & Lewis, 1969; Lewis & Rosenblum, 1974; Goldberg, this volume). These effects have been well documented.

Few studies have examined the effect of infant characteristics upon parenting behavior in teenage samples. Field's study comparing teenage mothers interactions with their preterm and term infants described earlier may be the only example. Of particular interest is whether or not teenage parents would be more or less sensitive to altering behavior as a function of infant characteristics than older mothers. Available evidence suggests that teenage parents may have difficulty in fine-tuning their behavior, given their lack of knowledge about normative development, their possible denial of the problems of their infants, and/or their concentration on problems in their own life.

Historical and Cohort Changes

Changes have occurred in social structural variables associated with parenthood in the last several decades. It is believed that these changes affect parental practices, although few studies look at direct links between the two (Brooks-Gunn, 1985). Four of the major changes include changes in family size, maternal employment patterns, single parenthood, and teenage pregnancy. The number of children per family in the United States has decreased over the last 20 years. For example, the birth rate per woman was 3.6 children in 1960, as compared to 1.8 children in 1976. The number of children expected by married women aged 18 to 24 decreased from 3.1 children in 1960 to 2.1 children in 1976. At the same time, maternal employment has increased. For example, the percentage of mothers with children under 18 who are employed has doubled in the last 20 years. When looking at school-age children, more than one-half of all mothers are currently employed. Single-parent households also have become more common. For example, in 1960, 8% of all children were living with one parent only while in 1978, 19% were. Projections for 1990 are that 25% of all children will be living in a single-parent household. To look at the demographic trends another way, in 1960, 73% of all children were living with their two natural parents; in 1978, 63% were; and in 1990, it is expected that 56% of all children will be living with their two natural parents (Glick & Norton, 1978). Increases in children residing in single-parent households are primarily due to increases in the divorce rate. Single-parent households typically mean those headed by women; it also means the high likelihood of residing in a poverty household.

Teenage mothers are more likely to be unmarried and to be heads of their household than older mothers; in addition, coupled with the greater likelihood of not completing high school, teenage mothers are more likely to rely on public assistance or to work in unskilled jobs (Furstenberg & Crawford, 1981; Moore & Burt, 1982). In brief, teenage mothers are more likely to be living in poverty than are older mothers from the same neighborhoods.

These changes may affect parental behavior such as time spent with the child or responsivity to the child. While the reduction in the number of children per family might increase the time that any one individual child spends with the parent, the increase in employment, divorce, and single-parent households may contribute to having less time to spend with the child. Even if this is the case, we have no evidence to suggest the working mother spends less time in direct interaction with her child than does the nonworking mother. For example, when mothers and young children have been observed in the home over long stretches of time (up to 8 hours), the great proportion of the day is not spent in face-to-face vocalization or play between preschool children and their mothers (Clarke-Stewart, 1973). Furthermore, direct interaction, not total time spent together, seems to be the key parenting factor that enhances intellectual and linguistic development (Coates & Lewis, 1984).

Of particular interest with regard to teenage parents is the fact that preschool children do not necessarily fare better when their mothers are available full-time than part-time. For example, in the Baltimore Study, preschoolers whose mothers headed single-parent households and/or who were on public assistance performed less well intellectually than children whose mothers were employed or married. In the first case, that of the employed mother heading a single-parent household, other adults were involved in child care (daycare, female relatives). In the latter case, the married mother was less likely to work, but another adult also was available. Child outcome is probably enhanced by having multiple caregivers, although the mechanisms underlying this phenomenon are not well understood (Furstenberg, 1976).

Negative Life Events

The socioeconomic context in which an early pregnancy occurs has repeatedly been shown to affect later parent and child outcomes. Less attention has been directed toward the occurrence of negative life events or the strains of daily living often associated with the life of poverty, a life in which the teenage mother is likely to find herself, or toward the possible influence of these events upon her adjustment to parenthood or parental behavior.

The literature on the relationship of life events to psychological well-being may give us clues as to the importance of life events to parenting. The occurrence of negative life events is moderately related to psychological adjustment (Dohrenwend & Dohrenwend, 1974; Mueller, Edwards, & Yarvis, 1977; Ross & Mirowski, 1979). In addition, undersirable life events are more prevalent in the economically disadvantaged, the poorly educated, the female, the young, and the unmarried (Brown, Bhrolchain, & Harris, 1975; Pearlin & Johnson, 1977; Pearlin & Lieberman, 1977; Thoits, 1982). Obviously, then, the teenage parent is likely to experience undersirable life events and strains of daily living, given their possession of many of these characteristics.

Not only are certain groups likely to experience negative events, but these very same groups may be more vulnerable to them: That is, they will be more likely to exhibit psychological disturbance when confronted with negative events, as Kessler (1979; Kessler & Cleary, 1980) has suggested. Such vulnerability may be due, at least in part, to the unavailability of personal and social resources needed to cope with the stresses associated with negative events (Kessler & Essex, 1982). This has been demonstrated elegantly in several studies, where the joint occurrence of many stressful events and low social support are more predictive of psychological distress than either separately (Kessler & Essex, 1982; Liem & Liem, 1978; Thoits, 1982).

With regard to teenage mothers, several approaches have been taken to study the possible effects of undesirable life events. Pregnancy, childbirth, and parenting are considered to be stressful events in and of themselves. The distinction between desirable and undesirable life events has been made, since the latter are more likely to predict psychological problems than the former (Mueller et al., 1977; Ross & Mirowski, 1979; Thoits, 1981). The question arises, then, as to the desirability of pregnancy. In planned pregnancies of married, economically stable couples, desirability is assumed. The teenage parent presents a different case, however. Early pregnancy is assumed to be undesirable; as we have seen, the adolescents in the Baltimore Study were not particularly happy about becoming pregnant, even though they accepted it. However, initial unhappiness was not related to parenting, at least at the 4 year follow-up. Likewise, virtually all of the adolescents' mothers accepted the pregnancy and the baby, after their initial disappointment (Furstenberg, 1976). In a similar vein, unplanned pregnancies may be the norm in some groups: In the Harlem Study, three-quarters of the pregnancies were unplanned, across all age groups (McCormick et al., 1983). However, little stigma was associated with this state of affairs; indeed, community advocates believe that the concept of planning a pregnancy is not relevant or may be untenable in their community.

With regard to stresses occurring in conjunction with pregnancy, it is not clear that the teenager experiences more stress than the unmarried young adult, at least within a disadvantaged community. No differences in number of negative life events was found in the Harlem Study as a function of maternal age (Brooks-Gunn et al., 1984).

Finally, one study has explicitly examined the relative contribution of life events and psychological adjustment in pregnancy, finding the expected relationship (Turner & Noh, 1981). Interestingly, when social support and perceived personal control were examined as possible mediators of the life stress-psychological adjustment relationship, high support and personal control reduced the impact of negative life events significantly. One would expect this effect to occur regardless of maternal age.

Social Support

As the preceeding discussion implies, the availability and use of social support may buffer the individual from the possible deleterious effects of negative life events (Cassel, 1976; Cobb, 1976; Thoits, 1982). Indeed, some research validates this claim, even though questions have been raised as to whether or not what is being measured is a direct effect of life events upon social support or an interaction of events and support (Thoits, 1982, p. 143–146). In addition, social support may affect psychological functioning more directly, rather than through interaction with life events.

Social support, as related to pregnancy and early parenting, has not been studied extensively, although the evidence to date suggests that it plays an important role. For example, in an often quoted study, antepartum social support was related to positive pregnancy outcomes (Nuckolls, Cassel, & Kaplan, 1972). In the teenage pregnancy literature, the child's developmental functioning is related to the presence of another adult in the household or at least the presence of a significant other in child care (Furstenberg, 1976; Kellum, Ensminger, & Turner, 1977). The presence of another may (1) act as a buffer, in lessening the psychological or economic impact of negative events upon the family (as illustrated by the Turner and Noh study); (2) act as a source of socioemotional support for the mother (which results in indirect benefits to the child; increased maternal well-being due to support may result in more interest in or responsivity to the child (Lewis & Feiring, 1981); and/or (3) act as a direct source of support for the child. In any case, social support may be critical to teenage parents, whether it affects their parental practices directly or indirectly.

CONSEQUENCES OF PARENTING UPON CHILDREN'S DEVELOPMENT

It is believed that children's development is affected negatively by teenage parenthood. However, the risk associated with teenage parenthood has not been calculated except for neonatal morbidity and mortality (McCormick, Shapiro, & Starfield, 1984). With regard to later health status, social problems, or cognitive functioning, little is known. In addition, whether or not effects are equally distributed as a function of child's age, gender, or birth order is not studied. Finally, individual differences among children of teenage parents have not been examined; the characteristics of teenage mothers that predict later child dysfunction and those that foretell future success need to be identified.

Neonatal Status

In general, when medical care is adequate, little or no risk is found in terms of the health of neonates born to teenage mothers (Broman, 1981; McCormick et al., 1984; Sandler et al., 1981). Earlier studies reporting adverse health outcomes did not control for quality and quantity of obstetrical care (Baldwin & Cain, 1981). Obstetric risk factors predict neonatal mortality and morbidity better than does maternal age. However, an increased risk of neonatal mortality has been associated with race, maternal age at the extremes, low maternal educational attainment and prior adverse obstetric outcome (i.e., fetal death). The neonatal mortality rates of these groups are accounted for primarily by low birth weight, which is associated with these factors (McCormick, 1985; McCormick et al., 1984; Shapiro et al., 1980). The birth weight differentials account for race, adolescent motherhood, and low maternal education effects on neonatal mortality (McCormick, 1985).

Thus, it is not surprising that when ethnic and socioeconomic backgrounds are controlled, neonatal morbidity and mortality differences between teenage and older mothers disappear (Broman, 1981; Monkus & Bancalari, 1981). The only exception may be very young mothers, (under 15). Most studies have been unable to look at very young mothers, given the small number of them in any sample. This is the group most likely to conceal their pregnancy, and thus may begin their antenatal care later than older teenagers. This hypothesis was not substantiated in the Collaborative Perinatal Study, however. Broman (1981) examined 12–15, 16–17, and 20–29 year-old mothers. The black 16–17 year-olds had fewer antenatal visits than did the 12–15 or 20–24 year-olds. In addition, the young and old teens did not differ with respect to neonatal morbidity rates.

Other studies have examined neonatal outcomes in hospitals offering special antenatal programs or a uniformly high level of prenatal care. Again, no neonatal health differences as a function of maternal age are found (Mednick, Brock, & Baker, 1979; Sandler et al., 1981; Zackler, Andelman, & Bauer, 1969).

Infant Status

In general, health status does not differ for infants of teenage and older mothers. In one study where a composite physical health score was calculated for babies at one year of age, those infants raised by single teenage mothers were less healthy than those raised in teenage parent households with another adult present, either grandmother or father (Mednick et al., 1979).

In terms of developmental status, as measured by infant intelligence tests, babies of teenage and older mothers do equally well, when controlling for social class and/or maternal education (Broman, 1981; Marecek, 1979). In fact, infants born to younger mothers tend to have slightly higher scores on the motor and mental scales in both of these studies. These differences may be meaningless in terms of functional status (for example, the 8-month Bayley means for children of black 12–15, 16–17, and 20–29 year-olds were 79, 79, and 78, respectively; Broman, 1981). Also, infant intelligence test scores do not predict later intellectual functioning (Lewis, 1983), suggesting that the small early differences do not forecast higher functioning later on. Indeed, these differences may be due to teenagers' slightly different treatment of their infants than older mothers. Early tests are comprised of more motoric than verbal items. If teenage as compared to older mothers are talking less but playing equally with their infants, they may facilitate early motoric development. One would expect the children of teenage mothers to be at a disadvantage when language becomes more prominent.

The temperamental characteristics of infants born to teenage and older mothers may differ. Field's teenage mothers report that their 4-month-olds are more distractible and less adaptable; it is possible that the young mothers' passivity in face-to-face interactions contribute to these possibly less desirable infant characteristics. No differences were found in the Nashville Study (Sandler et al., 1981). In the Collaborative Perinatal Study, testers rated the infants of teenage mothers as less likely to be hypoactive, unresponsive, or slow to respond than infants of older mothers (Broman, 1981). These findings are consistent with those of Field's: More active infants may be rated as more distractible and less adaptable. In addition, they may be more likely to exhibit motoric competence given their higher activity levels.

Preschool Years

Intellectually, the functional status of children born to teenagers and older mothers begins to diverge in the preschool years. In the Collaborative Perinatal Study, Stanford-Binet IQ scores were 87 for black children of 12–15 year-old mothers, 89 for 16–17 year-olds, and 92 for 20–29 year-olds. Similar findings were found for the white sample. Within social classes, the same trends were found, even though social class accounted for more IQ variation than did maternal age. In both samples, the effects were *most* pronounced in the highest of three social classes.

Broman (1981) also examined the number of children with IQ's under 70, a clear measure of developmental dysfunction. As can be seen in Fig. 9.4 (which presents the data for black 16–17 and 20–29 year-old mothers), maternal age is related to mental retardation in the children. Marecek (1979) reports lower Stanford-Binet IQ scores for 4-year-old boys but not girls born to teenage than older mothers in the Philadelphia sample of the Perinatal Project. In the Baltimore Study, cognitive functioning was not related to age *within* a sample of teenage mothers, although social class and childrearing shared with another adult (father or female relative) were positively related to 4-year-old cognitive functioning (Furstenberg, 1976).

Elementary School Years

By 7-years-of-age, IQ performance is depressed for children of teenage mothers in the Philadelphia, but not in the National Perinatal sample, across social classes. In the Collaborative Perinatal Study, lower IQ scores were found for children of the teenage than older mothers in the highest but not lowest social class.

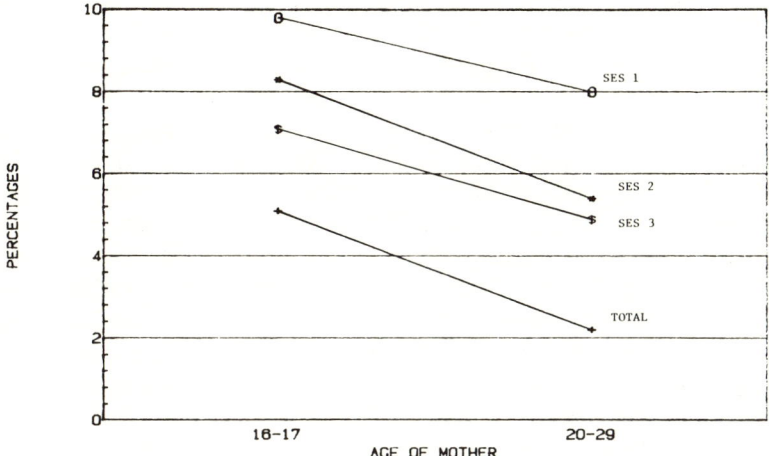

FIG 9.4. Percentage of black 4-year-olds with Stanford-Binet IQ scores under 70, by maternal age and social class (SES 3 = highest social class). (Broman, 1981)

School achievement, as tapped by Wide Range Achievement Test scores, was depressed by teenage parenthood in the Collaborative Study also. However, this effect was primarily accounted for by social class.

With regard to behavior problems, children of teenage rather than older mothers were more active, had less impulse control, and were more hostile during the testing session (Marecek, 1979), had more difficulty adapting to school (Kellum et al., 1977), and were more likely to be rated as hyperactive (Broman, 1981). Overall ratings of suspect or abnormal behavior, based on testers' ratings, were more likely to occur in children of white teenage than older mothers even after controlling for SES (Broman, 1981). Such behavior problems may set the stage for later difficulties, as Kellem et al. (1977) have found in the Woodlawn Study.

Secondary School

Long-term effects of teenage parenting may be expected, given the patterns seen in elementary school. Elementary school adjustment predicted secondary school adjustment and deliquency in the Woodlawn Study (Kellum et al., 1977), with teenage parenthood being related to initial adjustment problems. In an analysis of the Project TALENT data on 375,000 teenagers in 1960, those whose mothers were teens at their birth had lower cognitive scores and were more likely to have become teen parents themselves (Card, 1977). Presser (1978), in a sample of women in New York City, found maternal age at first birth to be the best predictor of the subjects' age at first birth.

Finally, we are conducting a 15 year follow-up of the original teenage mothers in the Baltimore Study; 80% of the original teenage mothers and their first born children, who are now adolescents themselves, have been reinterviewed. Preliminary analyses of their school-related behavior indicates a high level of maladjustment. Forty percent of the 15- to 16-year-olds reported that their parents came to the school because of a problem in the past year. Over one-quarter had skipped school and 28% had fought at school in the past year. The mothers reported that 49% of the adolescents had been suspended or expelled from school in the past 5 years, and 56% had received a note from the school about a behavior problem in the past 5 years. The figures were compared with those for the black subsample of the National Survey of Children (NSC; Furstenberg, Winquist-Nord, Peterson, & Zill, 1983). The Baltimore Study adolescents were compared with the NSC adolescents also born to teenagers and those born to older mothers. The results for the Baltimore Study were almost identical to those of the NSC early childbearers. In contrast, the 15- to 16-year-olds born to later childbearers exhibited much less school misbehavior: Seven percent had skipped school, 20% had fought, and 14% had their parents brought to school in the past year because of a behavior problem. Only 25% had been expelled in the past 5 years. In a similar vein, 15- to 16-year-olds whose mothers were early childbearers were much more likely to have repeated a grade than those whose mothers were later childbearers (see Fig. 9.5). It is possible that these negative findings for the adolescents of early childbearers are accounted for by maternal education and socioeconomic status; further analyses will control for maternal status.

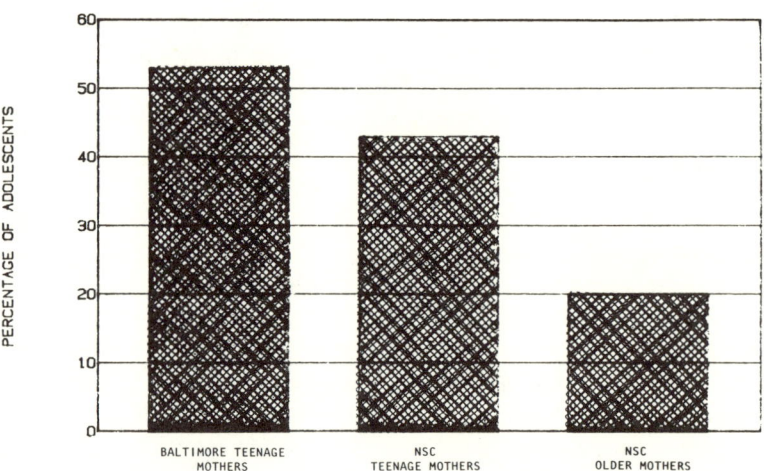

FIG 9.5. Percentage of 15- to 16-year-olds having repeated a grade in school.

ISSUES IN TEENAGE PARENTING

Relative Effects of Maternal Age

The literature to date does not address a major question: What is the effect of maternal age on child outcome, relative to other influences, such as education, poverty, and residence in single-parent households? In the well-studied case of low birth weight and births, maternal age has little effect when controlling for other influences. The higher incidence of LBW in neonates born to teenage mothers (at least those over age 15) is not due to a biological condition, but is associated with behavioral and environmental characteristics. Teenagers may receive less adequate antenatal care, and receive it later, if special programs are not provided for them. The potential reasons are numerous—attempts to conceal or deny pregnancy, lack of initiative, ignorance about the availability of neighborhood health services, fear or distrust of the health system, and/or misinformation about the effects of inadequate care. From a structural point of view, women in poverty neighborhoods may have less access to quality obstetrical care. Economically, teenagers from poor families may be concerned about payment for care.

These possibilities underscore the need to elucidate the personal, structural, and economic factors contributing to antenatal care differences. We know that enrollment in special obstetrical clinics for teenagers lowers the incidence of LBW births. However, how these programs do so is not known; in other words, *which* of the personal and structural barriers may be overcome by special programs has not been documented.

Comparison Groups

A related issue has to do with the appropriate groups with which to compare teenage mothers. As we have seen, teenage and older mothers may differ on a set of interrelated dimensions, making it difficult to attribute differences in parental practices to a single cause.

Typically, inferences are made about the consequences of teenage parenting by controlling for as many differences between younger and older mothers as possible. In general, young mothers are compared to older mothers holding education, work status, ethnicity and economic well-being constant, or using these variables as covariates. A problem exists with this approach, as major demographic variables used as covariates are typically in flux for the teenage mother. The teenage mother, at least when she is under 18, may not be classified as to high school completion, public assistance, or employment (Moore & Burt, 1982). For example, she may be on maternity leave from school, be in school, or have left school. Although teenage mothers are less likely to complete high school or to be employed, it is difficult to predict an individual's life course or even their status at age 20 on an a priori basis. Therefore, social structural factors known to affect child outcome may not be assessed very precisely in the teenage years (Furstenberg & Brooks-Gunn, in press).

Several approaches may overcome these limitations. First, individual differences may be examined within rather than across groups and over time. This approach has been used in the Baltimore Study. Second, comparisons can be made with older mothers from similar families of origin: Educational, occupational, economic, and marital status of the mothers' parents may be held constant. A variant of this approach would be to compare teenage mothers to their high school classmates who have children after their teen years. Classmates will have similar familial characteristics, being drawn from the same neighborhoods and will be from the same generational cohort (often a problem when teenage mothers are compared to mothers 5- and 10-years older). In the Baltimore Study, this approach was used very successfully to examine maternal attitudes and the outcomes of preschoolers (Furstenberg, 1976).

Third, comparisons may be made for mothers with special characteristics. For example, the impact of unwanted pregnancies (the modal situation for teenagers) upon parental practices may be examined by comparing teenage and older mothers who have unwanted pregnancies (McCormick et al., 1985). Another illustration of a more fine grain approach is the study by Field, in which teenage and older mothers with preterm and term infants were compared. Do teenage mothers alter their behavior, when confronted with the special needs of preterm infants, as older parents have been shown to do?

Outcomes of the Children

Setting aside the difficulty in obtaining comparison groups when studying teenage mothers, what may be said about the outcomes of their children? The meager literature suggests that differences become more pronounced as the children get older. If infants are affected, over and above the higher incidence of neonatal problems (specifically LBW), it is in the area of motor activity. Higher activity is also seen in the preschoolers of teenage mothers. Such behavior may set the stage for later school problems, as an inattentive, distractible, nonpersistent child is likely to have difficulty in the classroom setting.

Cognitive deficits first appear during preschool, at least in some studies. By elementary school, they are more consistently reported. Again, the child of the teenage mother may be at a disadvantage when entering school, a disadvantage that becomes exacerbated by the demands of school. By high school, the adolescent is faring poorly, in terms of deliquency, school achievement, and early childbearing. What transpired between elementary school and high school entrance to magnify the problems of the children is not known, and constitutes a large research gap.

Of particular interest is the fact that boys born to teenage mothers may be more at risk than their sisters. Males may be more likely to be affected by environmental events than girls, as literature on divorce and single-parent families suggests (Furstenberg et al., 1983). Whether or not the presence of a male in the household is more important for boys than girls is hotly debated, but unanswered. Finally, the "male effect" may be related to gender differences in the expression of problems: Boys are more likely to act out in aggressive ways than girls. Thus, their problems are more evident in school (hyperactivity, inattention, school expulsion, deliquency). Girls' problems may appear during adolescence, as expressed by early childbearing and school drop-out.

Finally, effects of teenage motherhood on children other than the first born have not been explored. It is possible that the teenager becomes a more effective parent with age and experience; in this scenario, her later children may be buffered from negative effects. On the other hand, the social and economic conditions under which later born children are reared may be more negative. With the first born, the teenager is likely to live in her mother's home, with all the social and economic supports offered by other adults. The second child is often not greeted as enthusiastically by the teenager's mother; indeed, the teenager is likely to set up her own household at this point (Furstenberg & Crawford, 1981). In any case, more information is needed about the later born children of teenage mothers.

Maternal Practices

Surprisingly, teenagers' parental practices are studied infrequently, even given the premise that they are sometimes inadequate parents. The exception involves parenting of infants. While few differences between teenage and older mothers have been found, the one that has, vocalization, may be directly linked to depressed cognitive scores in preschool and childhood. Maternal vocalization patterns to their infants are related to later linguistic competence (Cherry & Lewis, 1975). Therefore, early patterns may translate into later deficits, at least with respect to language. In addition, teenage mothers may interact more passively with their infants, which may affect later behavior. However, links between early parental practices and later child functioning have not been studied in teenage mothers.

It is possible that the influence of teenage parental behavior in the early years of the child's life is limited when another adult is present in the household. For many teenage mothers, the grandmother shares in, or does the majority of, the caregiving; unfortunately, the division of labor and time spent in caregiving in multigenerational families have not been systematically studied. In any case, the presence of other adults may ameliorate the negative consequences of teenage mothering, as Furstenberg (1976) has demonstrated.

With regard to older children, nothing is known about teenage parental practices. It is possible that individual differences among teenage mothers become more pronounced with time, given the variability of teenage mothers' life courses. Also, the problems seen at specific age points may be related to the transitions that the mother herself is making. For example, if teenage mothers are likely to be setting up their own households 5- to 6-years after the birth of their child, then the child is faced with a move to a new home and possibly neighborhood and the loss of his or her grandmother and other family members at the time of school entrance. Thus, the first grader of a teenage mother may have a particularly difficult time in the early grades, setting up a pattern of reoccurring school-related problems.

Summary

It is clear that many questions related to the consequences of teenage parenthood and parenting remain. We still have little information on teenager's parenting practices and the likely antecedents and consequences of them. As seen in this review, the relative effects of maternal age (over and above social and educational conditions associated with teenage parenting); possible differences in child outcome as a function of age, gender, birth order, parental practices of teenage mothers after the infancy period; and links between parental practices and child outcomes have not been systematically studied. In addition, research needs to explore the effect of changes in the mother's life on the child at different age points, in a manner analogous to the literature on divorce and child functioning.

REFERENCES

Baldwin, W., & Cain, V. (1981). The children of teenage parents. In F. F. Furstenberg, Jr., R. Lincoln, & J. Menken (Eds.), *Teenage sexuality, pregnancy, and childbearing*. Philadelphia: University of Pennsylvania Press.

Barglow, P., Bornstein, M., Exum, D. B. et al. (1968). Some psychiatric aspects of illegitimate pregnancy in early adolescence. *American Journal of Orthopsychiatry, 38*, 672–678.

Bell, R. W. (1968). A reinterpretation of the direction of effects in studies of socialization. *Psychological Review, 75*, 81–95.

Belsky, J. (1984). The determinants of parenting: A process model. *Child Development, 55*, 83–96.

Belsky, J., Robins, E., & Gamble, W. (1982). Characteristics, consequences and determinants of parental competence: Toward a contextual theory. In M. Lewis & L. Rosenblum (Eds.), *Social connections beyond the dyad*. New York: Plenum Press.

Broman, S. H. (1981). Longterm development of children born to teenagers. In K. Scott, T. Field, & E. Robertson (Eds.), *Teenage parents and their offspring*. New York: Grune & Stratton.

Brooks-Gunn, J. (1985). Maternal beliefs about sex-typing as they relate to differential treatment and outcomes. In I. Sigel (Ed.), *Parental belief systems: The psychological consequences for children*. Hillsdale, NJ: Lawrence Erlbaum Associates.

Brooks-Gunn, J., & Lewis, M. (1984). Maternal responsivity in interactions with handicapped infants. *Child Development, 55*(3), 782–793.

Brooks-Gunn, J., McCormick, M. C., & Heagarty, M. C. (1984, April). *The pregnancy experience of disadvantaged women: The role of life events and social isolation upon peri- and postnatal outcomes.* Paper presented in a symposium on Early Information Processing and Later Cognitive Functioning at the International Infancy Conference, New York City.

Brown, G. W., Bhrolchain, M. N., & Harris, T. (1975). Social class and psychiatric disturbance among women in an urban population. *Sociology, 9,* 225–254.

Brunnquell, D., Crichton, L., & Egeland, B. (1981). Maternal personality and attitude in disturbances of child rearing. *American Journal of Orthopsychiatry, 51,* 680–691.

Card, J. J. (1977). *Long-term consequences for children born to adolescent parents.* Final report to NICHD, American Institutes for Research, Palo Alto, CA.

Card, J. J., & Wise, L. (1981)eenage mothers and teenage fathers: The impact of early childbearing on the parents' personal and professional lives. In F. F. Furstenberg, Jr., R. Lincoln, & J. Menken (Eds.), *Teenage sexuality, pregnancy, and childbearing.* Philadelphia: University of Pennsylvania Press.

Cassel, J. (1976) The contribution of the social environment to host resistance. *American Journal of Epidemiology, 104,* 107–122.

Cherry, L., & Lewis, M. (1975). Mothers and two-year-olds: A study of sex-differentiated aspects of verbal interaction. *Developmental Psychology, 12*(4), 278–282.

Chilman, C. S. (1983). *Adolescent sexuality in a changing American society,* 2nd Edition. New York: John Wiley and Sons.

Clarke-Stewart, K. A. (1973). Interactions between mothers and their young children's characteristics and consequences. *Monographs of the Society for Research in Child Development, 38,* (6-7, Serial No. 153).

Coates, D. L., & Lewis, M. (1984). Early mother-infant interaction and infant cognitive status as predictors of school performance and cognitive behavior in six-year-olds. *Child Development, 55*(4), 1219–1230.

Cobb, S. (1976). Social support as a moderator of life distress. *Psychosomatic Medicine, 38*(5), 300–314.

Darabi, K., Graham, E., Namerow, P., Philliber, S., & Varga, P. (1984, November). The effect of maternal age on the well-being of children. *Journal of Marriage and the Family,* 933–936.

de Lissovey, V. (1973, July/August). Child care by adolescent parents. *Children Today,* 22–25.

Dohrenwend, B. S., & Dohrenwend, B. P. (1974). *Stressful life events: Their nature and effects.* New York: Wiley.

Epstein, A. S. (1979, March). *Pregnant teenagers' knowledge of infant development.* Paper presented at the Biennial Meeting of the Society for Research in Child Development, San Francisco.

Feldman, S. S., & Nash, S. C. (1984). The transition from expectancy to parenthood: Impact of the first-born child on men and women, *Sex Roles, 11.*

Feldman, S. S., & Nash, S. C. (1982). *Prediction of mothering behavior from pregnancy.* Unpublished manuscript, Stanford University.

Field, T. (1981). Early development of the preterm offspring of teenage mothers. In K. Scott, T. Field, & E. Robertson (Eds.), *Teenage parents and their offspring.* New York: Grune & Stratton.

Field, T., & Fogel, A. (Eds.). (1982). *Emotion and interaction: Normal and high risk infants.* Hillsdale, NJ: Lawrence Erlbaum Associates.

Furstenberg, F. F., Jr. (1976). *Unplanned parenthood: The social consequences of teenage childbearing.* New York: Free Press.

Furstenberg, F. F., Jr. (1981). The social consequences of teenage parenthood. In F. F. Furstenberg, Jr., R. Lincoln, & J. Menken (Eds.), *Teenage sexuality, pregnancy, and childbearing.* Philadelphia: University of Pennsylvania Press.

Furstenberg, F. F., Jr., & Brooks-Gunn, J. (in press). *Adolescent mothers in later life.* New York: Cambridge University Press.

Furstenberg, F. F., Jr., & Crawford, A. G. (1981). Family support: Helping teenage mothers to cope. In F. F. Furstenberg, Jr., R. Lincoln, & J. Menken (Eds.), *Teenage sexuality, pregnancy, and childbearing.* Philadelphia: University of Pennsylvania Press.

Furstenberg, F. F., Jr., Lincoln, R., & Menken, J. (Eds.). (1981). *Teenage sexuality, pregnancy, and childbearing.* Philadelphia: University of Pennsylvania Press.

Furstenberg, F. F., Jr. Winquist-Nord, C., Peterson, J. L., & Zill, N. (1983). The life course of children of divorce: Marital disruption and parental contact. *American Sociological Review, 48*(5), 656–668.

Glick, P. C., & Norton, A. L. (1978). Marrying, divorcing, and living together in the U.S. today. *Population Bulletin, 32*(5). Washington, D.C.: Population Reference Bureau.

Goldberg, S., & Lewis, M. (1969). Play behavior in the year-old infant: Early sex differences. *Child Development, 40,* 21–31.

Greenberg, N. H., Loesch, J. G., & Lakin, M. (1959). Life situations associated with the onset of pregnancy. *Psychosomatic Medicine, 21,* 296–310.

Grossman, F., Eichler, L., & Winickoff, S. (1980). *Pregnancy, birth, and parenthood: Adaptations of mothers, fathers, and infants.* San Francisco: Jossey-Bass.

Hamburg, B. A. (1980). Developmental issues in school-age pregnancy. In E. Purcell (Ed.), *Aspects of psychiatric problems of childhood and adolescence* (pp. 299–325). New York: Josiah Macy, Jr. Foundation.

Kasanin, J., & Handschin, S. (1941). Psychodynamic factors in illegitimacy. *American Journal of Orthopsychiatry, 11,* 66–84.

Kellam, S. G., Ensminger, M. E., & Turner, R. J. (1977). Family structure and the mental health of children. *Archives of General Psychiatry, 34,* 1012.

Kessler, R. C. (1979). A strategy for studying differential vulnerability to the psychological consequences of stress. *Journal of Health and Social Behavior, 20,* 100–108.

Kessler, R. C., & Cleary, P. D. (1980). Social class and psychological distress. *American Sociological Review, 45,* 463–478.

Kessler, R. C., & Essex, M. (1982). Marital status and depression: The role of coping resources. *Social Forces, 61*(2), 484–507.

Larsen, V. L. (1966). Stresses of the childbearing year. *American Journal of Public Health, 56*(1), 32–36.

Lavelle, N., & Keogh, B. K. (1980). Expectations and attributions of parents of handicapped children. In J. J. Gallagher (Ed.), *New directions for exceptional children* (Vol. 4). San Francisco: Jossey-Bass.

Leifer, M. (1977). Psychological changes accompanying pregnancy and motherhood. *Genetic Psychology Monographs, 95,* 55–96.

Lewis, M. (Ed.). (1983). *Origins of intelligence: Infancy and early childhood* (2nd Ed.). New York: Plenum.

Lewis, M., & Feiring, C. (1981). Direct and indirect interactions in social relationships. In L. Lipsitt (Ed.), *Advances in infancy research* (Vol. 1). New York: Ablex.

Lewis, M., & Rosenblum, L. (Eds.). (1974). *The effect of the infant on its caregiver: The origins of behavior,* Vol. 1. New York: Wiley.

Liem, R., & Liem, J. (1978). Social class and mental illness reconsidered: The role of economic stress and social support. *Journal of Health and Social Behavior, 19,* 139–156.

Mareck, J. (1979). Economic, social, and psychological consequences of adolescent childbearing: An analysis of data from the Philadelphia Collaborative Perinatal Project. Final report to NICHD.

McCormick M. (1985). What is low birthweight? *New England Journal of Medicine.*

McCormick, M. C., Brooks-Gunn, J., Shorter, T., Wallace, C., Holmes, J., & Heagarty, M. C. (1985). *The context of child-bearing among disadvantaged women: Planned vs. unplanned pregnancy.* Unpublished manuscript, University of Pennsylvania Medical School.

McCormick, M., Shapiro, S., & Starfield, B. (1984). High-risk young mothers: Infant mortality and morbidity in four areas in the United States, 1973–78. *American Journal of Public Health, 74,* 18–23.

Mednick, B., Brock, U., & Baker, R. (1979). *Infant caretakers: In praise of older women.* Paper presented at the annual meeting of the Western Psychological Association, San Diego.
Melges, F. T. (1968). Postpartum psychiatric syndromes. *Psychosomatic Medicine, 30*(1), 95–107.
Monkus, E., & Bancalari, E. (1981). Neonatal outcome. In K. G. Scott, T. Field, & E. Robertson (Eds.), *Teenage parents and their offspring,* New York: Grune & Stratton.
Moore, K. A., & Burt, M. R. (1982). *Private crisis, public cost: Policy perspectives on teenage childbearing.* Washington, D.C.: The Urban Institute Press.
Moore, K. A., & Caldwell, S. (1976). Out-of-wedlock pregnancy and childbearing. *Working Paper 992-02.* Washington, D.C.: The Urban Institute.
Mott, F., & Maxwell, N. (1981). School-age mothers: 1968 and 1979. *Family Planning Perspectives, 6*(Nov./Dec.), 287–292.
Mueller, D., Edwards, D. W., & Yarvis, R. M. (1977). Stressful life events and psychiatric symptomatology: Change or undesirability. *Journal of Health and Social Behavior, 18,* 307–316.
National Center for Health Statistics. (1981). *Vital Statistics of the United States.*
Nuckolls, K. B., Cassel, J., & Kaplan, B. H. (1972). Psycho-social assets, life crisis and the prognosis of pregnancy. *American Journal of Epidemiology, 95,* 431–441.
Osofsky, J. D. (Ed.). (1979). *Handbook of infant development.* New York: Wiley.
Osofsky, J., & Connors, K. (1979). Mother-infant interaction: An integrative view of a complex system. In J. Osofsky (Ed.), *Handbook of infant development.* New York: Wiley.
Osofsky, H. J., & Osofsky, J. D. (1970). Adolescents as mothers: Results of a program for low-income pregnant teenagers with some emphasis upon infants' development. *American Journal of Orthopsychiatry, 40*(5), 825–834.
Parke, R. D., Power, T. G., & Fisher, T. (1980). The adolescent father's impact on the mother and child. *Journal of Social Issues, 36*(1), 88–106.
Parlee, M. D. (1978). Psychological aspects of menstruation, childbirth, and menopause. In J. A. Sherman & F. L. Denmark (Eds.), *Psychology of women: Future directions of research.* New York: Psychological Dimensions.
Pauker, J. D. (1969). Girls pregnant out of wedlock. In M. LaBarre & W. LaBarre (Eds.), *The double jeopardy, the triple crisis-illegitimacy today.* New York: National Council on Illegitimacy.
Pearlin, L. I., & Johnson, J. S. (1977). Marital status, life strains, and depression. *American Sociological Review, 42,* 704–715.
Pearlin, L. I., & Lieberman, M. A. (1977). Social sources of emotional distress. In R. Simmons (Ed.), *Research in community and mental health.* Greenwich, CT: JAI Press.
Philliber, S., & Graham, E. (1981, February). The impact of age of mother on mother-child interaction patterns. *Journal of Marriage and the Family,* 109–115.
Presser, H. B. (1978). Social factors affecting the timing of the first child. In W. B. Miller & L. F. Newman (Eds.), *The first child and family formation.* Chapel Hill, NC: Carolina Population Center.
Quay, H. C. (1981). Psychological factors in teenage pregnancy. In K. Scott, T. Field, & E. Robertson (Eds.), *Teenage parents and their offspring.* New York: Grune & Stratton.
Robson, K. S., & Moss, H. A. (1970). Patterns and determinants of maternal attachment. *Journal of Pediatrics, 77*(6), 976–985.
Ross, C. E., & Mirowski, J. (1979). A comparison of life event weighting schemes: Change, undesirability, and effect-proportional indices. *Journal of Health and Social Behavior, 20,* 166–177.
Sameroff, A. J., & Feil, L. A. (1985). Parental concepts of development. In I. Sigel (Ed.), *Parent belief systems: The psychological consequences for children.* Hillsdale, NJ: Lawrence Erlbaum Associates.

Sandler, H., Vietze, P., & O'Connor, S. (1981). Obstetric and neonatal outcomes following intervention with pregnant teenagers. In K. Scott, T. Field, & E. Robertson (Eds.), *Teenage parents and their offspring.* New York: Grune & Stratton.

Schnur, E., Brooks-Gunn, J., & Shipman, V. (in preparation). Who attends Head Start?

Sears, R. R., Maccoby, E. E., & Levin, H. (1957). *Patterns of child rearing.* Stanford, CA: Stanford University Press.

Shapiro, S. et al. (1980). Relevance of correlates of infant deaths for significant morbidity at 1 year of age. *American Journal of Obstetrics and Gynecology, 136,* 363–373.

Sigel, I. (Ed.). (1985). *Parent belief systems: The psychological consequences for children.* Hillsdale, NJ: Lawrence Earlbaum Associates.

Spencer, M. B. (1982). Personal and group identity of black children: An alternative synthesis. *Genetic Psychology Monographs, 103,* 59–84.

Thoits, P. A. (1982). Conceptual, methodological, and theoretical problems in studying social support as a buffer against life stress. *Journal of Health and Social Behavior, 23,* 145–159.

Thoits, P. A. (1981). Undesirable life events and psychophysiological distress: A problem of operational confounding. *American Sociological Review, 46,* 97–109.

Turner, R. J., & Noh, S. (1981). *Class and psychological vulnerability among women: The significance of social support and personal control.* Paper presented at the meeting of the Society for the Study of Social Problems, Toronto, Ontario.

Wachs, T. D. (1982). *Early experience in human development.* New York: Plenum Press.

Zackler, J., Andelman, S. L., & Bauer, F. (1969). The young adolescent as an obstetric risk. *American Journal of Obstetrics and Gynecology, 103,* 305.

10
Nurturing Under Stress: The Care of Preterm Infants and Developmentally Delayed Preschoolers

Susan Goldberg
Sharon Marcovitch
The Hospital for Sick Children, Toronto.

The task of nurturing the young is a complex and difficult one under any circumstances. In this chapter we discuss examples of child rearing under conditions that further complicate the parent-child relationship, namely the presence of developmental problems on the part of the child. Two areas of research in which we have been directly engaged are presented: studies of parents of preterm infants and those of parents whose children are developmentally delayed as preschoolers. These serve here as examples from a larger class of biological impediments to the child's functioning which include acute or chronic illness, sensory and motor handicaps, and some behavioral disturbances and disabilities. Our purpose in examining the parent-child dyad in these circumstances is to understand how such biological impairments stress the parent-child dyad and how the dyad responds. In doing so, we expect to learn not only how individuals nurture under stressful conditions but about the normal adaptive capacities of parents.

Much of the work we present here began with the first author's studies of preterm infants and their parents begun in Boston in the mid-1970s. A subsequent move to join the research unit of Minde and his colleagues in 1981 provided the opportunity to study attachment behavior of preterm infants and to follow these same infants to 4-years-of-age, a project currently underway. In the interim, the collaboration of the two authors was established, beginning with the original study by Marcovitch (1983) and leading to a joint study still in progress (Goldbert & Marcovitch, 1982). This chapter offers the opportunity to integrate these seemingly diverse studies under the theme of "nurturing under stress."

THE PARENT-CHILD DYAD

In order to provide a framework for this integration, it is necessary to understand the parent-child dyad as a biobehavioral system and to discuss a general model of the effect of biological impairment of the child on the parents' ability to nurture. In Western industrialized settings where the vast majority of infants survive and develop into adulthood without major impediments, it is easy to lose sight of the biological functions of the parent-child dyad, because they can be taken for granted. It is important to remember that the survival, growth, and development of a child depends on appropriate care from adults. Nevertheless, as developmental psychologists now emphasize, adult care is not imposed upon a passive recipient (Bell, 1968; Goldberg, 1977; Lewis & Rosenblum, 1974; Sameroff, 1975). In order for adults to deliver appropriate care, the newborn infant, and later the child, must provide nurturing adults with clear signals of needs and adults must be able to recognize, interpret, and respond to those signals (Goldberg, 1982). Furthermore, when one of the partners is limited in these behavioral competencies, the other must make some compensatory adjustments if the dyad is to continue to function effectively. A review of studies of infants with diagnosed problems, those considered at high risk for problems, and those exposed to biological trauma (e.g., obstetric complications) indicates that such events are accompanied by behavioral manifestations that impair infants' abilities to provide adults with clear signals, and to respond to adult caregiving and social interactions (Goldberg, 1982). Thus, the burden of adjustment in these dyads falls to the parents.

Effective functioning of the parent-infant dyad is understood in terms of its ability to serve its biological goals: (1) to ensure survival of the child; (2) to promote normal growth and development; and (3) to ensure the development and maintenance of emotional bonds that will keep parent and child together until the child is sufficiently mature to survive independently. These goals form a hierarchy such that energy can be chanelled to higher functions only when lower ones are well established. Thus, growth and development become a focus for parents when survival can be taken for granted and enduring social relationships are addressed when normal growth and development are established. Of course, survival, growth, and development are life-long tasks that are never fully completed and in some of the families we discuss, normal growth and development can never be ensured. In such families, we suggest, emotional bonds and social relationships will flourish only after parents have established expectations of growth and development that are adjusted for their child's situation. As long as prognosis is a major uncertainty, parents will direct their energies to facilitation of growth and/or development. The goals that most parents of normal children articulate as the outcome of their nurturing (e.g., success in school, job, personal life) are goals which are superordinate to these biological goals and become a preoccupation only when survival, growth, and development can be assumed.

STRESS AND SUPPORT

Thus far, we have considered the parent-child dyad in its own context. However, the dyad is embedded in a larger family system, which affects and is affected by the dyad. In turn, the family is nested within an ever-widening circle of social systems: the neighborhood, the community, the town or city, etc. The success of the parent-child dyad in fulfilling its biological function depends not only upon conditions internal to the dyad but on conditions in these external systems. These conditions, which may be internal or external, can impede the functioning of the dyad (stresses) or enhance it (supports).

Stress has traditionally been defined in two ways. The first focuses upon life conditions or events that make demands upon an individual. The amount of stress is presumed to vary with the intensity, duration, and number of such demands confronting an individual in any given period. Thus, in the first study of preterm infants conducted by the first author (Goldberg, Brachfeld, & DiVitto, 1980), infants were grouped according to how many medical problems they had. The more medical problems they had, the more stress they and their parents were considered to experience. Life event scales (e.g., Holmes & Rahe, 1967) reflect this approach to stress. Within this framework, the care of the child with developmental problems can be understood in terms of the conditions or events that are potential stessors for parents. Table 10.1 outlines some of these for three different groups that we discuss.

A second approach is concerned primarily with the individual's ability to meet the demands of his/her life (Cox, 1978; Marcovitch, 1983). It is assumed that distress in the form of physical or psychological symptoms reflects the presence of demands that exceed the person's ability to respond. In this approach, the more symptoms an individual reports, the more stressed s/he is assumed to be. Measures which reflect this approach to stress include the Rutter Health Questionnaire (Rutter, Graham, & Yule, 1970) and the Hopkins Symptom Checklist (Derogatis, Lipman, Rickols, Uhlenhuth, & Covi, 1977). Our current and prior work with developmentally delayed children (Goldberg & Marcovitch, 1982; Marcovitch, 1983) includes measures of parental distress as does our follow-up of preterm infants and their families at preschool age (Goldberg & Corter, 1983).

Individuals have resources for meeting the demands of their lives which we call supports. Some supports are internal (e.g., good social skills, high self-esteem) while others are external (attention from spouse, friends, professional services). Like individuals, we can also view the parent-child dyad as being subject to stresses and supports which may be external or internal.

A well-functioning parent-child dyad generates competence and confidence in its members (Goldberg, 1977; Lewis & Goldberg, 1969) that become resources for coping with new demands. A poorly functioning dyad creates its own stresses, is more vulnerable to external stress and has fewer internal resources for meeting those demands. However, such a fragile parent-child dyad can be ener-

TABLE 10.1
Stressors and Supports

	Preterm	Down's Syndrome	Other Delays
Birth experience	traumatic	normal	normal
Postpartum stress	traumatic infant's life threatened, loss of parental role, unresponsive baby	awkward treatment, initial worries about meaning of handicap, baby may seem normal-disbelief	normal
Supports	medical and nursing staff as resources, parent support group		
Infancy stress	baby slow to develop, more problematic to care for but generally catching up	baby will appear increasingly delayed	initial worries problems of getting confirmation and/or help
Supports	infant stimulation neonatal follow-up	infant stimulation programs, parent groups, books	
Preschool	child increasingly normal residual worries?	parents usually well connected with resources, concerns about eventual competence	delay confirmed and investigated possibility of services-type varies with diagnosis

gized or buffered against threats to its integrity by supports in the larger social systems that surround it. Table 10.1 also indicates some of the supports that may be available to parents in the three groups we are considering; those with preterm infants, children with Down's syndrome and those with delays of other etiologies.

A striking feature of Table 10.1 is that these three groups of parents experience different developmental histories for their child and correspondingly different patterns of stressors and supports. For purposes of exposition, we assume that these groups do not overlap although in actual experience some overlap occurs (e.g., some Down's syndrome children are born prematurely, some preterm infants have later delays).

PRETERM INFANTS

The largest group of children with developmental problems for whom parent-child relations have been studied are those born prematurely. By convention, this group includes all infants born before 37 weeks gestation and as medical technology has improved the quality of neonatal intensive care, it has included increasingly more infants born at gestational ages below 33 weeks and as young as 25–26 weeks, many of whom weigh less than 1500 grams at birth. While this is a heterogeneous group, even among the smallest and most vulnerable infants, the majority develop normally after recovery from initial complications. For our purposes, we focus upon this "normal" majority who become more and more like their full-term peers as they mature. As Table 10.1 indicates, the major stresses for parents occur at birth and in the postpartum period, which is much extended by the infant's hospitalization. After hospital discharge, these parents experience conditions that are more stressful than those of parents of full-term infants, but these stresses are expected to diminish with time. The services and supports available are also most institutionalized in the birth and postpartum period and there are fewer services available as the children are discharged and mature.

Birth

The birth of an infant before 37 weeks gestation is regarded by mental health professionals as a major emotional crisis (Caplan, 1960; Caplan, Mason, & Kaplan, 1965; Kaplan & Mason, 1960). Once premature labor begins and is recognized, parents are aware that this is not a normal event and that the life and health of their baby are threatened. The normal psychological processes of preparing for the birth are interrupted. Parents may not have completed prenatal classes (or even begun them). Major emotional investments in a relationship with a particular obstetrician, in a particular kind of birth or postpartum experience must be given up and parents often experience grief (for the normal baby they will not have), and feelings of failure (for their inability to produce that normal baby). Many have expressed concern for the lack of opportunity that parents have to "bond" with their baby and the impediment this might introduce to parent-child relationships (e.g., Klaus & Kennell, 1976, 1982). However, the majority of studies which attempted to explore this have not observed the first interactions of mothers and babies but rather observed dyads at later periods when many other events and experiences have made a contribution.

Postpartum

During the infant's hospitalization, the role that parents normally expect to play in their baby's life is "taken over" by medical and nursing professionas. While this is, in one sense, a support essential to the survival of the baby, it also emphasizes a loss for the parents who are confronted with another domain in which they are "incompetent." There are few opportunities to become acquainted with their baby, or to develop the care-taking skills that would enhance their sense of competence. When they visit their baby (and most hospitals now encourage parents to do so while their babies are still in intensive care) they may feel overwhelmed by the environment of the intensive care nursery, by the sight of their baby, and be disappointed in his/her inability to be alert and responsive to them.

Minde and his colleagues (Minde et al., 1978, 1980) have made extensive observations of parents interacting with their small preterm infants (those weighing less than 1500 grams at birth) while they are still in hospital. Parents and infants were observed one or more times per week by two observers who recorded parent and infant behavior. When infants were first visited, neither they nor their parents engaged in active social interactions, but as babies recovered, their parents' activity increased accordingly (Minde et al., 1978). Individual differences in parents' social activity with these small infants reflected maternal supports such as her relationships with her husband and other family members and her experiences of being mothered in her childhood (Minde et al., 1980).

In a more recent analysis of data from these observations, we have made comparisons of mothers from two different cultural groups in the original sample (West Indian and East Indian) with their Canadian counterparts (Jeffers, Goldberg, Goolam-Hoosen, & Minde, 1984). The pattern of initial low activity and subsequent increase with the infant's recovery was characteristic of all three subgroups. Furthermore, unlike most other cross-cultural comparisons of mother-infant interaction, we found few significant interactive differences between these subgroups when they were matched for infant status, family SES, and parents' age. Our interpretation of these findings is that this hospital experience is equally overwhelming for all parents regardless of their previous cultural experience. All are equally unprepared and recover as their babies recover.

However, when babies have been seriously ill for an extended period, there is evidence that this may have a continuing effect on parental reactions even after the baby has recovered. A system of scoring neonatal illness was developed (Minde, Whitelaw, Brown, & Fitzhardinge, 1983) in which each infant received a daily rating for the severity of 19 possible neonatal problems. A total score was generated by adding up the daily ratings over the entire hospital stay. At the initial observations, when all infants were ill and inactive, parents were also inactive. When observed in the home, after infants had recovered and there were no behavioral differences between infants who had been ill for a long time and those who had shorter illnesses, the parents in the long-illness group were less socially interactive than those in the short-illness group. This suggests that mothers may take longer to recover from the initial constriction of their nurturing behavior than their babies take to recover from the limitations of neonatal illness. A recent study by Greene, Fox, & Lewis (1983) indicates that neonatal illness in both full-term and preterm infants affects not only neonatal behavior (as assessed on the Brazelton Scales) but parent-infant interaction as late as 3 months post term. Similarly, Beckwith and Cohen (1978) found that those infants who experienced more neonatal complications received more caretaking 1 month post discharge. Note that whereas Minde and his colleagues described decreased social interaction, Beckwith and Cohen (1978) report an increase in caregiving. This is consistent with our notion that threats to infant survival will increase parent investment in physical care at the expense of social activity.

The First Year

Once the infant is discharged to the home, parents may at first feel the loss of supportive hospital staff keenly. In our first study, when we visited homes 10 days postdischarge, parents of both full-term and preterm infants were especially eager for our attention, advice, and information (Goldberg, 1979). There may be some insecurity about their ability to care for the infant without the equipment or trained staff that was available in hospital. Even other parents of hospitalized babies on whom they have relied for support may no longer be accessible. For those infants considered to be at risk for subsequent developmental problems, most intensive care units maintain a neonatal follow-up service to monitor infant growth and development as well as health. There may be continued involvement in a parent support group (Boukydis, 1982) or participation in infant stimulation programs.

In the first few months, preterm infants are less "efficient" feeders than full-term peers as they spend more time pausing and less time sucking when the nipple is available (DiVitto & Goldberg, 1983). Nevertheless, their parents, like those of full-term infants use infant feeding cues to organize their own behavior and adjust their behavior to developmental changes in infant feeding patterns. Other observations of parent-infant interaction with preterm infants after the neonatal period report that these parents take a more active role with their infants than do parents of full-term infants (Brachfeld, Goldberg, & Sloman, 1980; Brown & Bakeman, 1979; Crawford, 1982; Crnic, Ragozin, Greenberg, Robinson, & Basham, 1983). However, this more active role, which includes more time in proximity, more physical contact, and in some studies, more verbalization, is also accompanied by less positive affect (Brachfeld et al., 1980; Crawford, 1982; Crnic et al., 1983) for both parents and infants, suggesting that these parents invest more work and have less fun (Goldberg & DiVitto, 1983) than their full-term counterparts. According to the scheme outlined earlier, "having fun" can emerge as a goal only when concerns about development have been resolved. In one study which included preterm infants in their second year (Wasserman, Solomon-Scwerzer, Spicker, & Stern, 1980) this initial pattern of high-parental activity subsided and interactions were more like those of full-term dyads during the second year. In our own study (Brachfeld et al., 1980) we found that preterm and full-term dyads did not differ significantly when the infants were one year, although Crnic and his colleagues (1983) continued to find differences 12 months past term. Wasserman and her colleagues (1980) observed that the increased similarity in interaction patterns coincided with apparent "catch-up" in development by the preterm group. They suggest that parents were, in fact, carrying out a self-imposed stimulation program for which the need was eliminated when their infants were more comparable to their postnatal age mates. In our study as well (Brachfeld et al., 1980) a similar interpretation was offered.

While we have argued (Goldberg, 1982; Goldberg & DiVitto, 1983) that this high level of activity on the part of parents of preterm babies appears to have some adaptive value, others (e.g., Field, 1977) have suggested that it may be maladaptive. The data we have already presented indicating that interaction patterns seem to relate to the existence and diminution of developmental delays and are related to threats to survival are consonant with the view that this high level of activity does, in fact, serve a developmental function. We now have data in another domain which are important to consider: assessments of the quality of infant-mother attachment at 1 year in preterm infants.

Attachment at One Year

The formation of a secure emotional bond is one of the major tasks of the first year of life. This is, in fact, the third goal in our hierarchy of biological goals. If the almost universally reported high-activity level of parents with their preterm infants is maladaptive, we would expect to find more preterms than full-term infants who are insecurely attached at 1 year of age. Several studies of preterm infants including our own have utilized Ainsworth's strange situation paradigm to assess attachment in preterm babies (Bakeman & Brown, 1980; Minde, Corter, & Goldberg, 1983; Rode, Chang, Fisch, Sroufe, 1981). In all of these studies, the proportion of securely attached preterm babies has been similar to that of concurrently assessed full-term babies or published normative data: approximately 2/3. In our study, which included premature twins and singletons born at less than 1500 grams birthweight, the smallest and most vulnerable group that has been assessed, 71% of babies were securely attached. Twin and singleton groups did not differ in the proportion of insecurely attached babies. However, in the twin group, we found an unexpectedly large proportion of babies exhibited behavior patterns that placed them within the secure group but in a category that included some characteristics of insecure babies. We called these babies "marginally secure." In published normative data (Ainsworth, Blehar, Waters, & Wall, 1978) 20% of the secure babies were classified in this fashion while in our sample this was so for 33% of the larger secure group ($\chi^2 = 4.05, p < .05$). This suggests that while infant-mother attachment is a relatively robust phenomenon resistant to many of the stresses accompanying preterm birth and development, twins and their parents may experience somewhat more difficulty in this respect. Nevertheless, the general consistency of data on attachment of preterm babies indicates that the patterns of dyadic interaction described serve an adaptive a function as the majority of these dyads do achieve secure attachment as assessed by the strange situation paradigm.

Later Development

We are not yet in a position to provide data on social relations of parents and preterm infants in the preschool period. Although there are many studies of preterm infants that continue well into the school years, the focus of these follow-ups has been on cognitive and language skills with very little attention to social competencies or problems or to parents' experience and attitudes in these later years.

DEVELOPMENTAL DELAYS: DOWN'S SYNDROME AND OTHER ETIOLOGIES

We turn now to two other groups of parents who are nurturing under stress. In our work with both of these groups we have not collected data in the infancy period. For those parents whose children's delays are not caused by Down's syndrome, the majority in our study are not identified until the preschool period. In our interviews, we ask parents how they first became aware of their child's problems, how they sought help, what resources they located, and how useful these resources were. The following account is constructed from these retrospective interviews plus other studies in the literature. We present parallel accounts of the experiences of parents whose children have Down's syndrome with those of other etiologies

Down's syndrome is the single most common cause of mental retardation and affects approximately 1 in 600 babies. Although it accounts for only 5–6% of all mentally retarded individuals, it marks an easily recognizable and relatively homogenous group of children identifiable soon after birth. The majority of studies of retarded children or delayed infants and their parents have been based on this group, even where generalizations are made about the larger and more heterogeneous group of children (e.g., Mahoney, 1983). The initial study by Marcovitch included 62 families (20 with Down's syndrome) and our current study has now seen 50 families, (including 19 with Down's syndrome).

Birth

In the vast majority of cases, birth was routine and normal and there was nothing about the birth or the period in the delivery room that alerted parents or medical staff to possible problems.

Postpartum

In the Down's syndrome group parents were usually told about the baby's problem in the day or so following birth. In the "other" group, the postpartum period was routine. Several years later, most of the parents in the Down's syndrome group remember and vividly recount the details of receiving the information about their child. They describe the awkwardness of relations with the hospital staff who seemed to avoid them, the pain of telling family and friends, and helpful or hurtful things that family and friends said or did at the time. They remember their own emotions of disbelief, distress and anger and their dissatisfaction with the lack of information and support they received from hospital staff. Most felt that their babies seemed normal (although some had medical problems) but had vivid fantasies about the "monster" their child might become.

Infancy

Because they *are* identified early in infancy, the development of Down's syndrome infants and their interactions with parents have been a frequent subject of study. For the same reason, these parents have been able to make early use of services such as infant stimulation programs and parent support groups and can locate reading materials designed to inform and aid parents of Down's syndrome children (e.g., Hanson, 1977). Before turning to the contrasting experience of families whose children have other types of delay, it is useful to summarize what is known about infants with Down's syndrome and their parents' nurturing styles.

Infants with Down's syndrome, like those born prematurely, develop more slowly than their normal counterparts. However, unlike the majority of preterm babies who eventually "catch up" with their full-term peers, those in the Down's syndrome group fall increasingly behind their normal peers as they get older. Thus, the delays in reaching developmental milestones that can reassure parents of the child's progress increase. However, the parent of such a child may also learn to adjust developmental expectations in accordance with the child's rate of progress. In one intervention for parents with delayed infants of mixed etiologies, Moxley-Haegert and Serbin (1983) designed a program that helped parents to recognize and predict subtle patterns of developmental change in their infants. This group of parents was found to carry out a home treatment program more effectively (as assessed by the frequency with which they engaged in the assigned activities, their consumption of the supplies provided for these activities, and their child's acquisition of the target skills) than a group which was exposed to child management techniques or had only instruction in the treatment program. This finding indicates that the adjustment of expectations for their child's development can have a strong motivating effect on the parent and affect the infant's development.

In addition to developing more slowly than the normal infant, the behavior of Down's syndrome infants is qualitatively different from that of normal peers at the same developmental stage. Patterns of eye contact and vocalization differ (Berger & Cunningham, 1981, 1983) and there is less use of referential looking toward mother during play sessions (Jones, 1980; Krakow & Kopp, 1983). Emotional expressions are less intense than those of normal infants and this is seen in smiling and laughter (Cicchetti & Sroufe, 1976, 1978; Emde, Katz, & Thorpe, 1978) as well as cries (Cicchetti & Serafica, 1981; Fisichelli & Karelitz, 1963; Karelitz & Fisichelli, 1962; Lind et al., 1970; Freudenberg, Driscoll, & Stern, 1978). However, there is some evidence that parents adapt to these less intense signals and learn to respond at lower levels of intensity than parents of normal infants (Sorce & Emde, 1982).

Observational studies of interactions between parents and their Down's syndrome infants indicate that in comparison with parents of children of the same developmental level, they are more active and more directive (Berger & Cunningham, 1983; Jones, 1980). In addition, Jones (1980) interviewed mothers following interaction sessions and found that those in the Down's syndrome group were most likely to report "teaching" as the goal of their interactions while those with normal infants were most likely to stress "having fun." These observations are consistent with our hierarchy of parental biological goals that suggests that in dyads where development is problematic, "having fun" is likely to be deferred in favor of efforts to stimulate development.

These highly active and directive patterns of interaction have sometimes been interpreted as "insensitive." However, the work of Shaffer and Crook (1979) indicates that sensitivity and directiveness are not necessarily incompatible qualities. In a recent study of mother-infant interaction with Down's syndrome infants, Crawley and Spiker (1983) also reported that observer ratings of these qualities in maternal style were independent. Furthermore, individual differences in maternal style were related to the developmental competence of the child. Children with higher scores on the Bayley Mental Scale had mothers who were rated high in stimulation value and there was some evidence that mothers who were rated high in both directiveness and sensitivity had higher functioning children. Whether these features of maternal style were a causal factor in the child's development or a response to the child's level of functioning was not ascertainable from the data. Nevertheless, these findings indicate the importance of examining individual differences within the delayed group and the relationship between child competence and maternal style.

From this point of view it is especially important to differentiate the much-studied Down's syndrome group from children with other delays as their developmental course and that of their parents is quite different. In the group with delays of other etiologies that we have studied, there are no data about infant development because these children are not identified until late in infancy or the preschool period. Most of the parents we interviewed became aware during the child's infancy that there were reasons to be concerned about possible developmental problems. However, for the most part, these were difficult to corroborate with opinions of family, friends, or professionals and parents experienced a period of great uncertainty during which they could only "wait and see." During this time they could not make use of services, support groups, or gather information because they did not yet know what their problem was. Although we often caution each other about the detrimental effects of premature "labeling" (e.g., Kearsley, 1979), labels also serve some positive functions for parents in identifying services, supports, and information that is relevant to their situation. When these families arrived late in the infancy period or preschool age for their child's first full assessment in hopes of discovering a diagnosis and treatment, they were just embarking upon the long developmental process that began for parents in the Down's syndrome group several years earlier when they first learned of their baby's problem.

Preschool

In our first study (Marcovitch, 1983), 62 families of preschoolers with delays were interviewed. Twenty of these were families in which the child had Down's syndrome. A further breakdown was made in the group with other delays. One subgroup included those for which some medical diagnosis had been given (N = 22); usually of a neurological problem (e.g., seizure disorder, agenesis of the corpus colossum). The other included those who could not be given a diagnosis and whose delays were of unknown etiology. (N = 20).

They were selected from referrals to the Developmental Evaluation Unit at The Hospital for Sick Children. To qualify for the study, a child had to be delayed in two or more areas of development and be referred to the unit during the preschool period. These referral criteria provided a sample of moderately delayed children without major physical handicaps. Those with severe or profound retardation and those with physical handicaps have usually been identified and assessed prior to 2-years-of-age. Children with Down's syndrome and some additional children with other types of delay were also located through Toronto area programs for developmentally handicapped children.

All came from two-parent families with a range of occupational and socioeconomic backgrounds in all three groups. (See Marcovitch, 1983 for a more detailed description of sample characteristics.) The study was designed to assess whether maternal stress varied systematically among the three handicap groups (Down's syndrome, neurological, and unknown etiology) and whether these factors would be related to styles of mother-child interaction.

Three measures of stress were used. The Rutter Health Questionnaire (1970) is a symptom report checklist indicative of physical and psychological distresses related to emotional disturbance. The Hassles Scale (Kanner, Coyne, Schaefer, & Lazarus, 1981) reports occurrences of daily stressful events. On both of these measures, higher scores reflect greater amounts of stress, the Rutter representing greater distress and the Hassles representing greater accumulation of demands on parents. In addition, we assessed the number of daily activities (e.g., mealtime, bath time) that were pleasurable or frustrating for parents with the target child. This measure was scored on the basis of a brief interview with the mother constructed for the purpose of the study. It has been called the Parental Coping Index (Marcovitch, 1983) and the total score is the number of pleasurable daily experiences reported. Thus, on this index, higher scores indicated more pleasurable experiences and lower scores reflected greater frustration and less pleasure.

Comparison between groups on these three measures (Table 10.2) indicates that there is a common pattern. Scores most indicative of stress (high for the Rutter and Hassles scales and low for the Coping Index) are found in the unknown etiology group whereas scores least indicative of stress characterize the Down's syndrome mothers. However, only the Coping Index showed statistically significant differences between groups. Parents in the Down's syndrome group reported more pleasurable experiences than those in the other two groups. This may, in fact, reflect the differences we discussed earlier in the parents' developmental history. The process of accepting a child's handicap and establishing realistic developmental expectations that began in the Down's syndrome group several years ago has just begun for those in the other two groups. When asked whether they belonged to a parent support group, 55% whose children had Down's syndrome replied that they did, whereas 44% of mothers in the neurological handicap group and 15% of the mothers in the unknown etiology group reported such association. Thus, the greater isolation experienced by mothers in the two latter groups may also contribute to their greater frustration in caring for their delayed child.

On the basis of scores on the Rutter Health Questionnaire, a subsample of 21 mother-child pairs were selected for observation of mother-child interaction. This subsample included 7 low (≤ 2), 8 moderate (3-5) and 6 high (>6) stress mothers. The mean score for the low-stress group was 1.12, for the moderate

TABLE 10.2
A Comparison of Means and Standard Deviation
for Stress Measures Across Handicap Groupings

Stress Measures	Down's Syndrome (N = 20)		Neurological (N = 22)		Unknown Etiology (N = 20)		F-Value
	M	S.D.	M	S.D.	M	S.D.	
Rutter Health Questionnaire	3.35	2.70	4.04	3.06	4.75	4.33	.83
Hassles	21.85	20.43	22.04	12.49	30.80	20.16	1.62
Parental Coping Index	6.71	2.28	5.32	2.01	3.95	1.61	9.87*

*$p < .01$

group 3.60 and for the high group 8.44. Ten mothers of Down's syndrome children and 11 mothers of children with other developmental disabilities were included. Mothers and children were observed in a free play laboratory session that lasted 15 minutes. Videotapes of the play sessions were rated by trained observers (unfamiliar with the research hypotheses) for maternal behaviors such as facial and vocal animation, control of activities, turn-taking, and positive and negative affect. The child's activity level and responsiveness were also rated, although only maternal ratings are discussed here.

Interactive ratings were compared by using a multivariate analysis of variance for two diagnostic subgroups: Down's syndrome and other delays. A consistent pattern emerged with a significant overall F (24.95, $p < .001$). Mothers of Down's syndrome children are more likely to follow their child's initiative, more likely to position their child for easy access to both themselves and the materials, more likely to choose developmentally appropriate materials, and more expressive facially and vocally for both positive and negative affects. Although only one scale yielded statistically significant differences between handicap groups (developmental appropriateness of materials, $F = 4.32, p < .05$), 9 of 10 comparisons ($p < .02$) were indicative of more relaxed, responsive and animated interactive maternal behavior in the Down's syndrome group. The findings that mothers in the Down's syndrome group were less stressed and had more positive interactions with their children suggests that it is unwise to generalize from the frequently studied children with Down's syndrome to those with other types of delays. These parents who have had a longer developmental history of their understanding and acceptance of the child's problems and more supportive services may well have ascertained what can be reasonably expected for their child's growth and development and can begin to enjoy both the parental role and their interactions with their child.

Furthermore, these findings highlight the importance of assessing individual differences in mother-child interaction in the developmentally delayed population. They suggest that mothers in some groups encounter greater difficulty in interacting with their delayed child and require supportive services addressing their individual needs, not merely services to parents of delayed children in general.

SUMMARY

In this chapter we have considered the nurturing experience of several groups of parents confronted with children's developmental problems. We have suggested that such problems stress parents in a variety of ways and have argued that parents' developmental history of discovering the child's problem and finding supports is related to the amount of distress parents experience in the nurturing role. Parental distress affects parental nurturing style in two ways. First, parents adapt to distress arising directly from the child's problems by adjusting their priorities and goals for the child and their relationship with the child. Survival, growth and development become important foci of parental activity and more pleasurable parental activities such as social play diminish in importance. Second, parental distress is reflected in emotional expressiveness. Those parents assumed to experience more stress in the preterm studies, or reporting more stress in the preschool study, are less expressive and/or show less positive affect during interactions with their child. This then may be one of the ways in which parental stress is communicated to infants and young children—through parents' constricted affective behavior.

In the preterm studies, we have found that in spite of early difficulties, the majority of babies form secure emotional bonds with their parents, indicating that both parents and children can successfully adapt to nurturing under stress. In the study of delayed preschoolers evidence on the quality of attachment is not presently available. However, the perspective that we have presented suggests that investigation of the socioemotional development of children with handicaps as they relate to parental stress and nurturing style will become increasingly important.

Our understanding of the factors that generally affect the capacity to nurture or nurturing style is still quite limited. In a recent review, Belsky (1984) argues that three types of variables make major contributions: contextual support and stress, child characteristics, and psychological resources of parents, with the latter being the most influential. In the present framework, we have viewed both psychological resources and contextual support and stress as potential supporters and stressors of the parent-child dyad. We have also suggested that in the case of children with specific developmental problems and handicaps there is an associated history of development in the parental role that partially determines contextual support and stress.

A greater deal has been written about the emotional process of parental adjustment to a child's handicap (Blacher, 1984 reviews recent thinking in this domain), but this has not been related to parental behavior or style of parent-child interaction. The biosocial model we presented suggests that the goals of parental behavior are changed by by the presence of developmental handicaps. The criteria we usually use to evaluate optimal parenting may also need to be changed. It seems likely that the psychological resources of parents will play an important role in facilitating or impeding both emotional adjustment and cognitive shifts in parental goals for growth and development. The relative importance of contextual supports, child characteristics, and parental resources in shaping normal parental behavior remain to be demonstrated for normally developing children. Whether similar or different patterns emerge for handicapped children is also an empirical question. However, the study of parental behavior under extremely stressful circumstances provides a unique opportunity to study capacities for adaptation that might not emerge with normal children whose care does not demand them.

REFERENCES

Ainsworth, M. D. S, Blehar, M. C., Waters, E., & Wall, S. (1978). *Patterns of attachment.* Hillsdale, NJ: Lawrence Erlbaum Associates.

Bakeman, R., & Brown, J. (1980). Early interaction: Consequences for social and mental development at three years. *Child Development, 51,* 437–447.

Beckwith, L., & Cohen, S. E. (1978). Preterm birth: Hazardous obstetrical and postnatal events as related to caregiver-infant behavior. *Infant Behavior and Development, 1,* 403–412.

Bell, R. W. (1968). A reinterpretation of the direction of effects in studies of socialization. *Psychological Review, 75,* 81–95.

Belsky, J. (1984). The determinants of parenting: A process model. *Child Development, 85,* 83–96.

Berger, J., & Cunningham, C. (1981). The development of eye contact between mothers and normal versus mothers and Down's syndrome infants. *Developmental Psychology, 17,* 678–689.

Berger, J., & Cunningham, C. (1983). Development of early vocal behaviors and interactions in Down syndrome and non-handicapped infant-mother pairs. *Developmental Psychology, 19,* 822–331.

Blacher, J. (1984). Sequential stages of parental adjustment to the birth of a child with handicaps: Fact or artifact? *Mental Retardation, 22,* 55–68.

Boukydis, C. Z. (1982). Support groups for parents with premature infants in NICUs. In R. Marshall, C. Kasman & L. S. Cape (Eds.), *Coping with caring for sick newborns.* Toronto: W. B. Saunders.

Brachfeld, S., Goldberg, & Sloman, J. (1980). Parent-infant interaction in free play at 8 and 12 months. Effects of prematurity and immaturity. *Infant Behavior and Development, 3,* 289–305.

Brown, J. V., & Bakeman, R. (1979). Relationships of human mothers with their infants during the first year of life. In R. W. Bell & W. P. Smotherman (Eds.), *Maternal influences and early behavior.* Jamaica, NY: Spectrum.

Caplan, G. (1960)Patterns of parental response to the crisis of premature birth. *Psychiatry, 23,* 365–374.

Caplan, G., Mason, E., & Kaplan, D. M. (1965). Four studies of crisis in parents of prematures. *Community Mental Health Journal, 1,* 149–161.

Cicchetti, D., & Serafica, F. C. (1981). Interplay among behavioral systems: Illustrations from the study of attachment, affiliation and wariness in young children with Down's syndrome. *Developmental Psychology, 17,* 36–49.

Cicchetti, D, & Sroufe, L. A. (1976). The relationship between affective and cognitive development in Down's syndrome infants. *Child Development, 47,* 920–929.

Cicchetti, D., & Sroufe, L. A. (1978). An organization view of affect: Illustration from the study of Down's syndrome infants. In M. Lewis & L. Rosenblum (Eds.). *The development of affect.* New York: Plenum.

Cox, T. (1978). *Stress.* Baltimore: University Park Press.

Crawford, J. W. (1982). Mother-infant interaction in premature and full term infants. *Child Development, 53,* 957–962.

Crawley, S. B., & Spiker, D. (1983). Mother-child interactions involving two year olds with Down Syndrome. A look at individual differences. *Child Development,* 54:1312–1323

Crnic, K. A., Ragozin, A., Greenberg, M. T., Robinson, N. M., & Basham, R. B. (1983). Social interaction and developmental competence of preterm and full term infants during the first year of life. *Child Development, 54,* 1199–1210.

Dergatis, L. R. (1977). *SCL-90 Scoring Manual.* Baltimore, MD: John's Hopkins School of Medicine.

DiVitto, B., & Goldberg, S. (1983). Talking and sucking: Infant feeding behavior and parent stimulation in dyads with different medical histories. *Infant Behavior and Development, 6,* 157–165.

Emde, R. N., Katz, E. L., & Thorpe, J. K. (1978). Emotional expression in infancy. II Early deviations in Down's syndrome. In M. Lewis & L. A. Rosenblum (Eds.), *The development of affect*, New York: Plenum Press.

Field, T. (1977). Effects of early separation, interactive deficits and experimental manipulation on mother-infant interaction. *Child Development, 48*, 763–771.

Fisichelli, V., & Karelitz, S. (1963). The cry latencies of normal infants and those with brain damage. *Journal of Pediatrics, 62*, 924–734.

Freudenberg, R. P., Driscoll, J. W., & Stern, G. S. (1978). Reactions of adult humans to cries of normal and abnormal infants. *Infant Behavior and Development, 1*, 224–227.

Goldberg, S. (1977). Social competence in infancy: A model of parent-infant interaction. *Merrill-Palmer Quarterly, 23*, 163–177.

Goldberg, S. (1979). Pragmatics and problems of longitudinal research with high risk infants. In T. Field, S. Goldberg, A. Sostek, & H. H. Shuman. *Infants born at risk*. Jamaica, NY: Spectrum.

Goldberg, S. (1982). Some biological aspects of early parent-infant interaction. In S. G. Moore & C. R. Cooper (Eds.), *The young child: Reviews of research* (Vol. 3). Washington, D.C.: National Association for the Education of Young Children.

Goldberg, S., Brachfeld, S., & DiVitto, B. (1980). Feeding, fussing, and play: Parent-infant interactions in the first year as a function of early medical problems. In T. M. Field, S. Goldberg, D. Stern, & A. Sostek (Eds.), *Interactions of high risk infants and children*. New York: Academic Press.

Goldberg, S., & Corter, C. (1983). *Social competence in low birthweight twins and singletons*. Proposal to Ontario Mental Health Foundation.

Goldberg, S., & DiVitto, B. (1983). *Born too soon: Preterm birth and early development*. San Francisco: Freeman.

Goldberg, S., & Marcovitch, S. (1982). *Child characteristics, maternal stress and mother-child relationships in developmentally delayed preschoolers*. Proposal to Canada Health and Welfare.

Greene, J. G., Fox, N. A., & Lewis, M. (1983). The relationship between neonatal characteristics and three month mother-infant interaction in high risk infants. *Child Development, 54*, 1286–1296

Hanson, M. (1977). *Teaching your Down's syndrome infant*. Baltimore: University Park Press.

Holmes, T. H., & Rahe, R. H. (1967). The social readjustment rating scale. *Journal of Psychosomatic Research*, 11:213–218.

Jeffers, D., Goldberg, S., Goolem-Hoosen, I., & Minde, K. (1984). Mother-infant interaction in the neonatal intensive care unit: Cross cultural comparisons, submitted for publication.

Jones, O. H. K. (1980). Prelinguistic communication skills in Down's syndrome and normal infants. In T. Field, S. Goldberg, D. Stern, & A. Sostek (Eds.), *High risk infants and children: Interactions with adults and peers*. New York: Academic Press.

Kanner, A. D., Coyne, J. C., Schaefer, C., & Lazarus, R. (1981). Comparison of two modes of stress measurement: Daily hassles and uplifts versus life events. *Journal of Behavioral Medicine, 4*, 1–3a.

Kaplan, D., & Mason, E. (1960). Maternal reactions to premature birth viewed as an acute emotional disorder. *American Journal of Orthopsychiatry, 30*, 539–552.

Karelitz, S., & Fisichelli, V. R. (1962). The cry thresholds of normal infants and those with brain damage. *Journal of Pediatrics, 61*, 679–685.

Kearsley, R. B. (1979). Iatrogenic retardation: A syndrome of learned incompetence. In R. B. Kearsley & I. E. Sigel (Eds.), *Infants at risk: Assessment of cognitive functioning*. Hillsdale, NJ: Lawrence Erlbaum Associates.

Klaus, M. H., & Kennell, J. H. (1976). *Maternal infant bonding*. St. Louis: C. V. Mosby.

Klaus, M. H., & Kennell, J. H. (1982). *Parent-infant bonding*. St. Louis: C. V. Mosby.

Krakow, J., & Kopp, C. B. (1983). The effects of developmental delay on sustained attention in young children. *Child Development, 54*, 1143–1155.

Lewis, M., & Goldberg, S. (1969). Perceptual-cognitive development in infancy: A generalized expectancy model as a function of mother-infant interaction. *Merrill-Palmer Quarterly, 15,* 81–100.

Lewis, M., & Rosenblum, L. (1974). *The effect of the infant on its caregiver.* New York: Wiley.

Lind, J., Vuorenkoski, V., Rosberg, G., Partenen, T. J., & Wasz-Hockart, O. (1970). Spectrograph analysis of vocal response to pain stimuli in infants with Down's syndrome. *Developmental Medicine and Child Neurology, 12,* 478–486.

Mahoney, G. (1983, April). *Communication patterns between mothers and their developmentally delayed infants.* Paper presented at the meetings of the Society for Research in Child Development. Detroit, Michigan.

Marcovitch, S. (1983). *Maternal stress and mother-child interaction with the developmentally delayed preschool child.* Unpublished Ph.D. thesis. York University.

Minde, K., Corter, C., & Goldberg, S. (1983, March). *The effects of twinship and biological impediments to early interaction and attachment between premature infants and their mothers.* Paper presented at the Second Conference of the World Association of Infant Psychiatry, Cannes, France.

Minde, K., Marton, P., Manning, D., & Hines, B. (1980). Some determinants of mother-infant interaction in the premature nursery. Journal of the *American Academy of Child Psychiatry, 19,* 1–21.

Minde, K., Trehub, S., Corter, C., Boukydis, C., Celhoffer, L., & Marton, P. (1978). Mother-child relationships in the premature nursery: An observational study. *Pediatrics, 61,* 373–379.

Minde, K., Whitelaw, A., Brown, J., & Fitzhardinge, P. (1983). The effect of neonatal complications in premature infants on early parent-infant interaction. *Developmental Medicine and Child Neurology.* 25: 763–777.

Moxley-Haegert, L., & Serbin, L. A. (1983). Developmental education for parents with delayed infants: Effects on parental motivation and children's development. *Child Development, 54,* 1324–1331.

Rode, S., Chang, P., Fisch, R. O., & Sroufe, L. A. (1981). Attachment patterns of infants separated at birth. *Developmental Psychology, 17,* 188–192.

Rutter, M., Graham, P., & Yule, W. (1970). *A neuropsychiatric study in childhood. Clinics in developmental Medicine.* No. 35/36. London: SIMP Heineman.

Sameroff, A. (1975). Early influences on development: Fact or Fancy? *Merrill-Palmer Quarterly, 21,* 267–294.

Shaffer, H. R., & Crook, C. K. (1979). Maternal control techniques in a directed play situation. *Child Development, 50,* 989–996.

Sorce, J. H., & Emde, R. N. (1982). The meaning of infant emotional expression: Regularities in caregiving responses to normal and Down's syndrome infants. *Journal of Child Psychology and Psychiatry,* 23: 145–158.

Wasserman, G., Soloman-Scwerzer, C. R., Spicker, S., & Stern, D. (1980, March). *Maternal interactive style with normal and at risk toddlers.* Paper presented at the International Conference on Infant Studies, New Haven.

Author Index

A

Abramovitch, R., 3, 20, *23, 24,* 62, *66*
Abramson, D.C., 190, *250*
Ader, R., 143, *199*
Ainsworth, M.D.S., 266, *274*
Alberts, T.R., 143, *196, 200*
Alexander, G., 157, *196*
Alexander, M., *205*
Allin, J.T., 143, 159, *196*
Andelman, S.L., 247, *258*
Anderson, A., *203*
Anderson, C.O., 155, *196*
Aoki, 137, *137*
Applebaum, M., 9, *24*
Archer, J., 170, 182, *196*
Armitage, C., *202*
Aschenbrenner, B., 212, 214, 218, 228, *231*
Ascher, J.A., *203*
Ashe, T.H., 181, *202*
Axelrod, S., 219, *231*

B

Bacon, M., 96, *120*
Bakeman, R., 265–266, *274*
Baker, R., 247, *256*
Baker, T.M., *200*
Baldwin, W., 246, *254*
Bancalari, E., 247, *257*
Banks, E.M., 143, 159, *196*
Baranczuk, R., 154, *196*
Baras, S., 178, *196*
Barfield, R.J., 144, *198*
Barglow, P., 240, *254*
Barnett, C.R., *204*
Barry, H., 4, *23,* 96, *120*
Bashman, R.B., 265, *274*
Bauer, F., 247, *258*
Bauer, J.H., 173, *196*
Beach, F.A., 158–160, *196*
Beckwith, L., 264–265, *274*
Bekoff, M., 22, *23*
Bell, N.T., *196*
Bell, R., 69, *89*
Bell, R.W., x, xi, 151, 156, 159, *196, 205,* 239–242, *254,* 260, *274*
Belsky, J., x, xi, 209–210, 219, 222–223, 229, *231,* 235, 239, 242, *254,* 273, *274*
Bem, S., 221, *231*
Benedek, T., 193, *196*
Bennett, W.C., *200*
Berger, T., 269, *274*
Berk, M.L., 178–179, *196*
Berkson, G., 160, *205*
Berman, P., 5–6, *23,* 25, 28, 30, 32, 34, 38–41, 48–49, *50,* 62, *66,* 69, 71, 77–79, *89*
Bhrolchain, M.N., 244, *255*
Bibring, G.L., 193, *196*
Blacher, J., 273, *274*

277

AUTHOR INDEX

Blake, C.A., 147, *197*
Blakemore, J., 49, *50,* 62–62, *66*
Blanchard, D.C., 181, *197*
Blass, E.M., 142, *197, 200*
Blehar, M.C., 266, *274*
Boll, E., 4–5, *23*
Bornstein, M., *254*
Bossard, J., 4–5, *23*
Boukydis, C.Z., 265, *274*
Bourne, G.L., *202*
Bowlby, J., 101, *120*
Brachfeld, 261, 265–266, *275*
Brewster, J., 143, *197*
Brewsher, P.D., 188, *200*
Bridgeman, D., 98, *121*
Bridges, R.S., 147–150, 162, 166, 170, *197, 204*
Brock, V., 247, *256*
Brody, S., 219, *231*
Broman, S.H., 246–249, *254*
Bronfenbrenner, U., x, xi, 130, *137*
Brookman, A., 104, *120*
Brooks, A., 136, *137*
Brooks, J., 26, *50,* 70, *89*
Brooks-Gunn, J., 76, *90,* 233, 235, 241–243, 245, 252, *254, 255,* 257
Brown, G.W., 244, *255*
Brown, T.V., 265–266, *274*
Brown, J., 264, *276*
Brown, M., 4, *23*
Brucken, L., 49, *51*
Bruno, J.P., 143, *199*
Brunnquell, D., 219, 240, *231, 255*
Bryant, B., 4–6, 21, *23*
Budwig, N., 55, *67*
Burt, M.R., 233, 237–238, 243, 251, *257*
Busch-Rossnagel, N., 69, *90,* 209, *232*

C

Cain, V., 246, *254*
Caldwell, S., 236, *257*
Callahan, E.C., 176, *203*
Campbell, C.S., 161, *206*
Campos, T.T., 190, *206*
Capek, K., 143, *197*
Caplan, G., 263, *274*
Card, J.J., 234, 249, *255*
Carlson, N.R., 155, *206*
Carlsson, S.G., 186, 189, *197*
Cassel, J., 246, *255, 257*
Cernoch, J.M., 169, *203*

Chang, P., 266, *276*
Chee, P., 158, *199*
Cherry, L., 253, *255*
Chiba, T., 126, *138*
Child, I., 4, *23,* 96, *120*
Chilman, C.S., 233, *255*
Christie, J., 95, *120*
Cicchetti, D., 269, *274*
Cicirelli, V., 5–6, *23*
Clark, M.C., 153, *204*
Clarke-Stewart, K.A., 53, *66,* 244, *255*
Cleary, P.D., 245, *256*
Clifton, D.K., 148, *197*
Coates, D.L., 244, *255*
Cobb, S., 223–246, *231*
Cockshott, C., *200*
Cohen, J., 166, *197*
Cohen, S.E., 264–265, *274*
Collmer, C.W., 212, *232*
Connors, K., 239, *257*
Conrad, L.C.A., 177–178, 180, *197, 198*
Coover, G., 151, 181, *198, 205*
Copeland, J.R.M., *199*
Corter, C., 3, 20, *23–24,* 62, *66,* 261, 266, *274*
Cowan, C.P., 222, *231*
Cowan, P.A., 222, *231*
Coyne, T.C., 270, *275*
Cox, T., 261, *274*
Cramer, C.P., 142, *200*
Crary, D., 154, *207*
Crasset, J., 124, *138*
Crawford, A.G., 243, 253, *255*
Crawford, T.W., 265, *274*
Crawley, S.B., 269, *274*
Crichton, L., 219, 240, *231, 255*
Crnic, K.A., 265, *274*
Crockenberg, S., 223, *231*
Cronin, P., 160, *200*
Crook, C.K., 269, *276*
Croskerry, P.G., 143, 157, *201*
Cunningham, C., 269, *274*
Cummings, E., 46, *51,* 70, *90*
Cummings, L.A., 164, *198*
Cutrona, C., 69, 78, *89*

D

Danielsson, B., *197*
Davabi, K., 238, *255*
Davis, P.G., 184, *201*
deChateau, P., 186, 189–190, *198*

Deis, R.P., 147, *206*
deLissovey, V., 238–239, *255*
Denenberg, V.H., 142, 144, 146, 154, 159, *196, 198–199, 204, 206, 207*
Dennett, P.M., *202*
deOlmos, T.S., 179, *198*
Derogatis, 261, *274*
Deutsch, H., 193, *198*
Dickie, J.R., 222, *231*
Diskin, S., 210, 215, *232*
DiVitto, B., 261, 265–266, *274–275*
Doering, S., 210, 212, 214, 225–228, *231*
Doerr, H.K., 147, 150, *198*
Dohrenwend, B.P., 244, *255*
Dohrenwend, B.S., 244, *255*
Dollinger, M.J., 142, *198*
Donovan, W., 61, *67*
Driscoll, T.W., 269, *275*
Dunn, J., 4, 6–7, 10, 14, 20, *24*, 62, *66*
Dunn, T.L., *200*

E

Easterbrooks, M.A., 22, 219, *231–232*
Eden, R., 124, *138*
Edwards, C., 5–6, *24*, 65, *67*, 73, *89*, 99, 115, *120–121*
Edwards, D.W., 244, *257*
Egeland, B., 219, *231*, 240, *255*
Eichler, L., 241, *199*, 210, 215, *232, 256*
Eiseido, K., 126, *138*
Eisenberg-Berg, N., 54, 61, *66–67*
Elwood, R.W., 153, 157, 161, 168, *198*
Ember, C., 65, *66*, 96, 104, *120–121*
Emde, R.N., 190, *206*, 269, *275–276*
Ensmunger, M.E., 246, *256*
Entwisle, D., 210, 212, 214, 225–228, *231*
Epstein, A.S., 239, *255*
Erikson, E., 57, *66*
Erskine, M., 144, 169, *198*
Essex, M., 245, *256*
Ewer, R.F., 143, *198*
Exum, D.B., *254*

F

Fagerberg, H., *197*
Farooq, A., 154, *206*
Fawcett, C.P., *200*
Feder, H.H., 147, *197*
Feil, L.A., 59, *67*, 234, 242, *257*
Feiring, C., 70, *90*, 246, *256*

Feldman, S.S., 48, *50*, 62–63, *66*, 69, 71–72, 77–79, 83, *89*, 186, 191, 194–195, *198, 201*, 212–214, 217–219, 221–225, 227–229, *231*, 240–241, *255*
Fernander, L., 28, *50*, 71, *89*
Fernstrom, M., *205*
Ferron, S.A., *202*
Feshbach, N., 54, *66*
Field, T., 70, *89*, 235, 238–239, 243, 248, 252, *255*, 266
Finkelstein, T.A., 178–179, *196*
Fisch, R.O., 266, *276*
Fisher, T., 234, *257*
Fisichelli, V., 269, *275*
Fitzhardinge, P., 264, *276*
Fleischer, S., 174, *198*
Fleming, A., 143–145, 149, 152, 157–158, 162, 164, 166, 168, 170, 176–177, 180, 182, 184, 186, 191, *198, 199, 202–203*
Fogel, A., 61–64, *67*, 69–72, 74–75, 78–80, 82, *90*, 233, 239, *255*
Fox, N.A., 65, *67*, 264, *275*
Franklin, M., *202*
Frantz, A.G., 176, 178, *199, 201, 206*
Frendenberg, R.P., 269, *275*
Friedman, M.I., 142, *199*
Frideman, S.M., 46, *51*, 70, *90, 201*
Frodi, A., 61, *67*, 212, 216, *232*
Frodi, M., 212, 216, *232*
Fuchs, S., 147, *201*
Fullard, W., 26, *50*, 70, 72, *90*
Fuller, G.B., *196*
Furstenberg, F.F., Jr., 233–235, 241–246, 248, 250, 252–253, *255, 256*

G

Gaffori, O., 177, *199*
Gagnon, J., 48, *51*
Galef, B.G., Jr., 143, 181, *199*
Gallimore, R., 5, *24*, 96, *120–121*
Gallistel, C.R., 156, *199*
Gamble, W., 209, *231*, 239, *254*
Gandelman, R., 146, 159, 173, *199, 207*
Garbarino, J., x, xi
Gelden, M.G., *202*
Gelfand, D., 43, *51*
George, A.T., 188, *199*
Giordano, A.L., 157, *204*
Given, K., 210, 215, *232*
Glass, G., 85, *90*
Glick, P.C., 243, *256*
Goldberg, S., 243, *256*, 259–261, 264–266, *275–276*

Goldberg, W.A., 222, *231*
Goldman, B.D., 144, *198*
Goodman, V., 5, *23*, 28, 34, 38–41, 49, *50*, 62, *66*, 71, 78, 79, *89*
Goolam-Hoosen, I., 264, *275*
Goulds, S., *200*
Gorski, R.A., *200, 203*
Goyens, J., 153, *202*
Graham, E., 238, *255*
Graham, P., 261, *276*
Gray, T.A., 170, *199*
Greenberg, M., 191, *199*
Greenberg, M.T., 265, *274*
Greenberg, N.H., 240, *256*
Greene, T.G., 264, *275*
Greenwald, G.S., 153–154, 168, *196, 205*
Grimm, C.T., 148, *197*
Grossman, F., 210, 212, 215, 217–219, 221–222, 224–225, 227, *199, 232,* 241, *256*
Grossman, K.E., 190–191, *199*
Grota, L.T., 143, *199*
Gubernick, D.T., 141, 143, 169, *199–200*
Gundewall, C., *197*

H

Halaris, A., *202*
Hales, D.T., 186, 189–190, *200*
Hall, B.L., 194, *206*
Hall, W.G., 142, *200*
Hamburg, B.A., 240, *256*
Handley, S.L., 188, *200*
Handschin, S., 240, *256*
Hausen, S., 148, *200*
Hanson, M., 268, *275*
Harns, T., 244, *255*
Hartman, C.G., 154, *206*
Hartmann, D., 43, *51*
Hay, D., 25, *51*
Heagarty, M.C., *254*
Heinicke, C., 210, 212, 215, 217, 219, 227, *232*
Hendrickson, C.W., *200*
Herrenkohl, L.R., 158–160, *200*
Hershberger, W.A., 151, *205*
Hersher, L., 169, *200*
Herzig, A., 49, *51*
Hirai, N., 134, *138*
Hoffman, M., 54, *67*
Hoken Dojin-sha, 127, *138*
Holloway, W.R., 142, *198*
Holmberg, H., *198*

Holmes, T.H., 261, *275*
Hooley, R.D., 169, *203*
Hopkins, J.B., 190, *200*
Hopkins, T.B., 178, *200*
Horneman, G., *197*
How, J., 188, *200*
Huston, T.L., 212, 216–217, 221, 225, 229, *232*
Hwang, C., *197,* 212, *232*

I

Ikard, W.L., 170, *200*
Ikeda, Y., 127, *138*
Ingram, W.R., 179, *198*
Intans-Peterson, M., 76, *90*

J

Jacklin, C., 5, 13, *24,* 47, *51*
Jacobson, C.D., 176, *200*
Jakubowski, H., 165, *200*
Jans, E.T., 198, *200*
Jarvella, R., *204*
Jaynes, T.T., 158–160, *196*
Jeffers, D., 264, *275*
Jelivek, J., 143, *197*
Jerauld, R., *200*
Jimba, Y., 128, *139*
Johnson, E., 95, *120*
Johnson, T.S., 244, *257*
Jones, O.H.K., 209, *275*
Jones, S., 212, 216–218, 225, *232*

K

Kalra, P.S., 147, *200*
Kamaras, L., 148, *201*
Kanner, A.D., 270, *275*
Kaplan, B.H., 246, *257*
Kaplan, D.M., 263, *274*
Karelitz, S., 269, *275*
Kasanin, J., 240, *256*
Katagiri, S., 136–137, *138*
Katz, E.L., 269, *275*
Kaye, K., 55, *67*
Kearsley, R.B., 270, *275*
Keeble, S., 160, *200*
Keiner, M., 178, 184, *203*
Kendrick, C., 4, 6–7, 10, 14, 20, *24,* 62, *66*
Kennell, J.H., 186, 188, 190, 196, *200–201, 204, 205,* 263, *275*

Kellum, S.G., 246, 249, *256*
Kenyon, P., 160, *200*
Keogh, B.K., 240, *256*
Kessler, R.C., 245, *256*
Kimble, D.P., 174, *200*
King, R., 119, *121*
Klaus, M.H., 186–188, 190, 196, *200–201, 204–205,* 263, 275
Knapp, M.E., 178, *206*
Kobayashi, H., 132, *138*
Kohler, C.H., 148, *200*
Kojima, H., 133, *138*
Komisaruk, B.R., *203*
Kopp, C.B., 269, *275*
Koranyi, L., 148, 165, *201*
Koshinaga, J., 128, *138*
Kosugi, K., 134, *138*
Krakow, T., 269, *275*
Krebs, D., 54, *67*
Kreger, N.C., *200*
Krehbiel, D.A., 147, *201*
Krettek, J.E., 178, *201*
Kreistal, M.B., 148, *201*
Krulich, L., *200*
Kuhar, M., 178, *206*
Kuhn, D., 49, *51*
Kurahashi, S., 133, *138*

L

Lakin, M., 240, *256*
Lamb, M., 6–7, *24,* 61, *67, 90,* 190, 212, 216, 218–219, 225, *232*
Lando, B., 3, *23, 62, 66*
Larsen, V.L., 240, *256*
Larsson, K., *197*
Lavelle, N., 240, *256*
Lazarus, R., 270, *275*
Leavitt, L., 61, *67*
Legg, C., *202*
Lehman, M.N., 178, 180, *201*
Lehrman, D.S., 142–143, 151, 162, *204*
Leiderman, P.H., *204*
Leifer, M., 194–196, *201, 204,* 213, 220, *232,* 241, *256*
LeMoal, M., 177, *199*
LeNeindre, P., 154–155, 169, *203*
Lennon, R., 54, 61, *66*
Leon, M., 143, 146–147, 157, *197, 200, 201–202, 206*
Lerner, T., 210, *232*
Lerner, R., 69, *90*

LeRoy, L.M., 147, *201*
Levin, H., 242, *258*
Levin, R., 147, *202,* 209–210, *232*
LeVine, R., 116, *120*
Levine, S., 181, *198*
Lewis, M., x, xi, 26, *50,* 70, 76, *90,* 209, *232,* 239, 242–244, 246–247, 253, *255–256,* 259, 260–261, 264, *276*
Lieberman, M.A., 244, *257*
Liem, J., 245, *256*
Liem, R., 245, *256*
Lincoln, R., 233, *255*
Lind, J., 191, *199,* 269, *276*
Lisk, R.D., 155, *201*
Lissak, K., 148, *201*
Loesch, T.G., 240, *256*
Lorenz, K., 26, 47, *51,* 72, *90,* 101, *120*
Lott, D., 147–148, *201*
Lowe-Vandell, D., 6, *24*
Lozoff, B., *200*
Lubin, M., 146, *202*
Luebke, C., 144, 170, 177, *198*
Lundino, R.W., *200*

M

Maccoby, E.E., 5, 13, *24, 47, 50,* 242, *258*
MacFarlane, A., 210, *232*
MacKinnon, D.S., 144, 150, *205*
Maeda, H., 177, *201*
Magnus, E.M., 196, *201*
Mahoney, G., 267, *276*
Mali, J., 49, *51*
Mallafree, C.M., 157, *204*
Malsburgy, C.W., 176–178, *202*
Marcovitch, S., 259, 261, 267, 270–271, *275–276*
Marecek, J., 235, 247–249, *256*
Maretski, H., 104, *120*
Maretski, T., 104, *120*
Marques, D.M., 158, *201*
Martin, G.B., 169, *203*
Martyna, W., 221, *231*
Marvin, R., 62, *67*
Mason, E., 263, *274*
Matsunaga, G., 133, *138*
Mayer, A.D., 143, 145, 161, *203–204*
Maxwell, N., 238, *257*
McAlpine, W., *200*
McCann, S.M., 175, *200, 205*
McCall, R., 9, *24*
McCormick, M., 245–247, 252, *256*

McEwen, B.S., 184, *201*
McHale, S.M., 212, 216–217, 221, 225, 229, *232*
McLane, J., 55, *67*
McLaughlin, F.T., 169, *203*
McNamee, G., 55, *67*
Meed, M., 196, *201*
Mednick, B., 247, *256*
Melges, F.T., 240, *256*
Melson, G.F., 61–65, *67*, 69–72, 74–75, 77–80, 82, *90*, 233
Menken, J., 233, *255*
Menniti, F.S., 148, *204*
Miceli, M.O., 176–178, 180, 182, *199*, *202*
Miller, W., 49, *51*
Minde, K., 259, 264–266, *275–276*
Minnett, A., 6, *24*
Mirowski, T., 244–245, *257*
Mistry, J., 63, *67*, 69–71, 78, 82, 86–87, *90*, 233
Miura, K., 130–131, *138*
Mogenson, G.T., 177, *201*
Moltz, H., 146–148, 175, *202*, *205*
Monda, L., 30, 132, *50*, *62*, *66*
Monkus, E., 247, *257*
Monroe, Y.L., *203*
Moore, A.U., 169, *200*
Moore, C., 143, 169, *200*, *202*
Moore, K., 233, 236–238, 243, 251, *257*
Morelli, G.A., 143, *202*
Moretto, D., 168, 176, 182, 199, *202*
Morioka, K., 133, *138*
Morishige, W.K., 144, *202*
Morse, E., 125, 132, *138*
Moss, H., 195–196, *202*, *204*, 240, *257*
Moss, M., 212, 216–218, 225, *232*
Mott, F., 238, *257*
Moxley-Haegert, L., 268, *276*
Much, N., 97–99, *120–121*
Mueller, D., 244–245, *257*
Murray, H., 135, *138*
Mussen, P., 54, *67*
Myers, 159, *199*
Myerscough, R., 30, 32, *50*, *62*, *66*

N

Nachman, M., 181, *202*
Nagel, D.S., 177, *203*
Namerow, P., 238, *255*
Nash, S.C., 48–49, *50–51*, 62–63, *66*, 69, 71–72, 77–79, 83, 86, *89*, 191, 194, 195, *198*, *209*, 212–214, 217–219, 221, 225, 227, 228, *231*, 240–241
National Center for Health Statistics, 236, 250, *257*
Navojosky, B.H., *204*
Neff, C., 61, *67*
Nerlove, S., 96, *120*
Newman, L., 49, *51*
Newnham, J.P., 188, *202*
Newton, N., 196, *201*
Nishita, J.K., *201*
Nitschke, W., *196*
Niwa, Y., 130, *138*
Noh, S., 245–246, *258*
Noirot, E., 144, 153, 156, 159, 168, *202*
Norman, R.L., *197*
Norton, A.L., 243, *256*
Nott, P.N., 188, *202*
Nucci, L., 96–98, 109, *120*
Nuckolls, K.B., 246, *257*
Numan, M., 146–147, 176–177, 184, *202*, *203*
Nydegger, C., 102–103, 110–111, *120*
Nydegger, N., 102–103, 110–111, *120*

O

O'Connor, S., 235, *257*
Ohinata, M., 128, 135, *139*
Ohtoh, Y., 125–126, *138*
Ohtsu, T., 126, *138*
Orpen, G., 145, 149, 152, 184, *199*, *203*
Osofsky, H.T., 238, *257*
Osofsky, T.D., 238–239, *257*
Ostermeyer, M.C., 144, *203*
Owen, P., *206*

P

Paclik, L., 168, *202*
Parke, R., 211–212, 224, *232*, 234, *257*
Parlee, M.D., 240, *257*
Parsons, B., 184, *201*
Partenen, T.J., *276*
Pauker, T.D., 240, *257*
Pay, S., 178, *196*
Pearlin, L.I., 244, *257*
Pederson, C.A., 148, *203*
Pelchat, R., 143, *206*
Pepe, G., 145, *202–203*
Pepler, D., 3, 5, 18, 20, *23–24*
Peters, L.C., *201*

AUTHOR INDEX 283

Peterson, T.L., 250, *256*
Pfaff, D., 177–178, 180, 184, *197–198, 201, 203*
Phelps, C.P., 165, *201*
Philliber, S., 238, *255*
Phillipson, D.T., 177, *203*
Piaget, J., 97, *120*
Piorrata, S., 65, *67*
Pitt, B., 188, *203*
Plumb, N., *201*
Poindron, P., 153, 155, 169, *203*
Pool, D., 99, *120*
Porter, R.H., 142, 169, *203*
Power, T.G., 234, *257*
Powers, T.B., 178, *201, 203, 206*
Presser, H.B., 249, *257*
Pretlow, R.A., 3rd, *201*
Price, T.L., 178, *201*
Prime Minister's Office of Japan, 131, 133, *138*

Q

Quadaguo, D.M., 170, *203*
Quay, H.C., 240, *257*

R

Radke-Yarrow, M., 119, *121*
Radin, N., 211, *232*
Rahe, R.H., 261, *275*
Ragozin, A., 265, *274*
Ramsey-Klee, D., 210, 215, *232*
Reddel, M., 76, *90*
Rees, L.H., *202*
Reiling, A., 26, *50*, 70, 72, *90*
Reisbick, S., 143, 157, 161, *203*
Rheingold, H., 25, *51*
Richards, M.P.M., 153, 157, *203*
Richmond, T.B., 169, *200*
Ringler, N.M., 186, 190, *204*
Robins, E., 209, *231*, 239, *254*
Robinson, N.M., 265, *274*
Robson, K.S., 195, *204, 257*
Rode, S., 266, *276*
Rodholm, M., *197*
Rodriquez-Sierra, T., 147, *204*
Rogers, L., *200*
Rogoff, B., 65, *67*
Ronsheim, P.M., 148, *197*
Rosberg, G., *276*
Rosenberg, I., 191, *199*

Rosenberg, P.A., 158–160, *200*
Rosenblatt, T.S., 142–148, 150–153, 157–158, 171–162, 173, *197–199, 201, 203–206*
Rosenblum, L.A., x, xi, 154, *204*, 209, *232*, 239, 243, *256*, 260, *276*
Ross, C.E., 244–245, *257*
Ross, S., 148, 154, *200, 204, 207*
Roth, L.L., 148, *204*
Rothchild, I., 197, *202–203*
Rovine, M., 230, *231*
Rowell, T.E., 157, 161, *204*
Rowland, D., 175, *202, 205*
Rubin, B.S., 148, *204*
Ruble, D., 186, 191, *199*
Russell, C., 222, *232*
Russell, G., 211, 221, *232*
Rutter, M., 261, *276*

S

Sackett, G., 86, *90*
Sainsbury, R.S., 175, *206*
Sameroff, A., 59, *67*, 219, *232*, 234, 242, *257*, 260, *276*
Samuels, H., 4, *24*
Sandler, H., 235, 238–239, *257*, 246–248
Santrock, J., 6, *24*
Sasaki, Y., 128, *139*
Sawin, P.B., 154, *204, 207*
Sawyer, C.H., 148, 165, *197, 200, 201*
Scalia, F., 179, *204, 206*
Scanlon, J.W., 190, *205*
Schaefer, C., 270, *275*
Schaller, J., *197*
Schnur, E., 235, *257*
Seashore, M.J., 191, *204*
Sears, R.R., 242, *258*
Seifer, R., 219, *232*
Sellers, M., 65, *67*
Serafica, F., 269, *274*
Serbin, L.A., 268, *276*
Serizawa, M., 128, *139*
Shaffer, H.R., 269, *276*
Shaikh, A.A., *204*
Shapiro, S., 246–247, *256*
Sheard, N.M., 142, 157, *206*
Shereshefsky, P., 195–196, *204*, 211–212, 216–217, 227–228, *232*
Sherry, D., 61, *67*
Shields, S., 47, *51*
Shigetomi, C., 43, 46, *51*

Shimamura, T., 128, *138*
Shinagawa, N., 136–137, *138–139*
Shinano Kyoiku-Kai, 133, *139*
Shipman, V., 235, *257*
Shryne, J., *203*
Shweder, R., 97–99, 116, *120–121*
Siegel, H.I., 145, 147–148, 150, 152–154, 157, 165, 168, *198, 204, 205*
Sigel, I., 234, 242, *258*
Simon, W., 48, *51*
Sloan, V., 28, 30, 49, *50*, 71, *84*
Sloman, T., 265, *274*
Slotnick, B.M., 148, 174, *198, 205*
Smetana, J., 98–99, *121*
Smith, D.A., 180, *206*
Smith, G.K., 143, 157, *201*
Smith, H.G., 177, *203*
Smith, L., 160, *205*
Snipper, A., 96, 101, 103, *120–121*
Smotherman, W.P., 151, 158–159, *205*
Snyder, S., 178, *206*
Soloff, M., *205*
Soloman-Scwerzer, C.R., 265, *276*
Sorce, J.H., 269, *276*
Sosa, R., 186, *200, 205*
Sostek, A.M., 190, *205*
Speidel, G., 96, *120*
Spencer, M.B., 242, *258*
Spicker, S., 265, *276*
Spiker, D., 269, *274*
Sroufe, L.A., 266, 269, *274, 276*
Stamm, T.S., 174, *205*
Stanley, J., 85, *90*
Starfield, B., 246, *256*
Steele, M., 148, 175, *202, 205*
Steffa, M., *200*
Stein, G., 188, *205*
Stern, D., 265, *276*
Stern, G.S., 269, *275*
Stern, T.M., 144, 147, 150, 165, *205*
Steven, M.A., *201*
Stewart, R., 6, *24*, 49, 62, *67*
Suzuki, T., 129, *139*
Svare, B.B., 144, *206*
Svejda, M.J., 190, *206*
Swanson, L.T., 161, *206*
Swanson, L.W., 177, *206*

T

Takahashi, S., 128, *138*
Takano, A., 128, *139*

Takashima, H., 124, *139*
Tambosso, L., 158, *199*
Taylore, P.M., 194, *206*
Teicher, M.H., 142, *197*
Terkel, J., 146, 165, 173, *200, 206*
Terlecki, L.J., 175, *206*
Thane, K., 190, *199*
Tharp, R., 96, *120*
Thiessen, D.D., *206*
Thoits, P.A., 244–246, *257*
Thornburg, K., 49, *51*
Thoron, L., 178, *206*
Thorpe, T.K., 269, *275*
Tinkelpaugh, O.L., 154, *206*
Tinsley, B., 211, 224, *232*
Toda, S., 61, 63, 64, *67*, 74–75, *90*
Tolan, W., 209, *231*
Tomasu, V., 148, *201*
Tomlin, S., *202*
Trause, M.A., 188, *200–201*
Trost, R.C., *200*
Turiel, E., 96–99, 109, 116, *120–121*
Turner, B.H., 178, *206*
Turner, R.T., 245–246, 256, *258*

U

Uhl, G., 178, *206*
Urrutia, T.J., *205*
Ursin, H., 181, *198*

V

Vaccarino, F., 158, 180, *199*
Varga, P., 238, *255*
Vermouth, N.T., 147, *206*
Vietze, P.M., 190, *200*, 235, *257*
Voci, V.E., 155, *206*
Vuorenkoski, V., *276*

W

Wachs, T.D., 239, *258*
Wagatsuma, H., 127, *139*
Waldron, S., *200*
Wall, S., 266, *276*
Wallace, P., 153–154, *206*
Ward, M.J., 230, *231*
Wardlaw, A.E., 178, *206*
Wasserman, G., 265, *276*
Wasz-Hockart, O., *276*
Watanabe, K., 124, 126, 133, *139*

Waters, E., 26, *274*
Watson, C., 221, *231*
Watson, R., 224, *232*
Weeks, M., 49, *51*
Weingarten, H., 181, *206*
Weinstock, S., 44, *51*
Weisner, B.P., 142, 157, *206*
Weisner, T., 5, *24*, 96, *121*
Weller, K.L., 180, *206*
Wenger, M., 96, 107, *121*
Wertsch, J., 55, *67*
West, M., 25, *51*
Weston, D., 98, *121*
White, B., 7, *24*
White, S., 65, *67*
Whitelaw, A., 264, *276*
Whiting, B., 5–6, *24*, 48, *51*, 65, *67*, 96, 99–103, 105, *120–121*
Whiting, J., 5, *24*, 96, 99, 105, *121*
Whitney, T.F., *201*
Wiberg, B., 186, 189, 190, *198*
Willes, R., 124, *138*
Wilson, E., 54, *67*
Wilson, K.C.M., 154, *199*
White, N., 181, *206*
Winans, S.S., 178–180, *201, 203–204, 206*
Winberg, J., *198*

Winickoff, S., *199*, 210, 215, *232*, 241, *256*
Winquist-Nord, C., 250, *256*
Wise, L., 234, *255*
Wong, P.Y., 145, 149, 152, *203*
Woodside, B., 143, *206*

Y

Yanagita, K., 125, *139*
Yarirs, R.M., 244, *257*
Yarrow, M.R., 195–196, *204*, 211–212, 216–217, 227–228, *232*
Yule, W., 261, *276*

Z

Zachman, T.A., *196*
Zackler, T., 247, *258*
Zahn-Waxler, C., 6, *23*, 46, *50*, 70, *90*, 119, *121*
Zarrow, M.X., 146, 153–155, 159, *196, 199, 204, 206*
Zax, M., 219, *232*
Zemlick, M., 224, *232*
Zill, N., 250, *256*
Zuehlke, S., *201*

Subject Index

A

Abortion, 136–137
Adolescent parents, 92, 136–137, 235–238
Age effects on nurturance,
  Age interval between siblings, 6–13,
  Age of child, 1, 6–13, 25–50,
  Agonistic behavior, 7, 9–23, 80–88, 102–103, 107–109,
  Altruism, 43–44, 54–56, 69
Attachment, 266–267
Attitudes toward children,
  in Japan, 123–137
Attraction toward infants, 26, 47–48, 72
Audition, 159

B

Babyishness, 75, 101
Baby-sitting experience, 132–134
Brain (of rat), 174–185

C

Caretaking role assignment by adults, 4, 34–42, 95–119, 134–135
Child-care books, 127
Child-infant interactions outside the family, 1, 25–50, 69–89
Competence for nurturance, 53, 64, 91, 95–119

Contingent responsiveness to infant behavior, 83–88
Conventional moral rules, 96, 98–100
Cross-cultural comparisons, 5–6, 65–66, 92, 96–119, 123–137

D

Down's syndrome, 267–272

E

Ego strength, 240
Egocentrism, 4
Empathy, 46, 54–56, 69
Ethnographic description of child-infant interaction, 105, 125–127

F

Fathers, 211
  see sex differences in parenting, 130–131
Family size effects on nurturance, 132

H

Hormones, 92
  in animal responsiveness to young, 145–148, 151–155, 166–173, 182–185
  in human responsiveness to the young, 188–189

SUBJECT INDEX

I

Infant health, 247–248
Infanticide, 125–127
Infants,
    benefits of cross-age interaction, 70
    contribution to own nurturance, 2, 18–20, 69–89, 100
Interest in infants, 77–88

L

Lactation, 156–157

M

Maternal behavior,
    definition, 186–188
    effect of mood on, 191, 195
    in mammals, 153–155
    in rats, 142–153, 161–166, 169–172, 176–185
Methodological issues, 8–9, 22–23, 29–30, 34–35, 61–63, 71–72, 92
Moral rule learning, 91

N

Neonatal mortality, 247
Nurturance,
    and conception of human life, 135–137
    definition of, 2, 8, 54–59, 70–71, 100–102, 105–107, 135–137, 233–234

O

Olfaction, 158

P

Parenthood, 233–234
Parenting,
    antecedents of, 3, 47, 69, 92, 213–221, 239–243
    anxiety, 129–131
    child-rearing neurosis, 127–129
    dimensions of, 55, 260
    direct effects on, 213–226
    effects of child on, 211, 242–243
    effects of the marital relationship, 92
    effects of stress, 93, 129–131, 244–245
    indirect effects on, 226–229

    parent-child suicide, 128–129
    risk factors, 92
    sensitive period in, 189–191
    sex differences in, 230
    social influences on, 92, 221–224
Pregnancy,
    in humans, 193–195, 224–226, 230, 241–242
    in rats, 148–150
Preterm infants, 93, 262–267
Play, 95–96
Prosocial behavior, 4, 7, 9–23, 32–50, 80–88, 100–102, 109–112

R

Rational moral rules, 96, 98–100

S

Situational factors in responsiveness to infants, 1, 25, 31–50, 97–98, 129–135
Sex composition of child-infant pair, 3, 6–8, 13–15, 20
Sex differences,
    in children's responsiveness to infants, 1, 5–7, 13–15, 20, 25–50, 53–67
    in children's cognitions about infants, 76–77
    in parent's responsiveness to infants, 58, 130–131
Siblings, 1, 3–24
Social cognition,
    about infants, 72–77
    about caretaking, 59
Societal influences on nurturance, 65–66, 95–119, 123–137
Stability of individual differences, 16–17
Stress, 261–262
Support systems, 130, 245–246, 261–262

T

Teenage mothers,
    effects on children, 248–250, 252–253
    parenting practices, 238–239, 253–254
Touch, 160

V

Vision, 160